CHENG

"Bringing Asia to the World"™

Dekiru!
AN AP® JAPANESE PREPARATION COURSE

Hiromi Peterson
Naomi Hirano-Omizo
Junko Ady

AP® and Advanced Placement® are trademarks registered by the College Board, which is not affiliated with, and does not endorse, this product.

CHENG & TSUI

"Bringing Asia to the World"™

Copyright © 2018, 2009
by Hiromi Peterson

First Edition 2018

4th Printing, 2021

25 24 23 22 21   4 5 6 7 8

ISBN 978-1-62291-195-0

Publisher
JILL CHENG

Editorial Manager
BEN SHRAGGE

Editor
MIKE YONG

Cover Design
CHRISTIAN SABOGAL

Cheng & Tsui Company, Inc.
25 West Street
Boston, MA 02111-1213 USA
Phone (617) 988-2400 / (800) 554-1963
Fax (617) 426-3669
chengtsui.co

All rights reserved. No part of this publication may be reproduced or transmitted in any form or by any means, electronic or mechanical, including photocopying, recording, scanning, or any information storage or retrieval system, without written permission from the publisher.

All trademarks and references mentioned in this textbook are used for identification purposes only and are the property of their respective owners.

Further Adventures in Japanese
(Field Test Edition) 2009

Printed in the United States of America

Dekiru! CONTENTS

To the Student and the Teacher			v
Advice			ix
Acknowledgments			xvii
AP® 漢字表		AP® *Kanji* List	1
Lesson 1	自分と家族と友達	Self, Family, and Friends	55
Lesson 2	日常生活	Daily Life	77
Lesson 3	レジャーと趣味とスポーツ	Leisure, Hobbies, and Sports	97
Lesson 4	家でコミュニティーで	Home and Community	117
Lesson 5	都市と町と田舎	Cities, Towns, and Villages	139
Lesson 6	自然と環境	Nature and Environment	157
Lesson 7	学校と教育	School and Education	177
Lesson 8	服装	Clothing	197
Lesson 9	コミュニケーションとメディア	Communication and Media	215
Lesson 10	テクノロジー	Technology	235
Lesson 11	仕事とキャリア	Work and Career	255
Lesson 12	冠婚葬祭	Rites of Life	275
Lesson 13	祭りと年中行事	Festivals and Annual Events	297
Lesson 14	交通	Transportation	321
Lesson 15	天気と気候	Weather and Climate	341
Lesson 16	食物	Food	361
Lesson 17	買物	Shopping	383
Lesson 18	体と健康	Body and Health	403
Lesson 19	旅行	Travel	423
Lesson 20	日本と世界	Japan and the World	445
Appendices			
Verb Conjugation Charts			466
References			468

TO THE STUDENT AND THE TEACHER

Welcome to *Dekiru!*, a textbook for advanced learners of Japanese. The contents of this volume reflect our reconceptualization and reconfiguration of *Further Adventures in Japanese*, a textbook that has been in print for almost ten years. In this period, we have not only received invaluable feedback from students and teachers, but there have also been changes in the format of the Advanced Placement® (AP®) Japanese Language and Culture exam. We have sought to take the current needs of students and teachers of Japanese to heart, and have aimed to provide a textbook firmly based on the Japanese National Standards and ACTFL Proficiency Guidelines that is specifically designed to prepare students for the AP® Japanese Language and Culture exam. The change in title, from *Further Adventures in Japanese* to *Dekiru!*, reflects the fact that this textbook supports the learning of all advanced students of Japanese seeking to improve their proficiency, regardless of the textbook series with which they started. We aim to prepare students to function successfully in daily interactions at an advanced level and in culturally appropriate ways. Students using *Dekiru!* will be able to further sharpen their communicative skills in listening, reading, writing, and speaking, as well as enhance their cultural proficiency.

The goals of this textbook are manifold. First, we would like to aim for all users of this text to be skilled in communicating in Japanese at a multi-paragraph level: students should be able to comprehend, read, write (type), and speak at the paragraph level and be able to connect paragraphs into a cohesive whole when required. Second, we want to prepare students for success on the AP® Japanese Language and Culture exam. With this aim, we have designed lessons with exercises formatted in the same way as the actual exam. Twenty themes likely to be on the exam are featured independently in twenty lessons. Each lesson provides practice in the major components of the AP® exam: listening, reading, writing, and speaking.

For a meaningful and successful experience, we recommend that both students and teachers familiarize themselves with the features of this volume, discussed in the following pages.

Suggestions and Advice for the Student and Teacher

For the benefit of students and teachers, this section was developed and compiled based on several years of observing student preparation for the AP® Japanese Language and Culture Exam. We hope it is useful for other students and teachers. It includes helpful information and suggestions to heed when taking the AP® Japanese Language and Culture exam. The exam consists of five sections: Listening, Reading, Text Chat, Compare and Contrast, and the Conversation and Cultural Perspective Presentation.

In addition, the College Board provides assessment rubrics for each section of the exam. It is recommended that students and teachers familiarize themselves with the standards by which students are evaluated on each section of the exam, as well as each section's relative weight.

Kanji

A total of 410 *kanji* are on the recommended AP® list. A list of these *kanji* appears at the beginning of the textbook. For the benefit of students, *kanji* introduced in the *Adventures in Japanese* series, Volumes 1–3, Fourth Edition, are presented on this list. *Kanji* that appear on the AP® *kanji* list must be learned by all students. Students who have completed Adventures in Japanese, Volume 4 will have studied many additional *kanji*. Students may study the *kanji* at their own pace and teachers may introduce *kanji* as they wish as they teach through this textbook. Sample *kanji* quizzes are available to the teacher at chengtsui.co/dekiru.

Lessons

According to the College Board, the AP® exam tests each student's knowledge of Japanese language and culture based on selected cultural topics. Each lesson in *Dekiru!* is devoted to a particular cultural topic that is likely to be on the AP® exam. The instructor may select any lesson, or part of a lesson, and may present them in any sequence, according to the needs and interests of his or her class. Each lesson is independent of the others. The lessons and topics are:

Lesson 1: Self, Family, and Friends
Lesson 2: Daily Life
Lesson 3: Leisure, Hobbies, and Sports
Lesson 4: Home and Community
Lesson 5: Cities, Towns, and Villages
Lesson 6: Nature and Environment
Lesson 7: School and Education
Lesson 8: Clothing
Lesson 9: Communication and Media
Lesson 10: Technology
Lesson 11: Work and Career
Lesson 12: Rites of Life
Lesson 13: Festivals and Annual Events
Lesson 14: Transportation
Lesson 15: Weather and Climate
Lesson 16: Food
Lesson 17: Shopping
Lesson 18: Body and Health
Lesson 19: Travel
Lesson 20: Japan and the World

Each lesson consists of the following sections:

Task

Each lesson begins with a task that students can use as a guide for what they are expected to be able to do by the end of the lesson. These may be used for formative conversation practice and/or summative OPI (Oral Proficiency/Pro-Achievement Interview) exams at the end of the term.

Culture (in English)

Cultural information broadens students' perspectives on the language and promotes a deeper cultural understanding of Japan in the context of world cultures. The initial page of each lesson provides, in English, a cultural context for the lesson topic. It furnishes a foundation for students to formulate their own their own ideas for the Cultural Perspective Presentation section of the AP® exam. The cultural summary also provides an impetus for students to think more deeply about the "whys" of cultural practices so that they can be more open to cultural differences. Students are also encouraged to further research any topic on their own and enrich their background knowledge of any given cultural topic.

New Vocabulary

Approximately 30 new vocabulary items are introduced in each lesson. These allow students to communicate at a more advanced level on all topics of study. Please note that in the New Vocabulary sections, vocabulary items that appear in *kanji* without *hiragana* readings are those that appear in *Adventures in Japanese*; students ready for the AP® level are expected to have learned these vocabulary items in their prior years of study.

Grammar

The grammar structures that appear in *Dekiru!* are considered mostly a review. Most students are expected to have already been introduced to most of these grammatical structures, though simple grammatical explanations and ample practice sentences are offered, even if students have not learned them before. The concise treatment of grammar in this textbook also allows for easy comparisons among similar structures. Practice examples provide contexts for students to make distinctions among these similar forms.

Activities

Following the grammar section are a number of listening, reading, writing, and speaking activities that students can use to practice in class, individually, or in pairs. These practice activities all relate to the lesson's topic and require students to use the vocabulary and grammar introduced in the lesson while preparing to respond and interact through exercises similar to the AP® format. Many of the prompts help to guide students to respond in appropriate ways. Pre- and post-activity exercises are designed to accompany the AP® reading and listening samples in the next section.

Please note that in the Activities section, vocabulary items that appear in *kanji* without *hiragana* readings are those that appear in *Adventures in Japanese*.

Sample Test Questions

A valuable feature of *Dekiru!* are the near-authentic AP® sample test questions at the end of each lesson; these questions have been designed in the exact format of the AP® exam, and are intended to acclimate the student to answering questions on the actual exam. Each set of sample questions includes one listening test with five multiple-choice questions, one reading test with five multiple-choice questions, a Text Chat test, a Compare and Contrast test, a Conversation test, and a Cultural Perspective Presentation test. Of these, two test questions in each lesson (marked with a CD graphic) are accompanied by audio files available for download at chengtsui.co/dekiru. For more sample tests, please refer to *Strive for a 5: AP® Japanese Practice Tests.* We urge teachers to carefully follow the instructions on these tests, including the time requirements, to create an authentic test-taking situation for students. Please note that in the Sample Test Questions section, *hiragana* readings are not given for vocabulary items that contain *kanji* on the official AP® *kanji* list in order to offer a realistic simulation of the testing environment and to better prepare students for taking the test.

Scripts and Answers for the Sample Test Questions

For reference, scripts that accompany the audio files for the listening section and the conversation section (speaking), as well as answer keys to the multiple-choice listening and reading questions, are available on the companion website at chengtsui.co/dekiru.

Audio Recordings

Two audio files per lesson are available for download at chengtsui.co/dekiru. These are the files for the Listening and Conversation sample test questions. For the Listening section, students should take notes while listening, then answer the multiple-choice questions. For the Conversation section, we suggest that students record each spoken response within twenty seconds of being given the prompt.

Finally, we close by wishing all users of this text a successful journey as they advance through their study of Japanese. Please contact us with any comments or suggestions at editor@chengtsui.co. Thank you for choosing *Dekiru!*

〈聞く Listening アドバイス〉

You may download the audio recordings for this section from chengtsui.co/dekiru.

【Sample Stimulus Types】
- Conversation
- Debate
- Instructions
- Message
- Presentation
- Public announcement
- Radio broadcast

【Knowledge/skills】
- Interpretive communication
- Comprehension; inference

【Format】
- Multiple-choice questions
- Several listening selections: 30-35 questions, 25% of the final score, 20 minutes total. (Response time: 12 seconds per question)
- Each selection will be read once or twice.
- Taking notes is allowed. Notes will not be graded.
- Moving back and forth among questions is not allowed.

【Suggestions】
1. Take notes while listening.
2. The response time you are allowed for each multiple-choice question is 12 seconds. Follow the time limits during practice sessions.
3. On the AP® exam, the questions are not presented until after the listening portion is complete, so you should not look at the questions prior to listening to the passage.
4. Once you have answered an item, you will not be able to return and correct it. Be sure of your answer before making a choice.

<読む Reading アドバイス>

【Sample Stimulus Types】
- E-mail
- Instructions
- Letter
- News article
- Short story
- Travel brochure

【Knowledge/skills】
- Interpretive communication
- Comprehension; inference

【Format】
- Multiple-choice questions
- Several reading selections: 35-40 questions, 25% of the final score, 60 minutes total
- Moving back and forth among all the questions is allowed.

【Suggestions】
1. Learn the readings and the meanings of all 410 AP® *kanji*. A list of these *kanji*, along with compounds in which these *kanji* feature, is included with *Dekiru!*
2. Go through all the questions in order first, then go back and check your work.
3. Skim over the questions before reading, so you know what information to look for.

<書く Text Chat アドバイス>

【Knowledge/skills】
- Interpersonal communication
- Informing; describing; explaining; expressing a preference; elaborating; justifying an opinion; requesting; inviting; suggesting

【Format】
- 6 questions, 12.5% of the final score, 10 minutes total. (Response time: 90 seconds per question)

【Speech style】
When communicating with someone you don't know well, use the polite です/ます form. While the honorific usage is not required on the AP® exam, using it correctly and appropriately will benefit you. When communicating with someone close to you, use the informal form, although this is not commonly required on the AP® exam.

【Suggestions】
1. Every response is important. Elaborate and answer thoroughly. Do not leave any section unanswered.
2. When introducing yourself, it is polite and natural to say どうぞよろしくお願いします after giving your name.
3. At the very end of the conversation, show appreciation to the person with whom you are having the text chat. If you enjoyed the conversation, say 楽しかったです。 If you want to offer encouragement to your partner, say がんばって下さい。

<書く Compare & Contrast Article アドバイス>

【Knowledge/skills】
• Presentational communication
• Comparing; contrasting; describing; justifying an opinion

【Format】
• 1 question, 12.5% of the final score, 20 minutes
• Written article, 300 - 400 characters

【Speech style】
Use the です/ます form or the だ form consistently.

【Outline sample structure】
1. Opening:
   これから、AとBをくらべてみます。AとBは違うことも同じこともあります。
2. Three similarities and/or differences between A and B:
   まず 一つ目の違うことは、Aは〜ですが、Bは〜です。
   二つ目の違うことは、〜。
   そして、三つ目の違うことは、〜。
   or しかし、一つの同じことは、AもBも〜。
3. Your preference and reasons:
   （結論(けつろん)として）私はAの方がBより好きです。
   なぜなら、(reason) からです。

【Comparative patterns】
1. Between A and B, I like A more than B. AとBで、Aの方がBより好きです。
2. I don't like B as much as A. BはAほど好きではありません。
3. It's faster to go by car than to walk. 車で行く方が、歩くより速いです。
4. Walking is not as fast as going by car. 歩くのは、車で行くほど速くないです。

【Suggestion】
1. Make sure to note important items that you will write about. The outline will not be graded. No more than 5 minutes should be spent for outlining.
2. Use the AP® *kanji*.
3. Proofread well, especially for *kanji* and comparative grammar patterns. Check that you have not chosen the wrong *kanji*.

<話す Conversation アドバイス>

You may download the audio recordings for this section from chengtsui.co/dekiru.

【Knowledge/skills】
- Interpersonal communication
- Participate in conversations by responding appropriately

【Format】
- 4 prompts as part of 1 conversation
- 4 questions, 12.5% of the final score, 3 minutes total. (Response time: 20 seconds per question)

【Speech style】
Immediately decide on which speech style you should use, depending on the person to whom you are speaking.

【Responding appropriately to expressions】
1. 日本人：「ご協力お願いします。」
   答え：「はい、分かりました。何でも聞いて下さい。協力します。」
2. 日本人：「がんばってください。」
   答え：「はい、がんばります。」

【Polite style and informal style】
1. "Let me see..."
   Polite style: そうですねえ。。。
   Informal style (male): そうだねえ。。。
   Informal style (female): そうねえ。。。
2. "have to decide..."
   Polite style: 決めなければなりません
   Informal style: 決めなくちゃ

【Suggestions】
1. Make sure to speak loudly and clearly. Use a confident voice.
2. Begin with a cheerful greeting.
3. After introducing yourself, say どうぞよろしくお願いします。
4. Carry on a polite conversation.

5. At the end, close your conversation with a word of appreciation and a polite closing remark.
   Ex. どうも有難うございました。
6. When you don't know much about the topic asked, you may answer 「Topic についてよく知りませんから、私は答えられません。」
7. 「分かりません」and「もう一度言って下さい」do not count as correct answers.
8. Listen to the questions carefully. If you don't understand the question, repeat back the question. At minimum, say 「そうですねえ…」

【Suggestions for improving your listening skills】
1. Practice engaging in impromptu conversations in Japanese.
2. Listen to Japanese radio programs and Japanese songs, watch Japanese TV programs, Japanese movies, *anime*, etc.

＜話す Cultural Perspective Presentation アドバイス＞

【Knowledge/skills】
- Presentational communication (speaking)
- Describing and expressing opinions about a Japanese cultural practice or product

【Format】
- 1 question, 12.5% of the final score, 7 minutes (Preparation time: 4 minutes, Response time: 2 minutes)

【Speech style】
Use the polite です/ます style.

【Sample structure】
1. Begin with an appropriate introduction.
    これから、(topic) についてお話します。
2. Discuss five aspects/examples of the topic.
    1.) まず or 第一に、
    2.) 次に or 第二に、
    3.) 第三に、
    4.) 第四に、
    5.) 第五に、
3. Explain your view or perspective.
    私の考えとして、〜と思います。
4. End with a concluding remark.
    これで、(topic) についての発表を終わります。聞いて下さいまして、ありがとうございました。以上です。

【Helpful words】
1. Conjunction words
    a. それから、：Then,
    b. そのうえ、：Besides, moreover
    c. しかも、：Besides, moreover
    d. それとも、：Or,
    e. ですから、：Therefore,
    f. しかし、：However,
    g. 一般的〔いっぱんてき〕に言って、：Generally speaking,

  h. たとえば：For instance,
  i. なぜなら、〜からです。：That's because 〜
2. Uncertainty
  a. 日本人は魚をよく食べる<u>ようです</u>。Japanese seem to eat a lot of fish.
  b. 日本人は魚をよく食べる<u>らしいです</u>。Japanese seem to eat a lot of fish.
  c. 日本人は魚をよく食べる<u>かもしれない</u>。Japanese might eat a lot of fish.
  d. 日本人は魚をよく食べる<u>にちがいありません</u>。Japanese must eat a lot of fish.
  e. 日本人は魚をよく食べ<u>そうです</u>。It seems Japanese eat a lot of fish.
  f. 日本人は魚をよく食べる<u>そうです</u>。I heard that Japanese eat a lot of fish.

【Suggestions】
1. Make sure to speak loudly and clearly. Use a confident voice.
2. Learn about Japanese culture with accuracy and in detail.
3. Observe and think critically about reasons for Japanese cultural behavior.
4. If you are not sure about aspects of Japanese culture you are discussing, use grammar forms that express uncertainty.

ACKNOWLEDGMENTS

The authors of *Dekiru!* would like to express our appreciation to the following individuals for their invaluable contributions to this textbook.

- Michael Muronaka for the illustrations
- Keiko Kurose for reviewing the AP® *kanji* list and for the resource materials she sent from Japan
- Natsumi Watanabe, a one-year exchange student from Japan, for writing a passage and accompanying questions
- Ken Noguchi for granting us permission to use his work entitled 「あきらめないこと、それが 冒険だ」, which was used to create reading material
- Masahiro Sasaki, older brother of Sadako Sasaki, for sharing his speech about Sadako delivered at Stuyvesant High School in New York after a 9/11 memorial service
- Satomi Wise for creating reading materials and games
- Atsuko Motet for creating the vocabulary review section
- Rika Onchi and her students at Yuuhigaoka High School in Osaka for creating listening materials
- Douglas Kiang for recording the audio files
- Harry Kubo, Reona Ono, Keigo Sato, Yuki Balunso, Lisa Matsukata, Tetsuya Kose, Daisuki Kose, Gen Sakamoto, Aki Teshigahara, and Keiko Burgess for their voice recordings
- Norie Masamitsu for proofreading the life story of her father Soichiro Honda
- Gina Hara for proofreading the multiple-choice listening and reading questions
- Keiko Burgess for proofreading the listening and reading questions
- Leigh Omizo for proofreading the Culture Note sections
- Jill Cheng, our publisher, and the entire staff at Cheng & Tsui for their support in collaborating and coordinating the work for this textbook. In particular, we appreciate the diligent work of Mike Yong, who worked closely with us as our editor.
- Our colleagues and administrators at Punahou School for their contributions and their support throughout the work for *Adventures in Japanese* and *Dekiru!*
- Our families for their steadfast support in so many ways as we labored through writing the *Adventures in Japanese* textbooks over several decades.

With deepest gratitude,
Hiromi Peterson, Naomi Hirano-Omizo, and Junko Ady

AP® 漢字

After studying this book, you are expected to know the meaning of and be able to read and type the following *kanji*.

【タスク１：AP® *Kanji*】
Master the 410 AP® *kanji*. You should know the meanings of, and be able to read, the *kanji* compounds for each AP® *kanji*, and be able to type the *kanji* compounds properly.

Abbreviations used in the list:

- AP® #   = AP® *kanji* number
- 漢字   = AP® *kanji*
- AIJ-L. = AIJ Level and Lesson in which the *kanji* was introduced
- AIJ #   = AIJ *kanji* number
- 訓読み = *Kun* (Japanese) reading
- 音読み = *On* (Chinese) reading
   (The *kanji* are listed in あいうえお order by *on* reading.)
- 意味   = *Kanji* meanings
- 熟語   = Compound *kanji* words using the *kanji*
- X   = No reading

AP®#	漢字	AIJ-L	AIJ#	訓読み	音読み	意味	熟語
1	悪	II-12	161	わる(い)	あく	bad	悪い〔わるい〕is bad 悪人〔あくにん〕bad person
2	安	II-4	79	やす(い)	あん	cheap; peaceful	安い本〔やすいほん〕cheap book 安物〔やすもの〕cheap things 大安売り〔おおやすうり〕big bargain sale 安田〔やすだ〕さん Yasuda-san 安心〔あんしん〕する to be relieved 安全〔あんぜん〕safe 安藤〔あんどう〕さん Ando-san
3	暗			くら(い)	あん	dark	暗い〔くらい〕is dark 明暗〔めいあん〕light and dark
4	以	III-6	239	X	い	to the ～ of	以上〔いじょう〕more than ～ 以下〔いか〕less than ～ 以前〔いぜん〕before ～ 以後〔いご〕after ～ 以内〔いない〕within ～ 以外〔いがい〕except ～ 以来〔いらい〕since ～
5	意			X	い	meaning; mind	意味〔いみ〕meaning 意見〔いけん〕opinion 意外〔いがい〕unexpected; surprising
6	医			X	い	medical	医者〔いしゃ〕doctor 医学〔いがく〕medical study 医学部〔いがくぶ〕medical department
7	育			そだ(つ/てる)	いく	to raise (a child or pet)	育つ〔そだつ〕(someone) is raised 育てる〔そだてる〕raise (someone) 体育〔たいいく〕physical education 教育〔きょういく〕education
8	一	I-3	1	ひと	いち/いっ	one	一つ〔ひとつ〕one [general counter] 一人〔ひとり〕one person 一日〔ついたち〕first day of the month 一日〔いちにち〕one day 一月〔いちがつ〕January 一万〔いちまん〕ten thousand 一才〔いっさい〕one year old 一回〔いっかい〕one time

漢字

AP®#	漢字	AIJ-L	AIJ#	訓読み	音読み	意味	熟語
9	員	III-7	249	X	いん	member	社員〔しゃいん〕company employee 会員〔かいいん〕group member 銀行員〔ぎんこういん〕banker 駅員〔えきいん〕station employee 店員〔てんいん〕store clerk 全員〔ぜんいん〕everyone
10	引			ひ(く)	いん	to pull	ドアを引く〔ひく〕to pull (=open) the door 引き算〔ひきざん〕subtraction 辞書を引く〔じしょをひく〕to look up in the dictionary 風邪を引く〔かぜをひく〕to catch a cold 引き出し〔ひきだし〕drawer
11	飲	II-5	90	の(む)	いん	to drink	水を飲む〔みずをのむ〕to drink water 飲み水〔のみみず〕drinking water 飲酒運転〔いんしゅうんてん〕drunken driving 飲料水〔いんりょうすい〕drinking water
12	院			X	いん	institute	病院〔びょういん〕hospital 大学院〔だいがくいん〕graduate school 院長〔いんちょう〕a head of a hospital
13	右	II-2	65	みぎ	う/ゆう	right (side)	右手〔みぎて〕right hand 右足〔みぎあし〕right foot 右側〔みぎがわ〕right side 左右〔さゆう〕left and right
14	雨	II-4	75	あめ	う	rain	大雨〔おおあめ〕heavy rain 雨天〔うてん〕rainy weather 小雨〔こさめ〕drizzle 梅雨〔つゆ/ばいう〕rainy season
15	運			はこ(ぶ)	うん	to carry; luck	荷物を運ぶ〔にもつをはこぶ〕to carry luggage 運転〔うんてん〕driving 運動〔うんどう〕sports; exercises 運がいい〔うんがいい〕lucky 運が悪い〔うんがわるい〕unlucky
16	映	II-8	118	うつ(す)	えい	to project	映し出す〔うつしだす〕to project 映画〔えいが〕movie 映画館〔えいがかん〕movie theater 上映時間〔じょうえいじかん〕running time of a movie

AP®#	漢字	AIJ-L	AIJ#	訓読み	音読み	意味	熟語
17	泳			およ(ぐ)	えい	to swim	泳ぐ〔およぐ〕to swim 水泳〔すいえい〕swimming
18	英	II-7	103	X	えい	British; brave	英国〔えいこく〕England 英語〔えいご〕English 英会話〔えいかいわ〕English conversation
19	駅	III-7	248	X	えき	station	駅〔えき〕(railway) station 駅名〔えきめい〕station name 上野駅〔うえのえき〕Ueno Station 乗車駅〔じょうしゃえき〕boarding station
20	円	I-11	53	まる	えん	circle; yen	円山公園〔まるやまこうえん〕Maruyama Park 百円〔ひゃくえん〕100 yen 一万円〔いちまんえん〕10,000 yen 十万円〔じゅうまんえん〕100,000 yen 百万円〔ひゃくまんえん〕1,000,000 yen
21	園	II-10	141	その	えん	garden	園田〔そのだ〕さん Sonoda-san 公園〔こうえん〕park 上野公園〔うえのこうえん〕Ueno Park 動物園〔どうぶつえん〕zoo 園長〔えんちょう〕kindergarten principal 遊園地〔ゆうえんち〕amusement park
22	遠	III-5	228	とお(い)	えん	far	遠い〔とおい〕far 遠回り〔とおまわり〕detour 遠足〔えんそく〕hike; outing 遠慮〔えんりょ〕する to hesitate
23	横			よこ	おう	side	横山〔よこやま〕さん Yokoyama-san 横浜〔よこはま〕Yokohama 横綱〔よこづな〕sumo grand champion 横断歩道〔おうだんほどう〕pedestrian crossing
24	屋	II-7	110	や	おく	store; roof	花屋〔はなや〕flower shop 魚屋〔さかなや〕fish market 薬屋〔くすりや〕pharmacy 部屋〔へや〕room 屋根〔やね〕roof 屋台〔やたい〕cart; stand 屋上〔おくじょう〕rooftop 屋外〔おくがい〕outdoors

漢字

AP®#	漢字	AIJ-L.	AIJ#	訓読み	音読み	意味	熟語
25	温			あたた(かい)	おん	warm	温かい水〔あたたかいみず〕warm water 温度〔おんど〕temperature 気温〔きおん〕temperature (atmospheric) 地球温暖化〔ちきゅうおんだんか〕global warming
26	音	III-2	187	おと/ね	おん	sound	雨の音〔あめのおと〕sound of rain 本音〔ほんね〕true feeling 音楽〔おんがく〕music 音楽家〔おんがくか〕musician
27	下	II-2	64	した/お(りる)/さ(がる)/さ(げる)	か/げ	under	山下〔やました〕さん Yamashita-san 下りる〔おりる〕to go down 下げる〔さげる〕to lower 地下鉄〔ちかてつ〕subway 〜以下〔いか〕less than〜 下手〔へた〕unskillful
28	化	III-1	172	ば(ける)	か/け	to change	文字化け〔もじばけ〕gibberish 文化〔ぶんか〕culture 化学〔かがく〕chemistry 変化〔へんか〕する (something) changes 化粧〔けしょう〕cosmetics
29	何	II-3	72	なに/なん	か	what	何人〔なにじん〕What nationality? 何人〔なんにん〕How many people? 何時〔なんじ〕What time? 何回〔なんかい〕How many times? 何日〔なんにち〕What day of the month?
30	夏	III-2	180	なつ	か	summer	暑い夏〔あついなつ〕hot summer 夏休み〔なつやすみ〕summer vacation 真夏〔まなつ〕mid-summer 初夏〔しょか〕early summer 春夏秋冬〔しゅんかしゅうとう〕spring, summer, autumn and winter
31	家	II-6	102	いえ	か/け	house; person	大きい家〔おおきいいえ〕a big house 家族〔かぞく〕family 家内〔かない〕(own) wife 家庭〔かてい〕family; household 画家〔がか〕painter (artist) 小説家〔しょうせつか〕novelist 田中家〔たなかけ〕Tanaka family

漢字

AP®#	漢字	AIJ-L.	AIJ#	訓読み	音読み	意味	熟語
32	科			X	か	subject	科目〔かもく〕(school) subject 社会科〔しゃかいか〕social studies 科学〔かがく〕science
33	歌	III-3	195	うた/ うた(う)	か	song	歌を歌う〔うたをうたう〕to sing a song 校歌〔こうか〕school song 歌手〔かしゅ〕singer
34	火	I-5	13	ひ/ び	か	fire	花火〔はなび〕fireworks 火曜日〔かようび〕Tuesday 火事〔かじ〕fire; conflagration
35	花	III-1	173	はな/ ばな	か	flower	花子〔はなこ〕さん Hanako-san 花屋〔はなや〕flower shop 花火〔はなび〕fireworks 生け花〔いけばな〕flower arrangement
36	荷			に	か	luggage	荷物〔にもつ〕luggage; baggage 重荷〔おもに〕heavy burden
37	画	II-8	119	X	が/ かく	picture; stroke	映画〔えいが〕movie 日本画〔にほんが〕Japanese painting 洋画〔ようが〕Western paintings/movie 画家〔がか〕painter (artist) 漫画〔まんが〕comic; cartoon 画数〔かくすう〕number of strokes 計画〔けいかく〕plan
38	会	II-6	99	あ(う)	かい	to meet	会う〔あう〕to meet 教会〔きょうかい〕church 会に出る〔かいにでる〕to attend a meeting 会長〔かいちょう〕president (of an organization) 会場〔かいじょう〕meeting place 全国大会〔ぜんこくたいかい〕national meeting 司会〔しかい〕master of ceremonies
39	回	II-5	92	まわ(す)/ まわ(る)	かい	-time(s); to turn	右に回す〔みぎにまわす〕to turn to the right 回り道〔まわりみち〕detour 何回〔なんかい〕How many times? 今回〔こんかい〕this time 回転寿司〔かいてんずし〕conveyor belt sushi

漢字

AP®#	漢字	AIJ-L.	AIJ#	訓読み	音読み	意味	熟語
40	海	III-1	174	うみ	かい	sea; ocean; beach	広い海〔ひろいうみ〕spacious ocean 海の家〔うみのいえ〕beach house 海外旅行〔かいがいりょこう〕travel abroad 日本海〔にほんかい〕Sea of Japan 海水〔かいすい〕ocean water 海軍〔かいぐん〕navy 地中海〔ちちゅうかい〕Mediterranean Sea 海産物〔かいさんぶつ〕marine products
41	界	II-9	131	X	かい	boundary	世界〔せかい〕world
42	皆	III-3	194	みな/みんな	かい	everyone	皆さん〔みなさん〕everyone [polite, address form] 皆〔みんな〕everyone 皆川〔みながわ〕さん Minagawa-san
43	絵	II-12	162	え	かい	painting	絵を描く〔えをかく〕to paint a picture 絵文字〔えもじ〕pictograph 絵本〔えほん〕picture book 絵画〔かいが〕painting
44	開	II-9	123	あ(ける)/あ(く)/ひら(く)	かい	to open	戸を開ける〔とをあける〕to open a door 戸が開く〔とがあく〕door opens 花が開く〔はながひらく〕flowers open 開場時間〔かいじょうじかん〕opening time 開会式〔かいかいしき〕opening ceremony
45	階	III-4	210	X	かい/がい	floor	階段〔かいだん〕stairs 地下二階〔ちかにかい〕basement 2nd floor 三階〔さんがい〕3rd floor
46	外	II-3	68	そと	がい/げ	outside	家の外〔いえのそと〕outside of the house 外国語〔がいこくご〕foreign language 外国人〔がいこくじん〕foreigner 外出〔がいしゅつ〕する to go out 海外旅行〔かいがいりょこう〕travel abroad 外来語〔がいらいご〕word of foreign origin 外泊〔がいはく〕する to spend a night away from home 外食〔がいしょく〕eating out 外車〔がいしゃ〕foreign car 外見〔がいけん〕appearance 外交〔がいこう〕diplomacy 外科〔げか〕surgical department

漢字

AP®#	漢字	AIJ-L.	AIJ#	訓読み	音読み	意味	熟語
47	学	I-10	47	まな(ぶ)	がく	to learn	学ぶ〔まなぶ〕to study/learn (in depth) 学校〔がっこう〕school 学期〔がっき〕semester 学生〔がくせい〕student (college) 学長〔がくちょう〕university president 学者〔がくしゃ〕scholar 大学院〔だいがくいん〕graduate school 工学部〔こうがくぶ〕school of engineering 言語学〔げんごがく〕linguistics 男女共学〔だんじょきょうがく〕co-education 修学旅行〔しゅうがくりょこう〕school excursion 学士号〔がくしごう〕bachelor's degree
48	楽	III-2	188	たの(しい)	がく/らく	enjoyable	楽しい〔たのしい〕enjoyable 音楽〔おんがく〕music 楽器〔がっき〕musical instrument 楽な椅子〔らくないす〕comfortable chair
49	活	III-3	200	X	かつ	active; live	生活〔せいかつ〕living 活動〔かつどう〕activity 部活〔ぶかつ〕club activity
50	寒	III-8	274	さむ(い)	かん	cold	寒い風〔さむいかぜ〕cold wind 寒冷前線〔かんれいぜんせん〕cold front
51	漢	III-1	163	X	かん	Chinese	漢字〔かんじ〕Chinese characters 漢方薬〔かんぽうやく〕Chinese medicine 漢和辞典〔かんわじてん〕Chinese character-Japanese dictionary
52	間	II-5	86	あいだ/ま	かん/げん	interval; space	夏の間〔なつのあいだ〕during the summer 洋間〔ようま〕Western-style room 床の間〔とこのま〕alcove 間に合う〔まにあう〕to be on time 仲間〔なかま〕group of friends 時間〔じかん〕time 何時間〔なんじかん〕How many hours? 人間〔にんげん〕human beings
53	関			せき/ぜき	かん	barrier	大関〔おおぜき〕second highest ranking in sumo wrestling 関東〔かんとう〕Kanto region [region of eastern Honshu including Tokyo] 関西〔かんさい〕Kansai region [region of western Honshu including Osaka and Kyoto] 関係〔かんけい〕relationship 玄関〔げんかん〕entrance way; foyer

漢字

AP®#	漢字	AIJ-L.	AIJ#	訓読み	音読み	意味	熟語
54	館	III-8	265	X	かん	building	図書館〔としょかん〕library 体育館〔たいいくかん〕gymnasium 映画館〔えいがかん〕movie theater 美術館〔びじゅつかん〕art gallery/museum 博物館〔はくぶつかん〕museum 水族館〔すいぞくかん〕aquarium 館内〔かんない〕in the building 開館〔かいかん〕opening of a building 閉館〔へいかん〕closing of a building 館長〔かんちょう〕superintendent
55	顔			かお	がん	face	顔を洗う〔かおをあらう〕to wash one's face 美顔〔びがん〕クリーム facial cream 洗顔石鹸〔せんがんせっけん〕facial soap
56	願			ねが(う)	がん	wish	お願いします〔おねがいします〕Please. [request] 願書〔がんしょ〕application form
57	期			X	き	term	学期〔がっき〕semester 秋学期〔あきがっき〕fall semester 春学期〔はるがっき〕spring semester 一学期〔いちがっき〕first semester 期末試験〔きまつしけん〕semester exam 期待〔きたい〕expectation; hope
58	機			X	き	machine	機械〔きかい〕machine 飛行機〔ひこうき〕airplane 機長〔きちょう〕pilot 洗濯機〔せんたくき〕washing machine 機会〔きかい〕opportunity
59	帰	II-4	81	かえ(る)	き	to return	家に帰る〔いえにかえる〕return home 帰宅時間〔きたくじかん〕time one returns home 帰国子女〔きこくしじょ〕child who has returned to his/her own country after living abroad
60	気	II-5	84	X	き/け	spirit	元気〔げんき〕healthy 天気〔てんき〕weather 天気予報〔てんきよほう〕weather forecast 気温〔きおん〕temperature 気分〔きぶん〕がいい to feel good 合気道〔あいきどう〕aikido 空気〔くうき〕air 電気〔でんき〕electricity 人気〔にんき〕がある is popular 気持ちが悪い〔きもちがわるい〕to feel sick 寒気〔さむけ〕がする to feel chilly

AP®#	漢字	AIJ-L.	AIJ#	訓読み	音読み	意味	熟語
61	記			X	き	to mark	日記〔にっき〕diary 伝記〔でんき〕biography 記号〔きごう〕symbol 記事〔きじ〕article; news story 記者〔きしゃ〕reporter 記録〔きろく〕record
62	起	III-3	187	おき(る)	き	to wake up	起きる〔おきる〕to wake up 早寝早起き〔はやねはやおき〕sleep early, get up early 起立〔きりつ〕Stand.
63	休	I-9	42	やす(む)	きゅう	to rest	夏休み〔なつやすみ〕summer vacation 冬休み〔ふゆやすみ〕winter vacation 春休み〔はるやすみ〕spring vacation 休み時間〔やすみじかん〕recess; break 休日〔きゅうじつ〕day off 定休日〔ていきゅうび〕regular day off
64	急			いそ(ぐ)	きゅう	to hurry	急がば回れ〔いそがばまわれ〕More haste, less speed; Haste make waste 急〔きゅう〕に suddenly 急行〔きゅうこう〕express 特急〔とっきゅう〕special express 急用〔きゅうよう〕urgent business 救急車〔きゅうきゅうしゃ〕ambulance
65	泣	II-12	155	な(く)	きゅう	to cry	泣く〔なく〕to cry 泣き虫〔なきむし〕crybaby 号泣〔ごうきゅう〕する to cry aloud
66	究			X	きゅう	to investigate	研究〔けんきゅう〕research
67	牛	I-12	56	うし	ぎゅう	cow	子牛〔こうし〕baby cow 牛の肉〔うしのにく〕cow meat 牛肉〔ぎゅうにく〕beef 牛乳〔ぎゅうにゅう〕(cow) milk 和牛〔わぎゅう〕Japanese beef steer 神戸牛〔こうべぎゅう〕Kobe beef 牛丼〔ぎゅうどん〕beef *donburi*
68	去	III-1	176	さ(る)	きょ/こ	to leave	去年〔きょねん〕last year 死去〔しきょ〕death 過去〔かこ〕the past

漢字

AP®#	漢字	AIJ-L.	AIJ#	訓読み	音読み	意味	熟語
69	魚	II-4	77	さかな	ぎょ	fish	魚料理〔さかなりょうり〕fish dish 魚屋〔さかなや〕fish store 魚釣り〔さかなつり〕fishing 金魚〔きんぎょ〕goldfish 人魚〔にんぎょ〕mermaid
70	京	III-6	244	X	きょう	capital	東京〔とうきょう〕Tokyo 京都〔きょうと〕Kyoto 京子〔きょうこ〕さん Kyoko-san
71	強	III-2	178	つよ(い)	きょう	strong	強い力〔つよいちから〕strong power 勉強〔べんきょう〕study 強風〔きょうふう〕strong wind
72	教	II-6	98	おし(える)	きょう	to teach	教える〔おしえる〕to teach 教室〔きょうしつ〕classroom 教科書〔きょうかしょ〕textbook 教育〔きょういく〕education 教師〔きょうし〕teacher 教授〔きょうじゅ〕professor 宗教〔しゅうきょう〕religion キリスト教〔キリストきょう〕Christianity
73	橋	III-7	256	はし/ばし	きょう	bridge	橋を渡る〔はしをわたる〕to cross a bridge 橋本〔はしもと〕さん Hashimoto-san 日本橋〔にほんばし〕Nihonbashi 歩道橋〔ほどうきょう〕pedestrian bridge
74	業			X	ぎょう	work; business	卒業〔そつぎょう〕graduation 授業〔じゅぎょう〕class 工業〔こうぎょう〕(manufacturing) industry 商業〔しょうぎょう〕business 開業〔かいぎょう〕opening of a business
75	局			X	きょく	office	郵便局〔ゆうびんきょく〕post office 放送局〔ほうそうきょく〕broadcast station 薬局〔やっきょく〕pharmacy
76	近	II-10	142	ちか(い)	きん/こん	near	近い店〔ちかいみせ〕nearby shop 近所〔きんじょ〕neighborhood 最近〔さいきん〕recently 近藤〔こんどう〕さん Kondo-san
77	金	I-5	16	かね	きん	gold; money	お金〔おかね〕money 金曜日〔きんようび〕Friday 貯金する〔ちょきんする〕to save money

漢字

AP®#	漢字	AIJ-L.	AIJ#	訓読み	音読み	意味	熟語
78	九	I-4	10	ここの	きゅう/く	nine	九つ〔ここのつ〕nine (general counter) 九日〔ここのか〕the 9th day of the month; 9 days 九人〔きゅうにん〕nine people 九月〔くがつ〕September 九時〔くじ〕9:00
79	空	III-7	258	そら/ぞら/から/あ(く)	くう	sky	青い空〔あおいそら〕blue sky 空手〔からて〕karate 空き缶〔あきかん〕empty can 空気〔くうき〕air 空港〔くうこう〕airport 日本航空〔にほんこうくう〕Japan Air Lines 航空会社〔こうくうがいしゃ〕airline company
80	係			かか(り)	けい	in charge	係りの人〔かかりのひと〕person in charge 関係〔かんけい〕relationship
81	兄	III-1	167	あに/にい	けい/きょう	older brother	兄〔あに〕(own) older brother お兄さん〔おにいさん〕(other's) older brother 父兄会〔ふけいかい〕PTA 兄弟〔きょうだい〕siblings
82	形	III-5	230	かたち	けい/ぎょう	shape	色と形〔いろとかたち〕color and shape 三角形〔さんかくけい〕triangle 人形〔にんぎょう〕doll
83	経			X	けい	to pass through	経済〔けいざい〕economics 経験〔けいけん〕experience 経営〔けいえい〕management 経営者〔けいえいしゃ〕manager
84	計			はか(る)	けい	to measure	計算〔けいさん〕する to calculate 計画〔けいかく〕plan 時計〔とけい〕clock
85	決			き(める/まる)	けつ/けっ	to decide	決める〔きめる〕to decide 決まる〔きまる〕(something) is decided 決心する〔けっしんする〕to decide 解決する〔かいけつする〕to solve
86	結			むす(ぶ)	けつ/けっ	to tie	結婚〔けっこん〕marriage 結論〔けつろん〕conclusion 結果〔けっか〕result

漢字

AP®#	漢字	AIJ-L.	AIJ#	訓読み	音読み	意味	熟語
87	月	I-4	12	つき	げつ/がつ	moon; month	月が出ている〔つきがでている〕The moon is out. お月見〔おつきみ〕moon viewing 三日月〔みかづき〕crescent moon 三カ月〔さんかげつ〕three months 満月〔まんげつ〕full moon 月末〔げつまつ〕end of the month 月謝〔げっしゃ〕monthly tuition fee 九月〔くがつ〕September
88	犬	II-7	105	いぬ	けん	dog	小さい犬〔ちいさいいぬ〕small dog 秋田犬〔あきたけん〕Akita dog (breed)
89	見	I-11	54	み(る)	けん	to see; to look; to watch	見つける〔みつける〕to find お花見〔おはなみ〕cherry blossom viewing 見物〔けんぶつ〕sightseeing 見学〔けんがく〕study by observation 意見〔いけん〕opinion
90	験		X	けん	testing	試験〔しけん〕exam 経験〔けいけん〕experience 体験〔たいけん〕personal experience 実験〔じっけん〕experiment
91	元	II-5	83	もと	げん/がん	origin	元田〔もとだ〕さん Motoda-san 地元〔じもと〕local 元気〔げんき〕healthy お中元〔おちゅうげん〕mid-summer gift 元旦〔がんたん〕the first day of the year
92	現		X	げん	to appear	表現〔ひょうげん〕expression 現実〔げんじつ〕reality 現在〔げんざい〕present; nowadays 現代〔げんだい〕modern
93	言	I-12	59	い(う)/こと	げん	to say	言う〔いう〕to say 言葉〔ことば〕word 言語学〔げんごがく〕linguistics 方言〔ほうげん〕dialect
94	個		X	こ	individual	一個〔いっこ〕one (general counter) 個人〔こじん〕individual, personal 個性〔こせい〕individual personality
95	古	III-5	232	ふる(い)	こ	old	古い本〔ふるいほん〕an old book 古本屋〔ふるほんや〕second hand bookstore 古新聞〔ふるしんぶん〕old newspaper 中古車〔ちゅうこしゃ〕second hand car

漢字

AP®#	漢字	AIJ-L.	AIJ#	訓読み	音読み	意味	熟語
96	五	I-3	5	いつ(つ)	ご	five	五日〔いつか〕the 5th day of the month; five days 五つ〔いつつ〕five (general counter) 五月〔ごがつ〕May 五分の一〔ごぶんのいち〕1/5
97	午	II-5	88	X	ご	noon	午前〔ごぜん〕a.m. 午後〔ごご〕p.m. 正午〔しょうご〕noon
98	後	II-5	89	うし(ろ)/ あと/ のち	ご	after	車の後ろ〔くるまのうしろ〕behind the car 後で〔あとで〕later 午後〔ごご〕p.m. 最後〔さいご〕last
99	語	I-12	60	かた(る)	ご	to talk; language	物語〔ものがたり〕story 英語〔にほんご〕English 外国語〔がいこくご〕foreign language 語学〔ごがく〕language study 単語〔たんご〕vocabulary
100	公	II-10	140	おおや(け)	こう	public	公立〔こうりつ〕public (institution) 公園〔こうえん〕park ハチ公〔ハチこう〕Hachiko (a statue of a dog) 公害〔こうがい〕pollution 公衆便所〔こうしゅうべんじょ〕public toilet
101	口	I-6	19	くち/ ぐち	こう	mouth	大きい口〔おおきいくち〕a big mouth 入口〔いりぐち〕entrance 出口〔でぐち〕exit 改札口〔かいさつぐち〕ticket gate 人口〔じんこう〕population
102	向			む(く)/ む(ける)/ む(かう)/ む(こう)	こう	to face	向井〔むかい〕さん Mukai-san 向こう〔むこう〕other side; beyond 向かい〔むかい〕other side (of) 若者向け〔わかものむけ〕for young people 方向〔ほうこう〕direction
103	好	I-8	34	す(き)/ この(み)/ よし	こう	like	好きな本〔すきなほん〕a book (I) like 大好き〔だいすき〕like very much お好み焼き〔おこのみやき〕*okonomiyaki* 三好〔みよし〕さん Miyoshi-san 好子〔よしこ〕さん Yoshiko-san 好物〔こうぶつ〕favorite food 格好〔かっこう〕appearance; look

漢字

AP®#	漢字	AIJ-L.	AIJ#	訓読み	音読み	意味	熟語
104	工			X	こう/く	industrial	工業〔こうぎょう〕(manufacturing) industry 工学部〔こうがくぶ〕department of technology/engineering 工芸品〔こうげいひん〕handicraft 工場〔こうじょう〕factory 工事中〔こうじちゅう〕under construction 大工〔だいく〕carpenter
105	広	III-4	205	ひろ(い)	こう	wide	広い庭〔ひろいにわ〕a spacious garden 広島〔ひろしま〕Hiroshima 広本〔ひろもと〕さん Hiromoto-san 広大〔こうだい〕なキャンパス huge campus
106	校	I-10	48	X	こう	school	学校〔がっこう〕school 小学校〔しょうがっこう〕elementary school 中学校〔ちゅうがっこう〕middle school 高校〔こうこう〕high school 校長先生〔こうちょうせんせい〕principal 校歌〔こうか〕school song
107	港			みなと	こう	harbor	港の船〔みなとのふね〕boat in the harbor 港町〔みなとまち〕harbor town 空港〔くうこう〕airport 成田空港〔なりたくうこう〕Narita Airport 関西空港〔かんさいくうこう〕Kansai Airport
108	考	III-6	235	かんが(える)	こう	to think	いい考え〔かんがえ〕a good idea 参考書〔さんこうしょ〕reference book
109	行	I-7	26	い(く)/ゆ(く)/おこな(う)	こう/ぎょう	to go	海へ行く〔うみへいく〕to go to the beach 東京行き〔とうきょうゆき〕bound for Tokyo 式を行う〔しきをおこなう〕to hold a ceremony 急行〔きゅうこう〕express (train, bus, etc.) 銀行〔ぎんこう〕bank 年中行事〔ねんちゅうぎょうじ〕annual event
110	降	III-7	252	ふ(る)/お(りる)	こう	to fall; to get off	雨が降る。〔あめがふる〕It rains. 電車を降りる〔でんしゃをおりる〕to get off the train 降り口〔おりぐち〕an exit (to a lower level) 降水量〔こうすいりょう〕precipitation
111	高	II-4	80	たか(い)	こう	tall; expensive	背が高い〔せがたかい〕tall (height) 高田〔たかた〕さん Takata-san 高校生〔こうこうせい〕high school student 女子高校〔じょしこうこう〕girl's high school 男子校〔だんしこう〕boy's school 最高〔さいこう〕the most

漢字

AP®#	漢字	AIJ-L.	AIJ#	訓読み	音読み	意味	熟語
112	号			X	ごう	#	ロボット第一号〔だいいちごう〕Robot No. 1 ひかり５６号〔ごじゅうろくごう〕Hikari No. 56 [*shinkansen*] ６号車〔ろくごうしゃ〕Car No. 6 番号〔ばんごう〕number 信号〔しんごう〕traffic light
113	合	III-4	218	あ(う)/ あ(い)	ごう	to match	待合所〔まちあいしょ〕waiting area 話し合い〔はなしあい〕discussion/conference 試合〔しあい〕(sports) game 合格〔ごうかく〕to pass (an exam)
114	国	II-7	104	くに/ ぐに	こく/ ごく	country	美しい国〔うつくしいくに〕a beautiful country 国々〔くにぐに〕countries 韓国〔かんこく〕South Korea 外国〔がいこく〕foreign country 国内〔こくない〕domestic 全国〔ぜんこく〕national 四国〔しこく〕Shikoku island 国語〔こくご〕national language 中国〔ちゅうごく〕China
115	黒	III-3	199	くろ/ ぐろ	こく	black	黒い犬〔くろいいぬ〕black dog 黒猫〔くろねこ〕black cat 黒字〔くろじ〕in the black (balanced budget) 目黒〔めぐろ〕(city in Tokyo) 黒人〔こくじん〕black person
116	今	I-9	39	いま	こん	now	今、何時？〔いまなんじ〕What time is it now? 今井〔いまい〕さん Imai-san 今川〔いまがわ〕さん Imagawa-san 今日〔きょう〕today 今週〔こんしゅう〕this week 今月〔こんげつ〕this month 今年〔ことし〕this year 今朝〔けさ〕this morning
117	困	III-5	219	こま(る)	こん	to be troubled	困っている〔こまっている〕troubled 困難〔こんなん〕difficulty
118	婚			X	こん	marriage	結婚〔けっこん〕marriage 婚約〔こんやく〕engagement 新婚旅行〔しんこんりょこう〕honeymoon 離婚〔りこん〕divorce 再婚〔さいこん〕する to re-marry 初婚〔しょこん〕first marriage 晩婚〔ばんこん〕late marriage

漢字

AP®#	漢字	AIJ-L.	AIJ#	訓読み	音読み	意味	熟語
119	左	II-2	66	ひだり	さ	left	左目〔ひだりめ〕left eye 左手〔ひだりて〕left hand 左側〔ひだりがわ〕left side 左利き〔ひだりきき〕left-handedness 左右〔さゆう〕left and right
120	最	III-5	221	もっと(も)	さい	most	最も安い〔もっともやすい〕cheapest 最高〔さいこう〕highest; the most 最近〔さいきん〕recent 最長〔さいちょう〕longest 最小〔さいしょう〕smallest 最大〔さいだい〕biggest 最後〔さいご〕last 最新〔さいしん〕newest 最前線〔さいぜんせん〕frontline
121	歳			とし	さい/ざい/せい	age; - years old	百歳〔ひゃくさい〕hundred years old 万歳〔ばんざい〕Hurray! 御歳暮〔おせいぼ〕year-end gift
122	祭			まつ(り)/まつ(る)	さい	festival	桜祭り〔さくらまつり〕Cherry Blossom Festival 祭日〔さいじつ〕national holiday 文化祭〔ぶんかさい〕cultural festival 学園祭〔がくえんさい〕school festival
123	際			きわ/ぎわ	さい	edge	山際〔やまぎわ〕さん Yamagiwa-san 国際〔こくさい〕international 国際空港〔こくさいくうこう〕international airport 国際問題〔こくさいもんだい〕international problem
124	作	II-2	146	つく(る)	さく/さっ	to make	作り方〔つくりかた〕how to make (something) 作文〔さくぶん〕composition 作家〔さっか〕writer; novelist 作詞〔さくし〕lyrics 作曲〔さっきょく〕musical composition 作品〔さくひん〕work; production 作田〔さくだ〕さん Sakuda-san 作物〔さくもつ〕crops
125	昨			X	さく	last preceding	昨日〔きのう/さくじつ〕yesterday 一昨日〔おととい/いっさくじつ〕the day before yesterday 昨年〔さくねん〕last year 昨夜〔さくや〕last night

漢字

漢字

AP®#	漢字	AIJ-L.	AIJ#	訓読み	音読み	意味	熟語
126	雑			X	ざつ	miscellaneous	雑誌〔ざっし〕magazine 複雑〔ふくざつ〕complicated 雑音〔ざつおん〕noise
127	三	I-3	3	み/ み(つ)/ みっ(つ)	さん	three	三つ〔みっつ〕three (general counter) 三日〔みっか〕the 3rd day of the month; three days 三日月〔みかづき〕crescent moon 三人〔さんにん〕three people 三月〔さんがつ〕March 三カ月〔さんかげつ〕three months 三年〔さんねん〕three years 三万円〔さんまんえん〕30,000 yen
128	山	I-7	29	やま	さん	mountain	山本〔やまもと〕さん Yamamoto-san 山々〔やまやま〕mountains 山登り〔やまのぼり〕mountain climbing 富士山〔ふじさん〕Mt. Fuji
129	残			のこ(す)/ のこ(る)	ざん	to leave	残り物〔のこりもの〕leftovers 残念〔ざんねん〕disappointing 残業〔ざんぎょう〕overtime work 残暑〔ざんしょ〕lingering summer heat
130	仕	II-12	158	つか(える)	し	to serve	仕事〔しごと〕job 運転の仕方〔うんてんのしかた〕how to drive 仕方〔しかた〕がない it cannot be helped 仕上げる〔しあげる〕to complete
131	使	II-11	147	つか(う)	し	to use	使う〔つかう〕to use 使用料〔しようりょう〕rental fee 大使〔たいし〕ambassador 大使館〔たいしかん〕embassy
132	四	I-3	4	よ/ よっ/ よん	し	four	四人〔よにん〕four people 四つ〔よっつ〕four (general counter) 四日〔よっか〕the 4th day of the month; four days 四才〔よんさい〕four years old 四月〔しがつ〕April 四季〔しき〕four seasons
133	始	III-2	185	はじ(める)/ はじ(まる)	し	to begin	始まる〔はじまる〕(something) begins 始める〔はじめる〕to begin (something) 始業式〔しぎょうしき〕opening ceremony (of the school term) 開始〔かいし〕する to start

漢字

AP®#	漢字	AIJ-L.	AIJ#	訓読み	音読み	意味	熟語
134	姉	III-1	165	あね/ねえ	し	older sister	上の姉〔うえのあね〕elder of 2 older sisters 下の姉〔したのあね〕younger of 2 older sisters お姉さん〔おねえさん〕(someone's) older sister 姉妹〔しまい〕sisters
135	子	I-8	32	こ	し/じ	child	子供〔こども〕child(ren) 花子〔はなこ〕さん Hanako-san 女子〔じょし〕girl 男子〔だんし〕boy 電子〔でんし〕レンジ microwave oven 障子〔しょうじ〕sliding paper door
136	市			いち	し	city	魚市場〔さかないちば〕fish market 市川〔いちかわ〕さん Ichikawa-san 京都市〔きょうとし〕Kyoto city 市長〔しちょう〕mayor 市内〔しない〕(within a) city
137	思	II-12	160	おも(う)	し	to think	思い出〔おもいで〕memory 思い出す〔おもいだす〕to recall; to remember 思考力〔しこうりょく〕ability to think
138	指			ゆび	し	finger	指輪〔ゆびわ〕ring 親指〔おやゆび〕thumb 中指〔なかゆび〕middle finger 薬指〔くすりゆび〕ring finger 小指〔こゆび〕little finger 指定席〔していせき〕reserved seat 指圧〔しあつ〕finger pressure massage
139	止	II-10	135	と(まる)/と(める)/や(む)	し	to stop	止まれ！〔とまれ！〕Stop! 通行止め〔つうこうどめ〕No thoroughfare. 雨が止んだ〔あめがやんだ〕It stopped raining. 中止〔ちゅうし〕する to cancel
140	私	II-2	61	わたし	し	I; private	私の本〔わたしのほん〕my book 私立〔しりつ/わたくしりつ〕private (establishment)
141	紙	III-6	233	かみ/がみ	し	paper	手紙〔てがみ〕letter 折り紙〔おりがみ〕origami (paper folding) 新聞紙〔しんぶんし〕newsprint (paper) 白紙〔はくし〕blank paper
142	試			ため(す)	し	to try	試合〔しあい〕game (sports) 試験〔しけん〕exam

漢字

AP®#	漢字	AIJ-L.	AIJ#	訓読み	音読み	意味	熟語
143	事	II-5	91	こと/ごと	じ	matter	どんな事〔こと〕what kind of matter? 仕事〔しごと〕job 事故〔じこ〕accident 工事中〔こうじちゅう〕under construction 事務所〔じむしょ〕office 年中行事〔ねんちゅうぎょうじ〕annual event 州知事〔しゅうちじ〕governor
144	字	III-1	164	X	じ	character	きれいな字〔じ〕beautiful handwriting 漢字〔かんじ〕Chinese character 字画〔じかく〕number of strokes in a character 数字〔すうじ〕numeral 赤字〔あかじ〕deficit
145	寺	II-6	94	てら/でら	じ	temple	お寺〔てら〕temple 寺田〔てらだ〕さん Terada-san 山寺〔やまでら〕mountain temple 本願寺〔ほんがんじ〕Honganji Temple
146	持	II-6	97	も(つ)	じ	to hold	持ち物〔もちもの〕one's property (お)持ち帰り〔(お)もちかえり〕takeout (food)
147	時	II-6	95	とき/と	じ	time	その時〔とき〕at that time 時々〔ときどき〕sometimes 時計〔とけい〕clock; watch 九時〔くじ〕nine o'clock 時間〔じかん〕time 時差〔じさ〕time difference
148	次	II-9	132	つぎ	じ	next	次の日〔つぎのひ〕next day 次郎〔じろう〕さん Jiro
149	治			なお(る)/なお(す)	じ/ち	to treat	治る〔なおる〕to be cured 政治〔せいじ〕politics 治療〔ちりょう〕treatment
150	自	II-10	137	X	し/じ	self	自然〔しぜん〕nature 自分〔じぶん〕oneself 自信〔じしん〕confidence 自動車〔じどうしゃ〕car 自転車〔じてんしゃ〕bicycle 自動改札口〔じどうかいさつぐち〕ticket gate 自動販売機〔じどうはんばいき〕vending machine
151	辞			X	じ	word	辞書を引く〔じしょをひく〕to look up (a word) in a dictionary 辞職〔じしょく〕する to resign 祝辞〔しゅくじ〕congratulatory address

AP®#	漢字	AIJ-L.	AIJ#	訓読み	音読み	意味	熟語
152	式			X	しき	ceremony	卒業式〔そつぎょうしき〕graduation ceremony 始業式〔しぎょうしき〕opening ceremony (of a school term) 結婚式場〔けっこんしきじょう〕wedding ceremony location 式服〔しきふく〕ceremonial dress (お)葬式〔(お)そうしき〕funeral 開会式〔かいかいしき〕opening ceremony (of a meeting) 終了式〔しゅうりょうしき〕closing ceremony (of a meeting)
153	七	I-4	8	なな/なの	しち	seven	七つ〔ななつ〕seven (general counter) 七日〔なのか〕the 7th day of the month; seven days 七月〔しちがつ〕July 七味〔しちみ〕seven spice condiment 七夕〔たなばた〕Star Festival (July 7th)
154	失			うしな(う)	しつ	to lose	子供を失う〔こどもをうしなう〕to lose a child 失礼〔しつれい〕rude 失業者〔しつぎょうしゃ〕unemployed person 失明〔しつめい〕する to lose one's eyesight
155	室	II-11	152	X	しつ	room	教室〔きょうしつ〕classroom 寝室〔しんしつ〕bedroom 図書室〔としょしつ〕library room 和室〔わしつ〕Japanese-style room 茶室〔ちゃしつ〕teahouse
156	実			み	じつ/じっ	truth	木の実〔このみ/きのみ〕nut 実は〔じつは〕as a matter of fact; by the way 現実〔げんじつ〕reality 事実〔じじつ〕fact; truth 実話〔じつわ〕true story 実力〔じつりょく〕true ability
157	写			うつ(す)	しゃ	to copy	写す〔うつす〕to copy 写真〔しゃしん〕photo 写生〔しゃせい〕する to sketch
158	社	III-8	272	X	しゃ/じゃ	company	社会〔しゃかい〕society 会社〔かいしゃ〕company 社長〔しゃちょう〕company president 社員〔しゃいん〕company employee 神社〔じんじゃ〕shrine

漢字

AP®#	漢字	AIJ-L.	AIJ#	訓読み	音読み	意味	熟語
159	者	III-8	263	もの	しゃ/じゃ	person	怠け者〔なまけもの〕lazy person 若者〔わかもの〕young person 学者〔がくしゃ〕scholar 医者〔いしゃ〕doctor 患者〔かんじゃ〕patient
160	車	I-7	28	くるま	しゃ	car	車に乗る〔くるまにのる〕to ride a car 電車〔でんしゃ〕electric train 自動車〔じどうしゃ〕automobile 中古車〔ちゅうこしゃ〕used car 新車〔しんしゃ〕new car 空車〔くうしゃ〕empty car 車内〔しゃない〕inside a car or train 駐車場〔ちゅうしゃじょう〕parking lot
161	若	II-9	126	わか(い)	じゃく	young	若さ〔わかさ〕youth 若者〔わかもの〕young person
162	主	III-4	213	おも	しゅ	main	主に〔おもに〕mainly 主人〔しゅじん〕(own) husband; master 主食〔しゅしょく〕staple (main) food 主役〔しゅやく〕main character
163	取	II-8	120	と(る)	しゅ	to take	日本語を取る〔にほんごをとる〕to take Japanese 取引〔とりひき〕business; dealings
164	手	I-6	22	て	しゅ	hand; person	右手〔みぎて〕right hand 左手〔ひだりて〕left hand 手前〔てまえ〕this side (of) 勝手〔かって〕selfish 上手〔じょうず〕skillful 下手〔へた〕unskillful 選手〔せんしゅ〕(sports) player; athlete 運転手〔うんてんしゅ〕driver 歌手〔かしゅ〕singer 手話〔しゅわ〕sign language 拍手〔はくしゅ〕する to applaud; to clap (for) 握手〔あくしゅ〕する to shake hands
165	酒			さけ/-ざけ	しゅ	alcohol	酒を飲む〔さけをのむ〕to drink alcohol 日本酒〔にほんしゅ〕Japanese rice wine 洋酒〔ようしゅ〕Western liquor ぶどう酒〔ぶどうしゅ〕wine 飲酒運転〔いんしゅうんてん〕drunken driving

漢字

AP®#	漢字	AIJ-L.	AIJ#	訓読み	音読み	意味	熟語
166	受			う(ける)	じゅ	to receive	試験を受ける〔しけんをうける〕to take an exam 受け取る〔うけとる〕to receive 受験〔じゅけん〕する to take an entrance exam 受験地獄〔じゅけんじごく〕examination hell
167	授			さず(かる)	じゅ	to receive	授業〔じゅぎょう〕class 授業料〔じゅぎょうりょう〕tuition 教授〔きょうじゅ〕professor 准教授〔じゅんきょうじゅ〕associate professor
168	州	III-6	246	X	しゅう	state	本州〔ほんしゅう〕Honshu; main island of Japan 九州〔きゅうしゅう〕Kyushu Island 州知事〔しゅうちじ〕governor 州立大学〔しゅうりつだいがく〕state university
169	秋	III-2	181	あき	しゅう	autumn	秋学期〔あきがっき〕fall semester 秋風〔あきかぜ〕autumn breeze 晩秋〔ばんしゅう〕late fall 秋山〔あきやま〕さん Akiyama-san 秋分の日〔しゅうぶんのひ〕Autumnal Equinox Day (holiday-Sept. 23 or 24)
170	終	III-2	186	お(わる)	しゅう	to end	終わる〔おわる〕(something) ends 終了式〔しゅうりょうしき〕closing ceremony 終電〔しゅうでん〕last train
171	習	III-2	190	なら(う)	しゅう	to learn	習う〔ならう〕to learn 習い事〔ならいごと〕lesson; practice 学習〔がくしゅう〕learning 練習〔れんしゅう〕practice 習字〔しゅうじ〕calligraphy
172	週	II-5	85	X	しゅう	week	今週〔こんしゅう〕this week 来週〔らいしゅう〕next week 先週〔せんしゅう〕last week 毎週〔まいしゅう〕every week 週末〔しゅうまつ〕weekend 一週間〔いっしゅうかん〕one week
173	集			あつ(まる)/あつ(める)	しゅう	to gather; collect	集まる〔あつまる〕(someone) gathers 集める〔あつめる〕to collect (something) 集会〔しゅうかい〕meeting 集合時間〔しゅうごうじかん〕meeting time 集中〔しゅうちゅう〕する to concentrate

AP®#	漢字	AIJ-L.	AIJ#	訓読み	音読み	意味	熟語
174	住	II-9	124	す(む)	じゅう	to live	住む〔すむ〕to reside 住田〔すみだ〕さん Sumida-san 三井住友銀行〔みついすみともぎんこう〕Mitsui-Sumitomo Bank 住所〔じゅうしょ〕address 住人〔じゅうにん〕resident
175	十	I-4	11	とお	じゅう	ten	十日〔とおか〕the 10th of the month; ten days 二十日〔はつか〕the 20th of the month 十分〔じゅうぶん〕enough 十人十色〔じゅうにんといろ〕To each his own. 十万円〔じゅうまんえん〕hundred thousand yen
176	重	III-4	208	おも(い)	じゅう/ちょう	heavy	重い〔おもい〕heavy 体重〔たいじゅう〕(body) weight 貴重〔きちょう〕valuable
177	宿			やど	しゅく/じゅく	inn	宿屋〔やどや〕inn 宿題〔しゅくだい〕homework 宿泊〔しゅくはく〕する to take lodging (at); to stay over (at) 原宿〔はらじゅく〕Harajuku 新宿〔しんじゅく〕Shinjuku
178	出	II-5	87	で(る)/だ(す)	しゅつ	to go out	家を出る〔いえをでる〕to leave home 出来る〔できる〕can do 出口〔でぐち〕exit 日の出〔ひので〕sunrise 宿題を出す〔しゅくだいをだす〕to turn in homework 出発〔しゅっぱつ〕する to depart 外出〔がいしゅつ〕going out 出身〔しゅっしん〕place of origin 出席〔しゅっせき〕attendance
179	術			X	じゅつ	art	美術〔びじゅつ〕fine arts 芸術〔げいじゅつ〕art 手術〔しゅじゅつ〕surgery
180	春	III-2	179	はる	しゅん	spring	春の花〔はるのはな〕spring flower 春分の日〔しゅんぶんのひ〕Vernal Equinox Day (holiday-March 20 or 21) 青春〔せいしゅん〕youth 思春期〔ししゅんき〕adolescence 春夏秋冬〔しゅんかしゅうとう〕spring, summer, autumn and winter

漢字

AP®#	漢字	AIJ-L.	AIJ#	訓読み	音読み	意味	熟語
181	初			はじ(め)/はつ	しょ	beginning	初〔はじ〕めまして How do you do? 初恋〔はつこい〕first love 最初〔さいしょ〕beginning; first 初夏〔しょか〕early summer
182	所	II-8	117	ところ/どころ	しょ/じょ	place	どんな所〔ところ〕What kind of place? 台所〔だいどころ〕kitchen 場所〔ばしょ〕place 住所〔じゅうしょ〕address 近所〔きんじょ〕neighborhood
183	暑	III-8	273	あつ(い)	しょ	hot	暑い夏〔あついなつ〕hot summer 暑中見舞い〔しょちゅうみまい〕summer greeting (card) 残暑〔ざんしょ〕lingering summer heat
184	書	II-3	71	か(く)	しょ/じょ	to write	書く〔かく〕to write 辞書〔じしょ〕dictionary 参考書〔さんこうしょ〕reference book 書道〔しょどう〕calligraphy
185	女	I-8	33	おんな	じょ	female	女の人〔おんなのひと〕woman 女子〔じょし〕girl 女性〔じょせい〕female 男女共学〔だんじょきょうがく〕co-ed 彼女〔かのじょ〕she; her
186	商			あきな(い)	しょう	commer-cial	商業〔しょうぎょう〕commerce 商売〔しょうばい〕business 商品〔しょうひん〕goods 商品券〔しょうひんけん〕gift certificate
187	小	I-10	44	ちい(さい)/お/こ	しょう	small	小さい〔ちいさい〕small 小川〔おがわ〕さん Ogawa-san 小山〔こやま〕さん Koyama-san 小人〔こども〕child [at the ticket window] 小型〔こがた〕small size 小学校〔しょうがっこう〕elementary school 小学生〔しょうがくせい〕elementary student
188	少	II-10	134	すく(ない)/すこ(し)	しょう	few	少ない〔すくない〕few 少し〔すこし〕a little 少々〔しょうしょう〕just a minute, a little 少年〔しょうねん〕juvenile 少女〔しょうじょ〕little girl 少人数〔しょうにんずう〕small group (of people) 多少〔たしょう〕more or less

漢字

AP®#	漢字	AIJ-L.	AIJ#	訓読み	音読み	意味	熟語
189	笑			わら(う)	しょう	to smile; laugh	笑う〔わらう〕to smile; to laugh
190	上	II-2	63	あ(がる)/うえ/かみ	じょう	top	上がる〔あがる〕to rise; to go up 上原〔うえはら〕さん Uehara-san 川上〔かわかみ〕さん Kawakami-san 上手〔じょうず〕skillful 上品〔じょうひん〕elegant
191	乗	III-7	251	の(る)	じょう	to ride	乗物〔のりもの〕vehicle 乗り場〔のりば〕place for boarding vehicles 乗車券〔じょうしゃけん〕passenger ticket
192	場	III-7	260	ば	じょう	place	場所〔ばしょ〕location 入場券〔にゅうじょうけん〕admission ticket 会場〔かいじょう〕meeting place
193	色	II-7	109	いろ	しょく/しき	color	黄色〔きいろ〕yellow 茶色〔ちゃいろ〕brown 三色〔さんしょく〕three colors 色紙〔しきし〕square drawing paper 景色〔けしき〕scenery
194	食	I-12	58	た(べる)	しょく	to eat	食べ物〔たべもの〕food 食事〔しょくじ〕meal 朝食〔ちょうしょく〕breakfast 昼食〔ちゅうしょく〕lunch 夕食〔ゆうしょく〕dinner 夜食〔やしょく〕night meal 食後〔しょくご〕after a meal 食券〔しょっけん〕meal ticket
195	信			しん(じる)	しん	to trust	信じる〔しんじる〕to believe; to trust 自信〔じしん〕confidence 信用〔しんよう〕trust 赤信号〔あかしんごう〕red light
196	寝	III-3	196	ね(る)	しん	to sleep	早寝早起き〔はやねはやおき〕Early to bed, early to rise. 朝寝坊〔あさねぼう〕(を)する to oversleep (in the morning) 寝室〔しんしつ〕bedroom 寝具〔しんぐ〕bedding
197	心	II-12	159	こころ	しん	heart	いい心〔こころ〕good heart 安心〔あんしん〕する to be relieved 心配〔しんぱい〕する to worry 中心〔ちゅうしん〕center

漢字

AP®#	漢字	AIJ-L.	AIJ#	訓読み	音読み	意味	熟語
198	新	III-5	231	あたら(しい)	しん	new	新しい〔あたらしい〕new 新聞〔しんぶん〕newspaper 新学期〔しんがっき〕new semester 新人〔しんじん〕newcomer 新入生〔しんにゅうせい〕first-year student 新入社員〔しんにゅうしゃいん〕new employee
199	森	III-2	184	もり	しん	forest	緑の森〔みどりのもり〕green forest 森川〔もりかわ〕さん Morikawa-san 青森〔あおもり〕Aomori 森林〔しんりん〕forest
200	神	III-8	271	かみ/かん	しん/じん	god	神様〔かみさま〕god 神田〔かんだ〕さん Kanda-san 神道〔しんとう〕Shintoism 神社〔じんじゃ〕shrine 神戸〔こうべ〕Kobe
201	親			おや	しん	parent	父親〔ちちおや〕father 母親〔ははおや〕mother 両親〔りょうしん〕parents 親戚〔しんせき〕relatives 親切〔しんせつ〕kind
202	身			み	しん	body	中身〔なかみ〕contents 身近〔みぢか〕close (relationship) 身長〔しんちょう〕(person's) height 出身〔しゅっしん〕person's origin
203	進			すす(む)	しん	to advance	進め！〔すすめ〕Advance! 前進〔ぜんしん〕advancement 行進〔こうしん〕parade 進学〔しんがく〕する to go on to college 進化〔しんか〕evolution
204	人	I-8	31	ひと	じん/にん	person	人々〔ひとびと〕people 日本人〔にほんじん〕Japanese person, people 人口〔じんこう〕population 何人〔なにじん〕what nationality? 何人〔なんにん〕how many people? 一人〔ひとり〕one person 二人〔ふたり〕two people
205	図			はか(る)	ず/と	chart	地図〔ちず〕map 図画〔ずが〕drawing 図書館〔としょかん〕library

AP®#	漢字	AIJ-L.	AIJ#	訓読み	音読み	意味	熟語
206	水	I-5	14	みず	すい	water	水を飲む〔みずをのむ〕to drink water 水曜日〔すいようび〕Wednesday 海水〔かいすい〕ocean water 水泳〔すいえい〕swimming
207	数	III-2	189	かず/かぞ(える)	すう	number; to count	数を数える〔かずをかぞえる〕to count the amount 数字〔すうじ〕numeral 数学〔すうがく〕mathematics 生徒数〔せいとすう〕number of students
208	世	II-9	130	よ	せ/せい	world	世の中〔よのなか〕society; world 世界〔せかい〕world 二世〔にせい〕second generation 20世紀〔にじゅっせいき〕20th century
209	制			X	せい	system	制服〔せいふく〕uniform 制度〔せいど〕system
210	成			な(る)/なり	せい	to become	成田空港〔なりたくうこう〕Narita Airport 平成時代〔へいせいじだい〕Heisei Period 成人の日〔せいじんのひ〕Coming of Age Day 成功〔せいこう〕success 成績〔せいせき〕results; scor; grades
211	晴	III-8	267	は(れ)/ば(れ)	せい	clear sky	晴れのち曇り〔はれのちくもり〕clear, later cloudy 秋晴れ〔あきばれ〕clear autumn weather 晴天〔せいてん〕fine weather
212	正	II-6	93	ただ(しい)	せい/しょう	correct	正しい〔ただしい〕correct 正座〔せいざ〕する to sit properly お正月〔おしょうがつ〕New Year's Day 正午〔しょうご〕noon
213	生	I-9	37	う(まれる)/い(きる)/なま	せい/じょう	to be born	生まれる〔うまれる〕to be born 生きる〔いきる〕to live 生け花〔いけばな〕flower arrangement 生たまご〔なまたまご〕raw egg 学生〔がくせい〕student (college) 生徒〔せいと〕student (high school and lower) 誕生日〔たんじょうび〕birthday
214	西	III-3	202	にし	せい/さい	west	西海岸〔にしかいがん〕West Coast 西洋〔せいよう〕the West 関西〔かんさい〕Kansai region [including Osaka, Kyoto, Nara, etc.]

漢字

AP®#	漢字	AIJ-L.	AIJ#	訓読み	音読み	意味	熟語
215	青	II-7	106	あお	せい	blue	青色〔あおいろ〕blue color 青空〔あおぞら〕blue sky 青木〔あおき〕さん Aoki-san 青森〔あおもり〕Aomori 青信号〔あおしんごう〕green light 青春〔せいしゅん〕youth
216	静	III-4	209	しず(か)	せい	quiet	静かな庭〔しずかなにわ〕quiet garden 静岡〔しずおか〕Shizuoka
217	昔			むかし	せき	long ago	昔話〔むかしばなし〕folk tale 昔々〔むかしむかし〕once upon a time
218	石	III-5	227	いし	せき/せつ	rock; stone	大きい石〔おおきいいし〕a big stone 石川〔いしかわ〕さん Ishikawa-san 石庭〔せきてい〕rock garden 宝石〔ほうせき〕jewel 石鹸〔せっけん〕soap
219	赤	III-3	198	あか	せき	red	赤色〔あかいろ〕red color 赤ちゃん〔あかちゃん〕baby 赤字〔あかじ〕deficit 赤信号〔あかしんごう〕red light 赤飯〔せきはん〕*mochi* rice steamed with red beans 赤道〔せきどう〕equator
220	切	III-5	229	き(る)/きり/きっ	せつ	to cut	紙を切る〔かみをきる〕to cut paper 締切〔しめきり〕deadline 切手〔きって〕(postage) stamp 切符〔きっぷ〕ticket 大切〔たいせつ〕important 親切〔しんせつ〕kind
221	接			X	せつ	to connect	直接〔ちょくせつ〕direct 間接〔かんせつ〕indirect 面接〔めんせつ〕interview 面接室〔めんせつしつ〕interview room
222	節			ふし	せつ	node; joint	節目〔ふしめ〕turning point 季節〔きせつ〕season 節分〔せつぶん〕Bean Throwing Celebration 関節〔かんせつ〕joints (knee, elbow) 節約〔せつやく〕する to economize
223	説			と(く)	せつ	to explain	説明〔せつめい〕explanation 小説〔しょうせつ〕novel 解説者〔かいせつしゃ〕commentator

漢字

AP®#	漢字	AIJ-L.	AIJ#	訓読み	音読み	意味	熟語
224	雪	II-6	101	ゆき	せつ	snow	雪が降る〔ゆきがふる〕to snow 大雪〔おおゆき〕heavy snow 雪祭り〔ゆきまつり〕Snow Festival 雪山〔ゆきやま〕snow-covered mountain 雪像〔せつぞう〕snow statue
225	先	I-9	37	さき	せん	first	お先に〔おさきに〕Excuse me for going/doing something first. 先生〔せんせい〕teacher 先月〔せんげつ〕last month 先週〔せんしゅう〕last week 先日〔せんじつ〕the other day
226	千	I-11	51	ち	せん	thousand	千代田区〔ちよだく〕Chiyoda Ward (Tokyo) 千円〔せんえん〕one thousand yen 三千〔さんぜん〕three thousand
227	専			X	せん	exclusive	専攻〔せんこう〕major (college) 専門店〔せんもんてん〕specialty store 専業主婦〔せんぎょうしゅふ〕housewife [full-time]
228	川	I-7	30	かわ/ -がわ	せん	river	川上〔かわかみ〕upper reaches of a river 川下〔かわしも〕downstream 川本〔かわもと〕さん Kawamoto-san 小川〔おがわ〕さん Ogawa-san 大井川〔おおいがわ〕Ooi River
229	洗	II-11	145	あら(う)	せん	to wash	洗う〔あらう〕to wash 洗濯機〔せんたくき〕washing machine 洗面所〔せんめんじょ〕washroom 洗顔石鹸〔せんがんせっけん〕facial soap
230	線	III-7	257	X	せん	line	線を引く〔せんをひく〕to draw a line 山手線〔やまのてせん〕Yamanote Line 新幹線〔しんかんせん〕bullet train 下線〔かせん〕underline 白線〔はくせん〕white line
231	選			えら(ぶ)	せん	to choose	選ぶ〔えらぶ〕to choose; to select 選手〔せんしゅ〕athlete 選挙〔せんきょ〕election
232	前	II-3	69	まえ	ぜん	before; front	寝る前〔ねるまえ〕before sleeping 病院の前〔びょういんのまえ〕front of the hospital 前川〔まえかわ〕さん Maekawa-san 前田〔まえだ〕さん Maeda-san 午前〔ごぜん〕a.m.

漢字

AP®#	漢字	AIJ-L.	AIJ#	訓読み	音読み	意味	熟語
233	然			X	ぜん	be as is	自然〔しぜん〕nature 全然〔ぜんぜん〕(not) at all 突然〔とつぜん〕suddenly
234	全	II-12	156	まった(く)/すべ(て)	ぜん	whole	全く〔まったく〕(not) at all 全て〔すべて〕all 全部〔ぜんぶ〕all 全体〔ぜんたい〕whole 全国〔ぜんこく〕entire nation 全員〔ぜんいん〕everyone 全然〔ぜんぜん〕(not) at all
235	組			くみ/ぐみ	そ	group	一年一組〔いちねんいちくみ〕1st year class, Group #1 テレビ番組〔ばんぐみ〕TV program 赤組〔あかぐみ〕red team
236	早	I-10	46	はや(い)	そう	early	早寝早起き〔はやねはやおき〕early to bed, early to rise 早川〔はやかわ〕さん Hayakawa-san 早春〔そうしゅん〕early spring 早朝〔そうちょう〕early morning 早退〔そうたい〕early departure
237	相			あい	そう	mutually	相手〔あいて〕partner; other party 相談〔そうだん〕する to consult 相撲〔すもう〕sumo wrestling
238	走	II-8	122	はし(る)	そう	to run	走る〔はしる〕to run 走者〔そうしゃ〕runner 暴走族〔ぼうそうぞく〕delinquent drivers
239	送	III-8	262	おく(る)	そう	to send	送る〔おくる〕to send 放送〔ほうそう〕broadcast 郵送〔ゆうそう〕する to send by mail 送料〔そうりょう〕postage 運送会社〔うんそうがいしゃ〕shipping company 送別会〔そうべつかい〕farewell party
240	贈			おく(る)	ぞう	to present	贈り物〔おくりもの〕gift 贈答品〔ぞうとうひん〕gift item
241	側			-がわ	そく	side	右側〔みぎがわ〕right side 東側〔ひだりがわ〕east side 向かい側〔むかいがわ〕other side 両側〔りょうがわ〕both sides

漢字

AP®#	漢字	AIJ-L.	AIJ#	訓読み	音読み	意味	熟語
242	足	II-8	114	あし/た(りる)	そく	foot; enough	右足〔みぎあし〕right foot 左足〔ひだりあし〕left foot 手足〔てあし〕hands and feet 足りない〔たりない〕not enough 寝不足〔ねぶそく〕lack of sleep
243	速	III-8	268	はや(い)	そく	fast	速い車〔はやいくるま〕fast car 速度〔そくど〕speed 早速〔さっそく〕immediately
244	族			X	ぞく	group	家族〔かぞく〕family 親族〔しんぞく〕relatives 暴走族〔ぼうそうぞく〕delinquent drivers
245	続			つづ(く)	ぞく	to continue	続く〔つづく〕to continue 続ける〔つづける〕to continue (something) 連続〔れんぞく〕ドラマ serial drama
246	卒			X	そつ	to graduate	卒業〔そつぎょう〕graduation 大卒〔だいそつ〕college graduate 高卒〔こうそつ〕high school graduate
247	村	III-6	243	むら	そん	village	村山〔むらやま〕さん Murayama-san 村人〔むらびと〕villager 村長〔そんちょう〕village chief
248	多	II-10	133	おお(い)	た	many	多くの人〔おおくのひと〕many people 多田〔おおた〕さん Oota-san 多分〔たぶん〕probably 大多数〔だいたすう〕great majority
249	太	II-12	153	ふと(る)	た/たい	to gain; thick	太る〔ふとる〕to gain weight 太郎〔たろう〕さん Taro-san 太平洋〔たいへいよう〕Pacific Ocean 太陽〔たいよう〕sun
250	打			う(つ)	だ	to hit	ボールを打つ〔うつ〕to hit a ball 打者〔だしゃ〕batter (baseball) 打率〔だりつ〕batting average 本塁打〔ほんるいだ〕home run (baseball)
251	体			からだ	たい	body	強い体〔つよいからだ〕strong body 体育〔たいいく〕physical education 体育館〔たいいくかん〕gym 全体〔ぜんたい〕entirety 体重〔たいじゅう〕(body) weight 体力〔たいりょく〕physical strength

漢字

AP®#	漢字	AIJ-L.	AIJ#	訓読み	音読み	意味	熟語
252	対			X	たい	vs.	反対〔はんたい〕opposition 絶対〔ぜったい〕に absolutely A対〔たい〕B A versus B 5対3〔ごたいさん〕5 to 3 (score)
253	待	II-6	96	ま(つ)	たい	to wait	待つ〔まつ〕to wait 待合室〔まちあいしつ〕waiting room 招待〔しょうたい〕する to invite
254	貸			か(す)	たい	to lend	お金を貸す〔おかねをかす〕to lend money 貸家〔かしや〕rental home
255	台	II-11	144	X	たい/だい	step; counter for large, mechanized items	台風〔たいふう〕typhoon 台湾〔たいわん〕Taiwan 台所〔だいどころ〕kitchen 一台の車〔いちだいのくるま〕one car
256	大	I-10	43	おお(きい)	たい/だい	big	大きい家〔おおきいいえ〕a big house 大変〔たいへん〕very; terrible 大学〔だいがく〕college 大学院〔だいがくいん〕graduate school 大学生〔だいがくせい〕college student 東大〔とうだい〕Tokyo University 大事〔だいじ〕important 大丈夫〔だいじょうぶ〕all right 大人〔おとな〕adult
257	第			X	だい	ordinal	第一日〔だいいちにち〕the first day 第一〔だいいち〕first 第二月曜日〔だいにげつようび〕second Monday
258	題	III-6	241	X	だい	title	題〔だい〕title 題名〔だいめい〕name of a title 宿題〔しゅくだい〕homework 問題〔もんだい〕problem 話題〔わだい〕topic 課題〔かだい〕theme; task
259	達			X	たち/だち/たつ	pluralizer; skilled	人達〔ひとたち〕people 友達〔ともだち〕friend 速達〔そくたつ〕special delivery 配達〔はいたつ〕する to deliver 配達人〔はいたつにん〕delivery person 料理の達人〔りょうりのたつじん〕iron chef 発達〔はったつ〕する to develop

漢字

AP®#	漢字	AIJ-L.	AIJ#	訓読み	音読み	意味	熟語
260	単			X	たん	single	単語〔たんご〕vocabulary 簡単〔かんたん〕simple 単位〔たんい〕credit
261	短			みじか(い)	たん	short	短い本〔みじかいほん〕a short book 短所〔たんしょ〕weak point 最短〔さいたん〕shortest distance 短文〔たんぶん〕short sentence
262	男	I-8	36	おとこ	だん	male	男の子〔おとこのこ〕boy 男子〔だんし〕boy 男性〔だんせい〕male 男女共学〔だんじょきょうがく〕co-education
263	知	II-11	148	し(る)	ち	to know	知らない〔しらない〕do not know 知人〔ちじん〕acquaintance 知事〔ちじ〕governor
264	地	III-6	238	X	ち/じ	land; ground	地下〔ちか〕basement 地下鉄〔ちかてつ〕subway 土地〔とち〕land 地球〔ちきゅう〕earth 地方〔ちほう〕area; locality 地震〔じしん〕earthquake 地元〔じもと〕local 地味〔じみ〕conservative
265	池	III-6	237	いけ	ち	pond	池の中〔いけのなか〕inside the pond 池田〔いけだ〕さん Ikeda-san 電池〔でんち〕battery
266	置	III-4	214	お(く)	ち	to put	チップを置く〔おく〕to leave a tip 位置〔いち〕location
267	遅			おく(れる)/おそ(い)	ち	to be late; late	遅れる〔おくれる〕to be late 遅い〔おそい〕late 遅刻〔ちこく〕tardiness
268	茶	III-5	224	X	ちゃ	tea	茶色〔ちゃいろ〕brown color 茶道〔ちゃどう/さどう〕tea ceremony 茶室〔ちゃしつ〕teahouse 抹茶〔まっちゃ〕powdered green tea for ceremony お茶漬け〔おちゃづけ〕tea over rice

漢字

AP®#	漢字	AIJ-L.	AIJ#	訓読み	音読み	意味	熟語
269	着	II-6	100	き(る)/ -ぎ/ つ(く)	ちゃく	to wear; to arrive	着る〔きる〕to wear [above the waist] 着物〔きもの〕kimono 下着〔したぎ〕underwear 着く〔つく〕to arrive 東京着〔とうきょうちゃく〕Tokyo arrival 到着〔とうちゃく〕arrival 着信〔ちゃくしん〕arrival of mail
270	中	I-10	45	なか	ちゅう/ -じゅう	inside	中村〔なかむら〕さん Nakamura-san 夜中〔よなか〕midnight 中学生〔ちゅうがくせい〕middle school student 中国〔ちゅうごく〕China 中止〔ちゅうし〕する to cancel 勉強中〔べんきょうちゅう〕in the midst of studying 一日中〔いちにちじゅう〕all day long
271	昼	III-1	170	ひる	ちゅう	noon	昼ご飯〔ひるごはん〕lunch 昼寝〔ひるね〕nap 昼食〔ちゅうしょく〕lunch
272	注			そそ(ぐ)	ちゅう	to pour	注意〔ちゅうい〕する to be careful 注文〔ちゅうもん〕する to order 特注〔とくちゅう〕special order
273	朝	III-1	169	あさ	ちょう	morning	朝ご飯〔あさごはん〕breakfast 朝日新聞〔あさひじんぶん〕Asahi newspaper 朝食〔ちょうしょく〕breakfast 早朝〔そうちょう〕early morning 今朝〔けさ〕this morning
274	町	III-6	242	まち	ちょう	town	町田〔まちだ〕さん Machida-san 町工場〔まちこうば〕small factory in town 町中〔まちなか〕midtown 町長〔ちょうちょう〕town chief
275	調			しら(べる)	ちょう	to check	調べる〔しらべる〕to check, search 調子〔ちょうし〕がいい in good condition 調和〔ちょうわ〕harmony 調味料〔ちょうみりょう〕seasoning (salt, sugar, etc.)

漢字

漢字

AP®#	漢字	AIJ-L.	AIJ#	訓読み	音読み	意味	熟語
276	長	II-11	151	なが（い）	ちょう	long; chief	長い間〔ながいあいだ〕for a long time 長崎〔ながさき〕Nagasaki 長島〔ながしま〕さん Nagashima-san 社長〔しゃちょう〕company president 会長〔かいちょう〕president (of an organization) 市長〔しちょう〕mayor 長所〔ちょうしょ〕good point
277	鳥	II-11	143	とり	ちょう	bird	青い鳥〔あおいとり〕a blue bird 小鳥〔ことり〕a small bird 焼き鳥〔やきとり〕grilled skewered chicken 鳥肉〔とりにく〕chicken (fresh) 一石二鳥〔いっせきにちょう〕Kill two birds with one stone.
278	痛	III-4	207	いた（い）	つう	painful	痛い〔いたい〕painful 痛み止め〔いたみどめ〕painkiller 頭痛〔ずつう〕headache 腹痛〔ふくつう〕stomach ache
279	通			とお（る）/かよ（う）	つう	to go through; to commute	通る〔とおる〕to go through 大通り〔おおどおり〕avenue 通う〔かよう〕to commute 交通〔こうつう〕transportation 通学〔つうがく〕commuting to school 通行人〔つうこうにん〕pedestrian 通行止め〔つうこうどめ〕road closure 普通〔ふつう〕ordinary 通知表〔つうちひょう〕report card
280	低			ひく（い）	てい	low	背が低い〔せがひくい〕short (height) 最低〔さいてい〕worst 低気圧〔ていきあつ〕low (atmospheric) pressure; bad temper
281	定			さだ（める）	てい	fixed	指定席〔していせき〕reserved seat 予定〔よてい〕plans 定期券〔ていきけん〕commuter pass 定休日〔ていきゅうび〕day off
282	庭	III-4	217	にわ	てい	garden	美しい庭〔うつくしいにわ〕beautiful garden 石庭〔せきてい〕rock garden 日本庭園〔にほんていえん〕Japanese garden 家庭〔かてい〕family; home; household 家庭科〔かていか〕home economics

漢字

AP®#	漢字	AIJ-L.	AIJ#	訓読み	音読み	意味	熟語
283	弟	III-1	168	おとうと	てい/だい/で	younger brother	弟〔おとうと〕younger brother 兄弟〔きょうだい〕siblings 弟子〔でし〕disciple; apprentice
284	的	III-4	216	まと	てき	- like; target	日本的〔にほんてき〕typically Japanese 印象的〔いんしょうてき〕impressive 目的〔もくてき〕purpose
285	天	I-12	55	あま	てん	heaven	天の川〔あまのかわ〕Milky Way 天気〔てんき〕weather 天国〔てんごく〕heaven 天才〔てんさい〕genius 天ぷら〔てんぷら〕tempura
286	店	III-7	254	みせ	てん	store	お店〔おみせ〕store 店長〔てんちょう〕shop manager 店員〔てんいん〕salesperson; clerk 本店〔ほんてん〕head office 開店〔かいてん〕opening of a shop 閉店〔へいてん〕closing of a shop
287	転			ころ(がる)	てん	to roll	運転〔うんてん〕する to drive 運転手〔うんてんしゅ〕driver 自転車〔じてんしゃ〕bicycle 回転寿司〔かいてんずし〕conveyor belt sushi
288	点	II-8	115	X	てん	point	十点〔じゅってん〕10 points 悪い点〔わるいてん〕bad score 満点〔まんてん〕perfect score
289	伝			つた(える)	でん	to convey	伝える〔つたえる〕to convey; to report 手伝う〔てつだう〕to help 伝統的〔でんとうてき〕traditional 伝言〔でんごん〕verbal message
290	田	I-8	35	た/-だ	でん	rice field	田中〔たなか〕さん Tanaka-san 吉田〔よしだ〕さん Yoshida-san 田舎〔いなか〕countryside
291	電	II-4	76	X	でん	electricity	電話〔でんわ〕telephone 電車〔でんしゃ〕electric car 電気〔でんき〕electricity 電力〔でんりょく〕electric power 電子〔でんし〕レンジ microwave oven
292	登			のぼ(る)	と/とう	to climb	登る〔のぼる〕to climb 登山〔とざん〕mountain climbing 登場人物〔とうじょうじんぶつ〕characters (in a play or novel)

AP®#	漢字	AIJ-L.	AIJ#	訓読み	音読み	意味	熟語
293	都	III-8	264	みやこ	と/つ	capital	都会〔とかい〕city; metropolis 京都〔きょうと〕Kyoto 東京都〔とうきょうと〕Tokyo Metropolitan area 都合〔つごう〕がいい convenient
294	度	III-8	270	たび	ど	- time(s)	行く度に〔いくたびに〕every time I go もう一度〔いちど〕one more time 温度〔おんど〕temperature 今度〔こんど〕this time; next time
295	土	I-5	17	つち	ど/と	soil	土田〔つちだ〕さん Tsuchida-san 土地〔とち〕land 土曜日〔どようび〕Saturday 本土〔ほんど〕mainland
296	冬	III-2	182	ふゆ	とう	winter	冬休み〔ふゆやすみ〕winter vacation 冬服〔ふゆふく〕winter clothing 真冬〔まふゆ〕midwinter 冬至〔とうじ〕winter solstice
297	島	II-11	143	しま	とう	island	広島〔ひろしま〕Hiroshima 島田〔しまだ〕さん Shimada-san 島々〔しまじま〕islands 半島〔はんとう〕peninsula
298	東	III-3	201	ひがし	とう	east	東山〔ひがしやま〕さん Higashiyama-san 東西南北〔とうざいなんぼく〕east, west, south and north 東京〔とうきょう〕Tokyo 東大〔とうだい〕Tokyo University 関東〔かんとう〕Kanto area [region of eastern Honshu including Tokyo]
299	答			こた(える)	とう	answer	答え〔こたえ〕answer 解答〔かいとう〕answer; solution
300	頭	III-7	255	あたま	とう/ず	head	頭がいい〔あたまがいい〕smart 一頭の馬〔いっとうのうま〕one horse 頭痛〔ずつう〕headache
301	働	III-5	226	はたら(く)	どう	to work	働く〔はたらく〕to work 働き者〔はたらきもの〕hard worker 労働時間〔ろうどうじかん〕working hours 労働者〔ろうどうしゃ〕laborer; worker

漢字

AP®#	漢字	AIJ-L.	AIJ#	訓読み	音読み	意味	熟語
302	動	III-5	225	うご(く)	どう	to move	動く〔うごく〕to move 自動車〔じどうしゃ〕automobile 運動〔うんどう〕exercise; sports 運動場〔うんどうじょう〕athletic field 動物〔どうぶつ〕animal 動物園〔どうぶつえん〕zoo 活動〔かつどう〕activity 動画〔どうが〕video; moving image
303	同	III-6	234	おな(じ)	どう	same	同じ〔おなじ〕same 同点〔どうてん〕tie (score) 同時〔どうじ〕simultaneous 同意〔どうい〕consent 同情〔どうじょう〕する to sympathize
304	道	II-10	138	みち	とう/どう	road; way	道〔みち〕road 道子〔みちこ〕さん Michiko-san 神道〔しんとう〕Shinto 道路〔どうろ〕road 横断歩道〔おうだんほどう〕pedestrian crossing 書道〔しょどう〕calligraphy 茶道〔さどう/ちゃどう〕tea ceremony 柔道〔じゅうどう〕judo 剣道〔けんどう〕kendo [way of the sword] 合気道〔あいきどう〕aikido 道場〔どうじょう〕dojo; hall used for martial arts 北海道〔ほっかいどう〕Hokkaido 道徳〔どうとく〕morals
305	特	III-5	220	X	とく	special	特に〔とくに〕especially 特急〔とっきゅう〕limited express 特別〔とくべつ〕special 特大〔とくだい〕extra big 特注〔とくちゅう〕special order
306	読	II-7	112	よ(む)	どく	to read	本を読む〔ほんをよむ〕to read a book 読み物〔よみもの〕a reading 読売新聞〔よみうりしんぶん〕Yomiuri Newspaper 読書〔どくしょ〕reading (as a hobby or interest) 音読〔おんどく〕reading aloud

漢字

AP®#	漢字	AIJ-L.	AIJ#	訓読み	音読み	意味	熟語
307	内	III-4	212	うち	ない	inside	山内〔やまうち〕さん Yamauchi-san 内田〔うちだ〕さん Uchida-san 内村〔うちむら〕さん Uchimura-san 家内〔かない〕(own) wife 家庭内暴力〔かていないぼうりょく〕domestic violence 内緒〔ないしょ〕secret; confidential
308	南	III-3	203	みなみ	なん	south	南口〔みなみぐち〕south gate 南田〔みなみだ〕さん Minamida-san 南極〔なんきょく〕South Pole 東南〔とうなん〕アジア Southeast Asia 南山大学〔なんざんだいがく〕Nanzan University
309	難			むずか(しい)/-がた(い)	なん	difficult	難しい〔むずかしい〕difficult 有難う〔ありがとう〕Thank you. 難問〔なんもん〕difficult question
310	二	I-3	2	ふた	に	two	二つ〔ふたつ〕two (general counter) 二人〔ふたり〕two (people) 二日〔ふつか〕the second day of the month 二月〔にがつ〕February 二週間〔にしゅうかん〕two weeks 二年〔にねん〕two years
311	肉	II-4	78	X	にく	meat	牛肉〔ぎゅうにく〕beef 豚肉〔ぶたにく〕pork 筋肉〔きんにく〕muscles
312	日	I-3	6	ひ/び/か	にち/じつ	day	日の丸〔ひのまる〕(name of) the Japanese flag お日様〔おひさま〕Sun 日曜日〔にちようび〕Sunday 定休日〔ていきゅうび〕regular day off 二日〔ふつか〕the 2nd day of the month 日米〔にちべい〕Japan-U.S. 何日〔なんにち〕what day?; how many days? 一日〔いちにち〕one day 一日〔ついたち〕the 1st day of the month; two days 祭日〔さいじつ〕festival day 祝日〔しゅくじつ〕holiday

漢字

AP®#	漢字	AIJ-L.	AIJ#	訓読み	音読み	意味	熟語
313	入	II-8	121	はい(る)/い(れる)	にゅう	to enter	入る〔はいる〕to enter 入れる〔いれる〕to put in 入口〔いりぐち〕entrance 入学式〔にゅうがくしき〕school entrance ceremony 入場券〔にゅうじょうけん〕admission ticket 入会〔にゅうかい〕する to join an organized group 入部〔にゅうぶ〕する to join a club 入試〔にゅうし〕entrance exam
314	熱			あつ(い)	ねつ	hot; fever	熱いお茶〔あついおちゃ〕hot tea 高い熱〔たかいねつ〕high fever 熱海〔あたみ〕Atami (place name)
315	年	I-9	41	とし	ねん	year	今年〔ことし〕this year 年を取っている〔としをとっている〕elderly お年寄り〔おとしより〕the elderly お年玉〔おとしだま〕New Year's monetary gift 去年〔きょねん〕last year 来年〔らいねん〕next year 毎年〔まいねん〕every year ２０２０年〔にせんにじゅうねん〕the year 2020 ３年生〔さんねんせい〕3rd grade student 年中行事〔ねんちゅうぎょうじ〕annual event 年末〔ねんまつ〕end of the year 中年〔ちゅうねん〕middle age 少年〔しょうねん〕boys; juveniles
316	背			せ	はい	back	背が高い〔せがたかい〕tall (height) 背中〔せなか〕back (of one's body)
317	配			くば(る)	はい/ぱい	to deliver	配る〔くばる〕to deliver; to distribute 心配〔しんぱい〕する to worry 配達人〔はいたつにん〕delivery person
318	買	II-4	82	か(う)	ばい	to buy	買う〔かう〕to buy 買物〔かいもの〕shopping
319	売	II-7	111	う(る)	ばい	to sell	安売り〔やすうり〕sale 売店〔ばいてん〕shop; stand 商売〔しょうばい〕trade; business 券売機〔けんばいき〕ticket vending machine 発売〔はつばい〕する to be for sale

AP®#	漢字	AIJ-L.	AIJ#	訓読み	音読み	意味	熟語
320	白	I-11	49	しろ	ばい/はく	white	白い〔しろい〕white 白人〔はくじん〕Caucasian 白紙〔はくし〕blank paper 紅白歌合戦〔こうはくうたがっせん〕Red & White Song Festival
321	八	I-4	9	やっ/よう	はち/はっ	eight	八つ〔やっつ〕eight (general counter) 八日〔ようか〕the 8th day of the month; 8 days 八月〔はちがつ〕August 八人〔はちにん〕eight people 八才〔はっさい〕eight years old 八百屋〔やおや〕greengrocer
322	発			X	はつ/ぱつ/はっ	to depart	発音〔はつおん〕pronunciation 東京発〔とうきょうはつ〕Tokyo departure 発明〔はつめい〕invention 出発〔しゅっぱつ〕departure 発車〔はっしゃ〕departure of a vehicle 発表〔はっぴょう〕する to present verbally; to announce 発達〔はったつ〕development 発見〔はっけん〕discovery
323	半	II-8	116	X	はん	half	半分〔はんぶん〕half 五時半〔ごじはん〕5:30
324	反			X	はん	against	反対〔はんたい〕する to oppose 駐車違反〔ちゅうしゃいはん〕parking violation
325	飯	III-3	191	めし	はん	cooked rice	焼き飯〔やきめし〕fried rice ご飯〔ごはん〕rice (cooked) 朝ご飯〔あさごはん〕breakfast 昼ご飯〔ひるごはん〕lunch 炊飯器〔すいはんき〕digital rice cooker
326	晩	II-7	192	X	ばん	evening	晩ご飯〔ばんごはん〕dinner 今晩〔こんばん〕tonight
327	番	II-7	107	X	ばん	number	一番〔いちばん〕best; first; No. 1; most 番号〔ばんごう〕number 番地〔ばんち〕house number 順番〔じゅんばん〕order; sequence 交番〔こうばん〕police box テレビ番組〔ばんぐみ〕TV program
328	非			X	ひ	non -	非常口〔ひじょうぐち〕emergency exit 非常に〔ひじょうに〕extremely 非売品〔ひばいひん〕article not for sale

漢字

AP®#	漢字	AIJ-L.	AIJ#	訓読み	音読み	意味	熟語
329	飛			と(ぶ)	ひ	to fly; jump	空を飛ぶ〔そらをとぶ〕to fly in the air 飛行機〔ひこうき〕airplane 飛行時間〔ひこうじかん〕flight time (length)
330	美	II-9	125	うつく(しい)	び	beautiful	美しい〔うつくしい〕beautiful 美人〔びじん〕beautiful woman 美術〔びじゅつ〕fine arts 美術館〔びじゅつかん〕art museum 美容院〔びよういん〕beauty salon
331	鼻			はな	び	nose	高い鼻〔たかいはな〕tall nose
332	必			かなら(ず)	ひつ	necessary	必ず〔かならず〕surely; definitely 必要〔ひつよう〕necessary 必勝〔ひっしょう〕certain victory 必須科目〔ひっすかもく〕required subjects
333	百	I-11	50	X	ひゃく/びゃく/ぴゃく	hundred	百円〔ひゃくえん〕100 yen 三百〔さんびゃく〕300 八百〔はっぴゃく〕800 八百屋〔やおや〕greengrocer
334	氷			こおり/-ごおり	ひょう	ice	氷〔こおり〕ice かき氷〔かきごおり〕shaved ice; snow cone 氷河〔ひょうが〕glacier
335	表			おもて	ひょう	front; chart	家の表〔いえのおもて〕frontside of the house 表を作る〔ひょうをつくる〕make a chart 発表〔はっぴょう〕する to present (orally); to announce 表現〔ひょうげん〕する to express
336	病	III-8	266	やま(い)	びょう	illness	病は気から〔やまいはきから〕Illness starts from the spirit. 病気〔びょうき〕illness 病院〔びょういん〕hospital 病名〔びょうめい〕name of a disease 病人〔びょうにん〕sick person 心臓病〔しんぞうびょう〕heart disease
337	品			しな	ひん	item	品物〔しなもの〕goods 品川駅〔しながわえき〕Shinagawa Station 化粧品〔けしょうひん〕cosmetics 商品券〔しょうひんけん〕gift certificate 食品〔しょくひん〕commodity 上品な人〔じょうひんなひと〕elegant person

AP®#	漢字	AIJ-L.	AIJ#	訓読み	音読み	意味	熟語
338	不			X	ふ/ぶ	non -	不便〔ふべん〕inconvenient 不公平〔ふこうへい〕unfair 不自由〔ふじゆう〕handicap 不安〔ふあん〕uneasy 不幸〔ふこう〕unhappy 不平〔ふへい〕complaint 睡眠不足〔すいみんぶそく〕lack of sleep
339	付			つ(く)	ふ/ぷ	attach	みそ汁付き〔みそしるつき〕with *miso* soup 気付く〔きづく〕to notice 付き合う〔つきあう〕to associate with 付近〔ふきん〕neighborhood; vicinity 添付〔てんぷ〕attachment
340	夫			おっと	ふ/ふう	man; (own) husband	私の夫〔わたしのおっと〕my husband ケネディー夫人〔ふじん〕Mrs. Kennedy 夫婦〔ふうふ〕married couple
341	婦			X	ふ	married woman	主婦〔しゅふ〕housewife 婦人〔ふじん〕woman 婦人服〔ふじんふく〕woman's clothing
342	父	I-6	23	ちち/とう	ふ/ぷ	father	父親〔ちちおや〕father 父方〔ちちかた〕father's side of the family お父さん〔おとうさん〕(someone's) father 祖父〔そふ〕(own) grandfather 父母〔ふぼ〕(own) parents 父兄会〔ふけいかい〕parents' association 神父〔しんぷ〕Catholic priest
343	部	II-12	157	へ/べ	ぶ	part	部屋〔へや〕room 子供部屋〔こどもべや〕child's room 全部〔ぜんぶ〕all 一部〔いちぶ〕one part 部分〔ぶぶん〕portion 部員〔ぶいん〕member 部活〔ぶかつ〕club activity
344	風	II-9	129	かぜ	ふう/ふ	wind	風〔かぜ〕wind 風邪〔かぜ〕a cold 強風〔きょうふう〕strong wind 台風〔たいふう〕typhoon 風力〔ふうりょく〕wind power 和風〔わふう〕Japanese style 洋風〔ようふう〕Western style 風呂〔ふろ〕bath

漢字

AP®#	漢字	AIJ-L.	AIJ#	訓読み	音読み	意味	熟語
345	服			X	ふく	cloth	制服〔せいふく〕school uniform 洋服〔ようふく〕Western-style clothes 和服〔わふく〕Japanese clothes 服装〔ふくそう〕clothing
346	払	III-7	257	はら(う)	ふつ	to pay	払う〔はらう〕to pay
347	物	II-10	139	もの	ぶつ/もつ	thing (tangible)	食物〔たべもの〕food 飲物〔のみもの〕drinks 着物〔きもの〕*kimono* [traditional Japanese wear] 買物〔かいもの〕shopping 乗物〔のりもの〕vehicle 洗濯物〔せんたくもの〕laundry 物語〔ものがたり〕tale, story 動物〔どうぶつ〕animal 動物園〔どうぶつえん〕zoo 植物〔しょくぶつ〕plants 物理〔ぶつり〕physics 生物〔せいぶつ〕biology 荷物〔にもつ〕luggage; baggage
348	分	I-7	25	わ(かる)/わ(ける)	ふん/ぶん/ぷん	to understand; to divide	分かる〔わかる〕to understand ゴミを分ける〔わける〕to sort trash 半分〔はんぶん〕half 四分の一〔よんぶんのいち〕1/4 多分〔たぶん〕probably 十分〔じゅうぶん〕enough 自分〔じぶん〕oneself 一分〔いっぷん〕one minute
349	文	III-1	171	ふみ	ぶん/も/もん	sentence	作文〔さくぶん〕composition 文化〔ぶんか〕culture 文化の日〔ぶんかのひ〕Culture Day (holiday: Nov. 3) 文化祭〔ぶんかさい〕cultural festival 文学〔ぶんがく〕literature 英文学〔えいぶんがく〕British literature 文字〔もじ〕character; letter (of alphabet) 注文〔ちゅうもん〕order
350	聞	II-4	74	き(く)	ぶん	to listen	聞く〔きく〕to listen; to ask 新聞〔しんぶん〕newspaper

AP®#	漢字	AIJ-L.	AIJ#	訓読み	音読み	意味	熟語
351	平	III-8	261	たい(ら)/ひら	へい/びょう	flat; peace	平ら〔たいら〕flat 平田〔ひらた〕さん Hirata-san 平和〔へいわ〕peace 平日〔へいじつ〕weekday 平気〔へいき〕calm; unconcerned; indifferent 平安時代〔へいあんじだい〕Heian Period (794-1185) 平成時代〔へいせいじだい〕Heisei Period (1989-present) 平家物語〔へいけものがたり〕Tale of the Heike 平等〔びょうどう〕equal
352	別			わか(れる)	べつ	to separate	別れる〔わかれる〕to separate 特別〔とくべつ〕special 別々〔べつべつ〕separate 別居〔べっきょ〕する to live separately 別室〔べっしつ〕separate room 差別〔さべつ〕discrimination
353	変	III-5	222	か(わる)/か(える)	へん	to change	変わる〔かわる〕(something) changes 変える〔かえる〕to change (something) 大変〔たいへん〕terrible; hard; very 変化〔へんか〕change; conjugation
354	便			たよ(り)	べん/びん	convenient	便利〔べんり〕convenient 不便〔ふべん〕inconvenient 便所〔べんじょ〕toilet 郵便局〔ゆうびんきょく〕post office ジャル8便〔はちびん〕JAL Flight #8
355	勉	III-2	177	つと(める)	べん	to study	勉強〔べんきょう〕study
356	歩	II-10	136	ある(く)	ほ/ぽ	to walk	歩く〔あるく〕to walk 横断歩道〔おうだんほどう〕pedestrian crossing 歩行者〔ほこうしゃ〕pedestrian 散歩〔さんぽ〕a walk; stroll
357	母	I-6	24	はは/かあ	ぼ	mother	母〔はは〕(own) mother お母さん〔おかあさん〕(someone's) mother 祖母〔そぼ〕(own) grandmother 父母〔ふぼ〕(own) parents

漢字

AP®#	漢字	AIJ-L.	AIJ#	訓読み	音読み	意味	熟語
358	方	II-7	108	かた/がた	ほう	person [polite]; way of doing; side	あの方〔かた〕that person over there 食べ方〔たべかた〕how to eat 夕方〔ゆうがた〕twilight; dusk どちらの方〔ほう〕which one (of two)? 方言〔ほうげん〕dialect 地方〔ちほう〕district 方向〔ほうこう〕direction
359	法			X	ほう/ぽう	law	法律〔ほうりつ〕law 方法〔ほうほう〕method 文法〔ぶんぽう〕grammar
360	忘			わす(れる)	ぼう	to forget	忘れる〔わすれる〕to forget 忘れ物〔わすれもの〕forgotten item 忘年会〔ぼうねんかい〕year-end party
361	忙			いそが(しい)	ぼう	busy	忙しい〔いそがしい〕busy 多忙〔たぼう〕very busy
362	北	III-3	204	きた	ほく/ぼく/ほっ	north	北〔きた〕north 北村〔きたむら〕さん Kitamura-san 北大〔ほくだい〕Hokkaido University 東北大学〔とうほくだいがく〕Tohoku University (in Sendai) 南北問題〔なんぼくもんだい〕North-South problem 北海道〔ほっかいどう〕Hokkaido 北極〔ほっきょく〕North Pole
363	本	I-5	18	もと	ほん/ぽん/ぼん	origin; book	山本〔やまもと〕さん Yamamoto-san 本を読む〔ほんをよむ〕to read a book 日本語〔にほんご〕Japanese language 本日〔ほんじつ〕today 一本〔いっぽん〕one (long objects) 三本〔さんぼん〕three (long objects)
364	妹	III-1	166	いもうと	まい	younger sister	妹〔いもうと〕(own) younger sister 姉妹〔しまい〕sisters
365	枚			X	まい	- sheet(s)	一枚〔いちまい〕one sheet

漢字

AP®#	漢字	AIJ-L.	AIJ#	訓読み	音読み	意味	熟語
366	毎	I-9	40	X	まい	every	毎日〔まいにち〕every day 毎週〔まいしゅう〕every week 毎月〔まいつき〕every month 毎年〔まいねん/まいとし〕every year 毎朝〔まいあさ〕every morning 毎晩〔まいばん〕every night 毎日新聞〔まいにちしんぶん〕Mainichi Newspaper
367	末			すえ	まつ	end	末っ子〔すえっこ〕youngest child (in a family) 週末〔しゅうまつ〕weekend 月末〔げつまつ〕end-of-month 年末〔ねんまつ〕end-of-year
368	万	I-11	52	X	まん/ばん	ten thousand	一万円〔いちまんえん〕10,000 yen 百万〔ひゃくまん〕1,000,000 万歳〔ばんざい〕Hurray!
369	味	III-5	223	あじ	み	taste	いい味〔あじ〕good taste 味見〔あじみ〕sampling 味の素〔あじのもと〕MSG 意味〔いみ〕meaning 中味〔なかみ〕contents 趣味〔しゅみ〕hobby 興味〔きょうみ〕interest 味噌汁〔みそしる〕*miso* soup
370	未			X	み	not yet	未来〔みらい〕future (distant) 未知〔みち〕unknown
371	無			X	む	nothing	無料〔むりょう〕free of charge 無理〔むり〕impossible 無力〔むりょく〕powerless 無口〔むくち〕reticence 無責任〔むせきにん〕irresponsible
372	名	II-3	67	な	めい	name	名前〔なまえ〕name 名古屋〔なごや〕Nagoya 氏名〔しめい〕full name 有名〔ゆうめい〕famous 名人〔めいじん〕expert 名物〔めいぶつ〕famous product 名門校〔めいもんこう〕famous school 名詞〔めいし〕noun 名刺〔めいし〕name card (business)

AP®#	漢字	AIJ-L.	AIJ#	訓読み	音読み	意味	熟語
373	明	II-9	127	あか(るい)/あき(らか)	めい	bright	明るい〔あかるい〕bright 明らか〔あきらか〕clear; obvious 明治時代〔めいじじだい〕Meiji Period (1868-1912) 説明〔せつめい〕explanation 明暗〔めいあん〕light and darkness 明日〔あした〕tomorrow
374	面			おも/おもて	めん	face	面白い〔おもしろい〕interesting 正面〔しょうめん〕front 表面〔ひょうめん〕surface 地面〔じめん〕ground 面接〔めんせつ〕interview 真面目〔まじめ〕serious
375	木	I-5	15	き	もく	tree	大きい木〔おおきいき〕big tree 木々〔きぎ〕trees 木本〔きもと〕さん Kimoto-san 木曜日〔もくようび〕Thursday
376	目	I-6	20	め	もく	eye	右目〔みぎめ〕right eye 左目〔ひだりめ〕left eye 目薬〔めぐすり〕eye drops 目的〔もくてき〕purpose 目次〔もくじ〕table of contents 目標〔もくひょう〕goal
377	問	III-6	240	と(う)	もん	to ask	問い合わせ〔といあわせ〕inquiry 問題〔もんだい〕problem 質問〔しつもん〕question 訪問〔ほうもん〕visit
378	門	II-4	73	X	もん	gate	門〔もん〕gate 校門〔こうもん〕school gate 正門〔せいもん〕front gate 専門〔せんもん〕speciality
379	夜	III-3	193	よる/よ	や	night	暗い夜〔くらいよる〕dark night 夜中〔よなか〕midnight 今夜〔こんや〕tonight 夜食〔やしょく〕night snack
380	野			の	や	field	野原〔のはら〕field 野中〔のなか〕さん Nonaka-san 野菜〔やさい〕vegetables 野球選手〔やきゅうせんしゅ〕baseball player 野球場〔やきゅうじょう〕baseball field 野菜〔やさい〕vegetable

漢字

AP®#	漢字	AIJ-L.	AIJ#	訓読み	音読み	意味	熟語
381	薬			くすり/ぐすり	やく/やっ	medicine	薬を飲む〔くすりをのむ〕to take medicine 薬指〔くすりゆび〕ring finger 風邪薬〔かぜぐすり〕cold medicine 薬剤師〔やくざいし〕pharmacist 麻薬〔まやく〕drug 薬局〔やっきょく〕pharmacy
382	友	II-8	113	とも	ゆう	friend	友達〔ともだち〕friend 友子〔ともこ〕さん Tomoko-san 友人〔ゆうじん〕friend 友情〔ゆうじょう〕friendship 親友〔しんゆう〕best friend
383	有	III-6	236	あ(る)/あり	ゆう	to have	有田〔ありた〕さん Arita-san 有難う〔ありがとう〕Thank you. 有名〔ゆうめい〕famous 有料〔ゆうりょう〕a charge
384	由			X	ゆう	reason	自由〔じゆう〕freedom 理由〔りゆう〕reason
385	遊			あそ(ぶ)	ゆう	to play	遊び場〔あそびば〕playground 水遊び〔みずあそび〕water play 遊園地〔ゆうえんち〕amusement park
386	夕	III-7	259	X	ゆう	evening	夕方〔ゆうがた〕early evening 夕食〔ゆうしょく〕dinner; supper 夕日〔ゆうひ〕sunset 七夕〔たなばた〕Star Festival (July 7)
387	予			X	よ	pre-	予習〔よしゅう〕preview 予定〔よてい〕plans 予選〔よせん〕preliminary 予約〔よやく〕reservation
388	曜	III-7	247	X	よう	day of week	何曜日〔なんようび〕What day of the week? 日曜日〔にちようび〕Sunday
389	様			さま	よう	polite equiv. of さん; manner	御客様〔おきゃくさま〕customers 様々〔さまざま〕various 様子〔ようす〕circumstances; condition
390	洋	III-4	215	X	よう	ocean	太平洋〔たいへいよう〕Pacific Ocean インド洋〔よう〕Indian Ocean 大西洋〔たいせいよう〕Atlantic Ocean 西洋〔せいよう〕the west 東洋〔とうよう〕the east 洋服〔ようふく〕Western-style clothes 洋子〔ようこ〕さん Yoko-san

漢字

AP®#	漢字	AIJ-L.	AIJ#	訓読み	音読み	意味	熟語
391	用			X	よう	task; use	用〔よう〕がある have things to do 用事〔ようじ〕がある have errands to do 台所用品〔だいどころようひん〕kitchenware 婦人用化粧室〔ふじんようけしょうしつ〕restroom for women 用紙〔ようし〕form
392	要			い(る)	よう	need	要る〔いる〕to need 必要〔ひつよう〕necessary 重要〔じゅうよう〕important
393	来	I-7	27	き/ く/ こ	らい	to come	来て。〔きて。〕Come. 来る〔くる〕to come 来ないで〔こないで〕Don't come. 来週〔らいしゅう〕next week 来月〔らいげつ〕next month 来年〔らいねん〕next year 未来〔みらい〕future (distant) 将来〔しょうらい〕future (near)
394	絡			X	らく	linkage	連絡〔れんらく〕contact
395	落			お(ちる)/ お(とす)	らく	to fall; to drop	落ちる〔おちる〕to fall 落とす〔おとす〕to drop (something) 落葉〔おちば〕fallen leaves 落選〔らくせん〕election loss 落語〔らくご〕traditional Japanese comic storytelling (*rakugo*)
396	利			X	り	advantage	便利〔べんり〕convenient 利用〔りよう〕する to use
397	理	II-11	150	X	り	reason	理科〔りか〕science 理想〔りそう〕ideal 理由〔りゆう〕reason 理解〔りかい〕する to understand 料理〔りょうり〕cooking
398	立	II-12	154	た(つ)	りつ/ りっ	to stand	立つ〔たつ〕to stand 起立。〔きりつ。〕Stand. 公立〔こうりつ〕public (institution) 私立〔しりつ/わたくしりつ〕private (institution) 市立〔しりつ/いちりつ〕municipal 州立〔しゅうりつ〕state (establishment) 国立公園〔こくりつこうえん〕national park 立派〔りっぱ〕sprendid; prominent

漢字

AP®#	漢字	AIJ-L.	AIJ#	訓読み	音読み	意味	熟語
399	留	III-8	269	とど(める)/とど(まる)	りゅう/る	to stop	留学〔りゅうがく〕する to study abroad 留学生〔りゅうがくせい〕foreign exchange student 留守〔るす〕not at home 留守番電話〔るすばんでんわ〕answering machine
400	旅	III-1	175	たび	りょ	travel	日本の旅〔たび〕Japan trip 旅人〔たびびと〕traveller 旅行〔りょこう〕travel; trip 旅行者〔りょこうしゃ〕traveller 海外旅行〔かいがいりょこう〕travel abroad
401	両			X	りょう	both	両方〔りょうほう〕both 両親〔りょうしん〕parents 両手〔りょうて〕both hands
402	料	II-2	149	X	りょう	material; fee	料理〔りょうり〕cooking 調味料〔ちょうみりょう〕seasoning 材料〔ざいりょう〕ingredients 料金〔りょうきん〕fare; fee 無料〔むりょう〕free of charge 授業料〔じゅぎょうりょう〕tuition 入場料〔にゅうじょうりょう〕admission fee
403	力	II-9	128	ちから	りょく	power	力持ち〔ちからもち〕strong person 協力〔きょうりょく〕する to cooperate 努力〔どりょく〕する to make efforts
404	林	III-2	183	はやし/ばやし	りん	forest	林〔はやし〕さん Hayashi-san 林田〔はやしだ〕さん Hayashida-san 小林〔こばやし〕さん Kobayashi-san 大林〔おおばやし〕さん Oobayashi-san 森林〔しんりん〕forest 林業〔りんぎょう〕forestry
405	冷	III-4	206	つめ(たい)	れい	cold	冷たい〔つめたい〕cold (to the touch) 冷蔵庫〔れいぞうこ〕refrigerator 冷凍庫〔れいとうこ〕freezer 冷凍食品〔れいとうしょくひん〕frozen food 冷房〔れいぼう〕air-conditioning
406	礼			X	れい	gratitude; paper bills	失礼〔しつれい〕rude お礼状〔おれいじょう〕thank you letter

漢字

AP®#	漢字	AIJ-L.	AIJ#	訓読み	音読み	意味	熟語
407	練			ね(る)	れん	to train	練習〔れんしゅう〕practice 連絡〔れんらく〕contact 訓練〔くんれん〕training
408	六	I-4	7	む/ むい/ むっ	ろく/ ろっ	six	六日〔むいか〕the 6th of the month; 6 days 六つ〔むっつ〕six (general counter) 六月〔ろくがつ〕June 六人〔ろくにん〕six people 六個〔ろっこ〕six (general counter)
409	和	III-4	211	X	わ	harmony; Japanese	和〔わ〕harmony 平和〔へいわ〕peace 和風〔わふう〕Japanese style 和食〔わしょく〕Japanese-style meal 和紙〔わし〕Japanese paper 和室〔わしつ〕Japanese-style room 和菓子〔わがし〕Japanese sweets 和楽器〔わがっき〕traditional Japanese musical instrument 和英辞典〔わえいじてん〕Japanese-English dictionary 英和辞典〔えいわじてん〕English-Japanese dictionary 和敬清寂〔わけいせいじゃく〕harmony, respect, purity and tranquility (tea ceremony teaching)
410	話	II-3	70	はな(す)	わ	to talk	話す〔はなす〕to talk 電話〔でんわ〕telephone 会話〔かいわ〕conversation 英会話〔えいかいわ〕English conversation 手話〔しゅわ〕sign language 世話〔せわ〕する to take care

| 1 課 | | 自分と家族と友達
Self, Family and Friends | |

> 【AP® タスク：自分と家族と友達】
> A Japanese magazine reporter is interviewing you for an article. You are a well known personality. The reporter wants to find out some personal information about you.
> 1. Personal information: age, birthdate, childhood, personal characteristics, hobbies, etc.
> 2. Family information: family members, relationships, their influence on you, things you appreciate about them.
> 3. Information about your best friend(s): how you became friends, things you appreciate about your friend(s).

【文化】 日本の家族：The Japanese Family

The contemporary Japanese family is typically a nuclear family, quite different from the larger multi-generational families of traditional Japan. Most families now consist of a father, mother, one or two children, and perhaps an in-law. In the cities, average Japanese families live in relatively small quarters. Most rural families still follow the traditional family structure. The birthrate of Japan is now one of the lowest in the world, at about 1.2 children per family. This rapidly declining birthrate has already affected Japanese society, and together with the increased graying of the Japanese population, poses a major problem for Japan.

The primary breadwinner of the family is still the father. His main responsibilities are to go to work and earn a good and steady income so that he can support his family. Although many changes are occurring in younger families, fathers are still treated with respect and are not expected to contribute significantly to daily household chores. The father is given the place of honor at home and others defer to his preferences. He spends most of his waking hours at work, though many younger fathers now spend more time at home with their families than in the past.

Mothers are still the primary household caretakers. They are up early preparing breakfast and lunches for their children and husbands. They do the bulk of the household chores, shopping, and family budgeting. It is the mother's responsibility to see that her children are educated well. They will go as far as staying up late at night to provide snacks for a child studying for exams. Mothers look after all of their children's needs, and if there are in-laws or elderly parents, it is also their responsibility to take care of them. Many mothers now work part-time to supplement the family income or volunteer in the community. This also gives a mother time to be out of the home and develop her own personal interests and relationships.

If there is a son in the family, his needs are still prioritized above the daughters'. He is often catered to, and rarely is expected to help with household chores. Parents may still believe that it is their son on whom they must depend for support when they become older. Many sons in Japan, particularly only sons, are spoiled and dependent on others to help them with daily responsibilities.

When daughters in the family reach their pre-teen years, they are expected to assist with household chores. Much more is demanded of daughters than sons. In recent years, though, girls may also be catered to by their parents.

Though far less common than before, some families still include one or possibly two grandparents, most often the parents of the father. When this grandparent is the mother-in-law to the young wife, there is often great conflict, as Japanese mothers-in-law traditionally wield much power. Although not as common as in the U.S., there are households now in Japan with single parents, unmarried singles, and adult singles living with their parents.

While the face of the Japanese family has changed significantly in the last generation or two, Japanese people still find the family to be a valuable source of support throughout life, with females still holding subordinate roles, and the aged still dominating over those who are younger.

Questions to ponder: What are some of the issues that Japanese families face in contemporary Japan? Why do you think the dominant status of males and the aged still prevails?

| 1 課 |

1課　復習単語

トピック：自分と家族と友達

1. 自己紹介(を)する	じこしょうかい(を)する	V3	(to) do a self-introduction
2. 紹介(を)する	しょうかい(を)する	V3	(to) introduce
3. (御)出身	(ご)しゅっしん	N	place of origin
4. 家族	かぞく	N	(my) family
5. 御家族	ごかぞく	N	(someone's) family
6. 先祖	せんぞ	N	ancestor
7. 親戚	しんせき	N	relatives
8. 祖父	そふ	N	(one's own) grandfather
9. 祖母	そぼ	N	(one's own) grandmother
10. おじいさん		N	grandfather; elderly man
11. おばあさん		N	grandmother; elderly woman
12. 両親	りょうしん	N	(own) parents
13. 御両親	ごりょうしん	N	(someone else's) parents [polite]
14. 主人	しゅじん	N	(own) husband
15. 御主人	ごしゅじん	N	(someone else's) husband
16. 家内	かない	N	(own) wife
17. 奥さん	おくさん	N	(someone else's) wife
18. 叔父	おじ	N	(one's own) uncle
19. 叔母	おば	N	(one's own) aunt
20. おじさん		N	uncle; man
21. おばさん		N	aunt; middle aged woman
22. 父	ちち	N	(own) father
23. 母	はは	N	(my) mother
24. 兄	あに	N	(own) older brother
25. 姉	あね	N	(own) older sisiter
26. 弟	おとうと	N	(own) younger brother
27. 妹	いもうと	N	(my) younger sister
28. お父さん	おとうさん	N	(someone's) father
29. お母さん	おかあさん	N	(someone's) mother
30. お兄さん	おにいさん	N	(someone's) older brother
31. お姉さん	おねえさん	N	(someone's) older sister
32. 弟さん	おとうとさん	N	(someone's) younger brother

1課

33. 妹さん	いもうとさん	N	(someone's) younger sister
34. 息子	むすこ	N	(own) son
35. 息子さん	むすこさん	N	(someone else's) son
36. 娘	むすめ	N	(own) daughter; young lady
37. 娘さん	むすめさん	N	(someone else's) daughter; young lady [polite]
38. 兄弟	きょうだい	N	(my) sibling(s)
39. 長男	ちょうなん	N	an eldest son
40. 長女	ちょうじょ	N	an eldest daughter
41. 次男	じなん	N	a second son
42. 次女	じじょ	N	a second daughter
43. 三男	さんなん	N	a third son
44. 三女	さんじょ	N	a third daughter
45. 末っ子	すえっこ	N	youngest child (in a family)
46. 一人っ子	ひとりっこ	N	only child
47. 双子	ふたご	N	twin
48. 赤ちゃん	あかちゃん	N	baby
49. いとこ	いとこ	N	cousin
50. 孫	まご	N	(own) grandchild(ren)
51. お孫さん	おまごさん	N	(someone else's) grandchild(ren)
52. 彼	かれ	N	he; him; boyfriend
53. 彼女	かのじょ	N	she; her; girlfriend
54. 主婦	しゅふ	N	housewife
55. 育てる	そだてる	V2	(to) raise (a person/pet)
56. (御)誕生日	(お)たんじょうび	N	birthday

| 1課 | ★★★ | 新しい単語 | ★★★ |

1. こちらこそ、どうぞよろしく。　　Exp　It is I, not you. [emphasis]
「初めまして。どうぞよろしく。」「こちらこそ、どうぞよろしく。」 "How do you do? Nice to meet you." "It is my pleasure."

2. おせわ＜世話＞になります。　　Exp　Thank you for your kindness. [from now on]
おせわ＜世話＞になりました。　　Exp　Thank you for your kindness. [until now]
(N1はN2の)せわ＜世話＞になる／なります　　V1　N1 will be taken care of by N2.
(N1はN2の)せわ＜世話＞をする／します　　V1　N1 takes care of N2.
私はホストファミリーのお世話になった。　I was taken care of by my host family.
ホストファミリーは私をよく世話してくれた。　My host family took good care of me.

3. けつろんとして＜結論として＞　　Exp　in conclusion
結論として、父も母も大事だと思う。　In conclusion, I think both fathers and mothers are important.

4. ふどうさん＜不動産＞　　N　real estate
父は不動産関係の仕事をしている。　My father is working at a real estate-related job.

5. にんげん＜人間＞　　N　human being
リンカーン大統領は人間として立派だったと思う。I think that as a person, President Lincoln was great.

6. ゆうじん＜友人＞　　N　friend [formal equivalent of 友達]
友人がたくさんいる。　I have lots of friends.

7. しんゆう＜親友＞　　N　best friend
何でも話せる親友がほしい。　I want a best friend to whom I can talk about anything.

8. ゆうじょう＜友情＞　　N　friendship
友情の大切さを感じる。　I feel the importance of friendship.

9. なかま＜仲間＞　　N　group of friends
仲間といる時が、最高に楽しい。　When I am with a group of my friends, it is the most enjoyable.

10. きっかけ　　N　initial opportunity; start; trigger
私達が友達になったきっかけは学校のダンスだった。　Our friendship first began at a school dance.

1課

11. もくひょう＜目標＞　N　goal
    今年の目標は大学に入学することだ。　My goal this year is to get into college.

12. きぼう＜希望＞ or のぞみ＜望み＞　N　hope; wish
    希望の大学に行きたい。　I want to go to the college of my choice.

13. せきにん＜責任＞　N　responsibility
    勉強することが今の私の責任だ。　Studying is my responsibility now.

14. やくわり＜役割＞　N　role
    親として父と母の役割は違う。　As parents, the roles of a father and a mother are different.

15. こじんてき＜個人的＞　Na　personal
    個人的な質問を聞いてもいいですか。　May I ask you a personal question?

16. きちょう＜貴重＞　Na　valuable
    「貴重なお時間を有難うございました。」　"Thank you for your valuable time."

17. おも＜主＞な　Na　main
    おも＜主＞に　Adv　mainly
    私の主な仕事は、掃除することだった。　My main job was cleaning.

18. (～と/に)にて＜似て＞いる／います　V2　to resemble (～); look alike (～)
    私は母によく似ていると言われる。　I have been told that I look a lot like my mother.

19. はげます＜励ます＞／励まします　V1　to encourage
    両親はいつもよくがんばるように私を励ましてくれる。　My parents always encourage me to do my best.

20. しっかりしている／しっかりしています　V2　to be reliable
    姉はしっかりしている。　My older sister is reliable.

21. たいがく＜退学＞する／します　V3　to drop out of school
    たいがく＜退学＞させられる／させられます　V3　to be made to drop out of school
    [passive causative form]
    友達は麻薬を持っていて退学させられた。　My friend was made to drop out of school because he possessed drugs.

22. (～に)じょうねつ＜情熱＞をかける／かけます　V2　to be passionate (about ～)
    今テニスに情熱をかけている。　I am passionate about tennis now.

23. (～を)しんよう＜信用＞する／します　V3　to trust (～)
    信用出来る友達がいる。　I have a friend whom I can trust.

1課

24. (のぞみ＜望み＞が)かなう＜叶う＞／叶います

    V1　(hope; wish) come true [intransitive]

    私の望みが叶いました。　My wish came true.

25. (のぞみ＜望み＞を)かなえる＜叶える＞／叶えます

    V1　to grant (hope; wish) [transitive]

    「望みを叶えて下さい。」 "Please grant my wish."

26. ていあん＜提案＞(を)する／します　V3　to suggest

    何かいい考えがあったら、提案してください。　If you have a good idea, please suggest it to me.

27. そうだん＜相談＞にのる／のります　V1　to guide

    そうだん＜相談＞(を)する／します　V3　to consult

    友達はいつも相談にのってくれる。　My friend always guides me.

28. ささえる＜支える＞／支えます　V2　to support

    父は家族を経済的に支えてくれる。　My father supports our family financially.

29. (〜が)そだつ＜育つ＞／育ちます　V1　(someone) grows [intransitive]

    (〜を)そだてる＜育てる＞／育てます　V2　to raise (someone) [transitive]

    私は東京で育った。　I grew up in Tokyo.

    祖母が私を育ててくれた。　My grandmother raised me.

30. すごす＜過ごす＞／過ごします　V1　to spend (time)

    仲間と過ごす時間が私には一番幸せな時だ。 "The time I spend with my group of friends is the happiest time for me."

1課

1課 文法

A. "do 〜 (as a favor)"

Giver は	Receiver (equal) に	Verb (TE form)	あげます。
Giver は	Receiver (inferior) に	Verb (TE form)	やります。
Giver は	Receiver (me) に/を	Verb (TE form)	くれます。
Receiver は	Giver に	Verb (TE form)	もらいます。

1. 私は友達にシャツを買ってあげました。   I bought a shirt for my friend (as a favor).
2. 私は妹に本を読んでやりました。   I read a book to my younger sister (as a favor).
3. 父は私を迎えに来てくれました。   My father came to pick me up (as a favor).
4. 私は姉に宿題を手伝ってもらいました。   I had my older sister help me with my homework (as a favor).

a. Complete the following sentences using appropriate verb TE forms + a giving/receiving verb.

1. 両親は私の授業料を _____。
2. 両親は私がほしい物を _____。
3. 友達は私の問題を _____。
4. 祖母が夕食を _____。
5. 私は両親に何も _____。
6. 私は弟におもちゃを _____。
7. 私は兄に車を _____。

b. Restate the following sentences in English.

1. 祖母が僕をよく世話してくれた。 _____
2. 友達は僕を励ましてくれた。 _____
3. 私を心配してくれた友人達がいた。 _____
4. 家族も本当によくしてくれた。 _____
5. 両親は僕を信用してくれた。 _____
6. 親友はいつも相談にのってくれる。 _____
7. 父は経済的に支えてくれる。 _____

1課

B. 敬語 Honorifics [recognition only]

a. Summary of honorific forms (尊敬語)

There are three ways to express respect to superiors (そんけい語) through verbs. When a verb has an irregular honorific form, use the irregular honorific form. If verbs do not have an irregular honorific form, use the honorific-passive form. The お＋Stem＋に なります form is the most formal and its usage is limited.

MASU form	Irregular Honorific Form	Honorific-Passive Form	お＋Stem＋に なります
食べます	めしあがります	食べられます	お食べになります
飲みます	めしあがります	飲まれます	お飲みになります
します	なさいます	されます	X
行きます	いらっしゃいます	行かれます	お行きになります
来ます	いらっしゃいます	来（こ）られます	X
います	いらっしゃいます	いられます	X
見ます	ごらんになります	見られます	X
言います	おっしゃいます	言われます	お言いになります
知っています	ごぞんじです	知っていられます	X

b. Review of some polite expressions (ていねい語):

Formal Speech Style	Informal Speech Style	Meaning
おはようございます。	おはよう。	Good morning.
ありがとうございます。	ありがとう。	Thank you.
お元気ですか。	元気？	How are you?
お好きですか。	好き？	Do you like it?
この方、こちら	この人	this person
こちら、そちら、あちら、どちら？	これ、それ、あれ、どれ？	this one, that one, that one over there, which one?
こちら、そちら、あちら、どちら？	ここ、そこ、あそこ、どこ？	here, there, over there, where?
いかが？	どう？	How?
どなた？	だれ？	Who?
どちら？	どっち？	Which?
何人様〔なんにんさま〕？	何人〔なんにん〕？	How many people?
お客様〔おきゃくさま〕	客〔きゃく〕	customer
ですから、	だから、	Therefore,
しかし、	でも、	However,
よろしいです	いいです	is good
Noun ＋ でございます	Noun ＋ です	is (copula)

1課

Change the underlined portions of the sentences to neutral -desu/-masu forms.

1.「初めまして。山田と申します。どうぞよろしくお願い致します。」

2.「どんなお仕事をして有名になられたんですか。」

3.「御両親のお仕事を教えて下さいませんか。」

4.「御自分の性格はどんな性格だと思われますか。」

5.「御家族でどなたに似ていらっしゃいますか。」

6.「個人的な質問ですみませんが、お子さんの時に御両親が離婚されたとか、再婚されたとかいう問題がございましたか。」

7.「これも大変失礼なんですが、たばこや麻薬を吸ってみたことがおありですか。」

8.「お友達の中で学校を退学させられた方を知っていらっしゃいますか。」

9.「親友と呼べる方がいらっしゃいますか。」

10.「親友になられたきっかけは何でしたか。」

11.「今、御両親に一番感謝されていることは何ですか。」

12.「今、情熱をかけてやっていらっしゃる事は何ですか。」

13.「今年の目標をお聞かせ下さい。」

14.「今日はどうも貴重なお時間を有難うございました。」

1課

C. Verb passive form （受身形）

Group 1 verbs:	のむ → のまれる	is drunk
Group 2 verbs:	たべる → たべられる	is eaten
Irregular verbs:	くる → こられる	come
	する → される	is done

1. 教科書がぬすまれた。　　　　　　　　My textbook was stolen.
2. お弁当は犬に食べられた。　　　　　　My box lunch was eaten by my dog.
3. 兄はどろぼうに自動車をぬすまれた。　My older brother had his car stolen by a thief.
4. 母は父に死なれて、生活は大変だったそうだ。
　　I understand that after my father died, my mother was left alone and life was difficult (for her).

Fill in the ( ) with correct particles and the blanks with correct passive forms.

1. 彼は私を信用した。＝ 私（ ）彼（ ）＿＿＿＿＿＿＿＿＿＿＿＿＿＿＿＿＿＿。
2. 彼は私をふった。＝ 私（ ）彼（ ）＿＿＿＿＿＿＿＿＿＿＿＿＿＿＿＿＿＿。
3. 祖母は私を育てた。＝ 私（ ）祖母（ ）＿＿＿＿＿＿＿＿＿＿＿＿＿＿＿＿。
4. 祖母は私を甘やかした。＝ 私（ ）祖母（ ）＿＿＿＿＿＿＿＿＿＿＿＿＿＿。
5. 母は私に勉強しなさいと言った。
　＝ 私（ ）母（ ）勉強しなさいと＿＿＿＿＿＿＿＿＿＿＿＿＿＿＿＿＿＿。
6. 両親はいつも私と姉を比べた。
　＝ 私（ ）姉（ ）いつも両親（ ）＿＿＿＿＿＿＿＿＿＿＿＿＿＿＿＿。
7. 友達は私を励ました。＝ 私（ ）友達（ ）＿＿＿＿＿＿＿＿＿＿＿＿＿＿＿＿。

D. Verb causative form （使役形）

Group 1 verbs:	いう → いわせる	make/let someone say
Group 2 verbs:	たべる → たべさせる	make/let someone eat
Irregular verbs:	くる → こさせる	make/let someone come
	する → させる	make/let someone do

1. 先生は生徒に漢字を書かせる。　　　　The teacher makes his/her students write *kanji*.
2. 両親は私を日本旅行に行かせてくれた。My parents let me go on a trip to Japan.
3. 母は私にピアノを練習させる。　　　　My mother makes me practice the piano.
4. 「お待たせしました。」　　　　　　　"I'm sorry for making you wait."

1課

Complete the sentences by using the causative form of the verb cues.

1. 先生は私達に日本語を＿＿＿＿＿＿＿＿＿＿＿＿＿＿＿＿＿。（話す）
2. 両親は毎晩私に皿を＿＿＿＿＿＿＿＿＿＿＿＿＿＿＿＿＿。（洗う）
3. 体育の先生は生徒をよく＿＿＿＿＿＿＿＿＿＿＿＿＿＿＿＿＿。（泳ぐ）
4. コーチは週末も私達を＿＿＿＿＿＿＿＿＿＿＿＿＿＿＿＿＿。（練習する）
5. 疲れているので、もっと＿＿＿＿＿＿＿＿＿＿＿＿＿＿下さい。（寝る）
6. 両親は授業料が高くても、大学に＿＿＿＿＿＿＿＿＿＿＿＿＿くれる。（行く）

E. Verb causative passive form [recognition only]

Group 1 verbs:	いう →いわせられる	be forced to say
Group 2 verbs:	たべる→たべさせられる	be forced to eat
Irregular verbs:	くる →こさせられる	be forced to come
	する →させられる	be forced to do

1. 友達は学校を退学させられた。　　　　　My friend was forced to drop out of school.
2. これは考えさせられる問題です。　　　　This is a problem that I am made to think about.

Restate in English.

1. 私達は毎日一時間もコーチに走らされた。　＿＿＿＿＿＿＿＿＿＿＿＿＿＿
2. 授業の後、先生に教室を掃除させられた。　＿＿＿＿＿＿＿＿＿＿＿＿＿＿
3. 友達に長い間、駅の前で待たされた。　　　＿＿＿＿＿＿＿＿＿＿＿＿＿＿

F. ～んです，～のです

The ～んです and ～のです endings are frequently used in conversation. When one of these endings appears in a statement form, it suggests that the speaker feels obligated to explain him/herself or his/her actions. When it appears in a question form, it serves the purpose of inviting an explanation from the listener.

～のです is used in formal situations and ～んです is used in less formal situations. The copula だ changes to な before ～んです and ～のです.

1. 友達が麻薬を使っているんですよ。　　　My friend is using drugs.
2. この本は本当に高かったんですよ。　　　This book was really expensive, you know.
3. 明日が試験なんですよ。　　　　　　　　Tomorrow is the exam day.
4. あの子が好きなんだ。　　　　　　　　　I like that person.
5. 僕はあの子が好きだったんだ。　　　　　I liked that girl.
6. 本当にいいんですか。　　　　　　　　　Is it really okay?
7. なぜ分からないんですか。　　　　　　　Why don't you understand it?

1課

a. Rewrite the underlined endings using 〜んです forms.

1. 母は教師<u>でした</u>。 →＿＿＿＿＿＿＿＿＿＿＿＿＿＿＿＿＿＿＿＿＿。
2. 兄はスキーが<u>上手です</u>。 →＿＿＿＿＿＿＿＿＿＿＿＿＿＿＿＿＿＿＿＿＿。
3. 祖父が<u>亡くなりました</u>。 →＿＿＿＿＿＿＿＿＿＿＿＿＿＿＿＿＿＿＿＿＿。
4. 祖母が私を世話をして<u>くれました</u>。 →＿＿＿＿＿＿＿＿＿＿＿＿＿＿＿＿＿＿＿＿＿。
5. 仲間がたくさん<u>います</u>。 →＿＿＿＿＿＿＿＿＿＿＿＿＿＿＿＿＿＿＿＿＿。
6. 車を買って<u>もらいました</u>。 →＿＿＿＿＿＿＿＿＿＿＿＿＿＿＿＿＿＿＿＿＿。

b. Restate the following sentences in English.

1. どんなお子さんだったんですか。 →＿＿＿＿＿＿＿＿＿＿＿＿＿＿＿＿＿＿＿＿＿
2. 母は郵便局で働いていたんです。 →＿＿＿＿＿＿＿＿＿＿＿＿＿＿＿＿＿＿＿＿＿
3. 祖父が事故で亡くなったんです。 →＿＿＿＿＿＿＿＿＿＿＿＿＿＿＿＿＿＿＿＿＿
4. 兄は麻薬を使い出したんです。 →＿＿＿＿＿＿＿＿＿＿＿＿＿＿＿＿＿＿＿＿＿
5. 俳優になったきっかけは何だったんですか。 →＿＿＿＿＿＿＿＿＿＿＿＿＿＿＿＿＿

1課

| 1課 | アクティビティー |

A. 日本文化：一人か二人ワーク→クラスワーク

Divide the topics below among your classmates and research your topic on the Internet. Using visuals, present your findings with your classmates.

1. 核家族〔かくかぞく〕
2. 嫁と姑〔よめとしゅうとめ〕
3. 少子化社会〔しょうしかしゃかい〕
4. 高齢化社会〔こうれいかしゃかい〕
5. 甘え〔あまえ〕
   (子が母に)甘える、(母が子を)甘やかす
   甘えん坊〔あまえんぼう〕
6. 教育ママ〔きょういくママ〕
7. 本音〔ほんね〕と建前〔たてまえ〕

B. 聞く Pre-Listening Activity：ペアワーク

Pair off with a partner. One partner will play the role of a famous person, and the other, an interviewer.

1.「初めまして。(Last name)と申します。どうぞよろしくお願い致します。」
2.「どんなお仕事をして有名になられたんですか。」
3.「御両親のお仕事を教えて下さいませんか。」
4.「御自分の性格はどんな性格だと思われますか。」
5.「御家族でどなたに似ていらっしゃいますか。」
6.「個人的な質問ですみませんが、お子さんの時に御両親が離婚されたとか、再婚されたとかいう問題がございましたか。」
7.「これも大変失礼なんですが、たばこや麻薬を吸ってみたことがおありですか。」
8.「親友と呼べる方がいらっしゃいますか。」
9.「親友になられたきっかけは何でしたか。」
10.「今、御両親に一番感謝されていることは何ですか。」
11.「今、情熱をかけてやっていらっしゃる事は何ですか。」
12.「今年の目標をお聞かせ下さい。」
13.「今日はどうも貴重なお時間を有難うございました。」

C. 聞く Post-Listening Activity：ペアワーク

After listening to the recording of the interview with the actor, have a conversation.

1. 渡部さんは子供の時にどんな問題がありましたか。
2. 渡部さんが問題があった時に、友達は何をしてくれましたか。
3. このインタビューからどんな感想を持ちましたか。

D. 読み Pre-Reading Activity：ペアワーク

Before reading *Naita Akaoni*, have a conversation with your partner.

1. 友達にどんな事をしてあげますか。
2. 友達はどんな事をしてくれますか。
3. 強い友情を感じたことがありますか。どんな時でしたか。

鬼

E. 読み Post-Reading Activity：ペアワーク

After reading *Naita Akaoni*, discuss the following questions.

1. 赤鬼の望みは何でしたか。
2. 赤鬼の望みを叶えるために、青鬼は赤鬼に何を提案しましたか。
3. 青鬼は赤鬼の望みが叶った時に、赤鬼にどんな手紙を書きましたか。
4. このお話を読んで、どんな感想を持ちましたか。

F. テキストチャット：ペアワーク

Pair off with a partner. One partner will provide the following prompts, and the other will respond in 20 seconds. After completing the list, switch parts.

1. 「初めまして。田中です。どうぞよろしく。」
2. 「個人的な質問をしてもいいですか。」
3. 「どんな性格をしていますか。」
4. 「自分の性格が好きですか。」
5. 「親との仲はどうですか。」
6. 「兄弟との仲はどうですか。」
7. 「問題があったら、親か友達のどちらに相談しますか。」
8. 「どんないい友人がいますか。」
9. 「今日はどうも有難うございました。」
10. 「日本の高校生について何か質問がありますか。」

1課

G. Compare & Contrast 「父と母」：ペアワーク

You will complete the following passage by selecting the correct answers from below. Write the correct letter in the ( ) and circle the correct particle from within the [ ].

(1._____)、父 [1. と　も] 母を (2._____) みます。私には父 [2. と　も] 母 [3. は　も] 大事ですから、比べることはとても難しいです。でも、父と母は (3._____) も同じこともあります。

まず、(4._____) の違いは、当たり前ですが、父は男で、母は女です。ですから、父の (5._____) が母 (6._____) 大きくて、力も強いです。父は私にスポーツを教えてくれましたが、母は私に音楽を教えてくれました。

(7._____) の違いは、父の主な責任は仕事をしてお金をもうけて家族を経済的に支えることですが、母の主な責任は子供を育てることです。特に子供が小さい時に、母は子供をよく世話します。赤ちゃんは母親がいなければ、育ちません。

しかし、(8._____) の同じことは、父も母も子供を愛してくれるということです。父親も母親も子供の幸福をいつも考えてくれます。それは、とても有難いことだと思います。

(9._____)、私には父も母もとても大事ですから、どちらの方が好き [4. とか] 決めることは出来ません。親として父と母の役割が違うと思います。しかし、私には母の方が父より近いです。(10._____)、もっと一緒に時間を過ごしてくれるからです。

| a. 一つ | b. 一つ目 | c. 二つ目 | d. これから | e. 結論として |
| f. なぜなら | g. より | h. 方 | i. 比べて | j. 違うこと |

Circle True or False based on the passage above.

1. (T F) This person feels closer to her mother than to her father.
2. (T F) This person likes both her father and her mother.
3. (T F) This person pointed out three differences between fathers and mothers.
4. (T F) This person is very appreciative of her parents.
5. (T F) This person thinks that mothers are more important for children than fathers.

1課

H. 会話：ペアワーク

Pair off with a partner. One partner will play a Japanese student on a homestay, while the other partner, playing a homestay host, will respond in 20 seconds. After you get to the last prompt, switch roles.

1. 「初めまして。太郎です。どうぞよろしくお願いします。」
2. 「少しですが、お土産をどうぞ。」
3. 「これからお世話になります。」
4. 「僕の目標は英語が上手になることです。」
5. 「でも、英語は難しいですね。」
6. 「学校のことをいろいろ教えて下さいね。」

I. 文化「日本の家族」：ペアワーク

Circle correct responses in the following statements about the Japanese family.

1. （父親　母親　息子　娘）は、外で仕事をしてお金を儲けて、家族を支える。
2. （父親　母親　息子　娘）は、週末に子供と時間を過ごすようにする。
3. （父親　母親　息子　娘）は、家事を手伝うはずだと思われている。
4. （父親　母親　息子　娘）は、たいてい朝昼晩の食事を作る。
5. （父親　母親　息子　娘）は、家事をして、奥さんを手伝う。
6. （父親　母親　息子　娘）は、子供の教育をよく見る。
7. （父親　母親　息子　娘）は、家事をあまり手伝わない。
8. （父親　母親　息子　娘）は、買物や料理や洗濯や掃除などの家事をする。
9. （父親　母親　息子　娘）は、お年寄りの世話をする。
10. （父親　母親　息子　娘）は、朝起きると子供の弁当を作る。
11. （父親　母親　息子　娘）は、勉強をしている息子におやつを持って行ってやる。
12. 日本の親は（子供が大学へ行くまで　大学を卒業した後も）子供の世話をする。

1課

<1課 - 聞く>
Listening: Movie Star Interview

12秒×5

【You may take notes while listening. Do not look at the questions below before listening. You will have 12 seconds to answer each question. You may NOT move back and forth among questions.】

(Narrator) Now you will listen once to an interview.

(Narrator) Now answer the questions for this selection.

1. What information is correct about the movie star's family?
   (A) His mother was a movie star.
   (B) His father worked at the post office.
   (C) He had no siblings.
   (D) He didn't have grandparents.

2. What information is correct about the movie star?
   (A) His mother died in a car accident.
   (B) His parents separated.
   (C) His parents divorced.
   (D) His father remarried.

3. Who helped him the most through his drug rehabilitation?
   (A) his mother
   (B) his grandmother
   (C) his father
   (D) his friends

4. What was the major reason for his recovery from drug abuse?
   (A) religion
   (B) friendship
   (C) a drug rehabilitation program
   (D) his career

5. Who recommended him for the acting job?
   (A) himself
   (B) his father
   (C) his friend's father
   (D) his teacher

1課

＜1課 - 読む＞

Reading: Children's Story

【You may move back and forth among all the questions.】

　昔々、山の崖のところに一軒のうちがありました。若くて元気な赤鬼が住んでいました。その鬼は、気持ちのやさしい親切な鬼でした。赤鬼は人間達と友達になりたいと思っていましたので、ある日、立て札を立てました。『心のやさしいおにのうちです。どなたでもおいでください。おいしいおかしもございます。おちゃもわかしてございます。あかおに』しかし、村の人はだれも赤鬼を信用しませんでした。赤鬼はおこって、立て札をこわしてしまいました。

　そこに、仲間の青鬼が雨雲に乗ってやって来ました。青鬼は友達の赤鬼に言いました。「たまに遊びに来てみると、ぷんぷんおこっているんだな。君らしくもない。どうしたの。」赤鬼は思っていることを正直に打ち明けると、青鬼は赤鬼に言いました。「では、こうしよう。ぼくが村に行って、あばれよう。そこに、君が来て、ぼくの頭をぽかぽかなぐるんだ。そうすれば、人間達は君を見て、君を信用するようになるよ。さあ、ぼくは村に出かけるから、後から、きっと来るんだよ。」

　青鬼は、村の小さなおうちに入って行くと、そこにいたおじいさんとおばあさんは、びっくりして、外に逃げ出して行きました。青鬼は、うちの中であばれて、家をめちゃくちゃにこわしました。そこに、赤鬼がやって来て、青鬼をぽかぽかなぐりました。青鬼は、逃げ出して行きました。それを見ていた村人は、赤鬼を信用するようになりました。そして、大人も子供も、赤鬼のうちへ遊びに行くようになりました。

　けれども、何日かして、赤鬼は、青鬼のことが心配になって来ました。あの時から、青鬼が全然遊びに来なくなったからです。赤鬼は村の人達に今日はるすにすると貼り紙をして、夜明けの雲に乗って、青鬼の住んでいる山の奥の岩のおうちに行きました。しかし、戸口は閉まって、開きません。赤鬼は戸口のそばに一枚の紙を見つけて、読みました。

　『赤鬼くん、人間達と仲良く暮らしなさい。君とぼくが仲良くしていれば、村の人達は、また君を信じなくなるでしょう。ぼくは長い旅に出ることにしました。ぼくは、どこにいようと、君の幸せをいつも祈っています。さようなら。体を大事にして下さい。いつまでも君の友達　青鬼』

　赤鬼は、だまってそれを三度も四度も読みました。そして、涙をぽろぽろ流して、泣きました。

浜田広介「泣いた赤鬼」より

1課

< 1課 - 読む (質問) >

Reading: Children's Story

(Narrator) Now answer the questions for this section.

1. What was Akaoni's wish?
   (A) Akaoni wanted to eat people.
   (B) Akaoni wanted to marry a human girl.
   (C) Akaoni wanted to make human friends.
   (D) Akaoni wanted to live in the human village.

2. What action did Akaoni take?
   (A) He put up a sign that invited people to visit him at his house.
   (B) He prepared tea and sweets, and put them outside of his house.
   (C) He went to meet with people in the village.
   (D) He asked Aooni to help him.

3. After listening to Akaoni's problem, what plan did Aooni suggest?
   (A) Aooni would explain how great Akaoni was to the village people.
   (B) Aooni would set a fire in the village, and then Akaoni would rescue the village people.
   (C) Aooni would enter and ransack someone's house in the village, and then Akaoni would attack Aooni.
   (D) Aooni would beat the village people, and then Akaoni would beat Aooni.

4. Why didn't Akaoni hear from Aooni for many days?
   (A) Aooni was sick from a cold.
   (B) Aooni was injured.
   (C) Aooni didn't want to associate with Akaoni.
   (D) Aooni could not go out because he could not walk.

5. Why did Akaoni cry after reading the letter from Aooni?
   (A) Akaoni was overjoyed with good news about Aooni.
   (B) Akaoni was sad because he didn't know why Aooni left home.
   (C) Akaoni was sad because Aooni told Akaoni they were no longer friends.
   (D) Akaoni was deeply moved by Aooni's true friendship.

<1課 - 書く (テキストチャット)>
Text Chat: Personal Life

90秒×6

You will participate in a simulated exchange of text-chat messages. Each time it is your turn to write, you will have 90 seconds. You should respond as fully and as appropriately as possible.

You will have a conversation about yourself with Kimi Yasuda, a student at your host school in Japan. She is researching American high school student life.

1. Respond. (90 seconds)
    初めまして。安田です。どうぞよろしく。今日は個人的な質問をしてもいいですか。
2. Give a specific example and respond. (90 seconds)
    まず第一の質問ですが、どんな性格をしていますか。自分の性格が好きですか。
3. Describe. (90 seconds)
    そうですか。次に、親や兄弟との仲はどうですか。
4. Explain your preference. (90 seconds)
    そうですか。第三に、問題があったら、親か友達、どっちに相談しますか。
5. Justify your opinion. (90 seconds)
    そうですか。最後に、どんないい友人がいますか。
6. Ask a specific question. (90 seconds)
    今日はいろいろ有難うございました。日本の高校生について何か質問がありますか。

<1課 - 書く (比較と対比)>
Compare and Contrast Article: Family and Friends

20分

Directions: You are writing an article for the student newspaper of your sister school in Japan. Write an article in which you compare and contrast similarities and differences between family and friends. Based on your personal experience, describe at least THREE aspects of each and highlight the similarities and differences between family and friends. Also state your preference for either and give reasons for it.

Your article should be 300 to 400 characters or longer. Use the *desu/masu* or *da* (plain) style, but use one style consistently. Also, use *kanji* wherever *kanji* from the AP Japanese *kanji* list is appropriate. You have 20 minutes to write.

【NOTES/OUTLINE: 自分の作文のアウトラインを書こう！】

Introduction:
_____

Three similarities/differences:

1. _____
2. _____
3. _____

Your preference and give reasons:
_____
_____

1課

＜１課 - 話す (会話)＞
Conversation: Introduction

20秒×4

You will participate in a simulated conversation. Each time it is your turn to speak, you will have 20 seconds to record. You should respond as fully and as appropriately as possible.

You will introduce yourself to Taro in a conversation. You are hosting Taro, a Japanese exchange student at your school.

(Taro)
(20 seconds)
(Taro)
(20 seconds)
(Taro)
(20 seconds)
(Taro)
(20 seconds)

＜１課 - 話す (日本文化)＞
Cultural Perspective Presentation: Japanese Family

4分+2分

Directions: Imagine you are making an oral presentation to your Japanese class. First, you will be instructed to read and listen to the topic for your presentation. You will then have 4 minutes to prepare your presentation. Then you will have 2 minutes to record your presentation. Your presentation should be as complete as possible.

Present your own view or perspective of the Japanese family. Discuss at least FIVE aspects or examples about the Japanese family.

Begin with an appropriate introduction, give details, explain your own view or perspective, and end with a concluding remark.

【Let's take notes!】

1. Begin with an appropriate introduction.

   _____

2. Discuss five aspects/examples of the topic.

   1.) _____
   2.) _____
   3.) _____
   4.) _____
   5.) _____

3. Explain your view or perspective.

   _____

4. End with a concluding remark.

   _____

１課

| 2課 | | 日常生活(じょう)
Daily Life | |

【AP® タスク：日常生活(じょう)】
Discuss the following topics with your partner.
1. Your most valued time of the day.
2. Things you have learned from experiencing what it would be like to live as a handicapped person.

【文化】 日本のトイレと風呂：Japanese Toilets and Baths

The Japanese bathroom and toilet culture is a fascinating one. Traditionally, bathing has played a significant role in the daily life of Japanese. "Bathing" traditionally meant taking a bath in the *furo* (風呂) or Japanese bathtub, though today, it may also mean taking a shower.

Most Japanese bathe every evening to cleanse themselves from the dirt and grime of a day spent out of the home. The Japanese preoccupation with cleanliness is traced to Shinto, the native religion. Purification was believed to be the way in which humans, nature and the gods could maintain harmony. To this day, Japanese habitually "purify" themselves with water or heat (steam) before entering temples and shrines. Bathing in the *furo* combines purification through fire (heat) and water.

Taking a bath in a *furo* is still the preferred way to bathe. At home, one enters the 風呂場 (*furoba*), leaves one's house slippers at the entrance to the bathing room, removes one's clothing and enters the area for washing. One sits on a low stool to soap with a long washcloth and to shampoo. One rinses off with a handheld shower or by pouring water over oneself using a small round container. After rinsing, one enters the tub, which is filled about two-thirds full with very hot water. Neither soap nor soapy towels is used in the bathtub. One soaks and relaxes while enjoying the warm bath that removes the day's stress. After the entire family has bathed in the hot bath, it is drained and the bathtub is cleaned. Because the water is used for the entire family, water use for baths is relatively small.

Showers are still a relatively new option. They are a way to rinse off before entering the *furo*, though more young adults now shower instead of taking a bath in the *furo*. The relative convenience of showers has also encouraged them to take morning showers. Many young girls now wash their hair in the morning for a fresh "blow dried hair" look. This is called *asashan* (朝シャン) or "morning shampoo."

The toilet in Japanese homes is located in a separate room from the bathing room. Before indoor plumbing, the toilet was located outside of the home, as it was regarded as unclean. Now, it still remains in a separate room. Before entering the toilet area, one removes one's house slippers and changes into plastic slippers reserved for the toilet area.

The toilet in a Japanese home takes many forms, but most families now own washlets or automated toilets with functions such as rinsing, drying, warming and massaging. An array of buttons located to the side of the toilet seat allows the user to choose from at least a dozen different options. Washlet toilets are now available at most public sites. Japanese enjoy the washlet for its luxury, cleanliness and the fact that they do not have to use paper.

Bath and toilet practices tell us much about the Shinto-based Japanese love for cleanliness and purity. Logistics of the toilet are remnants of the Japanese concepts of *uchi* (内) and *soto* (外) and their associations with cleanliness and impurity. Bathing is viewed by Japanese as a time of respite, relaxation and escape from the demands of one's daily life. Bathing and toilet practices also coincide with the Japanese concern for protecting the environment.

Questions to ponder: How is bathing perceived differently in Japan and in your country? Can you think of other practices that are examples of the Japanese appreciation of cleanliness and purity?

| 2課 | | 復習単語 | |

トピック：日常生活

1. 朝御飯	あさごはん	N	breakfast
2. 昼御飯	ひるごはん	N	lunch
3. 朝食	ちょうしょく	N	breakfast
4. 昼食	ちゅうしょく	N	lunch
5. 台所	だいどころ	N	kitchen
6. 家事	かじ	N	household chore; housework
7. (ゴミ)を出す	(ゴミ)をだす	V1	(to) take out (the garbage)
8. 電気製品	でんきせいひん	N	electric goods
9. 電子レンジ	でんしレンジ	N	microwave oven
10. 布団	ふとん	N	Japanese bedding
11. 布団を敷く	ふとんをしく	V1	(to) lay out the bedding
12. (風呂に)入る	(ふろに)はいる	V1	(to) take (a bath)
13. 通う	かよう	V	(to) commute
14. 週末	しゅうまつ	N	weekend

| 2課 | ★★★ | 新しい単語 | ★★★ |

1. にちじょうせいかつ＜日常生活＞　N　daily life
   私の日常生活は忙しすぎる。　My daily life is too busy.
2. すいみんぶそく＜睡眠不足＞　N　lack of sleep
   睡眠不足で眠い。　I am sleepy because of lack of sleep.
3. じょうほう＜情報＞　N　information
   インターネットで大学のいろいろな情報を集めている。　I am collecting information on various colleges on the Internet.
4. がんしょ＜願書＞　N　written application
   大学の願書を書かなければならない。　I have to write college applications.
5. しょうがいしゃ＜障害者＞　N　(physically) handicapped person
   障害者には親切にしてあげよう。　Let's be kind to handicapped people.
6. くるまいす＜車椅子＞　N　wheelchair
   祖父は車椅子を使っている。　My grandfather uses a wheelchair.
7. しゅわ＜手話＞　N　sign language
   祖母は耳が聞こえないので、私は手話で話す。　Since my grandmother cannot hear, I talk to her in sign language.
8. (お)ゆ＜(お)湯＞　N　hot water
   日本人はお風呂のお湯を家族皆で使う。　For Japanese, the entire family uses the hot bath water.
9. せっけん＜石鹸＞　N　soap
   日本人はお風呂の中で石鹸を使わない。　Japanese don't use soap in the bathtub.
10. へいじつ＜平日＞　N　weekday(s)
    平日は週末と比べてとても忙しい。　Weekdays are very busy compared to weekends.
11. りゆう＜理由＞　N　reason
    日本語を取った理由は、日本のアニメが分かりたいからだ。　The reason why I took Japanese is that I want to understand Japanese anime.
12. ほうそうきょく＜放送局＞　N　broadcast station
    紅白歌合戦はNHKの放送局で作られている。　The Red and White Song Contest is produced at the NHK broadcast station.
13. しょうたいけん＜招待券＞　N　complimentary ticket

しょうたいじょう＜招待状＞　N　invitation (card)
しょうたい＜招待＞(を)する／します　V3　to invite
映画の招待券を二枚もらった。　I received two complimentary tickets to the movie.

14. いつものところ＜いつもの所＞　N　the usual place
いつもの所で一時に会おう。　Let's meet at one o'clock at the usual place.

15. ふじゆう＜不自由＞　Na　disabled
祖母は耳が不自由だ。　My grandmother cannot hear.

16. むり＜無理＞　Na　impossible
これを全部するのは無理だ。　It is impossible to do all these.

17. ねむい＜眠い＞　A　be sleepy
眠そうな顔をしている。　You look sleepy.

18. (Dic./Nou＋の)たび＜度＞に　N　every time (one does ～); every ～
トトロのビデオを見る度に、嬉しくなる。　Every time I see the Totoro video, I become happy.
夏休みの度に、家族旅行に行く。　Every summer vacation, we go on a family trip.

19. ていしゅつ＜提出＞(を)する／します　V3　to submit
ていしゅつび＜提出日＞　N　due date
明日レポートを提出出来ない。　I cannot turn in the paper tomorrow.

20. てつや＜徹夜＞(を)する／します　V3　to be awake all night
ゆうべは徹夜で勉強していた。　I was studying without any sleep last night.

21. (あさ)ねぼう＜(朝)寝坊＞(を)する／します　V3　to oversleep (in the morning)
また今日も寝坊をしてしまった。　I overslept today again.

22. まにあう＜間に合う＞／間に合います　V1　to be on time
駅に走ったけど、間に合わなかった。　I ran to the station, but I didn't make it on time.

23. あう＜合う＞／合います　V1　to fit; to suit; to match
どんな大学が私に合っているかよく分からない。　I don't know what kind of college is a good fit for me.

24. のんびりする／のんびりします　V3　to be at leisure; to relax
のんびりする時間がほしい。　I want time to relax.

25. サボる／サボります　V1　to skip (class, work, etc.)
太郎は授業をサボって、海へ行った。　Taro cut class and went to the beach.

26. (illness が)なおる＜治る＞／治ります　V1　(illness) is cured [intransitive]
☞ (illness を)なおす＜治す＞／治します　V1　to cure (an illness) [transitive]

2課

やっと風邪が治った。 My cold has finally gotten better.

27. すすめる＜勧める＞／勧めます　V2　to recommend
先生は私達に日記を書くことを勧めた。 Our teacher recommended that we write a diary.

28. ボタンをおす＜押す＞／おします　V1　to push a button
ウォッシュレットのボタンを押すと、水が出て来る。 When you push a button on the washlet, the water comes out.

29. かんそう＜乾燥＞する／します　V3　to dry
ボタンを押すと、乾燥することも出来るから、紙が要らない。 When you push a button, you can also dry, so you don't need paper.

30. せつやく＜節約＞する／します　V3　to save; conserve
ウォッシュレットを使うと、紙を節約することが出来る。 When you use a washlet, you can save paper.

31. せいけつ＜清潔＞にする／します　V3　to keep clean; to keep sanitary
日本人は清潔好きだ。 Japanese like cleanliness.

32. クイズにあたる＜当たる＞／当たります　V1　to win a contest
クイズに当たって、日本行きの航空券を二枚もらった。 I won a contest and received two airline tickets for a trip to Japan.

【もっと単語】

1.	むね＜胸＞	N	chest
2.	しんぞう＜心臓＞	N	heart; cardio-
3.	えがお＜笑顔＞	N	smiling face
4.	ぶちょう＜部長＞	N	(club) president; department head
7.	ひっし＜必死＞	Na	desperate
8.	かんぜん＜完全＞	Na	perfect
5.	ありがたい＜有り難い＞	A	thankful
6.	ぐったりしている	V3	to be tired out
9.	(〜に)しゅうちゅう＜集中＞する	V3	to concentrate (on) 〜; to focus (on)
10.	はんせい＜反省＞する	V3	to think about oneself; reflect; regret
11.	まよって＜迷って＞いる	V1	to be puzzled (to be unable to decide what to do)
12.	からかう	V1	to tease
13.	ぐちをいう＜愚痴を言う＞	V1	to complain

2課

2課 文法

> A. Verb 1 (TE form) 、～　　　　　　　　　　"do V1, and do ～"
> Verb 1 (stem form) ＋ ながら、～　　　　　"While doing V1, does ～."
> 　　Used when one subject performs two actions concurrently.
> Verb 1 (informal form) ＋ 間に、～　　　　"While doing V1, does ～."
> 　　Used when one or two subject(s) exist and/or perform(s) two actions.
> Verb 1 (dictionary form) ＋ 前に、～　　　"Before doing V1, does ～"
> Verb 1 (TA form) ＋ 後で、～　　　　　　"After doing V1, does ～"
> Verb (TE form) ＋ から、～　　　　　　　"After doing V, does ～"
>
> 1. うちへ帰って、服を着替えた。　　　　I returned home and changed my clothes.
> 2. 運転をしながら、ラジオを聞く。　　　I listen to the radio while driving.
> 3. 日本にいる間に、いろいろな所へ旅行したい。
> 　　　I want to travel to various places while I am in Japan.
> 4. 母が朝食を作っている間に、父は本を読んでいた。
> 　　　While my mother was cooking breakfast, my father was reading the newspaper.
> 5. ゆうべ寝る前に、お風呂に入った。
> 　　　I took a bath before I went to bed last night.
> 6. 明日友達と映画を見た後で、友達のうちへ行くつもりだ。
> 　　　After seeing a movie with my friend tomorrow, I plan to go to my friend's house.
> 7. 昼食を食べてから、映画を見に行こう。
> 　　　Let's go watch a movie after eating lunch.

These are some activities you and/or your family members do in your daily life. Write sentences using all of the cues in the ( ). Use the forms above to conjoin your sentences.

1. (-て、シャワーをあびる、朝食を食べる)

　_____。

2. (-ながら、おどる、歌う)

　_____。

3. (-後で、宿題をする、おやつを食べる)

　_____。

4. (-前に、寝る、歯をみがく)

　_____。

5. (-間に、父、母、掃除する、車を洗う)

　_____。

B. 「どの大学へ行くか決めた？」　"Did you decide which university you are going to?"

1. 田中さんがパーティーに来るかどうか知りません。
   I do not know if Mr. Tanaka will come to the party or not.
2. 田中さんがパーティーに来るか来ないか知りません。
   I do not know if Mr. Tanaka will come or will not come to the party.
3. 東京駅までいくらか知っていますか。
   Do you know how much it costs to get to Tokyo Station?
4. いつ日本語の試験があるか覚えていますか。
   Do you remember when we are having our Japanese exam?

Combine the two sentences into one.
Ex. ダンスは何時に始まりますか＋知りません→ダンスが何時に始まるか知りません。
1. どの大学へ行きますか＋知りません
   →＿＿＿＿＿＿＿＿＿＿＿＿＿＿＿＿＿＿＿＿＿＿＿＿＿＿＿＿＿＿＿
2. その大学の授業料はいくらですか＋知りません
   →＿＿＿＿＿＿＿＿＿＿＿＿＿＿＿＿＿＿＿＿＿＿＿＿＿＿＿＿＿＿＿
3. 東海岸の大学へ行きたいですか＋知りません
   →＿＿＿＿＿＿＿＿＿＿＿＿＿＿＿＿＿＿＿＿＿＿＿＿＿＿＿＿＿＿＿
4. アメリカ史のレポートの提出日はいつですか＋知っていますか
   →＿＿＿＿＿＿＿＿＿＿＿＿＿＿＿＿＿＿＿＿＿＿＿＿＿＿＿＿＿＿＿

C. Verb potential form
Group 1 verbs:　　　話す　〔はなす〕→話せる　　〔はなせる〕　can speak
Group 2 verbs:　　　食べる〔たべる〕→食べられる〔たべられる〕can eat
Irregular verbs:　　　来る　〔くる〕　→来られる　〔こられる〕　can come
　　　　　　　　　　する　　　　　→出来る　　〔できる〕　　can do

1. 父は中国語が話せますが、私は話せません。　My father can speak Chinese, but I cannot.
2. 母はさしみが食べられません。　　　　　　My mother cannot eat raw fish.
3. 「この土曜日に家へ来られますか。」　　　"Can you come to my house this Saturday?"
　「はい、もちろん行けますよ。」　　　　　"Yes, of course I can."
4. 七時に予約出来ました。　　　　　　　　　I was able to make a reservation for 7 o'clock.

Complete the sentences using the potential form of a verb in the ( ).
1. 私は何も上手に＿＿＿＿＿＿＿＿＿＿＿＿＿＿＿＿＿＿＿＿。（しない）
2. 熱があって今日学校へ＿＿＿＿＿＿＿＿＿＿＿＿＿＿＿＿＿＿。（行かない）
3. だれにもほかの人の＿＿＿＿＿＿＿＿＿＿＿＿＿＿＿＿＿＿ことがある。（役に立つ）

2課

4. 祖母は足が悪くて＿＿＿＿＿＿＿＿＿＿＿＿＿＿＿＿＿＿＿＿。（歩かない）

5. 妹は病気でもっと生きたくても＿＿＿＿＿＿＿＿＿＿＿＿＿＿＿＿＿。（生きない）

6. 明日のパーティーにケーキを＿＿＿＿＿＿＿＿＿＿＿＿＿＿＿＿＿＿。（持って来ない）

D. Verb (Dic.) -ようになる
　　Verb (NAI-なく)なる
　　I Adj. -くなる
　　Na Adj. -になる

1. 車いすを使うようになった。　　I have come to use a wheelchair.
2. 歩けなくなった。　　　　　　　I am no longer able to walk.
3. 難しくなった。　　　　　　　　It has became harder.
4. 不便になった。　　　　　　　　It has become inconvenient.

---

a. Fill in the blanks with the correct verb form, using this sentence structure.

Ex. 私は前、日本語が話せなかったんですが、だんだん<u>話せるように</u>なったんです。

　　私は前、日本語が話せたんですが、使わなかったので、<u>話せなく</u>なったんです。

1. 祖母は前、歩けたのに、年を取って、だんだん＿＿＿＿＿＿＿＿＿＿＿なったんです。
2. 祖母は前、全然歩けなかったのに、今つえ(cane)を使って、少し＿＿＿＿＿＿＿＿＿＿
　なったんです。
3. 祖母は若いころ、漢字がたくさん書けたのに、漢字を使わないので、だんだん漢字が
　＿＿＿＿＿＿＿＿＿＿＿なったんです。
4. 祖母は若いころ、何でも上手に出来たのに、癌にかかって、何も
　＿＿＿＿＿＿＿＿＿＿＿なったんです。
5. 私は前、日本語の新聞は全然読めませんでしたが、毎日、日本語を勉強しているので、
　だんだん＿＿＿＿＿＿＿＿＿＿＿なったんです。

b. Fill in the blanks with the correct form of the word in the ( ).

Ex. 漢字の勉強が<u>おもしろく</u>なったんです。（おもしろい）

　　漢字の勉強が<u>好きに</u>なりました。（好き）

1. 難病にかかって、体がだんだん＿＿＿＿＿＿＿＿＿＿＿なりました。（不自由）
2. 書くことも＿＿＿＿＿＿＿＿＿＿＿なりました。（難しい）
3. 日記を書いて、＿＿＿＿＿＿＿＿＿＿＿なりました。（有名）
4. 掃除したので、部屋が＿＿＿＿＿＿＿＿＿＿＿なりました。（きれい）

2課

E. Polite form, informal speaking styles, and informal writing style

Modern young women tend to use male speech style.

	Polite 男女	Informal Speaking 男	Informal Speaking 女	Informal Writing 男女
Statements	食べます	食べる（よ）	食べる（よ/ね）	食べる
	今日です	今日だ（よ）	今日（よ）	テストだ
	好きです	好きだ（よ）	好き（よ）	好きだ
	高いです	高い（よ）	高い（よ）	高い
Questions	食べますか	食べる？↗	食べる？↗	食べるか
	テストですか	テスト？↗	テスト？↗	テストか
	好きですか	好き？↗	好き？↗	好きか
	高いですか	高い？↗	高い？↗	高いか
Negative statements	食べません	食べない（よ）	食べない（よ）	食べない
	今日ではありません	今日じゃない（よ）	今日じゃない（よ）	テストじゃない
	好きではありません	好きじゃない（よ）	好きじゃない（よ）	好きじゃない
	高くありません	高くない（よ）	高くない（よ）	高くない
Requests	がんばって下さい。	がんばって。	がんばって。	がんばって。
Others	はい、元気です	うん、元気だよ	ええ、元気よ	うん、元気だ
	いいえ、元気ではありません	ううん、元気じゃない（よ）	ううん、元気じゃない（のよ）。	ううん、元気じゃない
	そうですねえ。。。	そうだねえ。。。	そうねえ。。。	そうだねえ。。。
	では、さようなら	じゃね/じゃな	じゃね	じゃ、さようなら
	行くはずです	行くはずだ（よ）	行くはず（よ）	行くはずだ
	しかし	でも	でも	でも
	ですから	だから	だから	だから
	行くと言いました	行くって言った（よ）	行くって言った（よ）	行くって言った
	聞きましたが、分かりませんでした。	聞いたけど、分からなかった。	聞いたけど、分からなかった。	聞いたが、分からなかった。
	ありがとうございます	ありがとう	ありがとう	ありがとう

2課

| 2課 | | アクティビティー | |

A. 日本文化：一人か二人ワーク→クラスワーク

Divide the topics below among your classmates and research your topic on the Internet. Using visuals, present your findings with your classmates.

1. 先輩〔せんぱい〕と後輩〔こうはい〕
2. お風呂〔ふろ〕
3. ウォッシュレット
4. 神道〔しんとう〕の清め〔きよめ〕

B. 家族：ペアワーク

Narrate Ken's day with your partner. Use a variety of patterns: 〜て(から), 〜間に, Stem + ながら, TA + 後で, Dic. + 前に. Include as many details as you can.

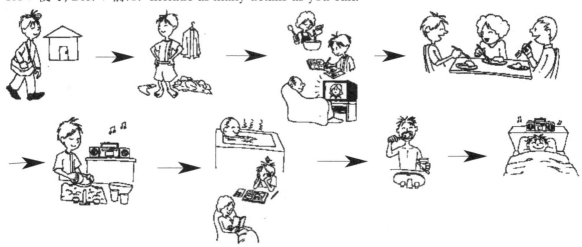

C. 聞く Pre-Listening Activity「高三の生活」：ペアワーク

Have a conversation with your partner using the following questions. Elaborate.

1. 最近、朝寝坊〔ねぼう〕して、学校に間に合わなかったことがある？
2. 最近、私は眠〔ねむ〕そうな顔〔かお〕をしている？
3. 最近、時々徹夜〔てつや〕をする？
4. 最近、睡眠不足〔すいみんぶそく〕？
5. もうすぐ何かレポートを提出〔ていしゅつ〕しなきゃいけない？
6. 大学の情報〔じょうほう〕をどうやって集〔あつ〕めてる？
7. どんな大学が自分に合ってると思う？
8. 願書〔がんしょ〕をいくつぐらいの大学に出そうと思ってる？
9. 大学の推薦状〔すいせんじょう〕は、もう先生にお願〔ねが〕いした？

2課

10. 時々のんびりすることがある？

11. クラスをサボったことがある？

D. 聞く Post-Listening Activity 「高三の生活」：ペアワーク

Compare and Contrast: High School Freshman Life and Senior Life
Based on your personal experience, describe at least THREE aspects of life as a freshman and life as a senior in high school. Highlight the similarities and differences. Also state your preference and give reasons for it. You will have 4 minutes to prepare and 2 minutes to present.

Introduction:
_____

Three similarities/differences:
   1. _____
   2. _____
   3. _____

Your preference and give reasons:
_____
_____

E. 読み Pre-Reading Activity 「一リットルの涙〔なみだ〕」：ペアワーク
What does it feel like to be physically handicapped? Try and experience it.

1. 目をつぶって見よう。目が不自由な人の気持ちを分かろう。
   Put on a blindfold (目かくし). Your partner will give you directions in Japanese. Walk around the classroom. Find your seat and sit down. Remove the blindfold. Share your experiences and your feelings with the class in Japanese.
   (目をつぶって。= "Close your eyes."　どいて。= "Move.")

2. 耳をふさいでみよう。手話で話してみよう。耳が不自由な人の気持ちを分かろう。
   Wear earplugs. Discuss each of the following topics with your partner. Try to read your partner's lips, use sign language and communicate by writing or any means of communication other than listening.
   (ふさぐ: "to plug")

   Topic 1: 放課後にすることを決める。

   Topic 2: 週末に行く所を決める。

   Topic 3: 今、一番興味を持っていることについて話し合う。

   Remove the earplugs. Share your experiences and your feelings with the class in Japanese.

2課

F. 読み Post-Reading Activity 「一リットルの涙〔なみだ〕」：ペアワーク

Presentation: Japanese Drama "One Liter of Tears"

Read the movie review of "One Liter of Tears," then present your view on this drama. Discuss at least FIVE aspects of this drama. Begin with an appropriate introduction, give details about the five aspects, explain your own view or perspective, and end with a concluding remark. You will have 4 minutes to prepare and 2 minutes to present. Your presentation should be as complete as possible.

1. Begin with an appropriate introduction.
   _____

2. Discuss five aspects/examples of the topic.
   1.) _____
   2.) _____
   3.) _____
   4.) _____
   5.) _____

3. Explain your view or perspective.
   _____

4. End with a concluding remark.
   _____

G. テキストチャット：ペアワーク

Pair off with a partner. One partner will provide the following cues by speaking. The other will not look at the book, and must respond in 20 seconds. Switch after finishing all.

1. おひさしぶりですね。
2. そちらの生活はどうですか。
3. ちゃんと食事していますか。
4. 皿洗〔さら〕いとか食事の片付〔かたづ〕けを手伝〔つだ〕っていますか。
5. ちゃんと部屋を掃除〔そうじ〕したり、洗濯〔せんたく〕をしたりしていますか。
6. どんな運動〔うん〕していますか。
7. 今、趣味〔しゅ〕と勉強とどっちの方が大事だと思いますか。
8. では、元気でね。
9. こちらの皆について何か聞きたいことがありますか。

2課

H. Compare & Contrast 「平日と週末〔しゅうまつ〕」：ペアワーク→クラスワーク

Prepare a compare and contrast presentation on weekday routines and weekend routines with your partner. Include an introduction, describe three similarities and differences with details, state your preference and give reasons for it. Take 5 minutes to prepare the presentation and present it in class in 3 minutes.

1. Introduction: _____

2. 一つ目の違いは、_____

   Details: _____

   二つ目の違いは、_____

   Details: _____

   三つ目の違いは or 一つの同じ事は、

   _____

   Details: _____

3. Preference: 結論〔けつろん〕として、私達は_____方が_____より好きです。

4. Reasons: その理由〔ゆう〕は、_____

   からです。

I. 友達との会話：ペアワーク

   a. The following statements are given in informal style. Change the underlined portions to the *desu/masu* style.

1. <u>あのね</u>、行きたい<u>って</u>言っていたあのコンサートの<u>招待券〔しょうけん〕がね</u>、ラジオ局のクイズで<u>当〔あ〕たったのよ</u>。

2. <u>でも</u>、今晩の<u>コンサートなのよ</u>。<u>二枚〔まい〕もらえるんだけど</u>、一緒に<u>行けない？</u>

3. <u>でもね</u>、<u>ちょっと</u>問題があって、この招待券〔しょうけん〕を今日午後４時までに放送局〔ほうきょく〕まで取りに行かなくちゃいけないのよ。<u>私、今日忙〔いそが〕しくて時間がないし、どうしよう</u>。

4. <u>じゃ</u>、いつもの所で六時に<u>待〔ま〕ち合わせようね</u>。ああ、今から<u>ドキドキしちゃう</u>。

   b. Have a conversation in the informal style with your partner. Speak at a natural speed.

J. ウォッシュレットの使い方：ペアワーク→クラスワーク

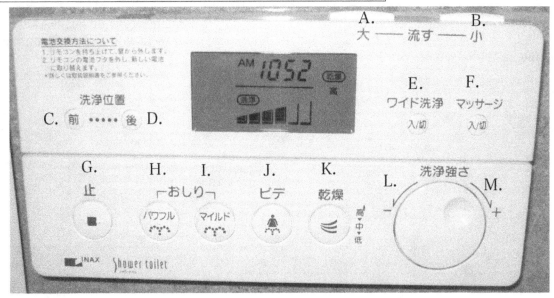

Identify the following buttons from the photo of the washlet above. Write the matching letters.

1. Front cleansing ( )
2. Rear cleansing ( )
3. Dryer ( )
4. Rear cleansing: Gentle ( )
5. Rear cleansing: High ( )
6. Stop ( )
7. Water pressure adjustment: High ( )
8. Water pressure adjustment: Low ( )
9. Wide cleaning ( )
10. Massage ( )
11. Big flush ( )
12. Little flush ( )

K. 日本のお風呂とトイレ：ペアワーク→クラスワーク

Circle the correct responses.

a. 日本のお風呂とトイレ：
1. 日本のお風呂とトイレは同じ所に（ある　ない）。
2. 日本のお風呂のお湯の中で石鹸やタオルを（使ってもいい　使ってはいけない）。
3. 日本のお風呂のお湯は、（家族全員　一人）が使った後、捨てる。
4. 日本のお風呂に入る前に、体を（洗わなくてはいけない　洗わなくてもいい）。
5. 日本人はたいてい（朝　昼　夜）お風呂に入る。
6. 日本人はたいてい（お父さん　お母さん　子供）からお風呂に入る。

b. 日本のトイレ：
1. 日本の最近のトイレは（ハイテク　まだ昔と同じ）トイレだ。
2. 日本の最近のトイレは、トイレットペーパーが（必要だ　必要ではない）。
3. 日本の最近のトイレは、（ボタン　スイッチ）を押すと、水が出て洗ってくれる。
4. 日本のトイレの戸は、使っていない時、（閉めておく　開けておく）べきだ。
5. 日本のトイレで使うスリッパは、うちの中で（はいてもいい　はいてはいけない）。

2課

<2課 - 聞く>

Listening: Senior Life

12秒×5

【You may take notes while listening. Do not look at the questions below before listening. You will have 12 seconds to answer each question. You may NOT move back and forth among questions.】

(Narrator) Now you will listen once to a conversation.

(Narrator) Now answer the questions for this selection.

1. What is the relationship between Momo and Tanaka?
    (A) Momo is younger than Tanaka and was on the same high school basketball team.
    (B) Momo and Tanaka are classmates in high school.
    (C) Momo is a high school student and Tanaka is her teacher.
    (D) Momo is a high school student and Tanaka is her basketball coach.

2. Where and when did they meet?
    (A) They met on the street in the morning.
    (B) They met on the train in the morning.
    (C) They met on the street on the way home in the late afternoon.
    (D) They met on the train on the way to school in the early afternoon.

3. Which is true about Momo?
    (A) Momo's basketball team is strong.
    (B) Momo is a leader of her basketball team.
    (C) Momo didn't sleep last night because she has two exams today.
    (D) Momo is supposed to turn in a physics paper today, but she was not able to finish it.

4. Where in the college application process is Momo now?
    (A) Momo has completed collecting all the necessary college information.
    (B) Momo already has asked her teachers to write her college recommendations.
    (C) Momo has already sent out her college application forms.
    (D) Momo is still working hard on all of the above.

5. What was Tanaka's suggestion to Momo?
    (A) Momo should study harder.
    (B) Momo should sleep more.
    (C) Momo should smile more.
    (D) Momo should go out with friends more.

<2課 - 読む>
Reading: Movie Review
【You may move back and forth among all the questions.】

　最近見た「一リットルの涙」というテレビドラマについて紹介します。このドラマは本当にあったお話で、普通の明るくにぎやかな家族に突然ひとつの出来事が起こりました。長女の亜也さんは１５歳の時、難病にかかって、医者から治らないと宣言されました。体がだんだん不自由になって、２５歳で亡くなりました。彼女は日常生活でごく当たり前と思うことがだんだん出来なくなり、苦しみました。少しずつ歩けなくなって、車いすを使うようになりました。そして、話せなくなっていきました。書くことも難しくなりました。でも、頭は正常です。亜也さんが歩けなくなっていった時に、自分がまだ歩けることを嬉しく思いました。亜也さんが学校へ行けなくなった時に、私はまだ学校へ行けるんだと喜びました。亜也さんが友達に「親切にしてくれてありがとう」と言ったり、いつも彼女の気持ちや悩みを聞いてくれる男友達に「いつもそばで話を聞いてくれてありがとう」と言ったりするたびに、私自身は誰にも感謝していないなあって反省させられました。そして、亜也さんのために何でもしてあげる家族の愛から、家族の有り難さを感じました。亜也さんが「自分は人のために役に立つことをしたいと思っていたけど、何にも出来ないよ。」とお母さんにぐちを言った時、お母さんは亜也さんに日記を書くことを勧めました。亜也さんの書いた日記は多くの人を励ましました。だれでも人の役に立てるんですね。「生きる」ということがどういうことか考えさせられ、今を大事に生きようと思いました。

　このドラマは２００５年に「親が子供に見せたいテレビ番組」の一位に選ばれました。亜也さんの言葉に、多くの人達が励まされたからだと思います。彼女の言葉の一つです。「胸に手をあててみる。ドキドキ、ドキドキ、音がする。心臓が動いている。嬉しい。私は生きている。」

　皆さんもぜひこのドラマを見て下さい。

＜２課 - 読む (質問)＞

Reading: Movie Review

(Narrator) Now answer the questions for this section.

1. How old was Aya when she became ill?
   (A) 5
   (B) 10
   (C) 15
   (D) 25

2. Even though Aya gradually could not do what she normally had done, what was she still able to do?
   (A) walk
   (B) talk
   (C) think
   (D) write

3. What made Aya write her journal?
   (A) She enjoyed writing.
   (B) Her mother advised her to.
   (C) Her friend encouraged her.
   (D) Her teacher advised her to.

4. How did Aya's life change the writer's life?
   (A) The writer decided to make more friends.
   (B) The writer decided to write a journal.
   (C) The writer decided to write thank-you cards to her family and friends.
   (D) The writer decided to live every moment fully.

5. Who in particular wanted to show this drama to children?
   (A) parents
   (B) teachers
   (C) students
   (D) Department of Education

２課

<2課 - 書く (テキストチャット)>

90秒×6

Text Chat: Daily Life

You will participate in a simulated exchange of text-chat messages. Each time it is your turn to write, you will have 90 seconds. You should respond as fully and as appropriately as possible.

You will have a conversation with Mrs. Kondo, who was your host mother in Japan last summer.

1. Respond. (90 seconds)
   おひさしぶりですね。そちらの生活はどうですか。
2. Respond. (90 seconds)
   ちゃんと食事していますか。皿洗いとか食事の片付けを手伝っていますか。
3. Respond. (90 seconds)
   ちゃんと部屋を掃除したり、洗濯をしたりしていますか。
4. Give a specific example and explain. (90 seconds)
   どんな運動していますか。
5. Justify your opinion. (90 seconds)
   今、趣味と勉強とどっちの方が大事だと思いますか。
6. Ask a specific question. (90 seconds)
   では、元気でね。こちらの皆について何か聞きたいことがありますか。

<2課 - 書く (比較と対比)>

20分

Compare and Contrast Article: Weekday Routines and Weekend Routines

Directions: You are writing an article for the student newspaper of your sister school in Japan. Write an article in which you compare and contrast weekday routines and weekend routines. Based on your personal experience, describe at least THREE aspects of each and highlight the similarities and differences between weekday routines and weekend routines. Also state your preference for either and give reasons for it.

Your article should be 300 to 400 characters or longer. Use the *desu/masu* or *da* (plain) style, but use one style consistently. Also, use *kanji* wherever there are *kanji* from the AP Japanese *kanji* list. You will have 20 minutes to write.

【NOTES/OUTLINE: 自分の作文のアウトラインを書こう！】

Introduction:
_____

Three similarities/differences:

1. _____
2. _____
3. _____

Your preference and reasons:
_____
_____

2課

＜2課 - 話す (会話)＞
Conversation: Concert

`20秒×4`

You will participate in a simulated conversation. Each time it is your turn to speak, you will have 20 seconds to record. You should respond as fully and as appropriately as possible.

You will have a conversation with Yumi, your Japanese friend, about a concert.

(Yumi)
(20 seconds)
(Yumi)
(20 seconds)
(Yumi)
(20 seconds)
(Yumi)
(20 seconds)

＜2課 - 話す (日本文化)＞
Cultural Perspective Presentation: Japanese Toilets and Baths

`4分+2分`

Directions: Imagine you are making an oral presentation to your Japanese class. First, you will read and hear the topic for your presentation. You will have 4 minutes to prepare your presentation. Then you will have 2 minutes to record your presentation. Your presentation should be as complete as possible.

Present your own view or perspective on Japanese toilets and baths. Discuss at least FIVE aspects or examples of Japanese toilets and baths.

Begin with an appropriate introduction, give details about your example, explain your own view or perspective, and end with a concluding remark.

【Let's take notes!】

1. Begin with an appropriate introduction.

   _____

2. Discuss five aspects/examples of the topic.

   1.) _____
   2.) _____
   3.) _____
   4.) _____
   5.) _____

3. Explain your view or perspective.

   _____

4. End with a concluding remark.

   _____

2課

3課　　レジャーと趣味とスポーツ　
Leisure, Hobbies and Sports

【AP® タスク：レジャーと趣味とスポーツ】

Discuss your interests. What are you passionate about now? When and how did you become interested in it? Who encouraged you to start it? Were you recognized or did you receive any award for it? What have you gained by engaging in this activity? What challenges have you experienced in relation to this interest? What goals do you still want to accomplish?

【文化】 日本のスポーツ：Japanese Sports

Japanese love sports. Almost any sport one can think of can be found in Japan. Japan's national sport is *sumo*. Other traditional "sports" are popular martial arts such as *judo*, *kendo*, *karate*, and *aikido*. The most popular sports imported from abroad are baseball, soccer and golf.

Sumo is a form of wrestling with a history of more than 1,000 years. It traces its roots to a time in which Japanese society was mainly agrarian. *Sumo* tournaments were a way to thank gods for a fruitful harvest. They are thus filled with rituals associated with Shinto practices. *Sumo* wrestlers, known for their hefty bare bodies, compete in snugly fitting silk belts with their bare hands. A wrestler faces his opponent in a *dohyo*, or ring, and loses if he is the one who first is pushed out of the ring, or first hits the ground with any part of his body other than his feet. Currently, the traditional sport is undergoing challenges as a result of scandals, fewer followers, and foreign wrestlers who find the *sumo* world stifling. It will, however, always hold a special place in Japan's world of sports.

The most popular Japanese martial art is *judo*, though there are also many followers of *kendo*, *karate*, *aikido* and other martial arts in Japan and throughout the world. *Judo* has won its place on the world scene, as it is recognized as an Olympic sport. The martial arts in Japan are not considered merely sports. Their roots are in training for military combat, and they are also viewed by faithful followers as a spiritual path.

Although *sumo* is the official national sport of Japan, the most popular sport over many decades has been baseball. Baseball, known as 野球 (*yakyuu*) in Japan, was introduced to Japan from the U.S. during the Meiji period. Baseball is played by everyone, from the youngest children on school teams to professionals. Games of two professional baseball leagues, each with six teams, capture television and radio audiences during the baseball season. In Japan, high school baseball is also extremely popular. National high school tournaments are played at Koshien, a large baseball stadium near Kobe. American players now play professionally in Japan, and Japanese players play on professional teams in the U.S.

Competing with baseball as Japan's favorite sport is soccer. The sport is commonly referred to these days as サッカー (*sakkaa*). Soccer, like baseball, is a favorite spectator sport, and is also played by children, young adults, non-professionals and professionals. The J-League, a professional soccer league, was established in 1993 and the sport has since taken off in popularity. The Japanese quickly rose to the international soccer scene when Japan participated in the World Cup for the first time and co-hosted the World Cup with South Korea in 2002.

The third most avidly followed sport introduced from the West is golf. Golfing, however is a luxury sport in Japan, as due to limited space, land prices are very high. Membership to golf clubs are exceedingly expensive and out of reach for most Japanese, but many Japanese enjoy golf by going to numerous golf ranges that dot many city, suburban and rural areas. Many are several-storied structures wrapped in green nets, which allow many golfers to practice at one time in an enclosed area.

Sports serve as a healthy outlet for the Japanese. Much like major sports such as football that capture nationwide interest in the U.S., most sports create intense interest in Japan, and very few Japanese do not follow major sports events. Sports foster a feeling of solidarity and belonging among the Japanese.

Questions to ponder: How do traditional Japanese "sports" differ from Western sports in Japan? Why have baseball and soccer become popular in Japan, in comparison to other Western sports?

| 3課 | | 復習単語 | |

トピック：レジャーと趣味とスポーツ

1.	娯楽	ごらく	N	entertainment
2.	趣味	しゅみ	N	hobby
3.	パーティー		N	party
4.	ピクニック		N	picnic
5.	キャンプ		N	camp
6.	プール		N	pool
7.	コンサート		N	concert
8.	ゲーム		N	game
9.	ゲームをする		V3	(to) play a game
10.	テレビ		N	TV
11.	テレビゲーム		N	video game
12.	漫画	まんが	N	comics
13.	動物園	どうぶつえん	N	zoo
14.	映画	えいが	N	movie
15.	映画館	えいがかん	N	movie theater
16.	歌舞伎座	かぶきざ	N	*kabuki* theater
17.	歌	うた	N	song; singing
18.	歌う	うたう	V1	(to) sing
19.	ギター		N	guitar
20.	弾く	ひく	V1	(to) play (a string instrument)
21.	劇	げき	N	stage play
22.	劇をする	げきをする	V3	(to) give/put on a stage play
23.	ダンス		N	dance; dancing (Western)
24.	ピアノ		N	piano
25.	美術	びじゅつ	N	art
26.	絵	え	N	painting; drawing
27.	(絵を)描く	(えを)かく	V1	(to) draw; paint a picture
28.	読書	どくしょ	N	reading
29.	生け花	いけばな	N	flower arrangement
30.	踊り	おどり	N	dance
31.	園芸	えんげい	N	gardening; landscaping; horticulture
32.	陶芸	とうげい	N	ceramics

3課

33. スポーツ		N	sports
34. フットボール		N	football
35. バレー(ボール)		N	volleyball
36. バスケット(ボール)		N	basketball
37. サッカー		N	soccer
38. テニス		N	tennis
39. ゴルフ		N	golf
40. 野球	やきゅう	N	baseball
41. プロ野球	プロやきゅう	N	professional baseball
42. 水泳	すいえい	N	swimming
43. 泳ぐ	およぐ	V1	(to) swim
44. 剣道	けんどう	N	kendo [Japanese fencing]
45. 選手	せんしゅ	N	(sports) player
46. チーム		N	team
47. ユニフォーム		N	(sports) uniform
48. 試合	しあい	N	(sports) game
49. (試合に)出る	(しあいに)でる	V2	(to) participate in a (sports) game
50. 優勝(を)する	ゆうしょう(を)する	N	(to) win a championship
51. スコア		N	score
52. ～対～	～たい～	PN	～to～; ～vs.～
53. ～点	～てん	Nd	～point(s)
54. 運動	うんどう	N	exercise
55. 運動(を)する	うんどう(を)する	V3	(to) exercise
56. 運動靴	うんどうぐつ	N	sports shoes

3課

| 3課 | ★★★ | 新しい単語 | ★★★ |

1. おしかった＜惜しかった＞ですねえ。　Exp　How regrettable!
「一点差で負けたんだよ。」「惜しかったねえ。」 "We lost by only one point." "How regrettable!"

2. りょうかい＜了解＞しました or です。　Exp　I understand.; I agree. [formal]
「パーティーは明日の６時になりました。」「了解です。」 "It was decided that the party will be at 6:00 tomorrow." "O.K."

3. ～のけん＜件＞ですが、　Exp　As for ～
「明日のパーティーの件だけど、プレゼントに何がいいと思う？」"As for the party tomorrow, what do you think would be good as a gift?"

4. もくてき＜目的＞　N　purpose
柔道の目的は心も体も強くすることだ。 The purpose of judo is to strengthen the mind and the body.

5. もよおし(もの)＜催し(物)＞　N　event; entertaiment
秋には催し物が多い。 There are lots of events in the fall.

6. げんだい＜現代＞　N　modern; contemporary; present-day
現代美術館でヨーロッパ美術展をやっている。 There is a European art exhibition at the modern art museum.

7. とうげいてん＜陶芸展＞　N　ceramics exhibition
　-てん＜-展＞　Na　- exhibition
母は陶芸展に作ったお皿を出している。 My mother is displaying the dishes she made at the ceramics exhibition.

8. にゅうじょうりょう＜入場料＞　N　admission fee
にゅうじょうけん＜入場券＞　N　admission ticket
ただの入場券をもらった。 I received free admission tickets.

9. こうどう＜講堂＞　N　auditorium
コンサートは講堂であった。 The concert was held at the auditorium.

10. にんぎょう＜人形＞　N　doll
ぬいぐるみ(にんぎょう)＜縫いぐるみ(人形)＞　N　stuffed doll
「今もぬいぐるみ人形が大好きよ。」 "I still love stuffed dolls."

11. (お)といあわせ＜(お)問い合わせ＞　　N　inquiry
    お問い合わせはこの電話番号にどうぞ。　Please call this number for inquiries.

12. にちじ＜日時＞　　N　date and time (of an event)
    パーティーの日時は５月５日土曜日の午後４時です。　The party date and time is 4:00 p.m. on Saturday, May 5th.

13. しょうご＜正午＞　　N　noon
    正午にお昼を食べよう。　Let's eat lunch at noon.

14. れい＜零＞　　N　zero
    私の電話番号は午前零時から896-0329に変わった。　From midnight, my phone number has changed to 896-0329.

15. よか＜余暇＞　　N　leisure time
    余暇があれば、のんびり音楽を聴きたい。　When I have free time, I want to leisurely listen to music.

16. きゅうじつ＜休日＞　　N　holiday; day off
    休日には、うちでのんびり過ごしたい。　I want to relax on my days off.

17. あいて＜相手＞　　N　partner; opponent
    次の試合の相手はとても強そうだ。　The opponent of my next match looks very strong.

18. けっしょうせん＜決勝戦＞　　N　final (match; game)
    じゅんけっしょう＜準決勝戦＞　　N　semifinal
    準決勝戦で勝って、決勝戦で負けた。　We won the semifinals, but lost the finals.

19. いってんさ＜一点差＞　　N　one point difference
    一点差で負けた。　We lost by one point.

20. いっぱん＜一般＞　　N　general (people)
    いっぱんてきにいって＜一般的に言って＞　　Ex　Generally speaking
    一般的に言って、コンサートの切符は高すぎると思う。　Generally speaking, concert tickets are too expensive.

21. きゅうよう＜急用＞で　　N+P　on urgent business
    「ごめん、急用で行けなくなっちゃった。」　"Sorry, I cannot go because of unexpected business."

22. れいぎただしい＜礼儀正しい＞　　A　courtesy; good manners
    武道をしている人達はとても礼儀正しい。　People who do martial arts are very polite in their manners.

3課

23. しきゅう＜至急＞　Adv　immediately; without delay [formal]

「至急、お母さんに電話して。」"Please call your mother immediately."

24. かんげい＜歓迎＞(を)する／します　V3　to welcome

かんげいかい＜歓迎会＞　N　welcome party

どなたでも歓迎です。　We welcome everyone.

25. かつやく＜活躍＞(を)する／します　V3　to be active in ～

兄はフットボール選手として活躍している。　My older brother is active as a football player.

26. はつばい＜発売＞する／します　V3　to be for sale

はつばいちゅう＜発売中＞　N　for sale; on the market

そのコンサートの切符はもう発売されている。　Tickets for that concert are already for sale.

27. かいさい＜開催＞(を)する／します　V3　to hold (an event)

かいさいきかん＜開催期間＞　N　duration (of an event)

生け花展の開催期間は二週間だそうだ。　I heard that the flower arrangement exhibition will be on for two weeks.

28. おこなう＜行う＞　V1　to hold (an event) [formal]

コンサートは講堂で行われた。　The concert was held at the auditorium.

29. (～と)きょうそう＜競争＞(を)する／します　V3　to compete with ～

きょうそう＜競争＞がはげしい＜激しい＞　A　competitive (not for person)

山田さんと競争したくない。I don't want to compete against Yamada.

有名大学への入学は競争がとても激しい。It's very competitive to get into famous colleges.

30. ゆうしょう＜優勝＞(を)する／します　V3　to win a championship

じゅんゆうしょう＜準優勝＞(を)する／します　V3　to be in second place

決勝戦で負けて、準優勝した。　We lost the final game and came in second.

31. (～に)しゅつじょう＜出場＞(を)する／します　V3　to participte in (tournament)

このゴルフ大会には多くの有名選手が出場している。　Many famous golfers are participating in this golf tournament.

32. (～が)ちゅうし＜中止＞になる／なります　V1　～ will be canceled

(～を)ちゅうし＜中止＞する／します　V3　to cancel ～

「試合は大雨で中止になりました。」"The game was canceled because of heavy rain."

3課　　　　　　　　　　　文法

> A. 〜は、Nounです。
> 　　〜は、Verb dictionary form+ことです。
> 1. 趣味は音楽です。　　　　　　　　My hobby is music.
> 2. 趣味はピアノを弾くことです。　　My hobby is playing the piano.

Fill in the blanks with responses based on your personal circumstances.

1. 私の趣味は＿＿＿＿＿＿＿＿＿＿＿＿＿＿＿＿＿＿＿＿＿＿＿＿ことです。
2. 私の今年の目標は＿＿＿＿＿＿＿＿＿＿＿＿＿＿＿＿＿＿＿＿＿ことです。
3. 私の将来の夢は＿＿＿＿＿＿＿＿＿＿＿＿＿＿＿＿＿＿＿＿＿＿ことです。
4. 父の責任は＿＿＿＿＿＿＿＿＿＿＿＿＿＿＿＿＿＿＿＿＿＿＿＿ことです。
5. 友情は＿＿＿＿＿＿＿＿＿＿＿＿＿＿＿＿＿＿＿＿＿＿＿＿＿＿ことです。
6. 教育の目的は＿＿＿＿＿＿＿＿＿＿＿＿＿＿＿＿＿＿＿＿＿＿＿ことです。

> B. Noun＋を＋する Verbs
> 　勉強をする。　　　　　　　　　I study.
> 　日本語を勉強する。　　　　　　I study Japanese.
> 　日本語の勉強をする。　　　　　I will do a study of Japanese.

Fill in the ( ) with correct particles.

1. 大学で化学（　　）専攻（　　）するつもりだ。
2. 毎日ピアノ（　　）練習（　　）する。
3. 昨日、部屋（　　）掃除（　　）した。
4. 母に友達（　　）紹介（　　）した。

> C. "Want"
> 1. 水がほしい。　　　　　　　　　　　　I want water.
> 2. 水が(orを)飲みたい。　　　　　　　　I want to drink water.
> 3. あなたに水を飲んでほしい。　　　　　I want you to drink water.
> 4. 田中さんは水をほしがっている。　　　Mr. Tanaka (seems to) want water.
> 5. 田中さんは水を飲みたがっている。　　Mr. Tanaka (seems to) want to drink water.

3課

Fill in the blanks with the correct answers from the list.

1. 私は自分の車が_____。
2. 兄も自分の車を_____。
3. 私は自分の車を_____。
4. 兄も自分の車を_____。
5. 私は父に車を_____。
6. 兄も父に車を_____。

a. ほしい
b. 買いたい
c. 買ってほしい
d. ほしがっている
e. 買いたがっている
f. 買ってほしがっている

D. 習えば習うほど、〜　　The more I learn, the more 〜

1. 日本の文化を習えば習うほど、日本の事をもっと知りたくなる。
    The more I learn about Japanese culture, the more I want to know about Japanese things.
2. 暑ければ暑いほど、冷たい飲物がほしくなる。
    The hotter it is, the more I want cold drinks.
3. 図書館が静かなら静かなほど、よく勉強出来る。
    The quieter the library is, the better I can study.

Fill in the blanks using the cues in the ( ).

1. ピアノを_____ _____ほど、難しくなる。（練習する）
2. _____ _____ほど、スープが飲みたくなる。（寒い）
3. ゴルフが_____ _____ほど、もっと上手になりたいと思う。（上手）
4. 日本語は_____ _____ほど、上手になる。（話す）
5. _____ _____ほど、太る。（食べる）

E. Verb OO Form

Group 1 verbs:　　のむ　→のもう　　　let's drink
Group 2 verbs:　　たべる →たべよう　　let's eat
Irregular verbs:　　くる　→こよう　　　let's come
　　　　　　　　　する　→しよう　　　let's do

1. 今、行こうか。　　　　Shall we go?
2. うん、行こう。　　　　Yes, let's go.

3課

Fill in the blanks by changing the verbs in the ( ) to the correct -OO form.

1. パーティーに持って来る物を_____。（決めましょう）
2. 明日のバスケットの試合を応援に_____。（行きましょう）
3. どこで_____。（待ち合わせましょうか）
4. 明日の試合は絶対_____。（勝ちましょう）
5. 日本の武道についてインターネットで_____。（調べてみましょう）

F. 「起きなさい。」 "Wake up!"

These informal command forms are used by superiors to persons of lesser status (parent to child; boss to subordinate, etc.).

Superior males use the command forms and the negative command form ("Don't do 〜."). These forms are also used on public signs, e.g., とまれ (for "Stop.") or およぐな ("No swimming.").

The -なさい (command) and negative form, -ないで, are polite commands which are used by superiors such as parents or teachers to their inferiors (= people of younger age and of lower rank). These forms may also be used in written instructions, i.e., instructions on a test.

	Dic. Form	Command	Neg. Command	Polite Command	Polite Neg. Command
Group 1 Verbs	話す	話せ Speak! - e	話すな Don't talk! Dic. form + な	話しなさい Speak. Stem form + なさい	話さないで Don't talk. NAI form + で
Group 2 Verbs	食べる	食べろ Eat! Stem form + ろ	食べるな Don't eat! Dic. form + な	食べなさい Eat. Stem form + なさい	食べないで Don't eat! NAI form + で
Irregular Verb	する	しろ Do it!	するな Don't do it! Dic. form + な	しなさい Do it. Stem form + なさい	しないで Don't do it. NAI form + で
Irregular Verb	来〔く〕る	来〔こ〕い Come!	来〔く〕るな Don't come! Dic. form + な	来〔き〕なさい Come. Stem form + なさい	来〔こ〕ないで Don't come. NAI form + で

1. 父はいつももっと勉強しろと言う。

   My father always tells me to study harder.

2. 私が運転する時、両親はいつもスピードを出すなと言う。

   Whenever I drive, my parents always tell me not to speed.

3. 私が外へ出かける時、母はいつも「気をつけなさい」と言う。

   When I go out, my mother always tells me, "be careful."

3課

Fill in the blanks with an appropriate command form.

1. 母は私が遅くまで寝ていると、「＿＿＿＿＿＿＿＿＿＿＿＿＿＿＿」と言う。
2. 父は私が遅く家に帰ると、「＿＿＿＿＿＿＿＿＿＿＿＿＿＿＿」と言う。
3. 母は私が遅くまで起きていると、「＿＿＿＿＿＿＿＿＿＿＿＿＿＿＿」と言う。
4. 父は私の成績が悪いと、「＿＿＿＿＿＿＿＿＿＿＿＿＿＿＿」と言う。
5. 母は私が夕食を食べないで、ケータイで友達と話していると、
   「＿＿＿＿＿＿＿＿＿＿＿＿＿＿＿」と言う。
6. 父は私が宿題をしないでテレビを見ていると、「＿＿＿＿＿＿＿＿＿＿＿＿＿」と言う。

G. Review of Speech Styles

	Polite 男女	Informal Speaking 男	Informal Speaking 女	Informal Writing 男女
1.	きめましょう	きめよう	きめよう	きめよう
2.	かてるでしょうか	かてるかな	かてるかな/かしら	かてるかな
3.	だいじょうぶです	だいじょうぶだ	だいじょうぶ	だいじょうぶだ
4.	メールを下さい	メールをくれ（よ）	メールをちょうだい	メールをくれ
5.	送って下さい	送って	送って	送って
6.	送ってくれませんか	送ってくれないか	送ってくれない？	送ってくれないか
7.	帰らなければなりません	帰らなきゃ/帰らなくちゃ	帰らなきゃ/帰らなくちゃ	帰らなければならない
8.	早く帰りなさいと言っています	早く帰れって言ってる	早く帰りなさいって言ってる	早く帰りなさいと言っている
9.	しています	やってる	やってる	やっている
10.	がっかりです	がっかりだ（よ）	がっかり（よ）	がっかりだ
11.	好きですか	好き？↗	好き？↗	好きか
12.	好きです	好きだ（よ）	好き（よ）	好きだ
13.	一点だけでした	一点だけだった	一点だけだった	一点だけだった
14.	楽しみにしています	楽しみにしてる（よ）	楽しみにしてる（ね）	楽しみにしている

| 3課 | | アクティビティー | |

A. 日本文化：一人か二人ワーク→クラスワーク

Divide the topics below among your classmates and research your topic on the Internet. Using visuals, present your findings with your classmates.

1. 武道〔ぶどう〕、「道〔どう〕」の教え
2. 相撲〔すもう〕、心技体〔しんぎたい〕
3. 柔道〔じゅうどう〕
4. プロ野球、大リーグ、高校野球、甲子園〔こうしえん〕
5. Ｊリーグ
6. 習い事〔ならいごと〕（書道、華道/生け花、茶道など）
7. ポップカルチャー（Ｊポップ、アニメ、マンガ、ビデオゲームなど）

B. 聞く Pre-Listening Activity「催し案内〔もよおしあんない〕」：ペアワーク

Read the following announcement about a special event, and conduct a conversation in plain form based on the questions below.

中国現代陶芸展〔げんだいとうげいてん〕について

場所〔ばしょ〕：現代美術館〔げんだいびじゅつ〕

開催期間〔かいさいきかん〕：４月４日〜２４日

開館時間：月、火、水、金、土曜日　10:30 a.m. - 4:30 p.m.
　　　　　日曜日　正午 - 5:00 p.m.
　　　　　木曜日休館

入場料〔いっぱん〕：一般 2,500円・シニア/学生1,000円・小人（１２歳以下）無料〔む〕

お問い合せ：941-0966

---

1. この催し〔もよお〕は何の催し〔もよお〕？
2. この催し〔もよお〕はどこでする？
3. この催し〔もよお〕はいつからいつまでやってる？
4. この催し〔もよお〕会場〔か〕の時間は？
5. この催し〔もよお〕会場がやってないのは、いつ？
6. この催し〔もよお〕の入場券〔けん〕は、いくら？
7. 電話番号が書いてあるけど、何のため？

C. 聞く Post-Listening Activity「催し案内〔もよおしあんない〕」:ペアワーク

Announce the following event to students from Japan. Your announcement should have an opening remark, details based on the notes, and a closing remark.

> Event: Basketball, vs. Lincoln High School at the Lincoln High School gym
> Date: Saturday, November 26, 4:30 p.m. - 7:00 p.m.
> Admission: Free of charge, but ticket required.
> School bus departure: 3:00 p.m. in front of the school auditorium.

D. 読む Pre-Reading Activity「イーメール」:ペアワーク

Match the Japanese words with their English equivalents.

1. 受信〔じゅしん〕   (   )   a. subject
2. 差出人〔さしだしにん〕 (   )   b. get mail
3. 件名〔けんめい〕   (   )   c. from
4. 日時〔にちじ〕   (   )   d. to
5. 宛先〔あてさき〕   (   )   e. new message
6. 返信〔へんしん〕   (   )   f. delete
7. 転送〔てんそう〕   (   )   g. reply
8. 添付〔てんぷ〕   (   )   h. date
9. 保存〔ほぞん〕   (   )   i. attachment
10. 削除〔さくじょ〕   (   )   j. forward

E. 読む Post-Reading Activity「イーメール」:ペアワーク→クラスワーク

Compare and Contrast: Using the Telephone and Email

Compare and contrast similarities and differences between using the telephone and email. Based on your personal experience, describe at least THREE similarities and differences between using the telephone and email. Also state your preference for either and give reasons for it. Take 4 minutes to prepare and 2 minutes to present.

Introduction:
_____

Three similarities/differences:

  1. _____
  2. _____
  3. _____

Your preference and reasons:
_____

3課

F. テキストチャット「余暇〔よか〕」：ペアワーク

Using the questions below as prompts, have a conversation. Use 20 seconds to respond to each question. Elaborate on your answers and give details.

1. 平日、暇な時間がありますか。
2. 週末は何をして過ごしていますか。
3. 休日の時、外に出かけるのと、うちにいるのと、どちらの方が好きですか。
4. 自分の余暇の過ごし方が好きですか。
5. もし、今、暇な時間があったら、何をしたいですか。
6. レジャーとして、家族と一緒にどんな所に出かけますか。
7. 日本人のレジャーの過ごし方を知っていますか。

G. Compare & Contrast「日米のポップカルチャー」：ペアワーク→クラスワーク

Compare American and Japanese pop culture. Use 30 seconds to respond to each question.

1. 日米の歌手はどう違う？
2. 日米の歌はどう違う？
3. 日米のアニメはどう違う？
4. 日米のマンガはどう違う？
5. 日米のポップカルチャーで似ていることがある？
6. 日米のポップカルチャーで、どちらの方が好き？

H. Compare and Contrast「スポーツと音楽」：ペアワーク

これから、スポーツ(1.)音楽を比べてみます。両方は皆さんが好きなものですが、スポーツと音楽は同じこと(2.)違うこと(3.)あります。

まず、一つ目(4.)違うことは、スポーツ(5.)体全体を使ってしますが、音楽(6.)体の一部を使ってします。スポーツをするためには、強い筋肉(7.)必要です。音楽をするためには、指や口だけを使います。

二つ目(8.)違いは、スポーツ(9.)相手と競争しますが、音楽(10.)だいたい競争しません。音楽は楽しむものです。

一つ(11.)同じことは、スポーツ(12.)音楽(13.)上手になればなるほど、もっと難しくなります。だれもがスポーツや音楽を子供の時に始めますが、プロになるためには、本当に上手でなければなれません。しかし、有名になればとてもいい給料がもらえます。

結論として、私はスポーツ(14.)音楽(15.)どちら(16.)好きです。なぜなら、ス

3課

ポーツは体を強くするし、音楽は心を和ませてくれるからです。スポーツも音楽もバランスのある生活をするために、私達に必要だと思います。

a. Fill in the blanks with the correct particle.
1. _____ 2. _____ 3. _____ 4. _____ 5. _____ 6. _____ 7. _____ 8. _____
9. _____ 10. _____ 11. _____ 12. _____ 13. _____ 14. _____ 15. _____ 16. _____

b. Mark the following statements True or False based on the passage above.
1. (T F) この人は音楽も強い筋肉が要ると思っている。
2. (T F) この人は音楽は競争するものではないと思っている。
3. (T F) この人は音楽もスポーツも練習すればするほど、だんだん難しくなると思っている。
4. (T F) この人は音楽がスポーツほど好きではない。
5. (T F) この人はスポーツや音楽のプロになりたがっている。

I. 会話「スポーツについて」：ペアワーク

Pair off with a partner. One partner should read the statements below and the other partner should respond as quickly as possible without looking at the book.

a. 先輩との会話：
1. 昨日のバスケットの準決勝で勝ったんですよ。
2. でも、決勝で負けてしまったんですよ。
3. でも、一点差だけだったんですよ。がっかりでした。
4. でも、昨日、弟はテニスの試合に優勝したんですよ。
5. 明日、野球の試合を応援に行きませんか。
6. スポーツは見るのと、するのと、どちらの方が好きですか。
7. では、どこで何時に待ち合わせましょうか。
8. 私を迎えに来てくれませんか。
9. では、楽しみにしていますね。

b. 友達との会話：
1. 昨日のバスケットの準決勝で勝ったんだよ(男)/勝ったのよ(女)。
2. でも、決勝で負けちゃったんだよ(男)/負けちゃったのよ(女)。
3. (男) でも、一点差だけだったんだよ。がっかりだよ。
   (女) でも、一点差だけだったのよ。がっかりよ。
4. でも、昨日、弟はテニスの試合に優勝したんだよ。(男)/優勝したのよ(女)。
5. 明日、野球の試合を応援に行かない？(男女)

3課

6. スポーツは見るのと、するのと、どっちの方が好き？(男女)
7. じゃ、どこで何時に待ち合わせようか(男女)。
8. (男) 僕を迎えに来てくれない？
   (女) 私を迎えに来てくれない？
9. じゃ、楽しみにしてるね(男女)。

J. 日本のスポーツ：ペアワーク
   Fill in the blanks with choices from the box below.

1. 日本の国の伝統的なスポーツは＿＿＿＿＿＿です。レスリングに似ていますが、＿＿＿＿＿＿の儀式 (ritual) に従います (follow)。最近、外国からの＿＿＿＿＿＿が多いです。

2. 日本の代表的な武道は＿＿＿＿＿＿です。オリンピックの種目 (event) でもあります。目的は相手に勝つだけでなく、自分の心を強く正しくすることです。

3. アメリカから日本に来て、人気があるチームスポーツは＿＿＿＿＿＿です。最近、アメリカ選手が日本のプロチームで、日本選手がアメリカ大リーグで活躍しています。甲子園球場で行われる全国高校＿＿＿＿＿＿は有名で、多くの日本人がテレビで見ています。

4. ヨーロッパから日本に来て、人気があるチームスポーツは＿＿＿＿＿＿です。Ｊリーグというプロのリーグが出来て、特に人気が出て来ました。＿＿＿＿＿＿にも出場するようになりました。

5. ヨーロッパから日本に来て、人気がある個人スポーツは＿＿＿＿＿＿です。日本の＿＿＿＿＿＿でプレイするのは、とても料金が高いです。多くの人は＿＿＿＿＿＿で練習しています。

6. 日本の伝統的なスポーツは、西洋のスポーツより、＿＿＿＿＿＿を大切にします。それから、とても＿＿＿＿＿＿正しく、相手を尊敬するはずです。

7. 一般的に言って、日本ではチームのスポーツの方が＿＿＿＿＿＿のスポーツより人気があるようです。日本人はグループですることが好きなのかも知れません。

> 神道　柔道　野球大会　サッカー　個人　相撲取り　野球
> ゴルフ　心　ワールドカップ　ゴルフ場　相撲　ゴルフレンジ　礼儀

3課

<3課 - 聞く>

Listening: Event Announcement

12秒×5

【You may take notes while listening. Do not look at the questions below before listening. You will have 12 seconds to answer each question. You may NOT move back and forth among questions.】

(Narrator) Now you will listen to an event announcement once.

(Narrator) Now answer the questions for this selection.

1. What kind of exhibition will be held at the Contemporary Art Museum?
    (A) jewelry
    (B) glass
    (C) painting
    (D) ceramics

2. When is the opening day of this exhibition and on which days is it closed?
    (A) The opening day is May 1st and it is closed on Sundays.
    (B) The opening day is May 2nd and it is closed on Mondays.
    (C) The opening day is May 3rd and it is closed on Sundays.
    (D) The opening day is May 4th and it is closed on Mondays.

3. How much is the admission fee for students?
    (A) 2,000 yen
    (B) 1,500 yen
    (C) 1,000 yen
    (D) free

4. Which of the following is NOT correct information?
    (A) Only children can enter the tournament.
    (B) The tournament is on May 8th.
    (C) The tournament is on Sunday afternoon.
    (D) The tournament is at the elementary school gym.

5. Which information about the concert is correct?
    (A) This jazz concert is held every year.
    (B) The concert will be held on Saturday evening.
    (C) The guest jazz pianist is from Boston.
    (D) Admission is free.

＜3課 - 読む＞
Reading: Emails
【You may move back and forth among all the questions.】

Read this set of emails.

受信箱

	差出人：	件名：	送信日時：
Message #1	大輔	RE:映画	5月7日
	了解。大丈夫だよ。実は、僕も急用が出来て、この週末行けなくなったんだよ。また今度な。		
Message #2	原田	RE:明日の試験	5月7日
	風邪で明日の物理の試験が受けられないって？大丈夫かい。学校に出られるようになったら、メールをくれないか。その時に決めよう。		
Message #3	高村	RE:宿題	5月7日
	スピーチの添付をありがとう。でも、この添付のファイルが開けられないから、もう一度送って。		
Message #4	まり	落とし物	5月10日
	今朝、かぎをなくしてしまったんです。三つのかぎがついてるキーチェーンで、トトロの小さな人形がついています。見つけた人は、至急知らせて下さい。		
Message #5	松本	キャンプ	5月10日
	明日のキャンプの件についてですが、台風接近のため、中止になりました。次のキャンプの日程は、決まり次第、知らせします。		
Message #6	かおり	野球	5月10日
	この土曜日の午後、野球の決勝戦に一緒に応援に行こうね。うちのチーム、勝てるかなあ。どこで待ち合わせようか。返事ちょうだいね。		

3課

<3課 - 読む (質問)>

Reading: Emails

(Narrator) Now answer the questions for this section.

1. Which message is an invitation to a baseball game?
   (A) Message #1
   (B) Message #3
   (C) Message #5
   (D) Message #6

2. Which message announces the cancellation of an activity?
   (A) Message #2
   (B) Message #4
   (C) Message #5
   (D) Message #6

3. Which is true about the lost keys?
   (A) The key chain has two keys.
   (B) The lost keys were found.
   (C) The key chain has a small Totoro charm.
   (D) This person lost her keys this afternoon.

4. What information is CORRECT about the exam this person is supposed to take tomorrow?
   (A) It is a biology exam.
   (B) This person cannot take the exam because of a cold.
   (C) This person cannot take the exam because of a car accident.
   (D) This person will take the exam as scheduled.

5. What happened to the attachment of a speech that was sent to this person?
   (A) The attachment was not attached.
   (B) The attachment file was blank.
   (C) The attachment file was the wrong life.
   (D) The attachment file could not be opened.

＜3課 - 書く (テキストチャット)＞

`90秒×6`

Text Chat: Leisure Time

You will participate in a simulated exchange of text-chat messages. Each time it is your turn to write, you will have 90 seconds. You should respond as fully and as appropriately as possible.

You will have a conversation about leisure with Ayumi Matsui, a student at your host school in Japan. She is doing some research on Americans.

1. Respond. (90 seconds)

   こんにちは。今、アメリカ人の余暇の過ごし方について調べています。御協力、お願いします。

2. Give a specific example and respond. (90 seconds)

   週末はたいてい何をして過ごしていますか。

3. Explain your preference. (90 seconds)

   休日の時、外に出かけるのと、うちにいるのと、どちらの方が好きですか。

4. Describe. (90 seconds)

   家族皆でいっしょにどんな所に出かけますか。

5. Give a specific example. (90 seconds)

   もし今、暇な時間があったら、何が一番したいですか。

6. Ask a specific question. (90 seconds)

   今日はどうも有難うございました。日本のレジャーについて何か質問がありますか。

＜3課 - 書く (比較と対比)＞

`20分`

Compare and Contrast: Japanese Pop Culture & American Pop Culture

Directions: You are writing an article for the student newspaper of your sister school in Japan. Write an article in which you compare and contrast similarities and differences between Japanese pop culture and American pop culture. Based on your personal experience, describe at least THREE aspects of each and highlight the similarities and differences between Japanese pop culture and American pop culture. Also state your preference for either and give reasons for it.

Your article should be 300 to 400 characters or longer. Use the *desu/masu* or *da* (plain) style, but use one style consistently. Also, use *kanji* wherever *kanji* from the AP Japanese *kanji* list is appropriate. You have 20 minutes to write.

【NOTES/OUTLINE: 自分の作文のアウトラインを書こう！】

Introduction:
_____

Three similarities/differences:

   1. _____
   2. _____
   3. _____

Your preference and reasons:
_____
_____

3課

＜3課 - 話す (会話)＞
Conversation: Sports

`20秒×4`

You will participate in a simulated conversation. Each time it is your turn to speak, you will have 20 seconds to record. You should respond as fully and as appropriately as possible.

You will have a conversation with Koji, your Japanese friend, about sports.

(Koji)
(20 seconds)
(Koji)
(20 seconds)
(Koji)
(20 seconds)
(Koji)
(20 seconds)

＜3課 - 話す (日本文化)＞
Cultural Perspective Presentation: Japanese Sports

`4分+2分`

Directions: Imagine you are making an oral presentation to your Japanese class. First, you will read and hear the topic for your presentation. You will have 4 minutes to prepare your presentation. Then you will have 2 minutes to record your presentation. Your presentation should be as complete as possible.

Present your own view or perspective of Japanese sports. Discuss at least FIVE aspects or examples of Japanese sports.

Begin with an appropriate introduction, give details, explain your own view or perspective, and end with a concluding remark.

【Let's take notes!】

1. Begin with an appropriate introduction.

   _____

2. Discuss five aspects/examples of the topic.

   1.) _____
   2.) _____
   3.) _____
   4.) _____
   5.) _____

3. Explain your view or perspective.

   _____

4. End with a concluding remark.

   _____

3課

4課 家でコミュニティーで
Home and Community

【AP® タスク：家でコミュニティーで】
Why do you think community service is important? What are your feelings and opinions about the community service activities you have participated in so far? What did you learn from performing community service?

【文化】 日本の家でのマナー：Manners in the Japanese Home

Visiting a Japanese home is a unique privilege. Most Japanese consider their homes private, and only family and close friends usually enter the most interior sections of the home. Most social encounters, even with friends, occur outside of the home. Once invited to a Japanese home, one is expected to follow some rules of basic etiquette.

First, all Japanese remove their shoes before stepping up into the home from the *genkan*, or foyer area. Upon removing one's shoes, it is most polite to also turn one's shoes around so that they face the doorway. As one does so, one should avoid facing one's back to the host. If one is carrying an umbrella, there is also usually an umbrella stand on which to leave it.

Upon stepping up from the *genkan*, the host will offer house slippers (スリッパ) to wear. The slippers are to be worn in hallways, uncarpeted areas or areas that are not covered with *tatami*. When one enters a carpeted or a Japanese style *tatami* room, one removes one's slippers outside of the doorway. When one enters the toilet area, one also removes the house slippers, leaves it outside the doorway and changes into bathroom slippers that are left just inside the toilet entrance. These slippers are usually made of rubber or plastic and are to be worn only in the toilet area. The toilet door is to be left closed even after one leaves the bathroom.

When one visits a Japanese home, it is customary to take a gift (手みやげ) to the host. Fruit, cakes or a gift from the visitor's country is ideal. The gift should be neatly wrapped. The gift is usually presented after one is invited and seated in the *zashiki*, or the traditional *tatami* room. As one sits facing the host, one presents the gift by gently sliding the gift slightly forward toward the host. As one does so, one should say, "*Sukoshi desu ga...*" or "*Tsumaranai mono desu ga...*" Japanese do not usually open gifts they receive in the presence of the giver.

Almost always, Japanese hosts will offer their guests a drink (such as coffee or tea, or a cold drink in the summer) and some sweets. It is always considered polite to first refuse the offer, but the host will always insist that the guest partake of the food offered. As in all cases when food is received, one should say "*Itadakimasu*" before consuming the food, and end with "*Gochisoosamadeshita.*" It is best not to time one's visit to coincide with a meal time. Before one leaves, one should warn the host of one's departure by saying "*Sorosoro shitsurei shimasu.*"

Guests to a Japanese home must be careful not to venture into the *tokonoma*, or alcove area of the *zashiki*. The *tokonoma* is a place of honor in which typically, a scroll, flower arrangement and special artifacts are adorned. It is considered rude to stand in the *tokonoma*. When several guests are seated in the *zashiki*, the person who is seated closest to the *tokonoma* is considered the most honored guest.

When one leaves one's host's home, one should always thank the host, and before exiting the door, say "*Ojama shimashita*," which literally means "I have been a nuisance."

A visit to a traditional Japanese home requires knowing proper etiquette in order to show one's appreciation of the invitation. Japanese etiquette at home reveals much about traditional values. The most prominent of these is how the concept of *uchi/soto* (内/外) is practiced.

Questions to ponder: What examples of uchi/soto are evident in Japanese home etiquette? How many of the above customs do you practice at your home? How many are different? What reasons can you think of that explain these differences in each culture?

4課

4課 ◆◆◆ 復習単語 ◆◆◆

トピック：家でコミュニティーで

1. 隣	となり	N	next to (neighboring)
2. 近所の人	きんじょのひと	N	person who lives in one's neighborhood
3. (お)年寄り	(お)としより	N	old person(s); senior citizen(s)
4. 社会福祉	しゃかいふくし	N	social welfare
5. ボランティア		N	volunteer
6. 寄付(を)する	きふ(を)する	V3	(to) donate
7. 公園	こうえん	N	park
8. 郵便局	ゆうびんきょく	N	post office
9. 有料	ゆうりょう	N	with a fee

| 4課 | ★★★ | 新しい単語 | ★★★ |

1. じつは＜実は＞　Exp　To tell (you) the truth; truthfully
   実はこの午後パーティーへ行かなきゃいけないんですよ。 To tell you the truth, I have to go to a party this afternoon.

2. いじょう＜以上＞です。　Exp.　That's all. [Used at the end of announcement.]
   これで発表を終わります。以上です。 I now end my presentation. That is all.

3. とくちょう＜特徴＞　N　characteristics
   日本の家でのマナーの五つの特徴についてお話します。I will talk about five characteristics of manners in the Japanese house.

4. しゅうかん＜習慣＞　N　customs
   日本人は誰かをうちに訪問する時、手土産を持って行く習慣がある。When Japanese people visit someone at home, it is customary to bring a small gift.

5. みため＜見た目＞　N　appearance
   日本では見た目がいいことが大事だ。In Japan, appearance is important.

6. りょうて＜両手＞　N　both hands
   かたて＜片手＞　N　one hand
   お土産をあげる時には、両手であげるはずだ。When you give a souvenir, you are supposed to give it with both hands.

7. しょうてんがい＜商店街＞　N　shopping arcade
   駅前にはたいてい商店街がある。 There is usually a shopping arcade in front of stations.

8. じゅうたくち＜住宅地＞　N　residential area
   留学センターは静かな住宅地にあります。The study abroad center is in a quiet residential area.

9. しょくどう＜食堂＞　N　dining room; cafeteria
   昼食はたいてい学校の食堂で食べる。 I usually eat lunch in the school cafeteria.

10. しせつ＜施設＞　N　facilities
    この学校にはいい施設がある。 There are good facilities at this school.

11. こくさい＜国際＞　N　international
    こくさいてき＜国際的＞　Na　international
    成田国際空港に着いた。 We arrived at Narita International Airport.

| 4課 |

12. しょくりょうひん＜食料品＞　N　groceries
デパートの地下はだいたい食料品を売っている。　They usually sell groceries in the basement of the department store.

13. かいがん＜海岸＞　N　beach; seashore; coast
海岸の掃除をしよう。　Let's clean the beaches.

14. ゴミひろい＜拾い＞　N　garbage pickup or clean-up
海岸のゴミ拾いをしよう。　Let's pick up the garbage at the seashore.

15. ひやけどめ＜日焼け止め＞クリーム　N　sunscreen
海へ行く時、日焼け止めクリームが必要だ。We need sunscreen when we go to the beach.

16. らくがき＜落書き＞　N　graffiti
落書きを消そう。Let's erase the graffiti.

17. しめきり＜締切＞　N　deadline
申込の締切は５月５日です。　The application deadline is May 5th.

18. もうしこみ＜申込＞　N　application
もうしこみようし＜申込用紙＞　N　application form
もうしこむ＜申し込む＞／申し込みます　V1　to apply
申込は５日までです。　The application is due by the 5th.

19. かぎ＜鍵＞をかける／かけます　V2　to lock
日本の畳の部屋は鍵がかけられない。Tatami rooms cannot be locked.

20. むける＜向ける＞　V2　to face (something) [transitive]
むく＜向く＞　V1　(someone) faces [intransitive]
玄関でくつをぬぐと、くつを戸に向けて置くはずだ。When you remove your shoes at the entrance, you are supposed to face them toward the door.

21. なげる＜投げる＞／投げます　V2　to throw
人に物を渡す時に、けっして投げてはいけない。　When you hand something to others, you should never throw it.

22. ちょきん＜貯金＞(を)する／します　V3　to save (money)
将来のために貯金をしている。　I am saving money for my future.

23. ペットをかう＜飼う＞／飼います　V1　to raise a pet
寮の部屋でペットを飼うことも禁止されている。　We are not allowed to raise pets in our dormitory rooms.

4課

24. くらす＜暮す＞／暮します　V1　to live
  東京は暮しやすいかな。　I wonder if it is easy to live in Tokyo.
25. にゅういん＜入院＞(を)する／します　V3　to be hospitalized
  友達が入院している。　My friend is in the hospital.
26. かっこう＜格好＞(を)する／します　V3　to appear (in a certain way)
  どんな格好をして行けばいいんですか。　What should I wear?
27. れんらく＜連絡＞(を)する／します　V3　to contact
  「何かあったら、連絡して。」　"If there is anything, contact me."
28. しゅうごう＜集合＞(を)する／します　V3　to gather
  七時に学校で集合した。　We gathered at school at 7:00.
29. きんし＜禁止＞(を)する／します　V3　to prohibit
  寮の部屋に友達を泊めることは禁止されている。　We are not allowed to have our friends sleep over in our room at the dormitory.
30. りよう＜利用＞(を)する／します　V3　to use [formal form of 使う]
  プールを無料で利用することが出来る。　We can use the pool for free.

【もっと単語】

1. やあ　　　　　　　　　　　　　　　　　Exp　Hi; What's new? [usually used by males]
2. かぐ＜家具＞　　　　　　　　　　　　　N　　furniture
3. ていきょう＜提供＞(を)する／します　　V3　to offer; to supply
4. (〜に)こえ＜声＞をかける／かけます　　V2　to let 〜 know
5. あぐらをかく／かきます　　　　　　　　V1　to sit cross-legged

4課　文法

> A. Permission, prohibition, obligation, non-obligation
> a. Polite form
> 1. Tシャツを着てもいいです。　　You may wear T-shirts. [Permission]
> 2. Tシャツを着てはいけません。　You may not wear T-shirts. [Prohibition]
> 3. Tシャツを着なければなりません。You have to wear T-shirts. [Obligation]
> 4. Tシャツを着なくてもいいです。　You don't have to wear T-shirts.
> b. Informal speaking form
> 1. Tシャツを着てもいいよ。　　　You may wear T-shirts. [Permission]
> 2. Tシャツを着ちゃいけないよ。　You may not wear T-shirts. [Prohibition]
> 3. Tシャツを着なきゃ/なくちゃ。 You have to wear T-shirts. [Obligation]
> 4. Tシャツを着なくてもいいよ。　You don't have to wear T-shirts.

a. You are talking to your teacher. Fill in the blanks with the correct form of the verbs in the ( ).
1. うちの中でぼうしを＿＿＿＿＿＿＿＿＿＿＿＿＿。（かぶる）
2. 畳の部屋でスリッパを＿＿＿＿＿＿＿＿＿＿＿＿。（はく）
3. 日本のお風呂の中で石鹸を＿＿＿＿＿＿＿＿＿＿。（使う）
4. 日本のうちに上がる時、くつを＿＿＿＿＿＿＿＿＿。（ぬぐ）
5. 日本で挨拶をする時、おじぎを＿＿＿＿＿＿＿＿＿。（する）
6. アメリカで机に座って＿＿＿＿＿＿＿＿＿＿＿＿＿。（話す）
7. アメリカで人に物を渡す時、物を＿＿＿＿＿＿＿＿。（投げる）

b. You are talking to your friend. Fill in the blanks with the correct form of the verbs in the ( ).
1. うちの中でぼうしを＿＿＿＿＿＿＿＿＿＿＿＿＿。（かぶる）
2. 畳の部屋でスリッパを＿＿＿＿＿＿＿＿＿＿＿＿。（はく）
3. 日本のお風呂の中で石鹸を＿＿＿＿＿＿＿＿＿＿。（使う）
4. 日本のうちに上がる時、くつを＿＿＿＿＿＿＿＿＿。（ぬぐ）
5. アメリカで挨拶をする時、おじぎを＿＿＿＿＿＿＿。（する）
6. アメリカで机に座って＿＿＿＿＿＿＿＿＿＿＿＿＿。（話す）
7. アメリカで人に物を渡す時、物を＿＿＿＿＿＿＿＿。（投げる）

4課

B. Transitive verbs and intransitive verbs
　　direct object を ＋ transitive verb
　　subject が ＋ intransitive verb

1. クラスは9時に始まるはずなのに、先生はいつもクラスを遅く始める。
　　The class is supposed to begin at 9:00, but the teacher always starts class late.
2. ドアが壊れているけど、誰がドアを壊したの。
　　The door is broken, but who broke the door?
3. お金を増やしたいけど、お金はなかなか増えないんだ。
　　I want to increase the amount of money I have, but money doesn't increase easily.
4. 体重を減らしたいけど、体重はなかなか減らないんだ。
　　I want to lose weight, but it doesn't decrease easily.

Fill in the blanks in the third column with the correct intransitive verb forms.

	Transitive verb 〜を	(someone) does (something)	Intransitive verb 〜が	(something) does
1.	〜を 始める	(SO) starts (ST)	〜が	(ST) starts
2.	〜を こわす	(SO) breaks (ST)	〜が	(ST) breaks
3.	〜を 見つける	(SO) finds (ST)	〜が	(ST) be found
4.	〜を 変える	(SO) changes (ST)	〜が	(ST) changes
5.	〜を おとす	(SO) drops (ST)	〜が	(ST) falls
6.	〜を 起こす	(SO) causes (ST)	〜が	(ST) happens
7.	〜を 開ける	(SO) opens (ST)	〜が	(ST) opens
8.	〜を 閉める	(SO) closes (ST)	〜が	(ST) closes
9.	〜を つける	(SO) turns on (ST)	〜が	(ST) turns on
10.	〜を けす	(SO) turns off (ST)	〜が	(ST) goes off
11.	〜を きめる	(SO) decides (ST)	〜が	(ST) is decided
12.	〜を あつめる	(SO) collects (ST)	〜が	(animate) gather
13.	〜を ふやす	(SO) increases (ST)	〜が	(ST) increases
14.	〜を へらす	(SO) decreases (ST)	〜が	(ST) decreases
15.	かぎを かける	(SO) locks (ST)	かぎが	(ST) be locked
16.	〜を むける	(SO) faces (ST)	〜が	(ST) faces
17.	〜を ならべる	(SO) arranges (ST)	〜が	(ST) lines up

4課

> C. (Subject が) ＋ Transitive verb (TE form) ＋ ある
>   has been done; be done
> Used to describe an existing state which is the result of an action previously done by someone.
> 1. 床の間に掛け軸がかけてある。　　　　　A scroll has been hung in the alcove.
> 2. パーティーの食べ物はもう買ってある。　Food for the party has already been bought.

Answer the following questions based on fact. Use the correct verb form in your answers.

1. 日本語の教室に日本語のポスターが貼ってありますか。 _____
2. 日本語の教室にお花が飾ってありますか。 _____
3. 日本語の教室はよく掃除してありますか。 _____
4. 日本語の教室にリサイクルの袋が置いてありますか。 _____
5. 日本語の教室は先生がいない時、鍵がかけてありますか。 _____

> D. Verb (TE form) ＋おく　　　　　　do something in advance
>   Means "do something in advance and leave as is for future convenience."
>   -ておく is often contracted or shortened to -とく in informal conversations.
>   Examples: 話しておく→話しとく　読んでおく→読んどく
> 1. いつか日本に留学したいので、日本語を勉強しておく。
>   Since I want to study in Japan someday, I will study Japanese (to prepare for it).
> 2. 母は今晩出かけるので、晩ご飯を作っておいてくれた。
>   Since my mother is going out tonight, she made our dinner ahead of time for us.
> 3. ドアに鍵をかけたら、鍵はマットの下に置いておく。
>   After locking the door, I put the key under the mat (for a family member).
> 4. 「トイレに行っとくね。」　"I will go to the bathroom ahead of time."
> 5. 「明日マラソンだから、今スパゲティーをたくさん食べとこう。」
>   "Since the marathon is tomorrow, let's eat lots of spaghetti now (to prepare for it)."

You are planning a birthday party at your house. Write three things you have to do to prepare for it using the -ておく pattern.

1. _____
2. _____
3. _____

4課

> **E. Intransitive verb (TE form) + いる   Description of a state**
>
> Used to describe a state. For example, to say, "The window is open," one would use the intransitive form of the verb (TE form) + いる. In intransitive sentences, the subject often takes the particle が.
>
> 1. 窓が 開いている。   The window is open.
> 2. 電気が ついている。   The electricity is on.
> 3. 電気が 消えている。   The electricity is off.

a. Describe the state of your classroom by filling in the blanks with an appropriate intransitive verb + いる form.

1. 教室の窓は、今_____。
2. 教室の戸は、今_____。
3. 教室の電気は、今_____。
4. 教室のコンピューターは、今_____。
5. 教室のエアコンは、今_____。

b. Circle the correct response.

1. 窓は今（開いて　開けて）いる。
2. 空き缶を（集めて　集まって）、リサイクルしている。
3. 「お金を（落として　落ちて）しまった。」
4. 「テレビを（つけて　ついて）おいて下さい。」
5. 「電気を（消して　消えて）下さい。」
6. 「レストランはもう（閉めて　閉まって）いるよ。」
7. 私の時計は今（壊して　壊れて）いるから、時間が分からない。
8. 友達がお金を（見つけて　見つかって）くれた。
9. 私は今日、交通事故を（起こした　起きた）。
10. 毎日アイスクリームやケーキを食べていたら、体重が（増やした　増えた）。
11. 次郎君はレスリングの試合の前に、いつも体重を（減らす　減る）。
12. 私の方に（向けて　向いて）座って下さい。

4課

| 4課 | | アクティビティー | |

A. 日本文化：一人か二人ワーク→クラスワーク

Divide the topics below among your classmates and research your topic on the Internet. Using visuals, present your findings with your classmates.

1. 玄関〔げんかん〕、下駄箱/くつ箱
2. 床の間〔とこのま〕、掛け軸、生け花
3. 押し入れ〔おしいれ〕、布団、枕
4. 座敷〔ざしき〕、畳、襖、障子、座布団〔ざぶとん〕
5. 日本庭園〔にほんていえん〕

B. 日本の家：ペアワーク→クラスワーク

Match the Japanese words with their English meanings.

1. 玄関〔げんかん〕 ( )
2. 床の間〔とこのま〕 ( )
3. 下駄箱/くつ箱 ( )
4. 傘立て〔かさたて〕 ( )
5. 押し入れ〔おしいれ〕 ( )
6. 座敷〔ざしき〕 ( )
7. 廊下〔ろうか〕 ( )
8. お風呂〔ふろ〕 ( )
9. トイレ ( )
10. カーペット ( )
11. 畳 ( )
12. スリッパ ( )
13. 襖 ( )
14. 障子 ( )
15. 生け花〔いけばな〕 ( )
16. 掛け軸 ( )
17. 布団 ( )
18. 枕 ( )
19. 座布団〔ざぶとん〕 ( )
20. 庭園 ( )

a. flower arrangement
b. Japanese-style room
c. toilet
d. framed and papered sliding door
e. garden
f. sliding paper door
g. Japanese cushion
h. pillow
i. footwear storage cabinet
j. bedclothes
k. entrance foyer
l. carpet
m. umbrella stand
n. alcove
o. Japanese straw mat
p. bath
q. scroll
r. slippers
s. closet
t. hallway

4課

C. 日本の家でのあいさつ：ペアワーク→クラスワーク

Match each expression with an appropriate situation.

1. ごめんください。　　　（　）
2. おじゃまします。　　　（　）
3. つまらない物ですが。　（　）
4. いただきます。　　　　（　）
5. ごちそうさまでした。　（　）
6. そろそろ失礼します。　（　）
7. おじゃましました。　　（　）

a. 訪問した家を出る時に言う。
b. 出された物を食べたり飲んだりした後に言う。
c. 帰る時を知らせる時に言う。
d. 御土産や手土産を渡す時に言う。
e. 出された物を食べたり飲んだりする前に言う。
f. 訪問したうちに入る時に言う。
g. 訪問したうちの玄関の外でうちの人を呼ぶ時に言う。

D. 日本の家の特徴〔とくちょう〕：ペアワーク→クラスワーク

Complete the following sentences with the correct responses. Circle the appropriate answers.

a. 日本の家：
1. (畳　カーペット) の部屋は伝統的である。
2. 風呂とトイレが (同じ　違う) 所にある。
3. 玄関に下駄箱という (傘　靴) を入れる所がある。
4. 床の間には (生け花　掛け軸) がかけてある。
5. (ふとん　ざぶとん) は朝起きた時に、押し入れに入れる。
6. 畳の部屋の戸は襖や障子で、鍵は (かけられる　かけられない)。

b. 日本の家でのマナー：
1. 挨拶する時に (握手をする　おじぎをする)。
2. 日本の家の中で靴を (はいていてもいい　はいていてはいけない)。
3. 靴をぬぐ時、靴は (玄関のドアに　家の中に) 向けて置くはずだ。
4. 畳の部屋でスリッパを (はいてもいい　はいてはいけない)。
5. 御土産をあげる時、(両手　片手) であげるはずだ。
6. 床の間に (立ってもいい　立ってはいけない)。
7. トイレを使っていない時、トイレの戸は (開けておく　閉めておく) べきだ。
8. 日本のお風呂の中で石鹸を (使ってもいい　使ってはいけない)。
9. 茶道で畳の上に座る時、女性は (あぐらをかいてもいい　あぐらをかいてはいけない)。
10. トイレのスリッパをほかの部屋で (はいてもいい　はいてはいけない)。
11. 襖や障子は足で (開けてもいい　開けてはいけない)。
12. うちの中で、ぼうしを (かぶっていてもいい　かぶっていてはいけない)。
13. 人に物を渡す時、(投げてもいい　投げてはいけない)。

4課

E. 聞く Pre-Listening Activity「ボランティア活動」：ペアワーク→クラスワーク

Mark each statement はい or いいえ depending on the kind of volunteer work you have done.
1. （はい　いいえ）病院で手伝ったことがある。
2. （はい　いいえ）海岸のゴミ拾いをしたことがある。
3. （はい　いいえ）老人ホームでお年寄りに手伝ったことがある。
4. （はい　いいえ）コミュニティーの催し物を手伝ったことがある。
5. その他：＿＿＿＿＿＿＿＿＿＿＿＿＿＿＿＿＿＿＿＿＿＿＿＿＿＿ことがある。

F. 聞く Post-Listening Activity「ボランティア活動」：ペアワーク→クラスワーク

Compare and Contrast: Doing Community Service and Having a Part-time Job

Compare and contrast similarities and differences between doing community service and having a part-time job. Based on your personal experience, describe at least THREE similarities and differences between doing community service and having a part-time job. Also state your preference for either and give reasons for your choice. Use 4 minutes to prepare and 2 minutes to share your presentation in class.

Introduction:
_____

Three similarities/differences:
1. _____
2. _____
3. _____

Your preference and reasons:
_____

G. 読む Pre-Reading Activity「コミュニティー」：ペアワーク→クラスワーク

Match each location with an appropriate description from the right.

1. 駅　　　　（　）　　a. いろいろな日常生活に便利な物を売っている所
2. 商店街　　（　）　　b. 家やアパートやマンションなどがある所
3. 書店　　　（　）　　c. 切手を買ったり、物を送ったりする所
4. スーパー　（　）　　d. お金を貯金したり出したりする所
5. コンビニ　（　）　　e. 電車に乗ったり降りたりする所
6. 住宅地　　（　）　　f. 安く食事が出来る所
7. 郵便局　　（　）　　g. 本や雑誌などを売っている所
8. 銀行　　　（　）　　h. いろいろな食料品や衣料品や家具などを安く売っている所
9. 食堂　　　（　）　　i. いろいろなお店が並んでいる所

4課

H. 読む Post-Reading Activity「コミュニティー」：ペアワーク→クラスワーク

Presentation: International Center

Present your view on the international center described. Discuss at least FIVE aspects of this center. Begin with an appropriate introduction, give details about the five aspects, explain your own view or perspective, and end with a concluding remark. You will have 4 minutes to prepare and 2 minutes to present. Your presentation should be as complete as possible.

1. Introduction: _____

2. Discuss five aspects of the topic.

   1.) _____
   2.) _____
   3.) _____
   4.) _____
   5.) _____

3. Explain your view.
   _____

4. End with a concluding remark.
   _____

I. テキストチャット「コミュニティーサービス」：ペアワーク→クラスワーク

You will have a conversation with Reiko Saito, the coordinator of a community service program. First, start a conversation with your partner using the sample response. Next, carry on the conversation with a response of your own. Each response should be answered within 20 seconds.

1. 「こんにちは。今日はお願いがあります。」
   例：「斉藤さん、こんにちは。いつも御苦労様です。お願いって何でしょうか。私で出来ることでしょうか。私で出来ることでしたら何でもしますから、言ってみて下さい。」

2. 「実は、この土曜日の午後、ボランティアがあと１０人必要なんです。」
   例：「ああ、ボランティアですか。どんなボランティアですか。土曜日の午後というのは、何時から何時までですか。どこでするんですか。私は土曜日の午後は暇ですから、参加しましょう。友達にも声をかけてみましょうか。」

3. 「有難う。海岸でゴミ拾いするのと、フェスティバルを手伝うのと、どちらの方が好きですか。」
   例：「どういたしまして。私はフェスティバルで手伝う方が、海岸でゴミ拾いするのより好きです。なぜなら、フェスティバルではいろいろな人に会えるから、楽しそうです。海岸でのゴミ拾いは、きたなくなるので、あまり好きではありません。」

4課

4.「皆ボランティア活動をするべきだと思いますか。」
　　例：「そうですねえ。。。ボランティア活動はとても大事だと思います。いろいろな人が助け合えば、社会はもっと暮しやすくなります。そして、私達は困っている人を手伝うべきだと思います。ボランティア活動をすると、自分の今の生活を感謝するようになると思います。」

5.「ほかにもどんなボランティア活動をして来ましたか。」
　　例：「そうですねえ。。。私は老人ホームでお年寄りの手伝いをしたり、病院に入院している子供達に本を読んであげたり、学校のリサイクルを手伝ったりしました。たくさんのボランティア活動をして、私はもっといい人間になったと思います。」

6.「有難う。何かこの土曜日のボランティア活動について質問がありますか。」
　　例：「どういたしまして。この土曜日のボランティア活動ですが、どこへ何時にどんな格好をして行けばいいですか。何か問題があったら、どこに電話すればいいですか。では、このボランティア活動を楽しみにしています。有難うございました。」

J. Compare & Contrast「デパートとコンビニ」：ペアワーク→クラスワーク

Complete the blanks with the appropriate words or sentences. Start with an introduction, then give two aspects of each and highlight differences and one similarity between department stores and convenience stores. Also state your preference for either and give reasons for it. Elaborate on each of your opinions.

　　　これから、デパートとコンビニを＿＿＿＿＿＿＿＿＿＿。デパートとコンビニは違うことも同じこともあります。
　　　まず、一つ目の違いは、デパートは＿＿＿＿＿＿＿＿＿＿＿＿＿＿＿＿＿＿が、コンビニは＿＿＿＿＿＿＿＿＿＿＿＿＿＿＿＿＿＿＿。＿＿＿＿＿＿＿＿＿＿
＿＿＿＿＿＿＿＿＿＿＿＿＿＿＿＿＿＿＿＿＿＿＿＿＿＿＿＿＿＿＿＿＿＿＿＿
　　　二つ目の違いは、デパートは＿＿＿＿＿＿＿＿＿＿＿＿＿＿＿＿＿＿＿が、コンビニは＿＿＿＿＿＿＿＿＿＿＿＿＿＿＿＿＿＿＿＿です。＿＿＿＿＿＿＿＿
＿＿＿＿＿＿＿＿＿＿＿＿＿＿＿＿＿＿＿＿＿＿＿＿＿＿＿＿＿＿＿＿＿＿＿＿
　　　しかし、一つの似ていることは、デパートもコンビニも＿＿＿＿＿＿＿＿＿＿
＿＿＿＿＿＿＿＿＿＿＿＿＿＿＿＿＿＿＿＿＿です。＿＿＿＿＿＿＿＿＿＿＿＿
＿＿＿＿＿＿＿＿＿＿＿＿＿＿＿＿＿＿＿＿＿＿＿＿＿＿。
　　　結論として、私は＿＿＿＿＿＿の方が＿＿＿＿＿＿より好きです。なぜなら、
＿＿＿＿＿＿＿＿＿＿＿＿＿＿＿＿＿＿＿＿＿＿＿＿＿＿＿＿からです。
＿＿＿＿＿＿＿＿＿＿＿＿＿＿＿＿＿＿＿＿＿＿＿＿＿＿＿＿＿＿＿＿＿＿＿＿

4課

K. 会話「ボランティア活動」：ペアワーク→クラスワーク

a. Change the underlined words in the informal style to their polite equivalents.

1. <u>やあ</u>、昨日はボランティアで公園の掃除をしに<u>行ったんだけど</u>、<u>疲れちゃったよ</u>。

2. 時々、ボランティア活動に<u>参加している</u>？

3. ところで、来週の<u>土曜日</u>に、川の掃除に<u>行くんだけど</u>、一緒に<u>行かない</u>？

4. <u>じゃ</u>、時間があったら、<u>連絡して</u>。僕の電話番号を<u>あげるから</u>。

b. Respond to each question in 20 seconds.

1. やあ、昨日はボランティアで公園の掃除をしに行ったんだけど、疲れちゃったよ。
　_____

2. 時々、ボランティア活動に参加している？
　_____

3. ところで、来週の土曜日に、川の掃除に行くんだけど、一緒に行かない？
　_____

4. じゃ、時間があったら、連絡して。僕の電話番号をあげるから。
　_____

L. 日本文化「日本の家でのマナー」：ペアワーク→クラスワーク

Write your own opinions in the blank sections below. Finish in 4 minutes.

1. Begin with an introduction: これから、日本の家でのマナーについて発表します。日本の家はアメリカの家とよく違うので、いろいろな違うマナーがあります。その５つの特徴についてお話します。

2. Discuss five aspects/examples of the topic:

　まず第一に、日本の家の中でくつをはいてはいけません。日本人は玄関でくつをぬいで、くつをドアの方に向けて置きます。帰る時に、くつをはきやすいからです。

　第二に、_____
_____

　第三に、_____
_____

4課

第四に、_____
_____

　　第五に、_____
_____

3. Explain your view or perspective.
　　結論として、_____
_____

4. End with a concluding remark.
　　これで、日本の家でのマナーについての発表を終わります。聞いて下さいまして、どうも有難うございました。

4課

<4課 - 聞く>

Listening: Community Service

12秒×5

【You may take notes while listening. Do not look at the questions below before listening. You will have 12 seconds to answer each question. You may NOT move back and forth among questions.】

(Narrator) Now you will listen to an announcement once.

(Narrator) Now answer the questions for this selection.

1. What kind of community service project is this?
    - (A) cleaning a park
    - (B) cleaning the beach
    - (C) helping the elderly
    - (D) planting

2. When is the community service project scheduled?
    - (A) Saturday, May 6th, 9:00 a.m. - 2:00 p.m.
    - (B) Saturday, May 8th, 8:00 a.m. - 3:00 p.m.
    - (C) Sunday, May 9th, 8:30 a.m. - 3:00 p.m.
    - (D) Sunday, May 7th, 8:30 a.m. - 12:00

3. When and where are the volunteers supposed to meet?
    - (A) at school, at 7:30 a.m.
    - (B) at school, at 7:00 a.m.
    - (C) at the beach, at 7:00 a.m.
    - (D) at the park, at 8:00 a.m.

4. What are the volunteers NOT advised to take with them?
    - (A) water
    - (B) sun screen
    - (C) hat
    - (D) slippers

5. What directions were NOT given to the volunteers?
    - (A) to write their names and cellular phone numbers on the sign up sheet with a black pen
    - (B) to sign up by May 2nd
    - (C) to call 936-8547 in case of a late cancellation
    - (D) to e-mail in case of a late cancellation

4課

＜4課 - 読む＞
Reading: A Letter
【You may move back and forth among all the questions.】

ジャック・ムーア様、

　初めまして。国際センターから連絡があったので、ムーア様が留学中に泊まられる国際センターについて紹介させていただきます。

　国際センターはJR北山駅から徒歩１５分の所にあります。東京からは４０分くらいです。駅前には商店街があり、レストラン、書店、スーパーなどがあります。センターは住宅地付近で、静かな所です。全館１０階の建物です。

　部屋にはベッドと机といすとテレビと冷蔵庫と電子レンジがあります。しかし、キッチンはありません。食事は二階の食堂で出来ます。朝食は無料ですが、昼食と夕食は有料です。但し、週末の夕食はありませんので、外食して下さい。お風呂とシャワーも部屋にあります。

　部屋に友達を泊めることは禁止されています。そして、ペットを飼うことや喫煙も禁止されています。

　国際センター内にはいろいろな施設があります。図書室、コンピュータールーム、スポーツセンターなどです。無料で利用することが出来ます。

　何かご質問がありましたら、お知らせ下さい。では、お越しをお待ちしております。

　　　　　　　　　　　　　　　　　　　　国際センター
　　　　　　　　　　　　　　　　　　　　山村まさみ

< 4課 - 読む (質問) >

Reading: A Letter

(Narrator) Now answer the questions for this section.

1. Where is the international center?
   (A) in Tokyo
   (B) a 15 minute train ride from the JR station
   (C) in a residential area
   (D) in a commercial area

2. What is the room NOT furnished with?
   (A) kitchen
   (B) desk
   (C) bath
   (D) refrigerator

3. What is allowed in the room?
   (A) pets
   (B) overnight stays by friends
   (C) smoking
   (D) using a microwave oven

4. What information is NOT correct about the international center?
   (A) There are many stores in front of the nearest station.
   (B) It has a dining room on the third floor.
   (C) It has a sports facility.
   (D) It is a ten story building.

5. What do the users of the international center have to pay?
   (A) Everything is free.
   (B) The users have to pay for using the sports center.
   (C) The users have to pay for all meals.
   (D) The users have to pay for dinner on weekends.

4課

<4課 - 書く (テキストチャット)>

Text Chat: Community Service

90秒×6

You will participate in a simulated exchange of text-chat messages. Each time it is your turn to write, you will have 90 seconds. You should respond as fully and as appropriately as possible.

You will have a conversation with Reiko Saito, the coordinator of a community service program.

1. Respond. (90 seconds)

   こんにちは。今日はちょっとお願いがあるんですが。

2. Volunteer. (90 seconds)

   実はこの土曜日の午後、ボランティアがあと十人必要なんですが。

3. Give your preference. (90 seconds)

   ありがとう。二つの活動があるんです。公園の落書(らくが)きを消(け)すボランティアと、老(ろう)人ホームへ行ってお年寄(よ)りの手伝いをするボランティアなんですが、どっちがいいですか。

4. Justify your opinion. (90 seconds)

   そうですか。ところで、なぜボランティア活動は大事だと思いますか。

5. Suggest. (90 seconds)

   なるほど。ほかにもどんなボランティア活動をしたらいいと思いますか。

6. Ask a specific question. (90 seconds)

   いろいろ有難う。何かこの土曜日のボランティア活動について質問がありますか。

<4課 - 書く (比較(ひかく)と対比(たいひ))>

20分

Compare and Contrast: Department Stores and Convenience Stores

Directions: You are writing an article for the student newspaper of your sister school in Japan. Write an article in which you compare and contrast similarities and differences between department stores and convenience stores. Based on your personal experience, describe at least THREE aspects of each and highlight the similarities and differences between department stores and convenience stores. Also state your preference for either and give reasons for it.

Your article should be 300 to 400 characters or longer. Use the *desu/masu* or *da* (plain) style, but use one style consistently. Also, use *kanji* wherever *kanji* from the AP Japanese *kanji* list is appropriate. You have 20 minutes to write.

【NOTES/OUTLINE: 自分の作文のアウトラインを書こう！】

Introduction:
_____

Three similarities/differences:

1. _____
2. _____
3. _____

Your preference and give reasons:
_____
_____

4課

<4課 - 話す (会話)>
Conversation: Community Service

`20秒×4`

You will participate in a simulated conversation. Each time it is your turn to speak, you will have 20 seconds to record. You should respond as fully and as appropriately as possible.

You will have a conversation with Masa, your Japanese friend, about community service.

(Masa)
(20 seconds)
(Masa)
(20 seconds)
(Masa)
(20 seconds)
(Masa)
(20 seconds)

<4課 - 話す (日本文化)>
Cultural Perspective Presentation: Manners at a Japanese Home

`4分+2分`

Directions: Imagine you are making an oral presentation to your Japanese class. First, you will be given a topic for your presentation. You will have 4 minutes to prepare your presentation. Then you will have 2 minutes to record your presentation. Your presentation should be as complete as possible.

Present your own view or perspective of manners at a Japanese home. Discuss at least FIVE aspects or examples of manners at a Japanese home.

Begin with an appropriate introduction, give details, explain your own view or perspective, and end with a concluding remark.

【Let's take notes!】

1. Begin with an appropriate introduction.
   _____

2. Discuss five aspects/examples of the topic.
   1.) _____
   2.) _____
   3.) _____
   4.) _____
   5.) _____

3. Explain your view or perspective.
   _____

4. End with a concluding remark.
   _____

`4課`

| 5課 | ●●● | 都市と町と田舎
Cities, Towns and Villages | ●●● |

【AP® タスク：都市と町と田舎】
Introduce your hometown, which you are proud of, to Japanese visitors. Where do you recommend that they visit? Why? What do you recommend that they taste? What do you recommend that they buy as souvenirs?

【文化】 日本の有名な都市：Japan's Famous Cities

Japan's most well-known cities lie in the eastern regions of the main island of Honshu. They are prominent for their geographical, historical, cultural and political significance. While many cities fit this description, we will focus on five main cities here: Nara, Kyoto, Osaka, Tokyo and Yokohama.

Nara was Japan's oldest permanent capital. Although not a heavily populated city, its long history and its deep connection to the introduction of Buddhism to Japan have made it well known. One of its most famous sites is Todaiji (東大寺), the largest wooden structure in the world. In it sits the largest image of Buddha in Japan, the Daibutsu (大仏), which has been named a National Treasure. Nara Park, which surrounds Todaiji, is home to hundreds of free-roaming deer. The stunningly beautiful Kasuga Shrine, and Horyuji, the oldest temple in Japan, are also recognized national treasures in Nara.

Kyoto, the capital of Japan for more than 10 centuries, is steeped in historical, religious, and cultural traditions like no other city in Japan. It ranks as Japan's seventh largest city. Some of its most famous sites are Kinkakuji (the famed Golden Pavilion), Nijo-jo (a castle known for its nightingale floors), Ryoanji (home of a meditatively elegant rock garden), Kiyomizudera (majestically set on the bluffs of Kyoto) and Fushimi Inari Jinja (mountaintop shrine with 10,000 vermillion gates). Kyoto hosts numerous culturally significant festivals and time-honored events. Kyoto is also known for its elegant handicraft, including silk, brocade, dyed fabric, porcelain, lacquer, fans, kimono, dolls and cloisonné.

Osaka is the commercial, industrial, economic and foreign trade giant of the Kansai region. It is the third largest city in Japan. The Kansai International Airport and a network of train lines, highways, and ships converge in and around vibrant Osaka. It is known for steel and iron manufacturing, fabric and textile industries, chemical industries, and food processing. Osaka Castle is the city's most significant historical site. It is now a museum dedicated to Toyotomi Hideyoshi, one of the most famous military leaders in Japanese history.

Yokohama is now one of the trendiest of the major cities of Japan. It recently became the second largest city in Japan, boasting a population of 3 million people. It lies southwest of Tokyo, about a 30 minute train ride away. Yokohama is historically known as a major port city and thus is strongly influenced by foreign cultures. One of the most famous sections of Yokohama is its Chinatown, which is likely one of the largest of its kind in the world. Yokohama is also known for its beautiful Sankeien Gardens as well as its ultra-modern and futuristic shopping and amusement centers.

Finally, Tokyo is the capital and largest city (population 13 million) of Japan. Before it became the capital, Tokyo was a castle town known as Edo. Tokyo is now the political, financial, commercial, educational, cultural and entertainment center of Japan. All major transportation systems feed into Tokyo. Its famous landmarks include the Imperial Palace, Meiji Shrine, Asakusa's Sensoji Temple, Ueno Park (the home of a zoo and several museums), and the Tsukiji Fish Market. Shopping abounds in Shibuya, Shinjuku, Ginza, Ikebukuro, Harajuku, Odaiba and Akihabara. Nearby are the famous historical cities of Nikko and Kamakura, and the popular Tokyo Disneyland.

Each city offers unique features to visitors as well as residents. All of Japan's cities, however represent a fascinating blend of old and new cultures. Japanese are proud of their country's rich cultural and historical heritage as well as its cutting-edge modern face.

Questions to ponder: How are Japanese cities a reflection of the Japanese and their attitudes and values? Why are the major cities located in clusters in the certain regions of Japan?

5課 復習単語

トピック：都市と町と田舎

1. 都会	とかい	N	(large) city; metropolis
2. ビル		N	building (Western style)
3. 便利	べんり	Na	convenient
4. 市	し	N	city
5. 市長	しちょう	N	(city) mayor
6. 村長	そんちょう	N	village chief
7. 田舎	いなか	N	countryside; hometown
8. 野原	のはら	N	field

| 5課 | ★★★ | 新しい単語 | ★★★ |

1. えんりょ＜遠慮＞しないで(下さい)。　　Exp　Please don't hesitate.
「お土産、何がいいか言ってね。遠慮しないで。」　"Tell me what you want for souvenirs. Don't hesitate."

2. ～ぶり　　Nd　after ～ (a long time)
「おひさしぶりです。一年ぶりですねえ。」"I haven't seen you for a long time. It's almost one year since the last time we met, isn't it?"

3. けん＜県＞　　N　prefecture
鹿児島県は九州の最も南にある。　Kagoshima Prefecture is at the southernmost (part) of Kyushu.

4. とし＜都市＞　　N　city
都市の生活は便利だ。　City life is convenient.

5. しゅと＜首都＞　　N　capital
京都は昔の日本の首都だった。　Kyoto was the capital of ancient Japan.

6. ふるさと＜故郷＞　　N　hometown
多くの日本人がお正月とお盆に故郷へ帰る。　Lots of Japanese go back to their hometowns during New Year's and the *Obon* (midsummer) season.

7. じもと＜地元＞　　N　local
地元の果物や野菜は本当においしい。The local fruits and vegetables are really tasty.

8. いなか＜田舎＞　　N　countryside
田舎の生活はのんびりしている。　Life in the countryside is relaxed.

9. こうがい＜郊外＞　　N　suburb
家は郊外にあって、朝夕の交通ラッシュが大変だ。My home is in the suburbs, and the traffic is terrible in the morning and evening.

10. かんこうち＜観光地＞　　N　tourist attractions
日本の有名な観光地を訪問したい。　I want to visit the famous tourist attractions in Japan.

11. けしき＜景色＞　　N　scenery
山からの景色はすばらしい。　The scenery from the mountains is wonderful.

12. めいぶつ＜名物＞　　N　special product (of a region)
鹿児島名物の黒豚を食べてみたい。　I want to try to eat the black pork that is a famous product of Kagoshima.

13. きこう＜気候＞　N　climate
日本の気候は、夏とても蒸し暑く過ごしにくい。As for the Japanese climate, summers are very hot and humid, and it is hard to spend (time there).

14. きおん＜気温＞　N　temperature (atmospheric)
地球の気温がだんだん高くなっているそうだ。I heard that the temperature of the earth is gradually getting higher.

15. (お)まつり＜(お)祭り＞　N　festival
お祭りがある度に、わくわくする。Every time we have a festival, I get excited.

16. ほうげん＜方言＞　N　dialect
　-べん＜-弁＞　N　～dialect
　かんさいべん＜関西弁＞　N　Kansai dialect
「ありがとう」のことを関西弁で「おおきに」と言う。 They say "*Ookini*" for "Thank you" in the *Kansai* dialect.

17. おぼうさん＜お坊さん＞　N　monk
日本のお坊さんはたいてい黒い着物を着ている。 Japanese monks usually wear black *kimono*.

18. せんきょうし＜宣教師＞　N　missionary
初めてのキリスト教の宣教師は１６世紀に日本に行った。The first Christian missionaries went to Japan in the 16th century.

19. すな＜砂＞　N　sand
鹿児島には砂の温泉があるそうだ。 I heard that there is a sand hot spring in Kagoshima.

20. しんちょう＜身長＞　N　height (stature)
私の身長は１６５センチだ。My height is 165 cm.

21. たいじゅう＜体重＞　N　(body) weight
体重は５０キロだ。My weight is 50 kilograms.

22. おすすめ＜お勧め＞　N　recommendation; recommended (something)
[☞すすめる＜勧める＞／勧めます to recommend (something)]
「この町のお勧めのレストランはどこですか。」"What restaurant do you recommend in this town?"

23. こうきしん＜好奇心＞　N　curiosity
妹は好奇心がいっぱいだ。My younger sister is full of curiosity.

5課

24. ぼうけん＜冒険＞　　N　adventure
   初めての日本旅行は冒険でいっぱいだった。My first trip to Japan was full of adventures.
25. かざん＜火山＞　　N　volcano
   日本には多くの火山がある。　There are lots of volcanoes in Japan.
26. ふんか＜噴火＞(を)する／します　　V3　to erupt
   桜島の火山は今も時々噴火する。　The volcano of Sakurajima sometimes erupts even now.
27. ふしぎ＜不思議＞　　Na　mysterious
   トトロは不思議な生き物だ。Totoro is a mysterious creature.
28. ふえ(をふく)＜笛(を吹く)＞／吹きます　　N　(to play) a flute [not a Western flute]
   トトロは木の上でオカリナという笛を吹いていた。Totoro was playing a flute called the ocarina in the tree.
29. つたえる＜伝える＞／伝えます　　V2　to convey
   メッセージを伝えたい。I want to convey my message.
30. こわがる＜怖がる＞／怖がります　　V1　to fear; to be afraid of
   竹中先生は猫が嫌いで、子猫さえ怖がる。Takenaka Sensei dislikes cats and she is even afraid of kittens.

【もっと単語】

1. だいこん＜大根＞　　　　　　　　N　　turnip
2. いも＜芋＞　　　　　　　　　　　N　　potato
3. じゃがいも＜じゃが芋＞　　　　　N　　(Irish) potato
4. さつまいも＜薩摩芋＞　　　　　　N　　sweet potato
5. てっぽう＜鉄砲＞　　　　　　　　N　　gun
6. うま＜馬＞　　　　　　　　　　　N　　horse
7. さむらい＜侍＞　　　　　　　　　N　　*samurai* warrior
8. どうぞう＜銅像＞　　　　　　　　N　　bronze statue
9. どんぐり　　　　　　　　　　　　N　　acorn
10. きのみ or このみ＜木の実＞　　　 N　　nut

【復習単語】

1. むら＜村＞　　　　　　　　　　　N　　village
2. まち＜町＞　　　　　　　　　　　N　　town

5課 文法

A. Noun 1 という Noun 2   Noun 2 called/ named Noun 1

Noun 1 identifies or clarifies Noun 2. Recall that 「Tree は日本語で何といいますか。」 means "How do you say 'tree' in Japanese?" Noun 1 という Noun 2 is a modifying clause derived from Noun 2 は Noun 1 といいます.

1. 「となりのトトロ」というアニメを見たことがありますか。
　　Have you ever seen the movie called "My Neighbor Totoro"?
2. 宮崎駿という監督を知っていますか。   Do you know the director named Hayao Miyazaki?
3. これは何という楽器ですか。   What is this musical instrument called?
4. 「おおきに」は関西弁で「ありがとう」という意味です。
　　"Ookini" means "thank you" in Kansai dialect.

Fill in the blanks with appropriate words from the list.

1. 桜島という＿＿＿＿＿＿＿を知っていますか。
2. 桜島大根というとても大きい＿＿＿＿＿＿＿が有名だ。
3. 鑑真という＿＿＿＿＿＿＿が仏教を日本に伝えた。
4. フランシスコ・ザビエルという＿＿＿＿＿＿＿がキリスト教を日本に伝えた。
5. 西郷隆盛という貧乏な＿＿＿＿＿＿＿が江戸時代を終わらせた一人だった。
6. トトロはオカリナという＿＿＿＿＿＿＿を吹くことが好きだ。

> 宣教師
> 笛
> 侍
> 火山
> お坊さん
> 大根

B.
～について   about ～
～として   as ～
～によると   according to ～
～によって   depending on ～

1. これから鹿児島について発表します。
　　I will now do a presentation about Kagoshima.
2. 鹿児島の名物として、黒豚が有名らしい。
　　Black pork seems to be famous as a special product of Kagoshima.
3. トトロの本によると、トトロは人間より年が多い。
　　According to the book Totoro, Totoro is older than human beings.
4. トトロは年によって、大きさが違う。
　　Depending on its age, Totoro's size is different.

Fill in each blank with について, として, によると or によって.
1. そちらの観光地_____教えて下さい。
2. お土産_____、お勧めは何ですか。
3. ガイドブック_____、七月に京都で祇園祭というお祭りがあるそうです。
4. 地元の果物_____、何が一番有名ですか。
5. 私の故郷は町_____は小さいですが、田舎ではありません。
6. 季節_____景色が違うそうだ。
7. 日本の気候は、季節_____とても違うそうだ。
8. 東京の大学に行っている友達_____、都会の生活はおもしろいらしい。

> **C. Indirect quotation (Plain form) ＋と＋思う/言う/答える/聞く**
>
> think/say/answer/hear that ～
>
> The subject of the sentence, that is, the person who thinks, says, answers, etc. is usually marked by the particle は. The subject of the quote, if different from the subject of the sentence, is followed by が.
>
> 1. 私はケンが日本へ行くと聞いた。　　　　　I heard that Ken will go to Japan.
> 2. 私はケンがやさしいと思う。　　　　　　　I think that Ken is nice.
> 3. ケンは日本が好きだと言った。　　　　　　Ken said that he likes Japan.
> 4. 私はケンがいい人だと思う。　　　　　　　I think Ken is a good person.
> 5. ケンは私が好きだったと思う。　　　　　　I think that Ken liked me.

Complete the sentences by using the cues given in the correct form.
1. 故郷はいい_____と思う。（所）
2. お祭りは_____と思う。（楽しい）
3. 田舎の空気は_____と思う。（きれい）
4. 母は以前_____と言った。（先生）
5. 夢はいい大学へ_____と答えた。（合格する）

> **D. Verb Stem ＋やすいです**　　　　　　　is easy to do ～
>
> **Verb Stem ＋にくいです**　　　　　　　　is hard/difficult to do ～
>
> To describe that an action is easy or difficult to do, use the verb stem ＋やすい or にくい. やすい and にくい conjugate as いadjectives. The original direct object of a sentence becomes either the topic or the subject in this construction. Thus, the particle used after the noun being described is は or が and <u>not</u> を. Other particles do <u>not</u> change to は or が.
>
> Ex. とうふを　はしで　食べます。　　　　I'll eat tofu with chopsticks.
>
> 　　とうふは　はしで　食べにくいです。　Tofu is hard to eat with chopsticks.

5課

1. このシャツはとても着やすいです。	This shirt is very easy to wear.
2. このペンは書きにくいですねえ。	This pen is hard to write with, isn't it?

Fill in the blanks with the cues in the correct やすい or にくい form.

1. 都会の人はあまり親切ではないので、＿＿＿＿＿＿＿＿＿＿と思う。（住む）
2. 都会は交通が便利なので、田舎より＿＿＿＿＿＿＿＿＿＿と思う。（住む）
3. 日本の首都の東京は物が高いので、東京は＿＿＿＿＿＿＿＿＿＿と思う。（暮す）
4. 田舎の野菜や果物は新しくて安いので、＿＿＿＿＿＿＿＿＿＿と思う。（暮す）
5. 田舎は空気がきれいで気持ちいいので、＿＿＿＿＿＿＿＿＿＿と思う。（過ごす）
6. 都会の夏は暑くて、クーラーがなければ、＿＿＿＿＿＿＿＿＿＿と思う。（過ごす）

E. ～かも 知れない／知れません	might ～; may ～
～だろう／でしょう	probably ～
～に違いない／違いありません	there is no doubt that ～; must be ～

These structures express different degrees of doubt.

1. 明日、雨が降るかも知れません。 It might rain tomorrow.
2. 明日、雨が降るでしょう。 It will probably rain tomorrow.
3. 明日、雨が降るに違いありません。 It will certainly rain tomorrow.

Write sentences about your future using the following structures.

1. ～かも知れません ＿＿＿＿＿＿＿＿＿＿＿＿＿＿＿＿＿＿＿＿
2. ～でしょう ＿＿＿＿＿＿＿＿＿＿＿＿＿＿＿＿＿＿＿＿
3. ～に違いありません ＿＿＿＿＿＿＿＿＿＿＿＿＿＿＿＿＿＿＿＿

5課

| 5課 | | アクティビティー | |

A. 日本文化：一人か二人ワーク→クラスワーク

Divide the topics below among your classmates and research your topic on the Internet. Using visuals, present your findings with your classmates.

1. 県〔けん〕
2. 鹿児島県
3. 日本の有名な都市：奈良、京都、大阪、横浜、東京
4. 日本の田舎
4. 温度（℃〔摂氏〕と°F〔華氏〕）
5. 身長（メートル、センチ）
6. 体重（キロ）

B. 聞く Pre-Listening Activity「鹿児島の発表」：ペアワーク→クラスワーク

Circle the correct responses.

1. 鹿児島県は（北海道　本州　四国　九州）の南にある。
2. 鹿児島の桜島は今も時々噴火している火山で、大きい（大根　いも　人参）が有名だ。
3. 鑑真というお坊さんは（神道　仏教　キリスト教）を中国から日本に伝えた。
4. フランシスコ・ザビエルという宣教師は（神道　仏教　キリスト教）をスペインから日本に伝えた。
5. （イギリス人　アメリカ人　ポルトガル人）が鉄砲を日本に伝えた。
6. 鹿児島県は（飛行機　馬　船）の時代に、日本の外国への窓口だったようだ。
7. 鹿児島で一番有名な人は（徳川家康　豊臣秀吉　西郷隆盛）で、銅像が建っている。
8. 侍の江戸時代を終わらせて、（明治　大正　昭和　平成）時代を始めた。
9. 鹿児島には温泉が多くて、砂の温泉もある。
10. 鹿児島の（観光地　名物　駅弁）として、黒豚とか魚から作られるさつま揚げとかかまぼこが有名だ。

C. 聞く Post-listening Activity「鹿児島の発表」：ペアワーク→クラスワーク

Introduce the place where you live. Prepare for 4 minutes and present for 2 minutes.

1. Introduction:_____
2. 1.) 故郷の地理 (geography/location)：_____
   2.) 故郷の気候：_____
   3.) 故郷の歴史：_____
   4.) 観光地：_____
   5.) 名物：_____
3. Perspective or view:_____
4. Concluding remark:_____

D. 読む Pre-Reading Activity「トトロ」：ペアワーク→クラスワーク
   1. Look at a picture of "Totoro." What kind of creature do you think it is?
   2. List any facts you know about "Totoro." Share them with the class.
   3. If you have seen the movie "*Tonari no Totoro*," what do you think is the theme (テーマ) of the movie? What did you think of the movie? Share your opinions and feelings in Japanese.

E. 読む Post-Reading Activity「トトロ」：ペアワーク→クラスワーク

Make an oral presentation about your favorite Japanese *anime*. Begin with an appropriate introduction, give five aspects of the *anime*, explain your own view or perspective, and end with a concluding remark. Prepare for 4 minutes and present for 2 minutes.

【Let's take notes!】

1. Begin with an appropriate introduction.
   _____

2. Discuss five aspects of the topic.
   1.) _____
   2.) _____
   3.) _____
   4.) _____
   5.) _____

3. Explain your view or perspective.
   _____

4. End with a concluding remark.
   _____

5課

F. テキストチャット「あなたの町」：ペアワーク→クラスワーク

Circle the correct choice or write an appropriate response in the blanks below. Share your highlights with your class.

1. 私の住んでいる所は（アメリカの東海岸　アメリカの西海岸　アメリカの中西部　アメリカの南部　太平洋　アラスカ　日本）にある。
2. 私の住んでいる所は（都会　郊外　田舎　町　その他：＿＿＿＿＿＿）だ。
3. 地元の気候が一番いい季節は（春　夏　秋　冬）だ。
4. 一番景色のいい所は＿＿＿＿＿＿＿＿＿＿＿＿＿＿＿＿＿＿＿＿だ。
5. この町のお勧めのレストランは＿＿＿＿＿＿＿＿＿＿＿＿＿＿＿＿＿＿＿＿だ。
6. 地元で有名なお土産は＿＿＿＿＿＿＿＿＿＿＿＿＿＿＿＿＿＿＿＿だ。
7. 一番のお祭りは＿＿＿＿＿＿＿＿＿＿＿＿＿＿＿＿＿＿＿＿だ。
8. 地元の一番の問題点は＿＿＿＿＿＿＿＿＿＿＿＿＿＿＿＿＿＿＿＿だ。

G. ディベート「町に住むのと田舎〔いなか〕に住むのとどちらの方がいいか」：グループワーク→クラスワーク

List the advantages of living in town and in the countryside. Have a debate.

a. 町に住むことの良い点：
1.) ＿＿＿＿＿＿＿＿＿＿＿＿＿＿＿＿＿＿＿＿。
2.) ＿＿＿＿＿＿＿＿＿＿＿＿＿＿＿＿＿＿＿＿。
3.) ＿＿＿＿＿＿＿＿＿＿＿＿＿＿＿＿＿＿＿＿。

b. 田舎に住むことの良い点：
1.) ＿＿＿＿＿＿＿＿＿＿＿＿＿＿＿＿＿＿＿＿。
2.) ＿＿＿＿＿＿＿＿＿＿＿＿＿＿＿＿＿＿＿＿。
3.) ＿＿＿＿＿＿＿＿＿＿＿＿＿＿＿＿＿＿＿＿。

H. 会話「町を訪問〔ほうもん〕」：ペアワーク→クラスワーク

Respond to this simulated conversation. Have a natural conversation with your partner. Each time, you will have 20 seconds to respond. You will have a conversation with Yuko, your Japanese host sister, who is an 8th grader. She will be visiting next week and will be staying with your family.

1. もしもし、優子です。おひさしぶり。一年ぶりね。元気？

2. 来週、そちらでお世話になりますが、よろしくお願いします。

3. 今、荷物を準備しているんだけど、どんな服を持って行ったらいいのか困ってるの。何を持って行ったらいいのかな？温度は何度ぐらい？

4. 何か日本からほしい物ない？お母さんがお土産に何がいいかなって困ってるから、

5課

ほしい物を教えて。遠慮(りょ)しないで。

I. 文化発表「日本の有名な都市」：ペアワーク→クラスワーク

List five famous cities in Japan. Discuss what you know about the cities and your view or perspective of each.

日本の都市〔とし〕	どんな所？	感想〔かんそう〕
1.		
2.		
3.		
4.		
5.		

5課

<5課 - 聞く>

Listening: Presentation on Kagoshima

12秒×5

【You may take notes while listening. Do not look at the questions below before listening. You will have 12 seconds to answer each question. You may NOT move back and forth among questions.】

(Narrator) Now you will listen to a presentation once.

(Narrator) Now answer the questions for this selection.

1. What kind of place is Kagoshima?
   (A) Kagoshima is in the northern part of Kyushu.
   (B) Kagoshima is cold compared to other prefectures.
   (C) Kagoshima produces big watermelons.
   (D) Kagoshima has an active volcano.

2. Which of the following is true about Kagoshima's history?
   (A) Buddhism arrived in Kagoshima in the 8th century.
   (B) Buddhism arrived in Kagoshima in the 16th century.
   (C) Christianity arrived in Kagoshima in the 18th century.
   (D) Guns were introduced to Kagoshima in the 18th century.

3. What information is CORRECT?
   (A) Ganjin was a monk from India.
   (B) Ganjin was a monk from China.
   (C) Francisco de Xavier was a missionary from Italy.
   (D) Francisco de Xavier was a missionary from France.

4. What is Saigo Takamori famous for?
   (A) He built ships.
   (B) He was one of the *samurai* who led Japan to the Meiji Era.
   (C) He was a strong *samurai*.
   (D) He made the famous *samurai* statues.

5. What is Kagoshima known for?
   (A) sand hot springs
   (B) black pork
   (C) fish products
   (D) all the above

<5課 - 読む>
Reading: Totoro
【You may move back and forth among all the questions.】

　「トトロ」が何か知っていますか。有名なアニメです。そのアニメの本当の名前は「となりのトトロ」と言います。私はこのアニメを何度も何度も見ました。好奇心いっぱいの妹のメイが可愛くて、その何も怖がらない冒険心が楽しくて、また不思議な生き物のトトロが現れたりして、最後には心が温かくなり、見るたびに元気が出て来ます。だから、トトロについていろいろ考えたし、本を読んだりもしました。

　そのアニメの制作者そして監督が宮崎駿という人ですが、宮崎駿さんが「トトロ」というアニメの中で伝えたかったメッセージは何なのでしょうか。

　「トトロ」って何でしょうか。私が読んだトトロの本によるとトトロは、人間より昔から住んでいる生き物。どんぐりなどの木の実を食べ、森でのんびり暮らしている。でも、普通は人間には見えない。昼間はたいてい寝ていて、月夜の晩に、オカリナという笛を吹くのが好き。空を飛ぶことも出来る。トトロというのは、メイ（４歳の女の子）がつけた名前。このアニメの中の大トトロは、1300歳ぐらいで、身長２メートル。中トトロは600歳ぐらい。小トトロは100歳ぐらいだそうです。小学４年生の姉のサツキと４歳の妹のメイは、困っている時に、いつもトトロに助けられました。

　私は宮崎駿さんが「自然を大切にしなさい。森を大切にしなさい。そうすれば、自然も森もあなたを助けてくれますよ。」と言っているような気がします。この変な生き物はいろいろな村にまだいるかも知れませんね。たぶん。

＜5課 - 読む (質問)＞
Reading: Totoro

(Narrator) Now answer the questions for this section.

1. What are the writer's thoughts about "Totoro"?
    (A) This is one of her favorite stories.
    (B) There are many things she did not understand.
    (C) There are some parts that need improvement.
    (D) This must be shown to both children and adults.

2. According to this writer, who is the most adventuresome in this story?
    (A) Totoro
    (B) Mei
    (C) Satsuki
    (D) the father

3. What is NOT a correct description of Totoro?
    (A) Totoro existed even before human beings.
    (B) Totoro eats leaves.
    (C) Totoro lives in a forest.
    (D) Totoro is usually invisible to people.

4. What is a correct description of Totoro?
    (A) Totoro sleeps at night.
    (B) Totoro likes to play the violin.
    (C) Totoro can fly.
    (D) Big Totoro is the youngest.

5. What is the author's opinion about the animator's intention in creating Totoro?
    (A) To respect nature
    (B) To respect animals
    (C) To take care of children
    (D) To promote family values

<5課 - 書く (テキストチャット)>
Text Chat: Your Town

`90秒×6`

You will participate in a simulated exchange of text-chat messages. Each time it is your turn to write, you will have 90 seconds. You should respond as fully and as appropriately as possible.

You will have a conversation about your town with Hideki Matsuo, a student at a Japanese school.

1. Respond. (90 seconds)

   それでは、よろしくお願いします。最初の質問です。住んでいらっしゃる所は何州の何市ですか。都会ですか。田舎(いなか)ですか。

2. Explain your preference. (90 seconds)

   一年の気候(こう)はどうですか。どの季節が一番いいですか。

3. Give specific examples. (90 seconds)

   町で一番有名な観光地(かんこう)やお祭りやお勧(すす)めのお土産(みやげ)などを紹介して下さい。

4. Give a specific example. (90 seconds)

   景色(け)の一番美しい所はどこですか。どんな景(け)色が見えますか。

5. State and justify your opinion. (90 seconds)

   高校生が卒業した後、地元にいた方がいいと思いますか。それとも、ほかの場所へ行った方がいいと思いますか。

6. Ask a specific question. (90 seconds)

   そうですか。ありがとうございました。では、何か僕達の町について質問して下さい。

<5課 - 書く (比較(ひかく)と対比(たいひ))>
Compare and Contrast Article: Living in the City and Living in the Countryside

`20分`

Directions: You are writing an article for the student newspaper of your sister school in Japan. Write an article in which you compare and contrast similarities and differences between living in the city and living in the countryside. Based on your personal experience, describe at least THREE aspects of each and highlight the similarities and differences between living in the city and living in the countryside. Also state your preference for either and give reasons for it.

Your article should be 300 to 400 characters or longer. Use the *desu/masu* or *da* (plain) style, but use one style consistently. Also, use *kanji* wherever *kanji* from the AP Japanese *kanji* list is appropriate. You have 20 minutes to write.

【NOTES/OUTLINE: 自分の作文のアウトラインを書こう！】

Introduction: _____

Three similarities/differences:

  1. _____
  2. _____
  3. _____

Your preference and reasons:
_____
_____

`5課`

＜5課 - 話す (会話)＞
Conversation: Visiting Town

`20秒×4`

You will participate in a simulated conversation. Each time it is your turn to speak, you will have 20 seconds to record. You should respond as fully and as appropriately as possible.

You will have a conversation with Yuko, your Japanese host sister, who is an 8th grader. She will be visiting next week and will be staying with your family.

(Yuko)
(20 seconds)
(Yuko)
(20 seconds)
(Yuko)
(20 seconds)
(Yuko)
(20 seconds)

＜5課 - 話す (日本文化)＞
Cultural Perspective Presentation: Famous Cities in Japan

`4分+2分`

Directions: Imagine you are making an oral presentation to your Japanese class. First, you will be given the topic for your presentation. You will have 4 minutes to prepare your presentation. Then you will have 2 minutes to record your presentation. Your presentation should be as complete as possible.

Discuss at least FIVE aspects or examples of famous cities in Japan. Present your own view or perspective of famous cities in Japan.

Begin with an appropriate introduction, give details, explain your own view or perspective, and end with a concluding remark.

【Let's take notes!】

1. Begin with an appropriate introduction.
   _____

2. Discuss five aspects/examples of the topic.
   1.) _____
   2.) _____
   3.) _____
   4.) _____
   5.) _____

3. Explain your view or perspective.
   _____

4. End with a concluding remark.
   _____

| 6課 | ●●● | 自然と環境(ぜん かんきょう)
Nature and the Environment | ●●● |

【AP® タスク：自然と環境(ぜん かんきょう)】
Discuss the environmental problems we face in the world. What do you think we should do in order to protect nature and the environment? What are you doing now to support this effort?

【文化】日本の地理：Japan's Geography

Both historically and in the modern day, Japan's geography has played a vital role in shaping the lifestyle and culture of the Japanese. Japan's location alongside its giant continental neighbors and Japan's own geographical characteristics make it a unique island country. It is a country known for its abundance of water - both sea water and fresh water.

Japan is an island country surrounded by the vast Pacific Ocean and the Sea of Japan. Within its own boundaries lies Setonaikai, an inland sea nestled between Honshuu and the island of Shikoku. In addition to the four main islands of Honshu, Hokkaido, Kyushu and Shikoku, hundreds of small islands dot the archipelago. Because of its abundant coastlines, Japanese people depend heavily on the ocean for food, industry, commerce and transportation. As an island country, Japan has been able to maintain considerable isolation from the rest of the world until recent generations. Its people are a relatively homogeneous ethnicity and its language and culture quite distinct from others.

It is a small country, only about 1/25 the size of its giant neighbor China and smaller in land area than the state of California. This compact country supports a population of 1.27 million people. Because of Japan's mountainous terrain, habitable spaces are extremely limited, and Japanese have had to learn to live harmoniously in heavily populated communities for centuries.

Japan, an extremely mountainous country, is known for its many active volcanoes. Its highest peak is the picturesque Mt. Fuji, an active volcano. About half of Japan's land area is mountainous, which leaves little arable land. Japan lies above the spot where several continental tectonic plates meet, and therefore experiences many earthquakes throughout the year. Because of its volcanic origins, hot springs are abundant throughout Japan. Many resorts throughout Japan have sprung up around these hot springs, called *onsen* (温泉).

Due to the relatively frequent rainfall through most of the year, rivers are plentiful throughout Japan. They rush down the steep slopes of the mountainous country. The rivers in Japan are relatively short and deep. The longest river, the Shinano River, is 227 miles long. At lower elevations, they form fertile plains, which are ideal for rice growing. Many of the major cities of Japan have sprung up near the mouths of rivers. Rivers have sustained the Japanese with food, transportation, commerce and recreation. Japanese have built dams to provide water for large populations and to furnish electricity.

Japan's position at the northwestern edge of the Pacific Ocean brings warm currents from the south. The climate on the southeastern coasts is therefore generally mild. Western Japan, however, faces the huge continent of Asia. Frigid northern winds from China and Siberia bring heavy snows to the northern and western regions of Japan. The collision of the two contrasting weather systems takes its toll on the island chain. Northernmost Hokkaido sits at the same general latitude as Portland, Oregon, while southernmost Okinawa is located at a latitude that lies just north of Hawaii. Consequently, the climate varies significantly across the archipelago.

The geographic location of Japan and its physical terrain have made an exceptional impact on the history, culture, daily lifestyle, attitudes and demeanor of the Japanese people. The Japanese reverence and worship of nature was born from the powerful influence of geography over the island chain.

Questions to ponder: What specific examples from Japan's history, culture and daily customs can you think of that can ultimately be traced to influences from Japan's geography? How do you think the character of the Japanese was influenced by Japan's geography? Was language influenced too?

6課 ◆◆◆ 復習単語 ◆◆◆

トピック：自然と環境

1. 地球	ちきゅう	N	Earth
2. 海	うみ	N	beach; ocean; sea
3. 山	やま	N	mountain
4. 自然	しぜん	N	nature
5. 環境	かんきょう	N	environment
6. 公害	こうがい	N	pollution
7. 空気	くうき	N	air
8. 影響	えいきょう	N	influence
9. 影響を与える	えいきょうをあたえる	V2	(to) influence
10. 影響を受ける	えいきょうをうける	V2	(to) be influenced
11. 缶	かん	N	can
12. 瓶	びん	N	bottle
13. ごみ		N	rubbish; garbage
14. (ゴミ)を出す	(ゴミ)をだす	V1	(to) take out (the garbage)
15. 燃えないゴミ	もえないゴミ	N	non-flammable garbage
16. 燃えるゴミ	もえるゴミ	N	flammable garbage
17. 問題	もんだい	N	problem
18. ペットボトル		N	plastic bottle
19. プラスチック		N	plastic (hard plastic material)
20. ビニール		N	soft plastic material
21. リサイクル		N	recycling

6課

| 6課 | ★★★ | 新しい単語 | ★★★ |

1. しぜんさいがい＜自然災害＞　N　natural disaster
   日本は自然災害が多い。There are many natural disasters in Japan.
2. じしん＜地震＞　N　earthquake
   東京に大きい地震が起きたら、どうなるんだろうか。I wonder what will happen if a big earthquake occurs in Tokyo.
3. しんど＜震度＞／マグネチュード　N　magnitude
   新潟の地震は震度７だったそうだ。I heard that the earthquake in Niigata was a magnitude 7.
4. しぼうしゃすう＜死亡者数＞　N　number of deaths
   交通事故の死亡者数は今年もう５００人以上だそうだ。I heard that the number of deaths from traffic accidents is already more than 500 this year.
5. ひがい＜被害＞　N　damage
   地震の被害もひどかったそうだ。I heard that the damage from the earthquake was terrible.
6. しげん＜資源＞　N　resources
   資源として、新聞紙をリサイクルしている。I am recycling newspapers as resources.
7. どうろ＜道路＞　N　road
   地震で道路は壊された。The roads were destroyed by the earthquake.
8. ちり＜地理＞　N　geography
   日本の地理をあまりよく知らない。I don't know much about the geography of Japan.
9. とち＜土地＞　N　land; property
   日本の土地は半分が山だそうだ。I understand that half of the land in Japan is mountainous.
10. しょくぶつ＜植物＞　N　plants
    植物からきれいな空気が作られる。One can create clean air from plants.
11. はいきガス＜排気ガス＞　N　(gas) exhaust
    公害の一つの原因は車からの排気ガスだ。One cause of environmental pollution is exhaust.
12. ちきゅうおんだんか＜地球温暖化＞　N　global warming
    地球温暖化によっていろいろな問題が起きている。Various problems are occurring as a result of global warming.
13. ぜんこく＜全国＞　N　nationwide
    地震の時、全国から寄付が送られた。At the time of the earthquake, donations were sent in from all over the nation.

6課

14. とうざいなんぼく＜東西南北＞　N　East, West, South, North
日本の国は東西より南北に長い。Japan is longer south to north than east to west.

15. おく＜億＞　N　one hundred million
日本の人口は1億二千万人ぐらいだ。Japan's population is about a hundred million.

16. おおぜい＜大勢＞　N　many (people)
大勢の人が死んだ。Lots of people died.

17. ほそながい＜細長い＞　A　long and narrow
日本は南北に細長い国だ。Japan is a long, narrow country from south to north.

18. ほうふ＜豊富＞　Na　abundant; wealthy
日本は海産物が豊富だ。Japan has an abundance of ocean products.

19. やく＜約＞〜／およそ〜　PN　about 〜; approximately; roughly
この学校の学生数はおよそ三千人だ。The number of students at this school is about 3,000.

20. おもに＜主に＞　Adv　mainly
日本は主に四つの大きな島からなっている。Japan mainly consists of 4 large islands.

21. (〜が)はっせい＜発生＞する／します　V3　(something) happens; occurs [intransitive]
地震の後、津波は発生しなかった。A tidal wave didn't occur after the earthquake.

22. おそう＜襲う＞／襲います　V1　to attack; assail
日本は毎年たくさんの台風に襲われる。Japan is attacked by many typhoons every year.

23. きゅうじょ＜救助＞(を)する／します　V3　to rescue
きゅうじょかつどう＜救助活動＞　N　rescue activity
多くの人が救助活動に参加した。Lots of people participated in the rescue activity.

24. ひなん＜避難＞(を)する／します　V3　to evacuate
大きい台風が来ているので、たくさんの人が学校の体育館に避難した。Because a large typhoon is coming, many people evacuated to the school gym.

25. (〜が)ふえる＜増える＞／増えます　V2　〜 increases [intransitive]
事故の数が増えている。The number of the accidents is increasing.

26. (〜を)ふやす＜増やす＞／増やします　V1　to increase 〜 [transitive]
「お金を増やしたいんだ。」"I want to increase the amount of money (I have)."

27. (〜が)へる＜減る＞／減ります　V1　〜 decreases [intransitive]
日本は子供の数が減っているそうだ。I heard that the number of children is decreasing in Japan.

6課

28. (～を)へらす＜減らす＞／減らします　V1　to decrease ～ [transitive]
「ごみを減らそう。」 "Let's decrease the trash (we produce)."

29. うえる＜植える＞／植えます　V2　to plant
木を植えて、緑を増やそう。 Let's plant trees and increase the greenery.

30. かんしん＜関心＞がある／あります　V1　to have a concern or interest
この環境問題に関心がある。 I have an interest in this environmental problem.

31. ちゅうい＜注意＞(を)する／します　V3　to warn; to caution
注意して下さい。 Please be careful.

32. フタ／ふた＜蓋＞　N　cover; lid; cap
ペットボトルを捨てる時に、フタは取るように。 When you throw away a water bottle, you should take off the cap.

33. (～に)かこまれている＜囲まれている＞　V1　be surrounded by ～ [passive form of かこむ／かこみます]
日本は海に囲まれている。 Japan is surrounded by ocean.

【もっと単語】

1. かん＜缶＞　　　　　　　　　　　　　N　　can
2. びん／ビン＜瓶＞　　　　　　　　　　N　　bottle
3. ペットボトル　　　　　　　　　　　　N　　plastic water bottle
4. ようき＜容器＞　　　　　　　　　　　N　　container; vessel
5. チラシ　　　　　　　　　　　　　　　N　　leaflet; flier
6. ダンボール＜段ボール＞　　　　　　　N　　cardboard
7. あきばこ＜空き箱＞　　　　　　　　　N　　empty box
8. かみパック＜紙パック＞　　　　　　　N　　(paper) cartons
9. ふるぎ＜古着＞　　　　　　　　　　　N　　old clothing
10. めん＜綿＞　　　　　　　　　　　　　N　　cotton
11. ひも＜紐＞　　　　　　　　　　　　　N　　string; cord
12. しばる＜縛る＞／縛ります　　　　　　V1　to bind; tie
13. つぶす＜潰す＞／潰します　　　　　　V1　to crush; smash
14. ちょうさ＜調査＞　　　　　　　　　　N　　investigate; examination
15. たいへいよう＜太平洋＞　　　　　　　N　　Pacific Ocean
16. たいせいよう＜大西洋＞　　　　　　　N　　Atlantic Ocean

6課

17.	しまぐに＜島国＞	N	island country
18.	かいさんぶつ＜海産物＞	N	ocean products
19.	えいきょう＜影響＞をあたえる＜与える＞／与えます	V2	to influence
20.	えいきょう＜影響＞をうける＜受ける＞／受けます	V2	to be influenced (by)
21.	トランジスタラジオ	N	transistor radio
22.	かいちゅうでんとう＜懐中電灯＞	N	flashlight
23.	こうじょう／こうば＜工場＞	N	factory
24.	わかもの＜若者＞	N	young people; youth
25.	かじ＜火事＞	N	fire [disaster]
26.	こうずい＜洪水＞	N	flood
27.	こおり＜氷＞	N	ice
28.	(〜が)とける＜溶ける＞／溶けます	V2	〜 melts [intransitive]
29.	きふ＜寄付＞をする／します	V3	to donate

6課

6課　　■■■　　　　　　　　　文法(ぶんぽう)　　　　　　　■■■

A. する/しない＋ように＋する　to make a (conscious) effort to do/not to do

Complete each sentence with the cues using this sentence construction.
1. 日本語のクラスでは日本語を_____。（話す）
2. 先生と出来るだけ英語を_____。（話す）
3. 運転(うんてん)しながらケータイを出来るだけ_____。（使う）
4. 車を運転(うんてん)する時、食べたり_____。（飲む）
5. 缶(かん)やペットボトルを_____。（リサイクルする）
6. 排気(はい)ガスをあまり_____。（出す）

B. する/しない＋ために　　in order to/not to do
　　Noun＋の＋ために　　for the sake of ～

Answer the questions in Japanese.
1. 地球温暖化(おんだん)を解決(かいけつ)するために、何をすべきですか。
_____。
2. 教室では何のために電気をたくさん使っていますか。
_____。
3. 環境(かんきょう)を良くするために、家族で何をしていますか。
_____。
4. 家でのゴミを増(ふ)やさないためには、何をすべきだと思いますか。
_____。

C. 友達からの電話　telephone calls from my friends

Restate in English.
1. コンピューターを使うための電気は地球温暖化(おんだん)の原因(げんいん)の一つだ。
_____
2. 環境(かんきょう)についての調査(ちょうさ)をがんばって下さい。
_____
3. 環境(かんきょう)についてのミーティングは何時から？　_____

6課

4. 日本は魚、貝、えび、たこ、いかなどの海産物が豊富だ。
___

5. 日本は地震や台風や火山噴火などの自然災害が多い国だ。
___

6. トランジスターラジオや懐中電灯や飲み水などの準備をしておくことが大事だ。
___

7. 住んでいる所に木や草などの緑の自然がどのくらいありますか。
___

D. 大勢の人   many people
    多くの人   many people
    一人の人   one person

Compare: 1a. パーティーに人が大勢来た。   Many people came to the party.
         1b. 大勢の人がパーティーに来た。   Many people came to the party.
         2a. パーティーに友達が一人来た。   One friend came to the party.
         2b. 一人の友達がパーティーに来た。   One friend came to the party.

Quantifier words such as たくさん、大勢、多く and 一人 are to be treated as nouns when they modify and immediately precede nouns. When they appear before the predicate, however, they are not followed by the particle の.

Circle the best response.

1. 地震で（多く　多くの）人が家をなくした。
2. （多く　多くの）家が火事で焼かれた。
3. ごみを（たくさん　たくさんの）捨てないようにしている。
4. （少し　少しの）人だけがミーティングに来た。
5. 日本は主に（四つ　四つの）大きな島からなっている。
6. （大勢　大勢の）地震で亡くなった。

E. 違うみたいだ。   It seems to be different. (informal)
    違うようだ。   It seems to be different. (formal)

You are talking to your teacher. Change the underlined portions to polite forms.

1.「最近は皆が環境に関心を持って来たみたいだね。嬉しいよ。」

2.「えっ、そう？　ちょっと遅くなったみたいだけど、ミーティングに行かなくちゃ。」

6課

F.	地震がよく起きるので、	Because earthquakes often occur,
	地震が多いので、	Because there are lots of earthquakes,
	地震は危険なので、	Because earthquakes are dangerous,
	地震の国なので、	Because it's a country of (many) earthquakes,

Write な or X (nothing) in the blanks, then choose the correct sentence endings and write the correct letter in the ( ).

1. 日本は海に囲まれている＿＿ので、（ ）　a. 場所によって気候がとても違う。
2. 日本は南北に細長い国＿＿ので、（ ）　b. 地震も多いが、温泉も多い。
3. 日本は資源が少ない＿＿ので、（ ）　c. 飲み水などを準備しておくことが大事だ。
4. 日本は火山が多い＿＿ので、（ ）　d. 地球の皆で協力すべきだ。
5. 日本は自然災害が多い国＿＿ので、（ ）　e. エコ車を買うことにした。
6. 排気ガスを減らしたい＿＿ので、（ ）　f. リサイクルすることが大事だ。
7. 環境は大事＿＿ので、（ ）　g. 海産物が豊富だ。

G.	日本は島国です。	Japan is an island country. (polite form)
	日本は島国だ。	Japan is an island country. (plain form)
	日本は島国である。	Japan is an island country. (expository form)

The polite form is used when speaking to those one is not very familiar with, or when one speaks or writes to an audience. Letters are usually written in the polite form. The plain form is used when speaking to those one is close to or in writing informal compositions, and the expository form is used when writing in a formal expository form.

です、ます体 Polite form	だ体 Plain form	論説体〔ろんせつたい〕 Expository form
知っていない人、目上の人に使う。	年下の人や友達に使う。	論文〔ろんぶん〕、新聞記事などに使う。
犬です。	犬だ。	犬である。
犬じゃありません。	犬じゃない。	犬ではない。
話す時は「ね、よ」などを文の終わりにつける	話す時は「ね、よ」などを文の終わりにつける。	書く時だけ使う。「ね、よ」などを文の終わりにつけない。

Change the following style of the article, written in the expository form, to the polite form.

日本は小さい国で、資源が少ないので、リサイクルはとても大事である。「まぜればゴミ、分ければ資源」という言葉を聞いたことがあるだろうか。いろいろな色の袋にゴミを分けるのは大変だが、ぜひ分けてほしい。皆でマナーを守ろう。

6課

6課 アクティビティー

A. 日本文化：一人か二人ワーク→クラスワーク

Divide the topics below among your classmates and research your topic on the Internet. Using visuals, present your findings with your classmates.

1. 東日本大震災、熊本地震、日本のプレート
2. 富士山噴火の歴史
3. 日本の台風シーズン、台風の数

B. 聞く Pre-Listening Activity「地震〔じしん〕」：ペアワーク→クラスワーク

What natural disasters occur in Japan and in the area where you live? Determine the 3 most common natural disasters you experience near your home. Mark the most common 1, next common 2, and the least common of the 3 with a 3.

日本の自然災害：

_____ 地震　　　_____ 津波　　　_____ 台風/ハリケーン　　_____ 竜巻 (tornado)
_____ 干ばつ (drought) _____ 山火事　_____ 噴火　　_____ 洪水 (flood)

私の住んでいる所の自然災害：

_____ 地震　　　_____ 津波　　　_____ 台風/ハリケーン　　_____ 竜巻 (tornado)
_____ 干ばつ (drought) _____ 山火事　_____ 噴火　　_____ 洪水 (flood)

C. 聞く Post-Listening Activity「地震〔じしん〕」：ペアワーク→クラスワーク

Make an oral presentation about Japan's natural disasters. Begin with an appropriate introduction, give five aspects of Japanese natural disasters, explain your own view or perspective, and end with a concluding remark. Prepare for 4 minutes and present for 2 minutes.

【Let's take notes!】

1. Begin with an appropriate introduction.
   _____

2. Discuss five aspects of the topic.
   1.) _____
   2.) _____
   3.) _____
   4.) _____
   5.) _____

3. Explain your view or perspective.
   _____

4. End with a concluding remark.
   _____

6課

D. 読む Pre-Reading Activity 「リサイクル」：ペアワーク→クラスワーク

Place a check before the items you recycle, then match each Japanese word with its English equivalent from the right.

資源として、リサイクルしていますか。

___ 1. アルミ缶　　　　　　（　）　　a. fliers
___ 2. スチール缶　　　　　（　）　　b. cartons
___ 3. ビン　　　　　　　　（　）　　c. old clothes (cotton)
___ 4. 油ビン　　　　　　　（　）　　d. magazines
___ 5. ペットボトル　　　　（　）　　e. books
___ 6. プラスチック容器　　（　）　　f. empty boxes
___ 7. 新聞紙　　　　　　　（　）　　g. cardboard boxes
___ 8. チラシ　　　　　　　（　）　　h. aluminum cans
___ 9. ダンボール　　　　　（　）　　i. newspapers
___ 10. 本　　　　　　　　（　）　　j. plastic bottles
___ 11. 雑誌　　　　　　　（　）　　k. oil bottles
___ 12. 空き箱　　　　　　（　）　　l. plastic containers
___ 13. 紙パック　　　　　（　）　　m. steel cans
___ 14. 古着（綿）　　　　（　）　　n. glass bottles

E. 読む Post-Reading Activity 「リサイクル」：ペアワーク→クラスワーク

Make an oral presentation about recycling in Japan. Begin with an appropriate introduction, give five aspects of Japanese recycling, explain your own view or perspective, and end with a concluding remark. Prepare for 4 minutes and present for 2 minutes.

【Let's take notes!】

1. Begin with an appropriate introduction.

_____

2. Discuss five aspects of the topic.

　　1.) _____
　　2.) _____
　　3.) _____
　　4.) _____
　　5.) _____

3. Explain your view or perspective.

_____

4. End with a concluding remark.

_____

6課

F. テキストチャット「地球温暖化〔ちきゅうおんだんか〕」：ペアワーク→クラスワーク
   a. Discuss the following topics with your partner and share them with your class.
1. 地球温暖化によってどんな問題が起きているか。
   a. 気温がもっと高くなっている。　　　　　　　　　　　　（はい　いいえ）
   b. 台風やハリケーンがもっと大きくなっている。　　　　　（はい　いいえ）
   c. 北極 (North Pole) や南極 (South Pole) の氷が溶け始めている。（はい　いいえ）
   d. 地震がもっと増えている。　　　　　　　　　　　　　　（はい　いいえ）
   e. その他 _____
2. 地球温暖化を起こしている原因は何か。
   a. 自動車からの排気ガス　　　　　　　　　　　　　　　　（はい　いいえ）
   b. 工場から出る CO_2　　　　　　　　　　　　　　　　　（はい　いいえ）
   c. コンピューターを使うための電気　　　　　　　　　　　（はい　いいえ）
   d. その他 _____
3. 私達は地球温暖化を解決するために何をするべきか。
   a. 木を植える。　　　　　　　　　　　　　　　　　　　　（はい　いいえ）
   b. 森の木を切る。　　　　　　　　　　　　　　　　　　　（はい　いいえ）
   c. 自動車の運転を減らす。　　　　　　　　　　　　　　　（はい　いいえ）
   d. ごみをたくさん捨てる。　　　　　　　　　　　　　　　（はい　いいえ）
   e. エアコンを使う。　　　　　　　　　　　　　　　　　　（はい　いいえ）
   f. その他 _____

b. Circle the responses that best describe your situation and fill in the blanks with your ideas.
1. 私は環境問題に関心（があります　はありません）。
2. 私は喜んで（協力します　協力しません）。
3. 私が住んでいる所には、木や草などの緑の自然が（多い　少ない）です。
4. 私が住んでいる所は、自然環境が（いい　悪い）です。
5. 私が住んでいる所は、空気や水が（きたない　きれい）です。
6. うちでは_____をリサイクルしています。
7. 学校では_____をリサイクルしています。
8. 地球温暖化についての私の考え：_____。
9. 日本の環境問題についての私の質問：_____。
10. 環境は大事ですから、話し合えて良かったです。この環境についての調査、
    （終わって下さい　がんばって下さい）。

6課

G. Compare & Contrast「植物〔しょくぶつ〕と動物」：ペアワーク→クラスワーク

Prepare a compare and contrast article about plants and animals. Fill in the blanks below. Complete your article in 5 minutes.

	One sentence	Elaborate.
Intro.	これから植物と動物をくらべてみます。	植物と動物は違うことも同じこともあります。
1st Similarity/ Difference	まず、一つ目の違うことは、植物は＿＿＿＿＿＿＿＿が、動物は＿＿＿＿＿＿＿＿。	
2nd Similarity/ Difference	次に、＿＿＿＿＿＿＿＿は、＿＿＿＿＿＿＿＿。	
3rd Similarity/ Difference	次に、＿＿＿＿＿＿＿＿は、＿＿＿＿＿＿＿＿。	
Preference	私は＿＿＿＿＿より＿＿＿＿＿の方が好きです。	
Reasons	なぜなら、＿＿＿＿＿＿＿＿＿＿＿＿＿＿＿＿＿＿＿＿＿＿からです。	

H. 会話「環境〔かんきょう〕」：ペアワーク→クラスワーク

a. Change the underlined sections to the appropriate polite forms.

1. 昨日、家族でハイブリッド車を<u>買ったんだ</u>。かっこ<u>いいよ</u>。

2. 家族で環境を良くするために何か<u>している</u>？

3. あっ、<u>そう？</u> アメリカ人も最近だんだん自然環境を<u>守らなくちゃいけない</u>と思って来たみたいで、<u>嬉しいよ</u>。

4. そうそう、今日の放課後、学校の環境についてのミーティングがある<u>そうだけど</u>、<u>行く</u>？

b. Carry on a conversation with your partner in the polite form first, then in the informal form. Each time, answer in 20 seconds. The answers should be as thorough as possible. Take turns.

6課

I. 文化発表「日本の地理」：ペアワーク→クラスワーク

a. Circle the correct responses.
1. 日本は（ほかの国に　海　山）に囲まれている。
2. 日本の南には（太平洋　大西洋　日本海　瀬戸内海）がある。
3. 日本は主に北海道、本州、四国、九州の四つの大きな（町　県　島）からなっている。
4. 日本は（東西　南北）に細長い島国である。
5. 日本の北と南の（気候）はよく違う。
6. 日本は魚、貝、えび、たこ、いかなどの（肉　野菜　海産物）が豊富である。
7. 日本の人口は（二千万　一億二千万　二億）ぐらいで、とても込んでいる。
8. 日本の土地のおよそ（半分　三分の一　四分の一）ぐらいは山である。
9. 日本の広さは（カリフォルニア　フロリダ　メイン）州ぐらいである。
10. 日本は火山が多いので、（津波　地震　台風）も多いが、温泉も多い。

b. Questions to ponder: Answer the following questions in Japanese.
1. What specific examples from Japan's history, culture and daily customs can you think of that can ultimately be traced to influences from Japan's geography?
   _____
   _____

2. How has the character of the Japanese been influenced by Japan's geography?
   _____
   _____

3. Has the language been influenced by Japan's geography? How?
   _____
   _____

6課

<6課 - 聞く>

Listening: Earthquakes

【You may take notes while listening. Do not look at the questions below before listening. You will have 12 seconds to answer each question. You may NOT move back and forth among questions.】

(Narrator) Now you will listen once to a report.

(Narrator) Now answer the questions for this selection.

1. When did the Kobe Earthquake happen?
    (A) January 19th, 1995
    (B) February 17th, 1995
    (C) January 17th, 1995
    (D) January 19th, 1985

2. What was the magnitude of the Kobe Earthquake?
    (A) Magnitude 7.0
    (B) Magnitude 7.2
    (C) Magnitude 8.0
    (D) Magnitude 8.2

3. What damage did NOT occur during the Kobe Earthquake?
    (A) Many buildings and roads were destroyed.
    (B) Many houses burned.
    (C) Almost 5,300 people died.
    (D) Many houses were destroyed by a tidal wave.

4. What did NOT happen soon after the Kobe Earthquake?
    (A) Many people evacuated to school gyms.
    (B) Many young volunteers went to Kobe to assist with the recovery.
    (C) Many young volunteers came from the Tokyo area.
    (D) Many people donated things and money to the people of Kobe.

5. What is the purpose of this announcement?
    (A) To ask people to evacuate in case of another possible disaster.
    (B) To explain the effects of the disaster and how to prepare for another possible disaster.
    (C) To explain the importance of community service and encouraging people to participate in it.
    (D) To report damage from earthquakes in Japan in general.

<6課 - 読む>

Reading: Web Page on Recycling

【You may move back and forth among all the questions.】

資源ゴミの分け方と出し方
「まぜればゴミ、分ければ資源」マナーを守りましょう。

緑色袋・・・缶・ビン

- [アルミ] [スチール] マークのある缶、ビン【※ 油ビンは赤袋に出す】
- 中身を空にし、洗って、水切りをする。

（注意！）ビンのフタは必ず取り外し赤袋に出す。

黄色袋・・・ペットボトル

- [PET 1] マークのあるもの。
- フタを取り、中身を空にし、洗って、水切りをする。
- つぶさない。

（注意！）フタ（プラスチック製キャップ）は必ず取り外し赤袋に出す。

水色袋・・・プラスチック類

- [プラ] マークのあるもの、又は、食品・商品の容器・包装に使われていたプラスチックやビニール
- 中身を空にし、洗って、水切りをする。

【※ 洗っても汚れの取れないものは、透明袋（燃えるゴミ）に出す】

ひもで十字にしばる・・・その他の資源ゴミ

- 新聞紙、折り込みチラシ
- ダンボール
- 本、雑誌、空き箱など　　　それぞれ別々にひもで十字にしばる。
- 紙パック
- 古着（綿100％のみ）

＜6課 - 読む (質問)＞

Reading: Web Page on Recycling

(Narrator) Now answer the questions for this section.

1. What color are the bags for empty cans and bottles?
   - (A) blue
   - (B) green
   - (C) yellow
   - (D) red

2. What color are the bags for old plastic trays and containers?
   - (A) blue
   - (B) green
   - (C) yellow
   - (D) red

3. What should you NOT do before putting empty plastic bottles in the bags?
   - (A) remove the caps
   - (B) wash the inside
   - (C) dry the inside
   - (D) crush the plastic bottles

4. Which should NOT be disposed of in the red bag?
   - (A) glass bottle caps
   - (B) plastic bottle caps
   - (C) dirty plastic trays and containers
   - (D) oil bottles

5. What does NOT have to be tied in bundles for recycling?
   - (A) newspapers
   - (B) empty boxes
   - (C) used 100% cotton clothes
   - (D) underwear

＜6課 - 書く (テキストチャット)＞

90秒×6

Text Chat: Environment

You will participate in a simulated exchange of text-chat messages. Each time it is your turn to write, you will have 90 seconds. You should respond as fully and as appropriately as possible.

You will have a conversation with Maki Tokuda, a student in your host school in Japan. She is researching environmental problems.

1. Respond. (90 seconds)
   初めまして。徳田です。どうぞよろしく。環境について調べています。御協力お願いします。
2. Describe. (90 seconds)
   今住んでいる所に、木や草などの緑の自然がどのぐらいありますか。
3. Describe. (90 seconds)
   住んでいる所の環境はどうですか。公害で空気や水はきたなくありませんか。
4. Give specific examples. (90 seconds)
   うちや学校でどんなリサイクルをしていますか。
5. State your opinion. (90 seconds)
   そうですか。最近、地球温暖化が問題になっていますが、御意見をお聞かせください。
6. Ask a specific question. (90 seconds)
   今日はどうも貴重な意見を有難うございました。日本の環境問題について何か質問がありますか。

＜6課 - 書く (比較と対比)＞

20分

Compare and Contrast Article: Plants and Animals

Directions: You are writing an article for the student newspaper of your sister school in Japan. Write an article in which you compare and contrast similarities and differences between plants and animals. Based on your personal experience, describe at least THREE aspects of each and highlight the similarities and differences between plants and animals. Also state your preference for either and give reasons for it.

Your article should be 300 to 400 characters or longer. Use the *desu/masu* or *da* (plain) style, but use one style consistently. Also, use *kanji* wherever *kanji* from the AP Japanese *kanji* list is appropriate. You have 20 minutes to write.

【NOTES/OUTLINE: 自分の作文のアウトラインを書こう！】

Introduction:
_____

Three similarities/differences:

 1. _____
 2. _____
 3. _____

Your preference and give reasons:
_____
_____

6課

＜6課 - 話す (会話)＞
Conversation: Environment

`20秒×4`

You will participate in a simulated conversation. Each time it is your turn to speak, you will have 20 seconds to record. You should respond as fully and as appropriately as possible.

You will have a conversation with Masa, your Japanese friend, about the environment.

(Masa)
(20 seconds)
(Masa)
(20 seconds)
(Masa)
(20 seconds)
(Masa)
(20 seconds)

＜6課 - 話す (日本文化)＞
Cultural Perspective Presentation: Japanese Geography

`4分+2分`

Directions: Imagine you are making an oral presentation to your Japanese class. First, you will read and hear the topic for your presentation. You will have 4 minutes to prepare your presentation. Then you will have 2 minutes to record your presentation. Your presentation should be as complete as possible.

Present your own view or perspective of Japanese geography. Discuss at least FIVE aspects or examples of Japanese geography.

Begin with an appropriate introduction, give details, explain your own view or perspective, and end with a concluding remark.

【Let's take notes!】

1. Begin with an appropriate introduction.

   _____

2. Discuss five aspects/examples of the topic.

   1.) _____
   2.) _____
   3.) _____
   4.) _____
   5.) _____

3. Explain your view or perspective.

   _____

4. End with a concluding remark.

   _____

6課

7課　学校と教育
School and Education

【AP® タスク：学校と教育】

Where are you in your college application process? What are the most important factors you will consider when selecting a college? What are the true goals of education? What are some of your immediate academic goals? Once you are admitted to the college of your choice, will you continue to be motivated to study? Do you think your attitude toward education after graduating from high school and after college will change? What are your life goals?

【文化】 日本の教育システム：Japanese Educational System

The modern Japanese school system was modeled after the European and American educational systems. Although there may soon be changes in the structure of the school system, it has traditionally been based on a 6-3-3-4 system, with elementary schools being 6 years, middle schools and high schools being 3 years each, and college being 4 years.

Before elementary school, many Japanese children attend preschool, called 保育園 (*hoikuen*) or kindergartens, called 幼稚園 (*yoochien*). Kindergarten is not compulsory, and thus most kindergartens and preschools are privately operated. *Hoikuen*, or child care centers, admit children at the age of one or younger. Children remain in *yoochien* until they are 6.

Elementary school (小学校), known as *shoogakkoo*, begins at grade one when children are 6 years old. Grades 1 through 9 are compulsory in Japan. The average class size for an elementary classroom is 30-40 students, and most subjects are the same as in American schools. In addition, elementary schools have begun to introduce English as a foreign language. Japanese children work in teams to clean their classrooms, halls and campuses. The students also serve the meals that is eaten in cafeterias or classrooms.

Middle school, or *chuugakkoo* (中学校), encompasses grades 7 through 9. At this point, more students switch to private schools, particularly among those whose parents want to spare their children the examination hell that accompanies entrance to top-tier schools. At most private schools attached to universities, students do not have to undergo competitive college entrance exams. Although Japanese are only required to complete grade nine, 98% of ninth graders advance to high school.

High schools, *kootoogakkoo* (高等学校), begin at the tenth grade. By this level, about 25% of students attend private schools, some of which are the most elite schools in Japan. There are also national high schools and public high schools. At this level, students are tracked and directed toward academic studies or specialized vocational studies based on their performance on exams. Students who wish to enter good high schools spend an inordinate amount of time preparing for entrance exams. They attend *juku* (cram schools) after regular classes and return home late to continue more studies.

If, after taking the infamous university exams, students are not admitted, they become what is known as *roonin*, 浪人, a term formerly used to describe masterless samurai. These students then spend the next year or more studying full-time at schools called *yobikoo*, which are private schools that prepare students for college entrance. About 45% of Japan's high school graduates advance to four-year colleges or junior colleges. Junior colleges and specialty schools train specialists in computer science, cooking, health sciences, and agriculture. There are about 710 four year universities in Japan, of which about three-quarters are private. Although many universities are now attempting to make changes, college in Japan is viewed as a playground, where students feel they can be rewarded for their years of study through high school. Only about 7% of college graduates continue on to graduate studies, as compared to 13% in the U.S.

In years past, Japan's educational system was revered, but in a rapidly changing world, Japan faces many issues, particularly with the decrease in the number of children in Japan. Some of Japan's most cherished values, such as educating its children about the value of consensus, hierarchy and in vs. out groups, may be seriously challenged.

Questions to ponder: Why do you think the educational system in Japan is being re-evaluated? What is the function of education in Japan?

7課		復習単語		

トピック：学校と教育

1. 学校	がっこう	N	school	
2. 公立	こうりつ	N	public	
3. 私立	しりつ	N	private	
4. 男子校	だんしこう	N	boy's school	
5. 女子校	じょしこう	N	girl's school	
6. (男女)共学	(だんじょ)きょうがく	N	co-educational	
7. 制服	せいふく	N	uniform (clothing)	
8. 先生	せんせい	N	teacher; Mr./Mrs./Ms./Dr.	
9. 生徒	せいと	N	student [non-college]	
10. 学生	がくせい	N	student [college]	
11. 幼稚園	ようちえん	N	kindergarten	
12. 何年生	なんねんせい	Ni	what grade	
13. 中学	ちゅうがく	N	intermediate school	
14. 中学生	ちゅうがくせい	N	intermediate school student	
15. 中学一年生	ちゅうがくいちねんせい	N	seventh grader	
16. 中学二年生	ちゅうがくにねんせい	N	eighth grader	
17. 中学三年生	ちゅうがくさんねんせい	N	freshman; ninth grader	
18. 高校	こうこう	N	high school	
19. 高校生	こうこうせい	N	high school student	
20. 高校一年生	こうこういちねんせい	N	high school sophomore; tenth grader	
21. 高校二年生	こうこうにねんせい	N	high school junior; eleventh grader	
22. 高校三年生	こうこうさんねんせい	N	high school senior; twelfthth grader	
23. 大学	だいがく	N	college; university	
24. 大学生	だいがくせい	N	college student	
25. 大学院	だいがくいん	N	graduate school	
26. 教育	きょういく	N	education	
27. 教える	おしえる	V2	(to) teach	
28. 教室	きょうしつ	N	classroom	
29. 教科書	きょうかしょ	N	textbook	
30. テキスト		N	textbook	
31. クラス		N	class	
32. 授業	じゅぎょう	N	class; instruction	

7課

33. 授業料	じゅぎょうりょう	N	tuition
34. 奨学金	しょうがくきん	N	scholarship
35. 学期	がっき	N	semester
36. 一学期	いちがっき	N	first semester
37. 今学期	こんがっき	N	this semester
38. 先学期	せんがっき	N	last semester
39. 来学期	らいがっき	N	next semester
40. 毎学期	まいがっき	N	every semester
41. 試験	しけん	N	exam
42. 試験を受ける	しけんをうける	V2	(to) take an exam
43. 小テスト	しょうテスト	N	quiz
44. 宿題	しゅくだい	N	homework
45. 成績	せいせき	N	grade
46. 専攻(を)する	せんこう(を)する	V3	(to) major (in)
47. 卒業する	そつぎょうする	V3	(to) graduate (from a school)
48. 卒業式	そつぎょうしき	N	graduation ceremony
49. 科目	かもく	N	subject
50. 外国語	がいこくご	N	foreign language
51. 英語	えいご	N	English
52. 日本語	にほんご	N	Japanese language
53. 中国語	ちゅうごくご	N	Chinese language
54. 韓国語	かんこくご	N	Korean language
55. フランス語	フランスご	N	French language
56. ドイツ語	ドイツご	N	German language
57. 文学	ぶんがく	N	literature
58. 数学	すうがく	N	math
59. 理科	りか	N	science (elementary and middle school)
60. 科学	かがく	N	science
61. 化学	かがく	N	chemistry
62. 物理	ぶつり	N	physics
63. 会計学	かいけいがく	N	accounting
64. エンジニア		N	engineer
65. 歴史	れきし	N	history
66. 社会	しゃかい	N	social studies; society
67. 音楽	おんがく	N	music
68. 体育	たいいく	N	P.E.

7課

#	漢字	かな	品詞	英語
69.	体育館	たいいくかん	N	gym
70.	運動場	うんどうじょう	N	athletic field
71.	図書館	としょかん	N	library
72.	カフェテリア		N	cafeteria
73.	スナックバー		N	snack bar
74.	ロッカー		N	locker
75.	寮	りょう	N	dormitory
76.	放課後	ほうかご	N	after school
77.	部活(動)	ぶかつ（どう）	N	club activity
78.	書道	しょどう	N	calligraphy
79.	茶道	さどう or ちゃどう	N	tea ceremony
80.	初級	しょきゅう	N	beginner level
81.	コンクール		N	competition [music]
82.	賞	しょう	N	award; prize
83.	塾	じゅく	N	cram school
84.	レポート		N	report; paper
85.	タイプ(を)する		V3	(to) type
86.	詩	し	N	poem
87.	訳	やく	N	translation
88.	訳す	やくす	V1	(to) translate
89.	英和辞典	えいわじてん	N	English-Japanese dictionary
90.	和英辞典	わえいじてん	N	Japanese-English dictionary
91.	漢字辞典	かんじじてん	N	*kanji* dictionary
92.	留学(を)する	りゅうがく(を)する	V3	(to) study abroad
93.	証明書	しょうめいしょ	N	I.D.
94.	推薦(を)する	すいせん(を)する	V3	(to) recommend
95.	推薦状	すいせんじょう	N	recommendation
96.	(お)休み	(お)やすみ	N	day off; vacation
97.	休み時間	やすみじかん	N	(a) break
98.	休む	やすむ	V1	(to) be absent (from〜)
99.	ホームルーム		N	homeroom
100.	スクールバス		N	school bus
101.	カンニング		N	cheating
102.	いじめ		N	bullying
103.	机	つくえ	N	desk
104.	ユニフォーム		N	(sports) uniform

7課

7課 ★★★　新しい単語　★★★

1. ほいくえん＜保育園＞　N　preschool; nursery school
   妹は家の近くの保育園に通っている。 My younger sister is attending a nearby preschool.
2. しゅうしごう＜修士号＞　N　master's degree
   姉は今、大学院で修士号を取っている。 My older sister is now pursuing a master's degree in graduate school.
3. はかせごう＜博士号＞　N　doctorate degree
   ゴードン博士は物理の博士号を持っているそうだ。 I understand that Professor Gordon has a Ph.D. in physics.
4. たんにん＜担任＞　N　in charge
   担任の先生はとてもやさしい。 The teacher in charge of us (i.e., homeroom teacher) is very kind.
5. せいとすう＜生徒数＞　N　number of students; enrollment
   学校の全生徒数はおよそ５００人ぐらいだ。 The total enrollment of the school is roughly 500.
6. めいもん＜名門＞　N　distinguished; prestigious
   めいもんこう＜名門校＞　N　well-known school
   プリンストン大学のような名門校に行きたい。 I want to go to a prestigious school like Princeton.
7. せいど＜制度＞　N　system
   日本の教育制度がいいかどうか知らない。 I don't know if Japan's educational system is good.
8. ぎむきょういく＜義務教育＞　N　compulsory education
   日本では高校は義務教育ではないそうだ。 I understand that in Japan, a high school education is not compulsory.
9. びょうどう＜平等＞　N　equal
   誰もが自由で平等な社会に住みたい。 Everyone wants to live in a free society.
10. だい＜題＞　N　title; topic
    大学エッセイの一つの題は私の好きな本についてだった。 One of the topics of the college essays was "my favorite books."
11. けっか＜結果＞　N　results
    試験の結果は悪くなかった。 The exam results were not bad.

12. かのうせい＜可能性＞　N　possibility
　　希望の大学に合格できる可能性は何パーセントぐらいかな。　I wonder what percent of a possibility I have of being admitted to the college of my choice?

13. げんきん＜現金＞　N　cash
　　現金は持って来ないで下さい。　Please do not bring cash.

14. ほうせき＜宝石＞　N　jewelry; jewel; gem
　　あの歌手は高価な宝石をしている。　That singer is wearing expensive jewelry.

15. どうぐ＜道具＞　N　equipment; tools; utensils
　　キャンプにゲームの道具を持って行く。　I will bring the equipment for the games to camp.

16. しょうひん＜賞品＞　N　prize
　　ゲームに勝って、いい賞品をもらった。　I won the game and received a good prize.

17. きんきょう＜近況＞　N　current situation; recent state (of things)
　　メールで近況を知らせて下さい。　Please inform me of the current conditions by e-mail.

18. じょうじゅん＜上旬＞　N　the first third of a month; beginning of the month
　　ちゅうじゅん＜中旬＞　N　the middle third of the month
　　げじゅん＜下旬＞　N　the last third of a month; end of the month
　　大学の結果は４月の上旬に知らされるそうだ。　I understand that we will be informed of the results from the college in the beginning of April.

19. すうねんご＜数年後＞　N　a number of years after; several years later
　　大学を卒業して数年後やっと仕事が見つかった。　After graduating from college, I finally found a job several years later.

20. こうか＜高価＞　Na　expensive
　　彼女は高価な指輪をしている。　She is wearing an expensive ring.

21. ねっしん＜熱心＞　Ns　enthusiastic; eager; earnest
　　母は教育に熱心だ。　My mother is enthusiastic about education.

22. つうち＜通知＞(を)する／します　V3　to notify; inform
　　つうちひょう＜通知表＞　N　report card
　　大学から４月の初めごろ通知をもらうらしい。　It seems we receive our report cards from the university about the beginning of April.

23. しんがく＜進学＞(を)する／します　V3　to advance to higher education; to be admitted to higher education.
　　大学進学について先生と相談した。　I consulted with the teacher about college admissions.

7課

24. めんせつ＜面接＞(を)する／します　V3　to interview
昨日ホテルで大学の面接があった。　Yesterday, I had a college interview at a hotel.

25. けんきゅう＜研究＞(を)する／します　V3　to research
父は薬について研究しているそうだ。　I understand my father is researching some drug.

26. さいかい＜再会＞(を)する／します　V3　to reunite
私は友達に１０年ぶりに再会した。　I reunited with my friends after 10 years.

27. にゅうがく＜入学＞(を)する／します　V3　to enter a school/college; matriculation
にゅうがくしけん＜入学試験＞　N　entrance exam
にゅうがくしき＜入学式＞　school entrance ceremonies; matriculation
この学校への入学は難しい。　Entrance into this school is difficult.

28. そうりつ＜創立＞(を)する／します　V3　to establish
そうりつしゃ＜創立者＞　N　founders (of an establishment or institution)
学校は１８６８年に宣教師によって創立された。　The school was founded in 1868 by missionaries.

29. まねく＜招く＞／招きます　V1　to invite [informal equivalent of 招待〔しょうたい〕する]
私はパーティーに招かれた。　I was invited to the party.

30. はなれる＜離れる＞／離れます　V2　to separate (from); to part (from)
来年大学に行くために、家を離れなければならない。　Next year, I have to leave home in order to go to college.

【もっと単語】

1. がんしょ＜願書＞　　　　　　　　　　　　N　application form
2. しめきり＜締切＞　　　　　　　　　　　　N　deadline
3. すいせんじょう＜推薦状＞　　　　　　　　N　recommendation
4. しょうがくきん＜奨学金＞　　　　　　　　N　scholarship
5. もうしこむ＜申し込む＞／申し込みます　　V1　to apply; submit an application
6. ごうかく＜合格＞(を)する／します　　　　V3　to be admitted (to a school); to pass an exam
7. ひやけどめ＜日焼け止め＞クリーム　　　　N　sunscreen; sunblock

7課 文法

> A. Verb (Dictionary form/Nai form) ＋こと   "(You) must/should do ～"
>   [instruction, direction, resolution, command]
>
>   Verb (Dictionary form/Nai form) ＋ように   "(You) must/should do ～"
>   [instruction, direction, urging, reminder]
>
> Although either may be used in some situations, ことmay be used when directing others to do something or resolving to do something oneself. ように is used to give direction to others in a way that urges others to do something and is less commanding in manner.
>   Compare:
>   1a.「宿題をする<u>こと</u>。」   "Do your/my homework."
>   1b.「宿題をする<u>ように</u>。」   "Do your homework."
>   2a.「宿題を忘れない<u>こと</u>。」   "Don't forget your/my homework."
>   2b.「宿題を忘れない<u>ように</u>。」   "Don't forget your homework."

a. You are writing your goals for your work in Japanese class. Fill in the blanks with the appropriate verb from the box and circle the correct ending.

1. 英語を＿＿＿＿＿＿＿（こと　ように）。
2. もっと日本語を＿＿＿＿＿＿＿（こと　ように）。
3. 漢字をもっと＿＿＿＿＿＿＿（こと　ように）。
4. いい成績を＿＿＿＿＿＿＿（こと　ように）。

| 話す |
| もらう |
| 話さない |
| 勉強する |

b. Your teacher is giving reminders to your classmates about Japanese language camp. Fill in the blanks with the appropriate verb from the list and circle the correct ending.

1. バス停に八時に＿＿＿＿＿＿＿（こと　ように）。
2. くつかサンダルを＿＿＿＿＿＿＿（こと　ように）。
3. ゲームを＿＿＿＿＿＿＿（こと　ように）。
4. ずっと日本語を＿＿＿＿＿＿＿（こと　ように）。

| はく |
| 話す |
| 集合する |
| 準備する |

> B. ～ように(と)言う   tell ～ to; say ～ in such a way
> ように follows verbs in the dictionary or NAI form. It is used when one states that a certain message has been conveyed by another person. When used with the NAI form, this form suggests that the message conveyed some kind of prohibition. と is optional.

Fill in the blanks with the appropriate verb from the list.

1. 両親はいつも運転には気をつけるように(と)＿＿＿＿＿＿＿。
2. お弁当を配達していただくように(と)＿＿＿＿＿＿＿。
3. 教室でケータイを使わないように(と)先生に＿＿＿＿＿＿＿。
4. もっと速く日本語を話すように(と)アドバイスを＿＿＿＿＿＿＿。

| 注意された |
| 言う |
| もらった |
| 頼んである |

7課

C. 〜と、
   〜たら、
   〜ば、

All of the above express as "If ..." Although they may be interchangeable in usage, there are certain restrictions on each.

a. Verb (Dictionary/ NAI form - Nonpast Plain form) ＋ と、Sentence 2.
Normally used when stating fact, mathematical or scientific principles. Is not generally used when expressing opinion or information of a personal nature.

1. 右にまがると、大きいデパートがある。
   If you turn right, there is a large department store.
2. 冬になると、雪が降る。
   When it becomes winter, it will snow.

b. Verb (TA/ NAKATTA form) ＋ら、Sentence 2.
Used to make general statements, often of a more personal nature. Sentence 2 (the main clause) may express volition, suggestion, invitation, request, permission, prohibition or opinion. Though it is considered a conditional, -たら is also often expressed as "When."

3. お酒を飲んだら、ぜったい車を運転してはいけない。
   When you drink alcohol, you definitely should not drive a car.
4. このハワイ旅行クイズが当たったら、一緒にハワイへ行こう。
   If I win this game for a trip to Hawaii, let's go to Hawaii together.

c. Verb (-ば)、Sentence 2.
Used in hypothetical statements, i.e., "if and only if . . ."
   いAdjective (-ば)、Sentence 2.
   なAdjective (なら)、Sentence 2.
   Noun   (なら)、Sentence 2.

5. (もし)試験が明日なら、今日勉強しなくちゃいけない。
   If the exam is tomorrow, I have to study today.
6. 日本の大学へ行けば、日本語が上手になるでしょう。
   If I go to college in Japan, my Japanese will probably become good.

Fill in the blanks with the appropriate form of the cues in the ( ).

1. もし明日雨が＿＿＿＿＿＿＿、キャンプは中止します。（降る）
2. ＿＿＿＿＿＿＿、さびしくなるなあ。（卒業する）
3. 彼に＿＿＿＿＿＿＿、嬉しくなる。（会う）
4. 今、千ドル＿＿＿＿＿＿＿、何を買う？（ある）
5. 銀行はこの道をまっすぐ＿＿＿＿＿＿＿、右側にあります。（行く）
6. 合格が＿＿＿＿＿＿＿、パーティーをしよう。（決まる）
7. 奨学金が＿＿＿＿＿＿＿、私は大学に行けない。（もらえない）
8. 毎年、春に＿＿＿＿＿＿＿、この公園は桜の花でピンクになる。（なる）
9. もしお天気が＿＿＿＿＿＿＿、ピクニックはやめよう。（悪い）
10. 将来もし日本に留学＿＿＿＿＿＿＿、ぜひ京都に行ってみたい。（出来る）

7課

> D. 〜んだって。　　(He/she) said that.../ (I) understand that... [informal use]
>
> This form is used informally when stating a quote or in stating information one has learned from a secondary source. It is used in situations similar to those used in the hearsay そうです construction. When one speaks to a person who is close, one uses the だって ending while the more polite ending is ですって. Plain verb forms, いadjective forms, なadjectives + な, and nouns + な, followed by ん appear before だって／ですって.
>
> | | | |
> |---|---|---|
> | Verb (plain form) ＋んだって。 | 行く／行かない＋んだって。 | |
> | | 行った／行かなかった＋んだって。 | |
> | いadjective ＋んだって。 | 安い／安くない＋んだって。 | |
> | | 安かった／安くなかった＋んだって。 | |
> | なadjective ＋ な ＋んだって。 | 好きな／好きじゃない＋んだって。 | |
> | | 好きだった／好きじゃなかった＋んだって。 | |
> | noun ＋ な ＋んだって。 | 三時な／三時じゃない＋んだって。 | |
> | | 三時だった／三時じゃなかった＋んだって。 | |

Change the underlined parts from the informal form to the polite form.

1. スタンフォード大学に合格したんだって？　すごいじゃない。

2. とってもダンスが上手なんだってね。　僕にも教えてよ。

3. 奨学金、もらえたんだってね。　良かったね。

4. 願書の締切って、この１５日なんだって？　早く書かなくちゃ。

> E. 〜によって＋Passive
>
> 〜によって is often attached to the noun that is the agent in a passive sentence. It is translated as "by," as in "by a certain person." 〜によって can be used in sentences which have an impersonal or formal agent, but is not used in sentences which have an agent that is considered "personal."
>
> Compare:　○ 私は母にしかられた。　　I was scolded by my mother.
> 　　　　　× 私は母によってしかられた。

Circle the correct word in the 〔 〕, then fill in the blanks with the passive form of the verb in the （ ）.

1. この学校は宣教師〔に　によって〕創立_____。（する）
2. この小説は有名な小説家〔に　によって〕_____。（書く）
3. 私の宿題は犬〔に　によって〕_____。（食べる）
4. 私の絵は先生〔に　によって〕_____。（ほめる）

| 7課 | | アクティビティー | |

A. 日本文化：一人か二人ワーク→クラスワーク

Divide the topics below among your classmates and research your topic on the Internet. Using visuals, present your findings with your classmates.

1. お受験〔おじゅけん〕
2. 塾〔じゅく〕、予備校〔よびこう〕
3. 短期大学〔たんきだいがく〕or 短大〔たんだい〕、専門学校〔せんもんがっこう〕
4. 給食〔きゅうしょく〕、上履き〔うわばき〕、掃除係〔そうじがかり〕、学校の制服〔せいふく〕
5. 少子化〔しょうしか〕

B. 学校関係の単語：ペアワーク→クラスワーク

〔　〕の中に読み方をひらがなで書きなさい。

	大学院〔　　　〕		博士号〔　　　〕
短期大学 or 短大 〔　　〕〔　　〕	大学〔　　　〕	専門学校〔　　　〕	修士号〔しゅうしごう〕
	高校〔　　　〕		学士号〔がくしごう〕
	中学校〔　　　〕		
	小学校〔　　　〕		
	幼稚園〔　　　〕		
	保育園〔　　　〕		

C. 大学進学について：ペアワーク→クラスワーク

Discuss the following with your partner and share your findings with your class.

1. 大学進学について先生と何度相談した？ ＿＿＿＿＿＿＿＿＿＿
2. 大学についてコンピューターでよく調べた？ ＿＿＿＿＿＿＿＿＿＿
3. 何校の大学に願書を送るつもり？ ＿＿＿＿＿＿＿＿＿＿
4. 最後の大学の願書の締め切りはいつ？ ＿＿＿＿＿＿＿＿＿＿
5. 大学の推薦状をもう先生にお願いした？ ＿＿＿＿＿＿＿＿＿＿
6. 大学のエッセイをもう書いた？題は何？ ＿＿＿＿＿＿＿＿＿＿
7. もう大学の面接をした？ ＿＿＿＿＿＿＿＿＿＿

7課

8. 大学からいつごろ結果の通知をもらう？　＿＿＿＿＿＿＿＿＿＿＿＿＿＿＿
9. 奨学金を申し込むつもり？　＿＿＿＿＿＿＿＿＿＿＿＿＿＿＿
10. 大学進学について何か親と問題がある？　＿＿＿＿＿＿＿＿＿＿＿＿＿＿＿
11. 希望の大学に合格出来る可能性は何パーセント？　＿＿＿＿＿＿＿＿＿＿＿＿＿＿＿
12. 最後に大学を決める時、一番大事な事は何？　＿＿＿＿＿＿＿＿＿＿＿＿＿＿＿
13. 大学では何を専攻するつもり？　＿＿＿＿＿＿＿＿＿＿＿＿＿＿＿
14. 将来はどこでどんな仕事をしたい？

＿＿＿

D. 聞く Pre-Listening Activity「キャンプ」：ペアワーク→クラスワーク

You are going to a Japanese language day camp at the beach.
日本語キャンプに必要だと思う物に○を、必要じゃないと思う物に×を書きなさい。

- a. iPod (　)
- b. 水着 (　)
- c. 飲物 (　)
- d. くつ (　)
- e. おやつ (　)
- f. シャツ (　)
- g. タオル (　)
- h. ケータイ (　)
- i. ショーツ (　)
- j. サングラス (　)
- k. サンダル (　)
- l. 現金 (　)
- m. カメラ (　)
- n. 昼食 (　)
- o. ゴミ袋 (　)
- p. 高価な宝石 (　)
- q. ゲームの道具 (　)
- r. 日焼け止めクリーム (　)
- s. ゲームの賞品 (　)
- t. コンピューター (　)

E. 聞く Post-Listening Activity「キャンプ」：ペアワーク→クラスワーク

Presentation: Japanese Language Camp

Present your views on this Japanese language camp. Discuss at least FIVE aspects of this camp. Begin with an appropriate introduction, give details about the five aspects, explain your own view or perspective, and end with a concluding remark. You will have 4 minutes to prepare and 2 minutes to present. Your presentation should be as complete as possible.

【Let's take notes!】

1. Begin with an appropriate introduction.

＿＿＿

2. Discuss five aspects/examples of the topic.

1.) ＿＿＿＿＿＿＿＿＿＿＿＿＿＿＿＿＿＿＿＿＿＿＿＿＿＿＿＿＿＿＿＿＿＿＿＿
2.) ＿＿＿＿＿＿＿＿＿＿＿＿＿＿＿＿＿＿＿＿＿＿＿＿＿＿＿＿＿＿＿＿＿＿＿＿
3.) ＿＿＿＿＿＿＿＿＿＿＿＿＿＿＿＿＿＿＿＿＿＿＿＿＿＿＿＿＿＿＿＿＿＿＿＿
4.) ＿＿＿＿＿＿＿＿＿＿＿＿＿＿＿＿＿＿＿＿＿＿＿＿＿＿＿＿＿＿＿＿＿＿＿＿
5.) ＿＿＿＿＿＿＿＿＿＿＿＿＿＿＿＿＿＿＿＿＿＿＿＿＿＿＿＿＿＿＿＿＿＿＿＿

7課

3. Explain your view or perspective.
_____

4. End with a concluding remark.
_____

F. 読む Pre-Reading Activity「オバマ大統領」：ペアワーク→クラスワーク

オバマ大統領について正しい説明と思う文に○をしなさい。

1. (　) オバマ大統領のお父さんはケニア人だった。
2. (　) オバマ大統領のお母さんはハワイ生まれの白人だった。
3. (　) オバマ大統領はハワイで生まれた。
4. (　) オバマ大統領はインドネシアに住んでいたことがある。
5. (　) オバマ大統領のお父さんは、ハワイ大学で博士号を取った。
6. (　) オバマ大統領の御両親は、離婚した。
7. (　) オバマ大統領のお母さんは教育に熱心な人だった。
8. (　) オバマ大統領はハワイのおじいさんとおばあさんと一緒に住んで、小学校に通った。
9. (　) オバマ大統領の担任の先生は、ケニアで研究生活を送った経験がある。
10. (　) オバマ大統領はお父さんとハワイで再会した。
11. (　) オバマ大統領のお父さんは、オバマ大統領のクラスに招かれ、ケニアについての話をした。
12. (　) オバマ大統領のお父さんは、ハワイで交通事故で亡くなった。

G. 読む Post-Reading Activity「オバマ大統領」：ペアワーク→クラスワーク

「オバマ大統領とあなたの子供時代」を比べなさい。4分準備、2分で発表しなさい。

Compare and contrast similarities and differences between President Obama's childhood and your childhood. Based on your personal experience, describe at least THREE aspects of each and highlight the similarities and differences between President Obama's childhood and your childhood. Also state your preference for either and give reasons for your choice.

Introduction:
_____

Three similarities/differences:

1. _____
2. _____
3. _____

Your preference and reasons:
_____

7課

H. テキストチャット「学校」：ペアワーク→クラスワーク

あなたの学校についての質問です。（　）の中から正しい言葉に○をし、下線には正しい説明を書きなさい。

1. 私の学校は（公立　私立）で、（男女共学　男子校　女子校）である。
2. 生徒数はおよそ_____人ぐらいで、（大きい　小さい）学校である。
3. 生徒は_____年生から_____年生までいる。
4. 授業料は年間およそ_____ドルぐらいで、入学は（難しい　やさしい）。
5. 学校の歴史は（古くて　新しくて）、_____年ごろに創立された。
6. 学校の創立者は（_____だった　知らない）。
7. 学校の行事の中で一番好きなのは、_____で、____月（____日　上旬　中旬　下旬）にある。
8. この行事を説明する。_____
_____
9. この学校のいい点の一つは、_____。
10. この学校の悪い点の一つは、_____。

I. Compare & Contrast「共学と男子校か女子校」：ペアワーク→クラスワーク

「共学と男子校か女子校」を比べなさい。4分準備して、2分でクラスで発表しなさい。

Compare and contrast similarities and differences between co-ed schools and boys' or girls' schools. Based on your personal experience and/or your background knowledge, describe at least THREE aspects of each and highlight the similarities and differences between co-ed schools and boys' or girls' schools. Also state your preference for either and give reasons for your choice.

Introduction:
_____

Three similarities/differences:
1. _____
2. _____
3. _____

Your preference and reasons:
_____

7課

J. 会話「大学」：ペアワーク→クラスワーク

With a partner, use these prompts to role play a conversation between a male Japanese teacher and his student. The prompts below are questions the teacher asks the student. The answers given by the student should be in the polite form. Questions must be answered in 20 seconds.

1. 希望の大学に合格出来たんだって？ おめでとう。

2. 全部でいくつの大学に願書を出して、いくつの大学に合格したの？

3. 大学では何が楽しみかな？ 何か心配してることもある？

4. 君達が卒業したら寂しくなるなあ。卒業しても時々メールで近況を知らせてくれよな。

K. 文化発表「日本の教育」：ペアワーク→クラスワーク

a. Fill in the ( ) with responses from the list.

1. 日本の学校制度は小学校、中学、高校の（　　）である。
2. 日本は中学までが義務教育で、（　　）は義務教育ではない。
3. 日本の学校では、生徒が教室とかトイレを（　　）しなければならない。
4. 日本の学校では、建物の中に入る時、たいてい（　　）に履き替えなければならない。
5. 日本の小中高では、たいてい（　　）を教室で食べる。
6. 日本の中高生は、たいてい（　　）を着て学校に通う。
7. いい学校に入るために、多くの日本の子供が放課後、（　　）へ通う。
8. 大学に合格出来なかった高校生は（　　）と呼ばれ、たいてい予備校に通って次の年の受験勉強をする。
9. 四年の大学へ進学しないで、（　　）や短大へ行く高校生もいる。
10. （　　）によって子供の数が減って来ているので、大学へ行く学生数も減って来ている。

```
a. 制服      b. 掃除      c. 塾      d. 浪人      e. 少子化
f. 専門学校  g. 6-3-3制   h. 上履き  i. 高校      j. 給食
```

b. Write about your perception of the Japanese school system.

_____
_____
_____

7課

<7課 - 聞く>
Listening: Camp Announcement

【You may take notes while listening. Do not look at the questions below before listening. You will have 12 seconds to answer each question. You may NOT move back and forth among questions.】

(Narrator) Now you will listen to some instructions once.

(Narrator) Now answer the questions for this selection.

1. When is the Japanese camp scheduled?
    (A) 7:00 a.m. - 2:30 p.m. on Saturday, May 2nd
    (B) 8:00 a.m. - 2:30 p.m. on Friday, May 20th
    (C) 7:00 a.m. - 3:00 p.m. on Sunday, May 20th
    (D) 8:00 a.m. - 3:00 p.m. on Friday, May 2th

2. What is NOT allowed at the camp?
    (A) shorts
    (B) hats
    (C) shoes
    (D) bare feet

3. What are the campers NOT allowed to take with them?
    (A) cameras
    (B) cellular phones
    (C) iPods
    (D) swimsuits

4. What is each group of students supposed to prepare for camping?
    (A) a game and prizes
    (B) lunch
    (C) drinks
    (D) snacks

5. What information is NOT correct about camping?
    (A) The teacher will grade students' efforts to speak Japanese.
    (B) Mrs. Matsumoto will deliver their lunch to the campsite.
    (C) Students are supposed to pay $8 for lunch.
    (D) In case of rain, they will postpone camping.

<7課 - 読む>
Reading: President Obama
【You may move back and forth among all the questions.】

オバマ大統領

　オバマ大統領のお父さんは黒人で、ケニア出身の経済学専攻の留学生だった。お母さんはカンザス州生まれの白人だった。二人はハワイ大学で知り合い、結婚し、1961年に大統領が生まれた。しかし、大統領が2歳の時に、お父さんはハーバード大学で博士号を取るために家を離れ、両親は離婚してしまった。お母さんはインドネシアからの留学生と再婚して、家族はインドネシアに住むことになった。しかし、お母さんはインドネシアでの大統領の教育を心配し、一週間に五日、朝4時に大統領を起こし、朝食を食べさせた後、学校へ行く前の3時間大統領に英語を教えた。教育に熱心なお母さんは10歳の大統領をおじいさんとおばあさんのいるハワイに送り、名門プナホウ学園に入学させた。小学五年生だった大統領はいつもニコニコ笑っている子だったが、友達もなく、学校になかなか馴染めなかった。担任のヘフティー先生は大統領を教える前年にケニアで一年間の研究生活を送っていて、自分のクラスにいた大統領にいろいろケニアのことについて話した。その年の12月に大統領のお父さんがハワイに一か月帰って来た。大統領はお父さんと8年ぶりに再会した。ヘフティー先生はお父さんをクラスに招き、ケニアのいろいろな歴史、文化、問題を子供達に話してもらった。その時、大統領はお父さんからの強い熱いメッセージを受け取ったようだ。お父さんはその後ケニアに帰り、数年後、交通事故で亡くなった。その30年後、大統領は人種に関係なく誰もが自由で平等に暮せる世界を目指して、大統領選に出馬した。

<7課 - 読む (質問)>
Reading: President Obama

(Narrator) Now answer the questions for this section.

1. What information is NOT correct about President Obama's father?
   - (A) His father majored in economics.
   - (B) His father was from Kenya.
   - (C) His father left his family in order to pursue a Ph.D. at Harvard University.
   - (D) His father died in Hawaii in a car accident.

2. What information is NOT correct about President Obama's mother?
   - (A) His mother was from Kansas.
   - (B) His mother was Caucasian.
   - (C) His mother met his father at the University of Hawaii.
   - (D) His mother remarried a professor from Indonesia.

3. What kind of childhood did President Obama have?
   - (A) His parents were divorced when he was 8 years old.
   - (B) He was sent to his grandparents' home in Hawaii to receive a better education.
   - (C) He started attending Punahou School in the 7th grade.
   - (D) He never had a chance to meet his father after his father left the family.

4. What did the President's mother do about his education while in Indonesia?
   - (A) His mother did not send her son to a local school.
   - (B) His mother woke her son at 6:00 a.m. for English lessons.
   - (C) His mother hired an English teacher for her son.
   - (D) His mother later sent her son to Hawaii for his education.

5. What is NOT correct about Mrs. Hefty?
   - (A) She was also from Kenya.
   - (B) She was President Obama's former homeroom teacher.
   - (C) She shared many things about Kenya with President Obama when he was a student.
   - (D) She invited the future President Obama's father to her class to give a talk about Kenya.

＜7課 - 書く (テキストチャット)＞

`90秒×6`

Text Chat: School

You will participate in a simulated exchange of text-chat messages. Each time it is your turn to write, you will have 90 seconds. You should respond as fully and as appropriately as possible.

You will have a conversation with Mari, a student at a Japanese school, about your school.

1. Start the conversation. (90 seconds)
   そちらの高校について教えて下さい。まず、どんな高校ですか。
2. Respond. (90 seconds)
   そうですか。次の質問です。授業料はいくらぐらいですか。入学は難しいですか。
3. Explain. (90 seconds)
   分かりました。次の質問です。学校の歴史(れきし)について教えて下さい。
4. State and explain your preference. (90 seconds)
   分かりました。次の質問に行きましょう。学校の行事で何が一番好きですか。
5. State your opinions. (90 seconds)
   そうですか。では、最後の質問です。学校のいい点と悪い点を一つずつ教えて下さい。
6. Ask a specific question. (90 seconds)
   ありがとうございました。ところで、日本の学校について何か質問がありますか。

＜7課 - 書く (比較(ひかく)と対比(たいひ))＞

`20分`

Compare and Contrast Article: Public Schools and Private Schools

Directions: You are writing an article for the student newspaper of your sister school in Japan. Write an article in which you compare and contrast similarities and differences between public schools and private schools. Based on your personal experience and/or your background knowledge, describe at least THREE aspects of each and highlight the similarities and differences between public schools and private schools. Also state your preference for either and give reasons for it.

Your article should be 300 to 400 characters or longer. Use the *desu/masu* or *da* (plain) style, but use one style consistently. Also, use *kanji* wherever *kanji* from the AP Japanese *kanji* list is appropriate. You have 20 minutes to write.

【NOTES/OUTLINE: 自分の作文のアウトラインを書こう！】

Introduction:
_____

Three similarities/differences:

1. _____
2. _____
3. _____

Your preference and give reasons:
_____
_____

`7課`

<7課 - 話す (会話)>
Conversation: College

20秒×4

You will participate in a simulated conversation. Each time it is your turn to speak, you will have 20 seconds to record. You should respond as fully and as appropriately as possible.

You will have a conversation with Mr. Matsuda, your Japanese teacher, about your acceptance to colleges.

(Teacher)
(20 seconds)
(Teacher)
(20 seconds)
(Teacher)
(20 seconds)
(Teacher)
(20 seconds)

<7課 - 話す (日本文化)>
Cultural Perspective Presentation: The Educational System in Japan

4分+2分

Directions: Imagine you are making an oral presentation to your Japanese class. First, you will read and hear the topic for your presentation. You will have 4 minutes to prepare your presentation. Then you will have 2 minutes to record your presentation. Your presentation should be as complete as possible.

Present your own view or perspective of the educational system in Japan. Discuss at least FIVE aspects or examples of educational system in Japan.

Begin with an appropriate introduction, give details, explain your own view or perspective, and end with a concluding remark.

【Let's take notes!】

1. Begin with an appropriate introduction.
   _____

2. Discuss five aspects/examples of the topic.
   1.) _____
   2.) _____
   3.) _____
   4.) _____
   5.) _____

3. Explain your view or perspective.
   _____

4. End with a concluding remark.
   _____

7課

| 8課 | | 服装
ふくそう
Clothing | |

【AP® タスク：服装ふくそう】

Discuss the pros and the cons of having school uniforms. How did your school decide on your present dress code? What are your feelings and opinions about your school dress code? What fashion is popular now? How does the media influence new fashions, and why? What is your opinion about present fashion trends?

【文化】 日本の制服せいふく：Japanese Uniforms

In comparison with people of other cultures, Japan is a country of people who tend to feel at ease wearing uniforms. In a relatively homogeneous culture that values conformity and identification by groups, it is not a surprising phenomenon.

As is obvious by the popular Japanese proverb "*Deru kugi wa utareru*," "The nail that sticks up gets hammered down," a Japanese who differs from others is made to conform to the prevailing group. Japanese have traditionally felt uneasy about being seen as different from others and prefer the outward appearance of belonging. This suggests loyalty, respect, cooperation and harmony with others. The Japanese are also generally ethnically homogeneous and therefore, are not markedly diverse in physical appearance. Uniforms are a form of identification that bonds those within a group and differentiates one group from other groups.

Uniforms serve another function. They are a form of behavior control and a way to maintain safety and order. Because those in uniform can quickly be identified as members of a certain group, should one become the "protruding nail" who wanders away or "breaks the rules," he will immediately be recognized and reined in or rescued. This is one reason why schoolchildren are frequently required to wear uniforms even when not in school.

Many students, particularly those in public schools, wear uniforms. As children grow older, more of them are required to wear uniforms in school. Most uniforms for girls consist of a blouse, skirt, blazer and possibly a beret. Many high school uniforms are now creations of popular fashion designers. Students also are required to wear a specified kind of shoes and socks. They must also follow strict rules about hairstyles and hair color, and usually are not allowed to wear makeup or jewelry. Boys traditionally wear dark pants, a white shirt and a blazer. Most uniforms include a tie and a hat/cap. Types of shoes are specified, as are socks. Rules on hair style, color and length are strictly enforced, though some students sometimes push these limits.

Many companies also require uniforms. Uniforms project professionalism, neatness and cleanliness. Although certain businesses such as banks and airlines give their employees some leeway in choosing to mix and match from a set of uniform pieces, the appearance of professionalism is still highly valued in Japan. Wearing uniforms at companies and businesses is a customer service strategy, so that customers can easily identify whom to ask for assistance.

Most Japanese who wear uniforms have two sets, a winter and summer uniform. Winter uniforms are usually made from wool, while cotton is used for most summer uniforms. Traditionally, all school students changed from their summer to winter, or winter to summer uniforms on the exact same day throughout Japan. The summer to winter date was usually October 1. It did not matter if the days were still hot or cold - everyone changed. Recently, however, school districts have determined their switchover days independently.

The uniform culture is still a major part of contemporary Japan today. It represents Japan's strong sense of group, and dynamics that are associated with group consciousness. While the younger generation tries to veer away from some of these traditions, they still preserve many of the same attitudes.

Questions to ponder: Are the purposes for wearing uniforms the same or different in Japan and your culture? Do you think uniforms have a place in any culture?

8課 ◆◆◆ 復習単語 ◆◆◆

トピック：服装（ふくそう）

1. 服	ふく	N	clothing
2. 服装	ふくそう	N	(the style of) dress; clothing; fashion
3. デザイン		N	design
4. サイズ		N	size
5. エムサイズ		N	medium size
6. エルサイズ		N	large size
7. エスサイズ		N	small size
8. ジャケット		N	jacket
9. セーター		N	sweater
10. シャツ		N	shirt
11. ズボン		N	pants
12. スカート		N	skirt
13. ワンピース		N	dress
14. Tシャツ		N	T-shirt
15. 浴衣	ゆかた	N	summer cotton *kimono*
16. ショートパンツ		N	shorts
17. ショーツ		N	shorts
18. パンツ		N	pants (underwear)
19. ソックス		N	socks
20. 靴下	くつした	N	socks
21. 靴	くつ	N	shoes
22. 帽子	ぼうし	N	cap; hat
23. 眼鏡	めがね	N	eyeglasses
24. ネックレス		N	necklace
25. 指輪	ゆびわ	N	ring
26. イヤリング		N	earrings
27. ピアス		N	pierced earrings

| 8課 | ★★★ | 新しい単語 | ★★★ |

1. とうろんかい＜討論会＞ N discussion; debate
   とうろん＜討論＞(を)する／します V3 to discuss
   「今日は制服について討論しよう。」 "Let's discuss school uniforms today."
2. きじ＜記事＞ N article
   このファッション記事によると、今年はグレーが流行するらしい。According to this fashion article, the color grey seems to be this year's fashion trend.
3. うでどけい＜腕時計＞ N wristwatch
   山田君は格好良い腕時計をしている。Yamada is wearing a nice looking wrist watch.
4. ぶたい＜舞台＞ N stage
   私は舞台に立つとあがってしまう。When I get up on stage, I end up losing my composure.
5. いしょう＜衣装＞ N costume; clothing
   ミュージカルの衣装はすばらしかった。The costumes for the musical were wonderful.
6. かつら N wig
   おばあさんはかつらをかぶっている。My grandmother is wearing a wig.
7. きんぱつ＜金髪＞ N blonde
   松川さんの奥さんは金髪の女性だ。Matsukawa's wife is a blonde woman.
8. しふく＜私服＞ N plain/private (own) clothes
   この高校は制服がなくて、皆私服を着ている。There is no school uniform at this high school and everyone wears their own clothes.
9. りゅうこう＜流行＞ N fashion
   りゅうこう＜流行＞(を)する／します V3 to be popular; to come into fashion
   はやる＜流行る＞／流行ります V1 to be popular; to come into fashion
   今、変なファッションが流行っている(or 流行している)。Strange fashions are now in style.
10. かっこう＜格好＞ N shape; appearance
    「変な格好をしないで下さい。」"Please don't wear something inappropriate."
11. せいしゅん＜青春＞ N youth
    友達と過ごした時間が青春の思い出だ。The times I spent with my friends are memories of my youth.
12. ほこり＜誇り＞ N pride
    この学校に誇りを感じる。I feel pride in this school.

13. こせい＜個性＞　N　individuality; personality
リサさんは個性が強くて、人とよくけんかをする。Lisa has a strong personality and often fights with people.

14. おそろい＜お揃い＞　N　suit; matching set (of clothing)
シャツとお揃いの緑の帽子をかぶっている。(She) is wearing a shirt and a matching green hat.

15. おしゃれ＜お洒落/オシャレ＞　Na　fashion-conscious
おしゃれ＜お洒落/オシャレ＞(を)する／します　V3　to dress up
姉はとってもオシャレです。My older sister is very fashionable.
姉は今日もおシャレをして、出かけた。My older sister dressed up today too, and went out.

16. けいざいてき＜経済的＞　Na　economical
制服と私服とどちらの方が経済的か分からない。I don't know which is more economical, (wearing) uniforms or one's own clothing.

17. せいけつ＜清潔＞　Na　clean; sanitary
⇔ふけつ＜不潔＞　Na　unclean; unsanitary
田中君はいつも同じシャツを着ていて洗濯しないみたいで、不潔な感じがする。Tanaka always wears the same shirt and does not seem to wash it, so I feel that he is unclean.

18. はで＜派手＞　Na　bright; showy
ケリーさんはいつも派手な服を着ている。Kelly always wears bright clothing.

19. じみ＜地味＞　Na　conservative
姉はいつも少し地味な服を着ている。My older sister always wears slightly conservative clothing.

20. ごうか＜豪華＞　Na　luxurious; splendid
ミュージカルの衣装は豪華だった。The costumes for the musical were splendid.

21. だらしない　A　loose; slovenly; sloppy
私服はだらしなく見えると思う。I think plain clothes look sloppy.

22. すがすがしい＜清々しい＞　A　refreshing; crisp; invigorating
清々しい朝だ。It is a crisp morning.

23. めずらしい＜珍しい＞　A　rare; unusual
めずらしく＜珍しく＞　Adv　rarely; unusually
彼は珍しく踊りを間違えた。Surprisingly, he made a mistake in dancing.

24. こい＜濃い＞　A　dark
⇔うすい＜薄い＞　A　thin; weak
濃い緑も薄い緑も大好きだ。I like both dark green and light green very much.

8課

25. おとなっぽい＜大人っぽい＞　　A　adult-like
化粧をして大人っぽくなった。　She wears makeup and has become more adult-like.

26. まよう＜迷う＞／迷います　　V1　to lose (one's way); to be perplexed; to be puzzled
☞まいご＜迷子＞になる／なります　　V1　to get lost (on the street)
制服があれば、朝何を着るか迷わなくてもいい。　If we had school uniforms, we wouldn't be undecided about what to wear in the morning.

27. しゅうちゅう＜集中＞(を)する／します　　V3　to concentrate; to focus
うるさいと、集中出来ない。　If it is noisy, I cannot focus.

28. あせをかく＜汗をかく＞／かきます　　V1　to perspire
汗をかいたので、シャツがちょっと臭い。　Because I perspired, my shirt is a little smelly.

29. そめる＜染める＞／染めます　　V2　to dye
田村さんは髪の毛を金髪に染めている。　Ms. Tamura has her hair dyed blonde.

30. にあう＜似合う＞／似合います　　V1　to match; to suit (someone)
赤いシャツはあなたによく似合う。　The red shirt suits you well.

31. あきる＜飽きる＞／飽きます　　V2　to tire (of)
もうインスタントラーメンに飽きてしまった。　I am tired of instant noodles.

32. さそう＜誘う＞／誘います　　V1　to invite
友達に映画に誘われた。　I was invited to the movie by my friend.

【もっと単語】

1. ふくそう＜服装＞	N	clothing
2. セーラーふく＜セーラー服＞	N	sailor suit
3. がくせいふく＜学生服＞	N	school uniform for boys [black color]
4. がら＜柄＞	N	design; pattern
5. しまもよう＜縞模様＞	N	striped (pattern)
6. みずたまもよう＜水玉模様＞	N	polka-dot (design)
7. おび＜帯＞	N	(kimono) sash or belt
8. げた＜下駄＞	N	Japanese wooden clogs
9. ぞうり＜草履＞	N	Japanese slippers
10. たび＜足袋＞	N	Japanese split-toe socks
12. もんつき＜紋付き＞	N	crested; with a (family) crest
13. はかま＜袴＞	N	Japanese split skirt

14. ほうせき＜宝石＞		N	jewel; jewelry
15. かちかん＜価値観＞		N	values
16. せいけつ＜清潔＞		N	purity; cleanliness
17. せいしき＜正式＞		Na	formal; official
18. (ぼうし＜帽子＞を)＜被る＞/被ります		V1	to wear (a hat) [over the head]
19. (めがね＜眼鏡＞を)かける/かけます		V2	to wear (glasses)
20. しめる＜締める＞		V2	to tighten; to tie (around)
21. そんざいかん＜存在感＞がある		V1	to have a presence

| 8課 | ■■■ | 文法(ぼう) | ■■■ |

A. "Wear" verbs

The verb "to wear" is expressed in many ways in Japanese, depending on where and how the item of clothing is worn. For example, if one wears something covering one's head, such as a hat or cap, the verb かぶる is used. If the clothing is worn in a way where it must be fastened or tightened around some part of the body, such as a belt or necktie, the verb しめる is used. If one wears clothing or accessories, e.g., glasses that suspend over a part of the body, the verb かける is used. 着る is the general term used to wear over the top, or over the entire body, as in wearing a shirt or a dress. はく is used when wearing clothing below the waist, such as pants, shoes, skirts or socks. The verb する is used when one wears accessories, such as jewelry, watches or hair accessories.

Fill in the blanks with the correct form of one of the verbs from the list.

1. サングラスを＿＿＿＿、帽子(ぼうし)を＿＿＿＿います。
2. ジーンズを＿＿＿＿、白いシャツを＿＿＿＿います。
3. スーツを＿＿＿＿、ネクタイを＿＿＿＿います。
4. 大きい眼鏡(めがね)を＿＿＿＿、金髪のかつらを＿＿＿＿います。
5. 金のネックレスを＿＿＿＿、三つのピアスも＿＿＿＿います。
6. 足袋(たび)を＿＿＿＿、着物を＿＿＿＿、帯(おび)を＿＿＿＿。

| 着る |
| はく |
| かぶる |
| かける |
| しめる |
| する |

B. 何か聞きたいこと   something you want to ask

This structure is constructed with a Question Word ＋ か ＋ Descriptor (Plain) ＋ Noun. It is translated as "something; some person, some place, etc." (depending on the question word) tall, quiet, I want to go, etc." The descriptor may be a noun ＋の, い-adjective, な-adjective ＋ な, or verb (plain) form.

Fill in the blanks with the correct question word ＋ か.

1. ＿＿＿＿分からないことがあったら、僕に聞いて。
2. 土曜日＿＿＿＿おもしろい所に行こうよ。
3. 青いシャツか黄色のシャツ、＿＿＿＿好きな方(き)に決めて。
4. ＿＿＿＿会いたい人がいたら、教えて。
5. ＿＿＿＿時間がある時に、一緒に食事しよう。

C. 何時に＋行けば/行ったら＋いい？   [Requesting a suggestion or advice]
What time should I go?

五時ごろに行けば/行ったら(＋どう)？ [Making a suggestion]
How about going around 5:00?

| 8課 |

For the first construction, which is used to solicit advice or a suggestion from the listener, one uses a question that ends in a verb in the conditional -ば or -たら form + いい(ですか). The second may be a response to the first, as it is used when giving advice or suggestions. It too, uses a verb in the -たら or -ば forms, and may end there when spoken informally in a upward intonation. It may also end with a どう？or more formally, with a どうですか.

Fill in the blanks with some good advice.

1. 「パーティーにどんな格好をして行ったらいいかなあ。」
   「何でもいいと思うけど、ちょっと格好いいドレスを_____どう？」
2. 「どうしよう？今日の午後、日本語の試験があるのに、まだ全然勉強していないんだ。」
   「まだ時間があるじゃない。_____どう？」
3. 「彼にね、土曜日のコンサートに誘われちゃったんだ。どうしたらいいかな？」
   「良かったじゃない。_____どう？」
4. 「ねえ、どうしよう？車の鍵が見つからないんだ。」
   「困ったねえ。_____どう？」

D. 子供っぽい   childish

The っぽい ending is generally used in informal situations and is attached to nouns or verb stems to describe a characteristic or tendency that usually has negative connotations. It is treated as an ーい adjective.

Fill in the blanks with the correct words from the list.

1. さゆりさんは化粧をしたら、すごく_____見える。
2. そんな_____いたずら(mischief)はやめなさい。
3. 祖母は最近_____、時々私の名前さえ忘れる。
4. 父は_____ので、あまり近くにいたくない。
5. 姉は_____、いつもすぐほかのことがしたくなる。

子供っぽい
おこりっぽい
大人っぽく
あきっぽくて
忘れっぽくて

E. どこの学校か分かりやすい   It's easy to understand what school it is.

When a question is embedded in a sentence, such as "what school is it" above, one uses the question in a plain form, attaches a か and uses it in the context of another sentence.

Insert a ▲ where か should be used.

例. 制服があれば、毎朝何を着る▲迷わなくてもいい。

1. 今どうしたらいい分からない。
2. どんな格好をしてパーティーに行けばいいの教えて。
3. こんな問題をだれに相談したらいいのなあ。
4. モモコというゴルファーを知っているって聞かれた。
5. どこの大学に行きたいまだ考えていない。

8課

8課　　　　　　　　　　　　　アクティビティー

A. 日本文化：一人か二人ワーク→クラスワーク

Divide the topics below among your classmates and research your topic on the Internet. Using visuals, present your findings with your classmates.

1. セーラー服、学生服
2. 最近の制服
3. 制服の夏服と冬服

B. 聞く Pre-Listening Activity「制服」：ペアワーク→クラスワーク

Do you support having a school uniform or not? Determine your three most important reasons for supporting or opposing school uniforms. Mark your choices 1, 2, and 3, with 1 being your most important reason. Finally, add your own reason.

a. 制服に賛成する理由：

___ 1. 制服を着ていると、どこの学校か分かりやすい。
___ 2. 制服は格好いいが、私服はだらしなく見える。
___ 3. 制服があれば、毎日何を着るか迷わなくていい。
___ 4. 制服は学生の時にだけ着られるので、青春の思い出になる。
___ 5. 制服は学校のシンボルだから、学校に誇りを持つようになる。
___ 6. 制服は私服より経済的だ。
___ 7. セーラー服は可愛い。
___ 8. 女子学生がセクシーな格好が出来ないので、勉強に集中出来る。
___ 9. その他の理由：_____

b. 制服に反対する理由：

___ 1. 皆が同じ服を着ていると、個性がなくなる。
___ 2. 制服ではオシャレが出来ない。
___ 3. 毎日同じ制服を着ると、飽きてしまう。
___ 4. 毎朝服装について考えなくていいので、ファッションセンスがなくなる。
___ 5. 制服は汗をかいてもあまり洗濯をしないから、不潔だ。
___ 6. その他の理由：_____

C. 聞く Post-Listening Activity「制服」：ペアワーク→クラスワーク

Presentation: My School's Dress Code

Present your view on your school's dress code. Discuss at least FIVE aspects of your school's dress code. Begin with an appropriate introduction, give details about the five aspects, explain your own view or perspective, and end with a concluding remark. You will have 4 minutes to prepare and 2 minutes to present. Your presentation should be as complete as possible.

【Let's take notes!】

1. Begin with an appropriate introduction.
   _____

2. Discuss five aspects/examples of the topic.
   1.) _____
   2.) _____
   3.) _____
   4.) _____
   5.) _____

3. Explain your view or perspective.
   _____

4. End with a concluding remark.
   _____

D. 読む Pre-Reading Activity「ファッション記事」：ペアワーク→クラスワーク

a. Circle the answer that best describes the clothes you have on now or your taste in clothes.

1. 私は今（白　黒　グレー　赤　黄色　緑　青　ピンク　紫）の（シャツ　ドレス）を着ている。
2. 私は今（白　黒　グレー　赤　黄色　緑　青　ピンク　紫）の（スカート　ズボン　ショーツ）をはいている。
3. 私は今、帽子をかぶって（いる　いない）。
4. 私は今、眼鏡をかけて（いる　いない）。
5. 私は今（ネックレス　腕時計　イヤリング　ピアス　ブレスレッド　ペンダント）をしている。
6. 私は今までかつらをかぶったこと（がある　はない）。
7. 私の髪の毛は金髪（だ　に染めたい　に染めたくない）。
8. 一般的に言って、私は（派手　地味）な服装が好きだ。
9. 服の柄として、私は（縞模様　水玉模様）が好きだ。

8課

b. Circle the correct words that pertain to wearing a Japanese *kimono*.

1. 私は着物を（着たことがある　着たことがない）。
2. 着物の上に（ベルト　おび）を締める。
3. 着物を着る時に（くつ　げた　ぞうり）をはく。
4. 着物を着る時に（色の　白い）（たび　ソックス）を履く。
5. 一般的に言って、着物を着る時に指輪とかネックレスなどを（しない　する）。
6. 男の正式な着物は紋付きと（スカート　袴）である。

E. 読む Post-Reading Activity「ファッション記事」：ペアワーク→クラスワーク

「洋服と着物」を比べなさい。４分準備して、２分で発表しなさい。

Compare and contrast similarities and differences between Western clothes and Japanese *kimono*. Based on the articles you read, describe at least THREE aspects of each and highlight the similarities and differences between Western clothes and Japanese *kimono*. Also state your preference for one and give reasons for your choice.

Introduction:
_____

Three similarities/differences:

1. _____
2. _____
3. _____

Your preference and reasons:
_____

F. 会話「ダンスパーティー」：ペアワーク→クラスワーク

a. Change the underlined sections to the correct polite form.

1. ねえねえ、聞いて。　彼にね、ダンスパーティーに誘われちゃったんだ。

2. でも、どんな格好して行けばいいのかなあ。

3. ドレスとか持っていないし、どうしよう。

4. 何か聞きたいことがあったら、相談にのってくれないかな。電話してもいい？

b. Using the informal questions above, create a dialog with a friend who will also respond informally.

8課

G. 文化発表「日本の学校の制服」：ペアワーク→クラスワーク

a. Fill in the blanks with the correct words from the box below.

1. 日本人は「ほかの人と同じことはいい」と思う（　）を持っているので、制服を着ることが好きらしい。制服を着ると、気持ちも「外」から「（　）」に入ることが出来るようだ。

2. 生徒が制服を着ていると、どこの（　）の生徒かすぐ分かるので、先生達は生徒の補導がしやすいし、生徒も悪いことをしにくい。

3. 制服だけでなく、日本の学校にはいろいろな服装の規則がある。制服の（　）の長さとか、髪の毛の長さとか、（　）をしてはいけないとか、髪の毛を（　）はいけないとか、（　）をしていはいけないとか、生徒も先生も規則を（　）ことにエネルギーを使う。

4. 日本人は会社でも制服を着る。（　）とかデパートとか航空会社とか、特にサービス業では制服を着て仕事をしている。制服は（　）感やプロ意識をお客さんに与えることが出来る。

5. 日本の制服は夏服と冬服があって、だいたい（　）に夏服から冬服に変わり、（　）に冬服から夏服に変わる。

a. １０月１日	b. ６月１日	c. 守る	d. 染めて
e. 宝石	f. 化粧	g. スカート	h. 内
i. 学校	j. 銀行	k. 清潔	l. 価値観

b. Write about your perspective on school uniforms in Japan.

_____
_____
_____

8課

<8課 - 聞く>

Listening: School Uniform Debate

12秒×5

【You may take notes while listening. Do not look at the questions below before listening. You will have 12 seconds to answer each question. You may NOT move back and forth among questions.】

(Narrator) Now you will listen once to a school debate between Ken and Mari.

(Narrator) Now answer the questions for this selection.

1. What kind of students are Ken and Mari?
    (A) Both Ken and Mari graduated from this school.
    (B) Both Ken and Mari are students at this school now.
    (C) Ken is a study abroad student and Mari graduated from this school.
    (D) Both Ken and Mari are study abroad students.

2. What is Mari's opinion about school uniforms?
    (A) Mari supports uniforms.
    (B) Mari thinks that students can express individuality with uniforms.
    (C) Mari thinks that students can dress up more with uniforms.
    (D) Mari thinks that students will get tired of uniforms.

3. What is Ken's opinion about school uniforms?
    (A) Ken does not like uniforms.
    (B) Ken thinks people cannot identify schools by students' uniforms.
    (C) Ken thinks uniforms look good.
    (D) Ken thinks that students who wear their own clothes look good.

4. Which statement is NOT correct?
    (A) Ken thinks that students don't have to worry about what to wear in the morning with uniforms.
    (B) Ken thinks wearing uniforms will become a memory of their youth.
    (C) Mari thinks uniforms become unsanitary from perspiration.
    (D) Ken thinks that students do not like uniforms.

5. What are Ken's and Mari's opinions about school uniforms?
    (A) Both Ken and Mari generally like uniforms.
    (B) Neither Ken nor Mari likes uniforms.
    (C) Only Ken likes uniforms.
    (D) Only Mari likes uniforms.

<8課 - 読む>

Reading: Fashions

【You may move back and forth among all the questions.】

森モモコ

今日のゴルフ場でのモモコさんは、今流行の緑と黄色の縞模様のシャツを着て、真っ白なミニスカートをはいていました。シャツの襟の内側はオレンジ色でした。帽子もシャツとお揃いの明るい緑色のをかぶっていました。金のネックレスをして、少し派手な大きめのイヤリングもしていました。そして、白い靴をはいていました。腕時計はしていませんでした。モモコさんのファッションは、ゴルフコースの芝生にマッチして、とてもすがすがしい印象で、モモコさんのイメージによく似合っていました。今日はスコアも良く、6アンダーの2位タイと最高のスタートを切りました。

小原さゆり

今日のさゆりさんは、日本舞踊の舞台で輝いていました。舞台での衣装は豪華でした。特に最後に着ていた桜の柄の着物は、とても華やかでした。帯は銀色で珍しく前で締めてありました。髪の毛は着物に似合ったアップのかつらをかぶり、顔は濃い化粧をしていたので、なかなか大人っぽく見えました。いつもは地味な感じのさゆりさんも、舞台に着物姿で立つと、存在感があって、これからの活躍が楽しみです。

＜8課 - 読む (質問)＞
Reading: Fashions

(Narrator) Now answer the questions for this section.

1. What color was Momoko's clothing today?
   (A) Her shirt was green and yellow.
   (B) The inside of her shirt was red.
   (C) She wore long white pants.
   (D) Her cap was white.

2. Which is correct?
   (A) Momoko also wore a small gold necklace.
   (B) Momoko wore no watch.
   (C) Momoko also wore a gold necklace and white earrings.
   (D) Momoko also wore yellow shoes.

3. What did Sayuri wear today on stage?
   (A) a kimono with a maple leaf design
   (B) a gold-colored sash
   (C) a blonde wig
   (D) heavy makeup

4. What was unusual about Sayuri's costume on stage today?
   (A) Sayuri's hair was long.
   (B) Sayuri's sash was tied in the front.
   (C) Sayuri wore a very simple colored *kimono.*
   (D) Sayuri's footwear was very colorful.

5. What impression did the article writer have of Momoko and Sayuri?
   (A) Momoko's fashion style was refreshing.
   (B) Momoko had a slow start today.
   (C) Sayuri looked younger on the stage.
   (D) Sayuri's future as a musical star is promising.

<8課 - 書く (テキストチャット)>
Text Chat: School Uniforms

90秒×6

You will participate in a simulated exchange of text-chat messages. Each time it is your turn to write, you will have 90 seconds. You should respond as fully and as appropriately as possible.

You will have a conversation with Kimi Nakata, a student at your host school in Japan, about American school uniforms.

1. Respond. (90 seconds)
   初めまして。中田です。どうぞよろしく。今日は制服について意見を聞かせて下さい。
2. Describe. (90 seconds)
   チャットではどんな服装をしている分かりませんね。今どんな格好をしているか説明して下さいませんか。
3. Respond and explain your opinion. (90 seconds)
   学校に制服がありますか。制服が好きですか。なぜ？
4. Give a specific example. (90 seconds)
   学校の服装について、どんな規則がありますか。
5. Explain your preference and justify your opinion. (90 seconds)
   学校に制服がある方がいいと思いますか。その理由は？
6. Ask a specific question. (90 seconds)
   今日はどうも有難うございました。日本の学校の制服について質問がありますか。

<8課 - 書く (比較と対比)>
Compare and Contrast Article: Uniforms and Own Clothes

20分

Directions: You are writing an article for the student newspaper of your sister school in Japan. Write an article in which you compare and contrast similarities and differences between wearing uniforms and your own clothes. Based on your personal experience, describe at least THREE aspects of each and highlight the similarities and differences between wearing uniforms and your own clothes. Also state your preference for either and give reasons for it.

Your article should be 300 to 400 characters or longer. Use the *desu/masu* or *da* (plain) style, but use one style consistently. Also, use *kanji* wherever *kanji* from the AP Japanese *kanji* list is appropriate. You have 20 minutes to write.

【NOTES/OUTLINE: 自分の作文のアウトラインを書こう！】

Introduction:
_____

Three similarities/differences:

   1. _____
   2. _____
   3. _____

Your preference and give reasons:
_____
_____

8課

＜8課 - 話す (会話)＞
Conversation: Dance Party

`20秒×4`

You will participate in a simulated conversation. Each time it is your turn to speak, you will have 20 seconds to record. You should respond as fully and as appropriately as possible.

You will have a conversation with Kei, your Japanese friend, about a dance party.

(Kei)
(20 seconds)
(Kei)
(20 seconds)
(Kei)
(20 seconds)
(Kei)
(20 seconds)

＜8課 - 話す (日本文化)＞
Cultural Perspective Presentation: School Uniforms in Japan

`4分＋2分`

Directions: Imagine you are making an oral presentation to your Japanese class. First, you will read and hear the topic for your presentation. You will have 4 minutes to prepare your presentation. Then you will have 2 minutes to record your presentation. Your presentation should be as complete as possible.

Present your own view or perspective of school uniforms in Japan. Discuss at least FIVE aspects or examples of school uniforms in Japan.

Begin with an appropriate introduction, give details, explain your own view or perspective, and end with a concluding remark.

【Let's take notes!】

1. Begin with an appropriate introduction.
   _____

2. Discuss five aspects/examples of the topic.
   1.) _____
   2.) _____
   3.) _____
   4.) _____
   5.) _____

3. Explain your view or perspective.
   _____

4. End with a concluding remark.
   _____

9課　●●●　コミュニケーションとメディア　●●●
Communication and Media

【AP® タスク：コミュニケーションとメディア】
What three cell phone functions are most useful to you? In what ways do you use your computer most? What ethical issues do you face when you use a computer? Which do you think is better, using the telephone or e-mail? Which do you think are better, printed newspapers or Internet newspapers?

【文化】 日本のテレビ番組：TV Programs in Japan

One of the most popular modern pastimes in Japan is watching television. In Tokyo, there are five private television channels and two nationally operated public NHK (Nihon Broadcasting System, or *Nihon Hoosoo Kyookai*) channels. NHK is broadcast throughout Japan, and various affiliates of the five private broadcasting systems are also aired. Japanese viewers also watch cable and satellite television.

The dominant news channel is NHK, though all of the privately operated stations also have ample news coverage. The Japanese are an avid early morning television audience, as detailed news coverage is broadcast all morning until about 9:00 a.m. The evening news is on at 6:00 p.m. National news is uniformly covered by all stations in Japan, but regional news is reported by regional affiliates throughout Japan. The morning news also covers extensive traffic reports (highway, bullet train and plane travel conditions), on which Japanese commuters depend heavily. A major part of the morning and evening news is devoted to detailed and precise weather reports. The broadcasts deliver daily weather forecasts, long term forecasts, national as well as regional weather, and ocean conditions. Japanese rarely leave their homes without knowing the weather forecast for the day, and are always appropriately prepared for the day's weather.

After the morning news and through the early afternoon, news stations feature "wide show" (ワイドショー) television programs, which are mainly targeted at housewives. These talk shows specialize in human interest feature stories on topics such as fashion trends, celebrity news, and popular events.

Another favorite television genre is the drama (ドラマ), or soap opera. Japanese dramas are short-term series that consist of only ten to twelve episodes. Because they are short term, writers are able to create fresh storylines that keep up with current topics, and use budding or currently popular actors and actresses as their main characters. The scenes are also shot at popular hot spots and feature fashionably dressed characters. Theme songs from ドラマ often become popular "top ten" songs.

Utabangumi (歌番組), or shows featuring singing, are also popular in Japan. The most famous, of course, is NHK's Red and White Song Contest or *Koohaku Uta Gassen* (紅白歌合戦) which airs every New Year's Eve. Families gather around the television to watch the four to five hour long production, an elaborate show with the most popular current and longstanding singers performing their hit songs. The friendly competition between the Red Team (female singers) and White Team (male singers) culminates with the announcement of the top scoring team at the end of the show.

Finally, an essential part of television programming is commercials. Commercials in Japan are sometimes viewed by Westerners as bordering on childish and silly, as is Japanese humor in general. Many of the commercials are of the "cutesy" type, accompanied by upbeat, cheerful music. Unlike Western commercials, there is very little negativity directed at the competition.

Television in Japan represents many of the values of contemporary Japanese culture, as it responds to the demands of its audience. Efficiency, uniformity, and solidarity are some of the qualities that identify Japanese television culture.

Questions to ponder: How is television culture in your country different from Japan? Why? What are some similarities?

| 9課 | | 復習単語(ふくしゅうたんご) | |

トピック：コミュニケーションとメディア

1. 新聞	しんぶん	N	newspaper
2. テレビ		N	TV
3. ラジオ		N	radio
4. (イー)メール		N	e-mail
5. 電話	でんわ	N	telephone
6. 携帯(電話)(けいたい)	けいたい(でんわ)	N	cell phone
7. ビデオ		N	video
8. 写真	しゃしん	N	photo
9. コマーシャル		N	commercial

| 9課 | ★★★ | 新しい単語 | ★★★ |

1. きのう＜機能＞　N　discussion; debate
「ケータイのどの機能を一番よく使っている？」"What cell phone function do you use most often?

2. じょうほう＜情報＞　N　information
個人の情報を盗まれてしまった。Personal information was stolen.

3. めざまし(どけい)＜目覚まし(時計)＞　N　alarm (clock)
寝る前に、目覚ましをセットする。I set the alarm before I go to bed.

4. ぼうすい＜防水＞　N　waterproof
防水時計をして海へ行く。I wear a water proof watch and go to the beach.

5. マナーモード　N　vibration mode
電車の中とかコンサート会場ではケータイをマナーモードに切り替える。In trains or in concert halls, I switch my cell phone to vibration mode.

6. へんじ＜返事＞　N　reply
友達にメールを送っても、返事はすぐ来ない。Even if I send an e-mail to my friend, she doesn't reply right away.

7. メロドラマ　N　melodrama
メロドラマは中年女性に人気があるようだ。It seems melodramas are popular among middle-aged women.

8. げいのう＜芸能＞　N　entertainment
げいのうじん＜芸能人＞　N　entertainers
芸能ニュースはいつも興味深い。News about entertainment is always very interesting.

9. しゅやく＜主役＞　N　leading role
この青春ドラマの主役は若い歌手に決まったそうだ。I understand it was decided that a young singer would have the lead role in this TV drama about young people.

10. しゅだいか＜主題歌＞　N　theme song
ドラマも主題歌も今ヒットしている。Both the TV drama and its theme song are hits now.

11. かし＜歌詞＞　N　lyrics
歌詞のいい歌が好きだ。I like songs with good lyrics.

12. しんはつばい＜新発売＞　N　newly released (for sale)
新発売のビデオゲームを早く買いたい。I want to buy the newly released video game early.

13. わだい＜話題＞　　N　topic (of discussion)
今話題の映画を早く見たい。I want to see the movie everyone is talking about right away.

14. しちょうりつ＜視聴率＞　　N　program rating
紅白歌合戦はいつも視聴率が高い。The ratings for the Red and White Song Contest are always high.

15. ちょうさ＜調査＞　　N　investigation; survey
今回の調査に御協力お願いします。We request your cooperation on this survey.

16. アンケート　　N　questionnaire
アンケートの結果をお知らせします。We will announce the results of the questionnaire.

17. ちほう＜地方＞　　N　region; district
全国ニュースも地方ニュースも放送している。Both the national news and regional news are being broadcast.

18. おおみそか＜大晦日＞　　N　New Year's Eve
紅白歌合戦はいつも大晦日の夜にやっている。The Red and White Contest is always broadcast on the evening of Dec. 31.

19. ひごろ＜日頃＞　　N　usually; (almost) always
日頃一番使っているケータイの機能はメールだ。Usually, the function I use most often on my cell phone is e-mail.

20. しよう＜使用＞　　N　usage
　　しようちゅう＜使用中＞　　N　in use
学校にはケータイ使用についての規則がある。There are rules about the use of cell phones in school.

21. しゅうかん＜習慣＞　　N　custom; practice
毎朝紙の新聞を読むのが私の習慣だ。It is my practice to read the printed newspaper every morning.

22. ユーモア　　N　(sense of) humor
日本人のユーモアを理解するのは難しい。It is difficult to comprehend the Japanese sense of humor.

23. りんり＜倫理＞　　N　ethics
　　りんりてき＜倫理的＞　　Na　ethical
ネット社会ではいろいろな倫理的な問題がある。There are various ethical problems in the world of the Internet.

9課

24. ぐたいてき＜具体的＞　Na　concrete
    ぐたいてきに＜具体的に＞　Adv　concretely; specifically
    どんな番組が好きか具体的に教えて下さい。Please tell me specifically what kind of (TV) programs you like.

25. ろくが＜録画＞(を)する／します　V3　to film; to video record
    ドラマは録画して、後で見る。I will videotape the drama, and watch it later.

26. さくし＜作詞＞(を)する／します　V3　to write the lyrics
    さっきょく＜作曲＞(を)する／します　V3　to compose music
    彼は全部自分の歌を作詞作曲して歌うそうだ。I understand he writes the lyrics and music for his songs and sings them.

27. せんでん＜宣伝＞(を)する／します　V3　to advertise; to publicize
    新しい映画をテレビで宣伝している。He is promoting his new movie on television.

28. しんか＜進化＞(を)する／します　V3　to progress; to evolve
    しんかろん＜進化論＞　N　theory of evolution
    テクノロジーは速く進化している。Technology is evolving quickly.

29. ついていく＜ついて行く＞／ついて行きます　V1　to keep abreast; to keep up
    テクノロジーの進化について行けない。I cannot keep up with the advancement of technology.

30. おこなう＜行う＞／行います　V1　to do; to conduct [formal]
    アンケートを行っていますので、どうぞよろしくお願いします。We are conducting a survey, so we request your help.

31. (〜に)はまっている／はまる／はまります　V1　to fit; to be obssessed (with)
    多くの日本の中年女性が韓国ドラマにはまっているそうだ。I understand that many middle-aged women in Japan are obsessed with Korean dramas.

32. とりあげる＜取り上げる＞／取り上げます　V2　to take (in one's hand); to confiscate
    授業中ケータイを使っていたら、先生に取り上げられてしまった。I was using my cell phone during class, so it was taken away by my teacher.

33. (〜が)なる＜鳴る＞／鳴ります　V1　to ring
    電話が鳴っている。The phone is ringing.

34. じろっとみる＜じろっと見る＞／見ます　V2　to stare at
    授業中ケータイが鳴った時に、皆にじろっと見られて恥ずかしかった。When my cell phone rang during class time, I felt embarrassed since everyone looked at me.

【もっと単語】

1. すみ＜隅＞からすみ＜隅＞まで		Exp	from corner to corner
2. ワープロ		N	word processor
3. (お)さいふ＜(お)財布＞		N	purse; wallet
4. だんゆう＜男優＞		N	(male) actor
5. じょゆう＜女優＞		N	actress
6. じだいげき＜時代劇＞		N	historical drama
7. チョンマゲ＜丁髷＞		N	topknot
8. ほうそうきょく＜放送局＞		N	broadcasting company
9. ホラーえいが＜ホラー映画＞		N	horror movie
10. どうろ＜道路＞		N	road
11. くに＜国＞		N	country
12. しゅふ＜主婦＞		N	housewife
13. こえ＜声＞		N	voice
14. ぎょうじ＜行事＞		N	event
15. とちゅう＜途中＞		N	along the way
16. むり＜無理＞		Na	impossible
17. だいたい		Adv	generally
18. おもに＜主に＞		Adv	mainly
19. すっかり		Adv	completely
20. じょうえい＜上映＞する／します		V3	to screen; to show
じょうえいちゅう＜上映中＞		N	is showing (now)
21. れんらくをとる＜連絡を取る＞／取ります		V1	to contact
22. やくにたつ＜役に立つ＞／役に立ちます		V1	to be useful
23. きりかえる＜切り替える＞／切り替えます		V2	to switch over; to change
24. ひろげる＜広げる＞／広げます		V2	to spread; to widen
25. うまくいく＜行く＞／行きます		V1	(something) goes well
26. ついている＜付いている＞／付いています		V2	(something) is attached
27. しゅうちゅう＜集中＞(を)する／します		V3	to focus; to concentrate

9課

9課　■■■　　　　　　　　　　　文法　　　　　　　　　　　■■■

> A. Verb (plain form) ＋ ような気がする　　to have a feeling that ～
> 　　いadjective
> 　　なadjective＋な
> 　　Noun＋の
> This construction is used to express one's "gut" feeling about a situation, thing or action. ような気がする is preceded by the plain forms of verbs, い adjectives, な adjectives (with な), and nouns (with の).

Fill in the blanks with the correct word from the box, then circle the correct particle.

1. ネットの新聞は、新聞を＿＿＿＿＿＿（な　の　X）ような気がしないんだ。
2. 電話で人の声を聞きながら話すのは、＿＿＿＿＿＿（な　の　X）ような気がする。
3. 母親はもうすっかり韓国ドラマに＿＿＿＿＿＿（な　の　X）ような気がする。
4. この歌は歌詞がとってもいいから、＿＿＿＿＿＿（な　の　X）ような気がしている。
5. このホラー映画は＿＿＿＿＿＿（な　の　X）ような気がする。
6. この歌は彼の作詞＿＿＿＿＿＿（な　の　X）ような気がする。

> 作曲　こわい　大事　はまっている　読んだ　ヒットする

> B. Verb (plain form) ＋といい(です)。　I hope/wish that ～
> 　　いadjective
> 　　なadjective＋だ
> 　　Noun＋だ
> This construction is used when one wants to express one's own hope or wish. It is preceded by the plain form of verbs, いadjectives, なadjectives (with だ) and nouns (with だ). Often, verbs appear in the potential form, especially when they refer to the speaker.

Fill in the blanks with the correct word from the box, then circle the correct particle.

1. 希望の大学へ＿＿＿＿＿＿（だ　X）といいね。
2. キャンプがいい＿＿＿＿＿＿（だ　X）といいね。
3. この調査が＿＿＿＿＿＿（だ　X）といいですね。
4. 母は好きなドラマがもっと＿＿＿＿＿＿（だ　X）といいと思っているようだ。
5. テレビ番組の途中のコマーシャルがもっと＿＿＿＿＿＿（だ　X）といい。
6. 図書館が＿＿＿＿＿＿（だ　X）だといいんですが。

> 続く　天気　静か　行ける　うまくいく　少ない

C. Conjunctions and adverbs

1. そして、	And,	8. それに、	Besides,
2. でも、	But,	9. それにしても、	Even so,
3. その次に、	After that,	10. 残念ながら、	Unfortunately
4. それから、	And then,	11. やっぱり	As (one) expected
5. ところで、	By the way,	12. すっかり	completely
6. だって、	That's because, [informal]	13. ぜったい	absolutely
7. それとも、	(Question 1). Or, (Question 2)		

Fill in the blanks with the most appropriate word from the above list.

1. このケータイ、防水の機能もついてるんだって。（　　　　）、私には必要ないな。
2. 一番よく使っている機能は電話。（　　　　）、メールかな。
3. 電話で話すのは大事だと思うよ。（　　　　）、ネットの新聞を読んでる？
4. 私はネットの新聞が好きよ。（　　　　）、最新のニュースがただで読めるから。
5. メールは手紙より速いし、（　　　　）、安い。
6. （　　　　）、テクノロジーの進化は速すぎて、私はついていけない。
7. 私は（　　　　）テクノロジーが苦手で、手伝ってあげられないよ。
8. この歌手の歌を聞いてから、（　　　　）ファンになってしまった。
9. 映画は映画館で見るのが好きですか。（　　　　）うちでＤＶＤを見るのが好きですか。

D. Sentence ending particles

1. よ	emphasis	4. かな	I wonder if 〜.
2. ね	seeking agreement or confirmation	5. かしら（女）	I wonder if 〜.
3. ねえ	admiration, surprise, exclamation	6. わ（女）	[sentence ending particle]

Choose the most appropriate sentence particle.

1. 女：ねえ、私の最新の携帯、見て。テレビがついてるんだ（よ　ね　ねえ）。
   男：わあ、すごい（よ　ね　ねえ）。
2. 女：週末、教えてくれたホラー映画を見た（よ　ね　ねえ）。
   　　とっても良かった（わ　かしら）。
   男：今度、一緒に映画を見に行こう（よ　ねえ）。
3. 男：この歌、ヒットする（かな　かしら　わ）。
   女：うん、歌詞がいいから、ぜったいヒットすると思う（よ　ねえ　かな）。

9課

4. 女：私はいつもネットの新聞を読んでる（よ　ね　ねえ）。
   男：そう？僕は紙の新聞を読まないと、読んだ気がしないんだ（よ　ね　ねえ）。
   これも習慣（かな　よ　ね　ねえ）。

> E. Conversation strategy:
>   1. Echo a question.
>   2. While thinking of an answer, use そうですねえ.
>   Ex.「学校に携帯の規則がありますか。」
>   "Are there any rules about cell phone (usage) at school?"
>   「携帯の規則ですか。そうですねえ。規則は先生によって違います。」
>   "Rules about cell phone (usage)? Let me see... Depending on the teacher, the rules differ."

Fill in the blanks with the appropriate response to echo the question.

1.「電話とメールとどっちをもっと使っていますか。」
　「＿＿＿＿＿＿＿＿＿ですか。そうですねえ。私は電話の方をもっと使っていますね。」
2.「テレビ番組のアンケートに御協力お願いします。」
　「＿＿＿＿＿＿＿＿＿ですか。分かりました。協力しましょう。」
3.「テレビのコマーシャルで、お好きなコマーシャルがありますか。」
　「＿＿＿＿＿＿＿＿＿ですか。そうですねえ。私はコマーシャルが好きじゃないです。」
4.「『初恋』というドラマの視聴率を調べています。毎週ご覧になっていますか。」
　「＿＿＿＿＿＿＿＿＿ですか。もちろん、毎週見ていますよ。」

> F. - させて＋いただきます　　　Very polite expression
>   1. 協力させていただきます。　　I will take the opportunity to cooperate.
>   2. 答えさせていただきます。　　I will take the opportunity to respond.
> This expression, which is used with verbs in the -te form, is used by a speaker to humbly express his/her willingness to do something when given the opportunity or when asked to do so.

Fill in the blanks with the the correct form of the verb in the ( ).

1. 生徒：「では、まず私から＿＿＿＿＿＿＿＿＿いただきます。」（紹介する）
2. 生徒：「今日は私の家族の先祖について＿＿＿＿＿＿＿＿＿いただきます。」
   （発表する）
3. 生徒：「出来るだけ、＿＿＿＿＿＿＿＿＿いただきます。」（協力する）
4. 店員：「探していらっしゃる品物が見つかりましたら、後ほど御自宅にお電話で
   ＿＿＿＿＿＿＿＿＿いただきます。（連絡する）

9課

G. Informal style and formal style

	Informal style	Formal style
1.	電話で話すって、大事だと思う。	電話で話すことは、大事だと思います。
2.	ネットでニュースが読めるじゃない。	ネットでニュースが読めませんか。
3.	いつも見てるよ。だって、おもしろいから。	いつも見ていますよ。なぜなら、おもしろいからです。
4.	母が見てるかも知れない。	母が見ているかも知れません。
5.	全部、自分で作曲してるんだって。	全部、自分で作曲しているそうです。
6.	すっかりファンになっちゃった。	すっかりファンになってしまいました。
7.	ねえ、見て見て。	すみません、見て下さい。
8.	どっちの方が好き？	どちらの方が好きですか。
9.	そうかい。（男）	そうですか。
10.	一緒に行こうね。	一緒に行きましょうね。

9課

| 9課 | | アクティビティー | |

A. 日本文化：一人か二人ワーク→クラスワーク

Divide the topics below among your classmates and research your topic on the Internet. Using visuals, present your findings with your classmates.

1. NHK、総合テレビ、教育テレビ、フジテレビ
2. テレビのニュース番組、交通情報、天気予報
3. ワイドショー、メロドラマ、有名な芸能人
4. 紅白歌合戦、大河ドラマ、時代劇、お笑いタレント
5. 日本のコマーシャル

B. Pre-Listening Activity「コミュニケーション」：ペアワーク→クラスワーク

Discuss the following questions with your partner and share your findings with your class.

1. ケータイの機能で何をよく使っていますか。よく使うベスト３に１～３の番号を書きなさい。

　　___電話　___テキストメール　___目覚まし　___インターネット　___時計
　　___カメラ　___音楽　___ゲーム　___おさいふケータイ
　　___ナビゲーター　___テレビ　___電車の改札　___防水

2. コンピューターで一番よく使っている機能は何ですか。

　　___情報　___ゲーム　___ワープロ　___ビデオ　___買物　その他：_____

3. コンピューターを使って、倫理的にどんな問題がありますか。
　　_____

C. Post-Listening Activity「コミュニケーション」：グループワーク→クラスワーク

討論をしよう。Prepare and debate the following topics.

1. 題：「電話」と「Eメール」とどちらの方がいいですか。

　電話の良い点：　_____
　電話の悪い点：　_____
　Eメールの良い点：　_____
　Eメールの悪い点：　_____
　どちらの方が好き？：　_____
　好きな理由：　_____

9課

2. 題：「紙の新聞」と「インターネットの新聞」とどちらの方がいいですか。
   紙の新聞の良い点： _____
   紙の新聞の悪い点： _____
   ネット新聞の良い点： _____
   ネット新聞の悪い点： _____
   どちらの方が好き？： _____
   好きな理由： _____

D. 読む Pre-Reading Activity 「イーメール」：ペアワーク→クラスワーク

Discuss the following questions with your partner in the informal style.

1. 韓ドラって何？
2. 韓ドラにはまっている人って、若い人？
3. どんなテレビ番組を録画している？
4. 誰のブログをよく見ている？
5. 自分の曲を作詞作曲して歌っている歌手を誰か知ってる？
6. 歌詞のいい曲を教えて。
7. 歌手の中で誰のファン？
8. ホラー映画が好き？
9. 好きな男優、女優は誰？
10. お笑いタレントって何をする人か知ってる？
11. 今よく宣伝している新発売の物って何かある？
12. コマーシャルの中で一番好きなコマーシャルは何？
13. 大河ドラマって、時代劇だけ？
14. 侍のチョンマゲを、どう思う？
15. 今、上映されている話題の映画は何？

9課

E. 読む Post-Reading Activity 「イーメール」：ペアワーク→クラスワーク

「映画と音楽」を比べなさい。4分準備して、2分で発表しなさい。
Compare and contrast similarities and differences between movies and music. Describe at least THREE aspects of each and highlight the similarities and differences between movies and music. Also state your preference for either and give reasons for your choice.

Introduction:
_____

Three similarities/differences:
  1. _____
  2. _____
  3. _____

Your preference and reasons:
_____

F. テキストチャット 「ケータイ」：ペアワーク→クラスワーク

Pair off with a partner. First, take turns reading the conversation. Next, one partner will read the questions out loud while the other partner will provide answers to the questions, incorporating the underlined phrases to formulate an original response. For each question, use 20 seconds to answer. Once you reach the end, switch roles. When answering, try to avoid looking at the book.

1. 質問：初めまして。渡辺です。どうぞよろしく。今日は携帯の使用についての質問に御協力下さい。
   答：初めまして。山本マークです。こちらこそ、どうぞよろしくお願いします。ケータイの使用についての質問ですね。分かりました。出来るだけ、協力させていただきます。

2. 質問：日頃よく使っている携帯の機能を三つ教えて下さい。
   答：ケータイの機能三つですね。私が日頃使っている機能は、電話とメールと目覚ましです。毎日ケータイを使っているので、今ケータイがないと、生活出来ないと思います。

3. 質問：携帯で電話とメールとどちらの方をもっと使っていますか。
   答：電話とメールですか。私は電話の方をメールよりもっと使っています。メールはすぐ返事が来ませんが、電話だと、すぐ返事が来ます。私の友達はあまりメールを見ていません。

4. 質問：学校で携帯使用について、どんな規則がありますか。
   答：学校のケータイの規則ですか。私の学校では先生によって規則は違います。きびしい先生は、教室で生徒がケータイを持っているだけで、ケータイを取り上げてしまいます。規則ではありませんが、マナーとして教室ではケータイをマナーモー

9課

ドに切り替えるはずです。ケータイが鳴ると、皆がじろっと見るので、恥ずかしくなります。

5. 質問：学校での携帯についての規則をどう思いますか。なぜですか。
   答：<u>学校でのケータイの規則ですね</u>。いいと思いますよ。ケータイは教室では必要ではありませんが、休み時間や放課後に親や友人と連絡を取るのに役に立ちます。授業中にケータイの音が鳴ると勉強に集中できませんから、教室での規則はきびしい方がいいと思っています。

6. 質問：どうも御意見を有難うございました。日本の携帯について何か質問がありますか。
   答：どういたしまして。お役に立てて嬉しいです。<u>日本のケータイについての質問ですが</u>、日本の学校でのケータイの規則は私の学校よりもっときびしいですか。どんな規則がありますか。今回の調査がうまくいくといいですね。また私でお役に立てることがありましたら、いつでも御連絡下さい。では、失礼します。

G. Compare & Contrast「ラジオとテレビ」：グループワーク→クラスワーク

討論をしよう。Prepare and debate the following topics.
題：「ラジオ」と「テレビ」とどちらの方がいいですか。

1. ラジオの良い点：＿＿＿＿＿＿＿＿＿＿＿＿＿＿＿＿＿＿＿
2. ラジオの悪い点：＿＿＿＿＿＿＿＿＿＿＿＿＿＿＿＿＿＿＿
3. テレビの良い点：＿＿＿＿＿＿＿＿＿＿＿＿＿＿＿＿＿＿＿
4. テレビの悪い点：＿＿＿＿＿＿＿＿＿＿＿＿＿＿＿＿＿＿＿
5. どちらが好き？：＿＿＿＿＿＿＿＿＿＿＿＿＿＿＿＿＿＿＿
6. 好きな理由：＿＿＿＿＿＿＿＿＿＿＿＿＿＿＿＿＿＿＿＿＿

H. 会話「テレビ番組」：ペアワーク→クラスワーク

Pair off with a partner. First, take turns reading the conversation. Next, one partner will read the questions out loud while the other partner will provide answers to the questions, incorporating the underlined phrases to formulate an original response. For each question, use 20 seconds to answer. Once you reach the end, switch roles. When answering, try to avoid looking at the book.

1. 質問：初めまして。テレビ番組についてアンケートを行っています。すみませんが、御協力お願いします。
   答：初めまして。山本マークです。こちらこそ、どうぞよろしくお願いします。<u>テレビ番組のアンケートですか</u>。おもしろそうですね。出来るだけ、協力させていただきます。

2. 質問：えー、視聴率を調べているんですが、一番好きなテレビ番組の名前と曜日と時間を教えて下さい。

9課

答：　ああ、視聴率ですか。私の一番好きなテレビ番組は「初恋」という番組で、日曜
　　　　　日の夜９時から１０時までやっています。ラブストーリーではまっちゃいました。
3. 質問：どんなコマーシャルがお好きですか。具体的に教えて下さい。
　　答：　コマーシャルですか。私はだいたいコマーシャルが好きじゃありませんが、最近
　　　　　やってる新発売の飲物のコマーシャルは、ペンギンが可愛くって好きですよ。
4. 質問：そうですか。テレビ番組について何かご希望がありますか。
　　答：　希望ですか。そうですねえ、私はコマーシャルが多すぎると思います。番組の途
　　　　　中のコマーシャルを少なくしてほしいです。どうも有難うございました。

I. 文化発表「日本のテレビ番組」：ペアワーク→クラスワーク

A. Fill in the (　) with the correct word from the box below.

1. NHKは日本放送協会のことで、(　　)の放送局である。
2. NHKには二つのチャンネルがあって、総合チャンネルと(　　)チャンネルがある。
3. テレビのニュース番組には世界のニュースも全国のニュースも(　　)のニュースも放送している。
4. ニュース番組には新幹線や道路の(　　)情報や天気予報なども放送している。
5. ニュース番組の後、ワイドショーをやっていて、主に(　　)が見ている。流行のファッションとか話題の芸能ニュースとかが多い。
6. 日本のテレビドラマはたいてい１０回から１２回のエピソードでお話が終わる。主演の俳優は可愛くて、カッコよく、ドラマの(　　)もよくヒットする。
7. (　　)も中年の主婦に人気があるようだ。
8. NHKの紅白歌合戦は毎年(　　)に行われる年中行事だ。
9. 紅白歌合戦は男性の白組と女性の赤組が歌で競い合うが、日本の有名な(　　)がだいたい出演する。視聴率も高い。
10. 日本のコマーシャルはとてもよく作られているが、アメリカ人から見ると、ちょっと子供っぽく見えるものも多いようだ。コマーシャルを見ると、日本人の(　　)のセンスがよく分かる。

a. 教育	b. 交通	c. 主題歌	d. 歌手	e. ユーモア
f. 地方	g. 国	h. 大晦日	i. 主婦	j. メロドラマ

b. Write your perspective or views on Japanese TV programs.

_____
_____
_____

9課

<9課 - 聞く>
Listening: Communication Tools

【You may take notes while listening. Do not look at the questions below before listening. You will have 12 seconds to answer each question. You may NOT move back and forth among questions.】

(Narrator) Now you will listen to a movie preview once.

(Narrator) Now answer the questions for this selection.

1. What are Kai's and Yuki's opinions about waterproof cellular phones?
   (A)   Both Kai and Yuki like them.
   (B)   Neither Kai nor Yuki like them.
   (C)   Only Kai likes them.
   (D)   Only Yuki likes them.

2. What cell phone function does Yuki use the most?
   (A)   text messaging
   (B)   telephone
   (C)   blog
   (D)   photo

3. What do Kai and Yuki think about text messaging?
   (A)   Kai does not like text messaging because he doesn't receive responses quickly.
   (B)   Kai likes text messaging because nobody bothers him.
   (C)   Yuki thinks it's important to have face to face communication.
   (D)   Yuki likes text messaging because she can check her messages any time.

4. What opinions do Kai and Yuki have about newspapers?
   (A)   Both Kai and Yuki like Internet newspapers.
   (B)   Neither Kai nor Yuki likes Internet newspapers.
   (C)   Only Kai likes Internet newspapers.
   (D)   Only Yuki likes Internet newspapers.

5. What is Kai's opinion about technology?
   (A)   Kai thinks that technology causes people more problems.
   (B)   Kai thinks that technology advances too quickly.
   (C)   Kai thinks that technology helps people's lives.
   (D)   Kai thinks that technology makes his life more interesting.

<9課 - 読む>
Reading: E-mails
【You may move back and forth among all the questions.】

Read this set of emails.

受信箱

	差出人：	件名：	送信日時：
Message #1	ユナ	RE:韓ドラ	１０月８日

そのドラマは残念ながら録画していないよ。私の趣味じゃないから。でも、うちの母親は韓ドラにはまってるから、ひょっとしたら録画してるかもしれないね。母に聞いてみる。

Message #2	かな子	RE:ブログ	１０月９日

教えてくれたブログを見たよ。この歌手、全部自分で作詞作曲しているんだってね。歌詞がとってもいいから、すっかりファンになっちゃった。彼女のコンサートがあったら、ぜったい一緒に行こうね。

Message #3	幸男	RE:映画	１０月９日

映画にさそってくれて有難う。そのホラー映画、主演男優も共演女優も大好きだから、見に行きたいんだけど、その日ほかに用があって、残念。また、今度な。

Message #4	健太	コマーシャル	１０月２０日

最近ラジオを聞いていたら、お笑いタレントのモンタがコマーシャルで新発売の飲み物の宣伝をしていたんだけど、何の飲み物か知ってる？

Message #5	ゆり	ビッグニュース	１０月２０日

今朝のネットの芸能ニュースによると、アイドル歌手のゴンタが来年のNHKの大河ドラマの主役に選ばれたんだって。時代劇らしいから、チョンマゲ姿のゴンタが見れるよ。今から楽しみ！

Message #6	夏美	アニメ	１０月２０日

あの今話題になっている宮崎駿監督のアニメ、この土曜から映画館で上映されるんだって、行ってみない？

＜９課 - 読む (質問)＞

Reading: Emails

(Narrator) Now answer the questions for this section.

1. Which message is an invitation to a movie?
   (A) Message #1
   (B) Message #3
   (C) Message #5
   (D) Message #6

2. Which message declines an invitation?
   (A) Message #1
   (B) Message #2
   (C) Message #3
   (D) Message #5

3. Who may have recorded the Korean drama?
   (A) Yuna
   (B) Yuna's mother
   (C) Yuna's sister
   (D) Yuna's friend

4. What did Kanako find out after looking at the singer's blog?
   (A) The singer is a male singer.
   (B) The lyrics of this singer's music are good.
   (C) This singer composes some of the songs.
   (D) This singer will have a concert soon.

5. What exciting news is revealed?
   (A) A famous comedian is singing in his commercial.
   (B) A famous horror movie will be on screening starting this Saturday.
   (C) A famous singer will be the main actor for a historical drama.
   (D) A famous movie star will have a concert.

＜9課 - 書く (テキストチャット)＞
Text Chat: Cell Phones

`90秒×6`

You will participate in a simulated exchange of text-chat messages. Each time it is your turn to write, you will have 90 seconds. You should respond as fully and as appropriately as possible.

You will have a conversation with Kimi Watanabe, a student at your host school in Japan, who is researching how cell phones are used by American high school students.

1. Respond. (90 seconds)
   初めまして。渡辺です。どうぞよろしく。今日は携帯の使用についての質問に御協力下さい。
2. Give specific examples. (90 seconds)
   日頃よく使っている携帯の機能を三つ教えて下さい。
3. Respond and explain your preference. (90 seconds)
   携帯で電話とメールとどちらの方をもっと使っていますか。
4. Give a specific example. (90 seconds)
   学校で携帯使用について、どんな規則がありますか。
5. Justify your opinion. (90 seconds)
   学校での携帯についての規則をどう思いますか。なぜですか。
6. Ask a specific question. (90 seconds)
   どうも御意見を有難うございました。日本の携帯について何か質問がありますか。

＜9課 - 書く (比較と対比)＞
Compare and Contrast Article: TV and Radio

`20分`

Directions: You are writing an article for the student newspaper of your sister school in Japan. Write an article in which you compare and contrast similarities and differences between TV and radio. Based on your personal experience, describe at least THREE aspects of each and highlight the similarities and differences between TV and radio. Also state your preference for either and give reasons for it.

Your article should be 300 to 400 characters or longer. Use the *desu/masu* or *da* (plain) style, but use one style consistently. Also, use *kanji* wherever *kanji* from the AP Japanese *kanji* list is appropriate. You have 20 minutes to write.

【NOTES/OUTLINE: 自分の作文のアウトラインを書こう！】

Introduction:
_____

Three similarities/differences:

　1. _____

　2. _____

　3. _____

Your preference and give reasons:
_____
_____

9課

＜9課 - 話す (会話)＞
Conversation: TV Programs

`20秒×4`

You will participate in a simulated conversation. Each time it is your turn to speak, you will have 20 seconds to record. You should respond as fully and as appropriately as possible.

You will have a conversation with a person who is conducting a survey for a TV station about media.

(Female)
(20 seconds)
(Female)
(20 seconds)
(Female)
(20 seconds)
(Female)
(20 seconds)

＜9課 - 話す (日本文化)＞
Cultural Perspective Presentation: Japanese TV Programs

`4分+2分`

Directions: Imagine you are making an oral presentation to your Japanese class. First, you will read and hear the topic for your presentation. You will have 4 minutes to prepare your presentation. Then you will have 2 minutes to record your presentation. Your presentation should be as complete as possible.

Present your own view or perspective of Japanese TV programs. Discuss at least FIVE aspects or examples of Japanese TV programs.

Begin with an appropriate introduction, give details, explain your own view or perspective, and end with a concluding remark.

【Let's take notes!】

1. Begin with an appropriate introduction.

   _____

2. Discuss five aspects/examples of the topic.

   1.) _____
   2.) _____
   3.) _____
   4.) _____
   5.) _____

3. Explain your view or perspective.

   _____

4. End with a concluding remark.

   _____

`9課`

10課　●●● テクノロジー ●●●
Technology

【AP® タスク：テクノロジー】
List three famous products that are examples of Japan's advanced technology. What special characteristics does each product have? Why do you think that the Japanese are skilled at developing advanced technological products?

【文化】 日本のテクノロジー：Japan's Technology

Japan is recognized as one of the countries at the cutting edge of technology. Japan's "love affair" with technology is not accidental. The characteristics of the Japanese people, society and its traditions have provided an excellent environment for technology to thrive in Japan. In a country which has for centuries nurtured sophisticated, precise and detailed arts and craftwork, it is not surprising that the contemporary "art" of technology has adapted itself well in Japan.

Marking the arrival of modernization in Japan was the *shinkansen* (新幹線), or bullet train. In 1964, when it made its debut, it received raves for its high speed of 125 mph (200 kph). The fastest *shinkansen* is now capable of reaching speeds of 600 km, or about 375 mph, or more than twice as fast. Japanese engineers continue to upgrade the *shinkansen* with advancements in not only its speed, but also control and functions, its quietness and general efficiency.

Japan is likely also the most advanced country in hybrid car technology. Hybrid cars were introduced in the West and resulted in small scale production in the U.S. and Europe, but Japan's car giants, Toyota and Honda, were the first to successfully market hybrid cars. Honda's release of the Insight and hybrid Civic and Toyota's release of the Prius have been welcomed by consumers for their quality, efficiency, and environmental friendliness. In 2004, the Toyota Prius II received the Car of the Year Award from Motor Trend and the North American Auto Show.

Japan's robot technology also leads the world. Robots in Japan are well accepted as friendly helpers and are not viewed as threats. Indeed, with the steep decline of a young, strong working force, and the ballooning number of older citizens who require help in and out of the home, robots are welcome in Japan today. In the 1970's, the earliest generation of robots in Japan was created to join factory workforces. Today, robots have entered the daily lives of many Japanese as office receptionists that serve tea and greet customers, or as pets, nursing staff at hospitals, companions and caretakers for the elderly and housecleaning maids at home.

Another area in which Japan dominates is the video game industry. Some of the earliest and most successful games, such as Pacman, Super Mario and Final Fantasy, have all emerged from Japan. Popular home consoles, such as Sony's PlayStation and Nintendo's DS and Wii, continue to be developed in Japan. The combination of *anime* TV and trading cards with video gaming, e.g., Pokemon and Yu-Gi-Oh, have fueled the popularity of games in Japan as well as throughout the world.

Smartphones in Japan have long been part of the lives of the Japanese. Functions and cosmetic features exceed those of phones in the West. Japan is, without doubt, a world leader in technology. The Japanese preference for precision, detail, compactness and efficiency, along with a sense of inventiveness and natural dexterity and skill, have all contributed to the extraordinary success of technology in Japan.

Questions to ponder: Can you think of other areas in which Japan is successful in technology? What physical or geographical features of Japan foster the characteristics listed in the last paragraph?

| 10課 | 復習単語(ふくしゅうたんご) |

トピック：テクノロジー

1. ビデオ　　　　　　　　　　N　　　video
2. カメラ　　　　　　　　　　N　　　camera
3. コンピューター　　　　　　N　　　computer

| 10課 | ★★★ | 新しい単語 | ★★★ |

1. そういえば＜そう言えば＞　Exp　As you mentioned,..., Come to think of it....
 「ああ、そう言えば、お金を借りてたね。ごめん。」　Oh, yes, come to think of it, I had borrowed some money from you, hadn't I?

2. どうしよう(か)。　Exp　What should I do?
 「あっ、鍵がない。どうしよう。」　"Oops, I don't have my keys. What should I do?"

3. 〜のほかに　Exp　other than...
 英和と和英のほかに、漢字辞書も使っている。　Other than an English-Japanese dictionary and a Japanese-English dictionary, I am also using a *kanji* dictionary.

4. でんしじしょ＜電子辞書＞　N　electronic dictionary
 電子辞書の英和、和英をよく使っている。　I often use a English-Japanese and Japanese-English electronic dictionary.

5. パソコン　N　laptop (computer)
 パソコンがあれば、どこに行っても仕事が出来る。　If you have a laptop, you can work no matter where you go.

6. こうげいひん＜工芸品＞　N　craft work
 日本の工芸品はすばらしい。　Japanese crafts are wonderful.

7. はなしあいて＜話し相手＞　N　person to talk with; companion
 お年寄りは話し相手がほしい。　Older people want people to talk to.

8. とうなん＜東南＞アジア　N　southeast
 日本には東南アジアからの移民が多い。　There are many immigrants from Southeast Asia in Japan.

9. しゅるい＜種類＞　N　variety
 日本のケータイは色もデザインも種類が多い。　Japan's cell phones come in many colors, designs and varieties.

10. ぎじゅつ＜技術＞　N　technique, art, skill
 多くの日本人がほかの国でいろいろな技術を教えている。　Many Japanese are teaching (sharing) many techniques in other countries.

11. しつ＜質＞　N　quality
 日本の車は質がいいようだ。　It seems that the quality of Japanese cars is good.

12. そくど＜速度＞　N　speed; velocity
新幹線の速度、デザイン、静かさには驚かされた。　I was surprised by the speed, design and quietness of the bullet train.

13. ひつじゅひん＜必需品＞　N　necessity
アメリカ人にとって自動車は必需品だ。　Cars are necessities for Americans.

14. しょうしか＜少子化＞　N　low birthrate; decline in the number of children
日本は少子化により子供の数が減っているそうだ。　I understand that in Japan, the number of children is declining due to low birthrates.

15. こうれいか＜高齢化＞　N　advancement of age; graying of a society
日本は高齢化によりお年寄りが多い社会になっている。　Because of the advanced age of people in Japan, it is becoming a society of many older citizens.

16. じじょう＜事情＞　N　circumstances; conditions
日本の車事情についてよく知らない。　I don't know much about the circumstances of cars in Japan.

17. つうきん＜通勤＞　N　commuting to work
つうがく＜通学＞　N　commuting to school
ほとんどの日本人が通勤通学に電車やバスを使っている。　Most Japanese people use trains and buses to commute to work and school.

18. なくてはならない　A　(something is) necessary; indispensible
ケータイは私になくてはならない物だ。　My cell phone is a necessity for me.

19. せいかく＜正確＞　Na　accurate; precise
新幹線は時間に正確だ。　The bullet train is always precisely on time.

20. きよう＜器用＞　Na　dextrous; skilled
日本人は手が器用らしい。　The Japanese are very skilled with their hands.

21. あいかわらず＜相変わらず＞　Adv　as always
生活は相変わらず忙しい。　As always, my life is busy.

22. える＜得る＞／得ます　V2　to gain; to acquire
インターネットから毎日の情報を得ている。　I get news (information) from the internet every day.

23. すぐれている＜優れている＞／優れています　V2　to excel; to surpass
日本の工芸品を作る技術は本当に優れている。　Japan's skills in technology are truly unsurpassed.

10課

24. かち＜価値＞がある／あります   V1   to have a value; valuable
この電子辞書は高かったが、その価値はある。   This electronic dictionary was expensive, but it has that value (it is worth it).

25. くふう＜工夫＞する／します   V3   to devise
日本人は工夫していい物を作り出すのが上手だ。   The Japanese are good at devising and making good things.

26. はったつ＜発達＞する／します   V3   to develop; to advance
日本の自動車技術はよく発達している。   Japan's automobile technology is well developed.

27. かいご＜介護＞(を)する／します   V3   to care (for)
お年寄りの介護をするのは大変な仕事だ。   Caring for older people is hard work.

28. もちはこぶ＜持ち運ぶ＞／持ち運びます   V1   to carry (around)
ケータイは小さいので、持ち運びに便利だ。   Since cell phones are small, they are easy to carry around.

29. へんしゅう＜編集＞(を)する／します   V3   to edit
コンピューターでビデオを編集する。   I will edit the video on the computer.

30. じゅうでん＜充電＞(を)する／します   V3   to charge; replenish
ケータイは毎晩充電しなければならない。   I have to charge my cell phone every night.

31. べんしょう＜弁償＞(を)する／します   V3   to compensate; reimburse
友達のゲーム器を壊したので、弁償するつもりだ。   Since I broke my friend's game console, I plan to pay her for it.

32. りよう＜利用＞(を)する／します   V3   to use; to utilize
多くのアメリカ人が通勤通学に自動車を利用する。   Many Americans commute to work and school by using cars.

33. きたい＜期待＞(を)する／います   V3   to expect; anticipate
いいロボットが作られることを期待している。   I anticipate that good robots will be made.

【もっと単語】

1. けつろん＜結論＞として   Exp   In conclusion
2. ひさしぶり＜久しぶり＞   Exp   (for) a long time
3. じつは＜実は＞   Exp   in reality; truthfully
4. にんげん＜人間＞   N   humans
5. とうろん＜討論＞   N   debate; discussion

6. かず＜数＞	N	amount; number
7. おとしより＜お年寄り＞	N	elderly persons
8. じんこう＜人口＞	N	population
9. いみん＜移民＞	N	immigrant
10. なんべい＜南米＞	N	South America
11. ちゅうとう＜中東＞	N	Middle East
12. せかいじゅう＜世界中＞	N	worldwide
13. せいかつ＜生活＞	N	lifestyle
14. けいざい＜経済＞	N	economy
15. ハイブリッドしゃ＜車＞	N	hybrid car
16. でんち＜電池＞	N	battery
17. ゲームき＜ゲーム器＞	N	game console
18. おてつだいさん＜お手伝いさん＞	N	maid
19. とちゅう＜途中＞	N	along the way
20. せいけつ＜清潔＞	Na	sanitary; clean
21. ひつよう＜必要＞	Na	necessary
22. (〜が)ふえる＜増える＞／増えます	V2	to increase
23. (〜が)へる＜減る＞／減ります	V1	to decrease
24. うけいれる＜受け入れる＞／受け入れます	V2	to accept; to receive
25. れんらく＜連絡＞(を)する／します	V3	to contact
26. さがす＜探す＞／探します	V1	to look for; search
27. けす＜消す＞／消します	V1	to turn off; erase; extinguish
28. のんびりする／のんびりします	V3	to relax
29. かりる＜借りる＞／借ります	V2	to borrow
30. かす＜貸す＞／貸します	V1	to lend
31. おとす＜落とす＞／落とします	V1	to drop (something)
32. (〜が)こわれる＜壊れる＞／壊れます	V2	(something) breaks
33. (〜を)こわす＜壊す＞／壊します	V1	to break (something)
34. たりる＜足りる＞／足ります	V2	to be sufficient
35. やくにたつ＜役に立つ＞／役に立ちます	V1	to be useful (to)
36. にんき＜人気＞がある／あります	V1	to be popular

10課

10課　文法

A.
| Noun 1 |
| Verb (plain form) |
| いadjective |
| なadjective ＋な |

だけでなく、(Noun 2 も) 〜。　　not only 〜, but also 〜.

This construction is used when the speaker wishes to emphasize that it is not only one thing, person, action or state that is being described, but that it is only part of a larger similar pool that shares a similar quality. The first part of the sentence follows the plain form of verbs, いadjectives, nouns or なadjectives with な. In the following independent clause, the particle も follows the noun that is being cited as also having the certain quality under discussion.

Circle the correct particles.

1. ビデオゲームは日本（な　X）だけでなく、世界（も　でも　X）人気がある。
2. 新幹線は時間に正確（な　X）だけでなく、とても清潔（な　も　X）だ。
3. 日本のケータイは色の種類が多い（な　X）だけでなく、デザインの種類（な　も　X）多い。
4. 受付の女性ロボットはあいさつをする（な　X）だけでなく、お茶（な　も　X）出すそうだ。
5. 日本は少子化で子供が減っている（な　X）だけでなく、高齢化でお年寄り（な　も　X）増えているそうだ。だれがお年寄りの世話をするんだろうか。

B. Sentence 1 し、Sentence 2。　　S1, and what's more S2.　Not only S1, but also S2, so . . .

In this sentence structure, the conjunction し is generally used after the plain forms. Occasionally, polite forms are used before し when speaking in formal situations. Using し emphasizes the speaker's desire to indicate that more than one thing has occurred, or is being described. し may occur more than once in a sentence. Sometimes, the final statement of this construction serves as a concluding remark. If a concluding remark is not stated, it is implied. The particle も (also) frequently appears in this sentence construction to serve as reinforcement.

All of the sentences should support one another in logic and lead up to a unified conclusion, whether that conclusion is stated or implied.

Circle the correct particles.

1. ケータイはいつでも使える（な　だ　X）し、どこでも使えるので、便利だ。
2. 新幹線は時間に正確（な　だ　X）し、清潔だし、それに、一時間に何本も走っている。
3. パソコンはコンピューターとして、小さい（な　だ　X）し、持ち運びが簡単なので、便利だ。

4. あのロボットはおじぎもする（な　だ　X）し、人間みたいに話すよ。
5. このロボットは掃除もしてくれる（な　だ　X）し、料理もしてくれるそうだ。
6. タックさんはお年寄り（な　だ　X）し、英語も話せない（な　だ　X）し、介護するのも大変だ。

C. どこにでも　to anywhere

The following chart summarizes the use of the common interrogative (question) words to which various particles may be attached. Here, you are able to compare all of the usages, their similarities and their differences. Differences lie in the particle(s) that follow the interrogative word and whether the predicate is affirmative or negative. Also, one must pay attention to the kind of verb one is using (action, existence or motion) and whether the interrogative functions as the place of action, destination, indirect object, etc. as opposed to the subject or direct object. That is, it is necessary to create multiple particles if particles other than を, が or は are involved. For example, to say "I won't go anywhere," one must be sure to say どこへも行かない rather than どこも行かない.

	no - - + neg.	some - - + aff.	any - - + aff.	all - - + aff.
何	何も + -ない nothing	何か something	何でも anything	全部、すべて everything
どこ	どこ（へ、で、etc.）も + -ない nowhere	どこか（へ、で、etc.） somewhere	どこ（へ、で、etc.）でも anywhere	どこ（へ、で、etc.）も everywhere
だれ	だれ（に、と、etc.）も + -ない nobody	だれか（に、と、etc.） someone	だれ（に、と、etc.）でも anyone	みんな、だれ（に、と、etc.）も everyone
いつ	いつも + -ない never	いつか sometimes	いつでも at any time	いつも always, all the time
どれ	どれも + -ない none of them	どれか some of them	どれでも any of them	どれも all of them

Circle the correct choice.

1. パソコンは小さいので、（どこかへ　どこへでも）簡単に持ち運べる。
2. ケータイは（いつも　いつか　いつでも）使えて、便利です。
3. ケータイがあれば、（どこかから　どこからでも）うちに連絡できる。
4. ケータイもパソコンも毎日使っていて、私には（どちらも　どちらか　どちらでも）必要だ。
5. 時々疲れて、（何も　何か　何でも）したくない時がある。
6. （だれか　だれでも）私のブログを見ることが出来る。

10課

D. Verb (TE form) ＋も、　　　　　　Even if/though one does/is ～,
　　いadjective (-くて) も、　　　　　Even if/though it is ～,
　　なadjective / Noun ＋ でも、　　　Even if/though it is ～,

This construction is used at the beginning of a sentence and means "Even if ～; Even though ～"
To form this sentence construction, attach も to TE forms of verbs, いadjectives base plus くて, nouns +で and なadjectives +で. Complete the sentence. The tense of the entire sentence is determined by the tense of the sentence ending.
Compare:
a. 日本語を三年、勉強しても、まだ上手ではありません。
　　Although I studied Japanese for three years, I am still not good at it.
b. 日本語を三年、勉強したのに、まだ上手ではありません。
　　Although I studied Japanese for three years, (despite my expectations), I am still not good at it.
The use of のに suggests that you had expectations that were not met, or that something did not turn out as you thought it might. The use of ても does not carry the implication of expectation.

Fill in the blanks with the correct verb in the (　) with the correct form.

1. ケータイがあれば、外に＿＿＿＿＿＿、連絡することが出来る。（いる）
2. メールを＿＿＿＿＿＿、友達はたいてい返事をくれない。（送る）
3. 友達はお金を＿＿＿＿＿＿、返さない。（借りる）
4. 弟はビデオゲームを買って＿＿＿＿＿＿、すぐ新しいのがほしくなる。（もらう）
5. 電子辞書は＿＿＿＿＿＿、それだけの価値があると思う。（高い）
6. 日本の電車はたいてい時間に＿＿＿＿＿＿、時々遅く来る。（正確）
7. 日本語があまり＿＿＿＿＿＿、日本旅行は楽しい。（分からない）

E. Question Word + (particle) + Verb -ても　　no matter ～

When one expresses "no matter where, who, what," etc. in Japanese, one should begin with the appropriate question word, and the correct particle (if necessary) depending on the verb with which it is used. The verb which follows appears in its Verb -ても form.

Fill in the blanks with the correct word from the box below.

1. パソコンがあれば、＿＿＿＿＿＿いても、タイプすることが出来る。
2. ＿＿＿＿＿＿高いコンピューターを買っても、使い方がよく分からない。
3. この単語の意味を＿＿＿＿＿＿聞いても、知らなかった。
4. 先生は＿＿＿＿＿＿メールを送っても、すぐ返事をくれる。
5. ロボットが＿＿＿＿＿＿をしてくれても、人間の友達の方がいい。
6. 弟はビデオゲームを＿＿＿＿＿＿しても、もっとしたくなるらしい。
7. 私は＿＿＿＿＿＿日本語を勉強しても、上手にならない。

　　　何人　いつ　何　何年　いくら　何回　だれに　どこに

10課

243

> F. 〜と(いうの)は、 Noun＋の/Sentence＋という＋ことだ。
> This structure is used in interpreting, explaining or defining a word, a phrase or a sentence.
> 1. デジカメと(いうの)は、デジタルカメラのことです。
>   *Dejikame* means digital camera.
> 2. 少子化と(いうの)は、子供がだんだん減るということです。
>   *Shooshika* is the phenomenon of the decrease of children (due to low birthrates.)
> 3. 「猿も木から落ちる」と(いうの)は、上手な人でも時々間違えるということです。
>   *Saru mo ki kara ochiru* (lit. even monkeys fall from trees) means that even a skillful person sometimes makes mistakes.

Fill in the blanks with the correct descriptions.

1. 高齢化社会と(いうの)は、＿＿＿＿＿＿＿＿＿＿＿＿＿＿＿＿＿＿＿＿＿ことです。
2. ウォッシュレットと(いうの)は、＿＿＿＿＿＿＿＿＿＿＿＿＿＿＿＿＿ことです。
3. トトロと(いうの)は、＿＿＿＿＿＿＿＿＿＿＿＿＿＿＿＿＿ことです。
4. 本音と(いうの)は、＿＿＿＿＿＿＿＿＿＿＿＿＿＿＿＿＿ことです。
5. 「笑う門には福来る」と(いうの)は、＿＿＿＿＿＿＿＿＿＿＿＿＿＿＿＿＿ことです。

10課　アクティビティー

A. 日本文化：一人か二人ワーク→クラスワーク

Divide the topics below among your classmates and research your topic on the Internet. Using visuals, present your findings with your classmates.

1. ロボット（介護ロボット、ペットロボット、災害救助ロボット、地雷除去ロボット）
2. テクノロジー（新幹線、ハイブリッド車、ビデオゲーム、ケータイ）
3. 日本の美（工芸品、陶器、匠の技）
4. 少子高齢化

B. 聞く Pre-Listening Activity「テクノロジー」：ペアワーク→クラスワーク

Carry on a conversation with your partner in the informal style. Elaborate.

1. 電子辞書を持っている？
2. 新幹線に乗ったことがある？
3. 新幹線は時間に正確？　清潔？　一時間に何本ぐらい走っている？
4. アメリカ人と日本人と、どちらの方が手が器用だと思う？
5. アメリカ人と日本人と、どちらの方が何か工夫をするのが上手だと思う？
6. アメリカの携帯と日本の携帯と、どちらの方がデザインや色や機能の種類が多い？
7. 人間みたいなロボットを見たことがある？
8. ハイブリッド車の技術は、アメリカと日本で、どちらの方が発達している？
9. ビデオゲームの中で、何が一番好き？
10. 日本とアメリカのビデオゲームを比べてみて。

C. 聞く Post-Listening Activity「テクノロジー」：ペアワーク→クラスワーク

討論をしよう。Discuss which country is more advanced in technology, Japan or America.

a. 日本の方がアメリカよりテクノロジーが発達していると思うグループ

　どんな物：＿＿＿＿＿＿＿＿＿＿＿＿＿＿＿＿＿＿＿＿＿＿＿＿＿＿＿＿＿＿＿＿＿＿

　なぜ　　：＿＿＿＿＿＿＿＿＿＿＿＿＿＿＿＿＿＿＿＿＿＿＿＿＿＿＿＿＿＿＿＿＿＿

　日本人の強さ：＿＿＿＿＿＿＿＿＿＿＿＿＿＿＿＿＿＿＿＿＿＿＿＿＿＿＿＿＿＿＿＿

b. アメリカの方が日本よりテクノロジーが発達していると思うグループ

　どんな物：＿＿＿＿＿＿＿＿＿＿＿＿＿＿＿＿＿＿＿＿＿＿＿＿＿＿＿＿＿＿＿＿＿＿

　なぜ　　：＿＿＿＿＿＿＿＿＿＿＿＿＿＿＿＿＿＿＿＿＿＿＿＿＿＿＿＿＿＿＿＿＿＿

　アメリカ人の強さ：＿＿＿＿＿＿＿＿＿＿＿＿＿＿＿＿＿＿＿＿＿＿＿＿＿＿＿＿＿＿

D. 読む Pre-Reading Activity「ロボット」：ペアワーク→クラスワーク

Discuss the following questions with your partner in the informal style.
1. 少子高齢化社会では、子供の数が（増える　減る）。
2. 少子高齢化社会では、お年寄りの数が（増える　減る）。
3. もうすぐ日本の人口の（10%　25%　40%）が60歳以上のお年寄りになるそうだ。
4. お年寄りの介護のために、日本は（南米　中東　東南アジア）からの若い移民を受け入れるかも知れない。

E. 読む Post-Reading Activity「ロボット」：ペアワーク→クラスワーク

Presentation: Japanese Robots

Present your view on Japanese robots. Discuss at least FIVE aspects of Japanese robots. Begin with an appropriate introduction, give details about the five aspects, explain your own view or perspective, and end with a concluding remark. You will have 4 minutes to prepare and 2 minutes to present. Your presentation should be as complete as possible.

【Let's take notes!】

1. Begin with an appropriate introduction.
   _____

2. Discuss five aspects/examples of the topic.
   1.) _____
   2.) _____
   3.) _____
   4.) _____
   5.) _____

3. Explain your view or perspective.
   _____

4. End with a concluding remark.
   _____

F. テキストチャット「ハイブリッド車」：ペアワーク→クラスワーク

Using the questions below as prompts, have a conversation. Use 20 seconds to respond to each question. Elaborate on your answers and give details.
1. こんにちは。阿部です。どうぞよろしく。
2. 今日は車について意見を聞かせて下さい。
3. 今、御家族はどんな車を運転しているんですか。
4. 日本の車とアメリカの車で、どちらの方が好きですか。
5. そうですか。ハイブリッド車はどう思いますか。

10課

6. 将来、自分の車が買えたら、どんな車を買うつもりですか。
7. 今日は有難うございました。
8. 僕はまだ車を運転していませんが、日本の車事情について何か質問がありますか。

G. Compare & Contrast 「ケータイとパソコン」：ペアワーク→クラスワーク

> ケータイもパソコンも私達の生活になくてはならない必需品ですが、違う点も似ている点もあります。これから、ケータイとパソコンを比べてみます。
> 　まず一つ目の違う点は、(1.)は(2.)より小さいので、どこにでも簡単に持ち運べて、本当に便利です。(3.)は、いつでもどこでも使うことが出来ます。友達や家族と連絡する時に、特に便利です。
> 　二つ目の違う点は、(4.)で簡単な情報を得るのは便利ですが、(5.)でレポートをタイプしたり、スライドショーを作ったり、ビデオを編集したりすることが出来ます。
> 　しかし、一つの同じことは、ケータイもパソコンもどちらも電池がなくなれば使えません。ソーラーパネルを利用した(6.)もあるようですが、いつも充電しなければなりません。
> 　結論として、私はケータイもパソコンもどちらも必要です。(7.)はだいたい外にいる時に人と連絡するために必要ですし、(8.)はレポートをタイプをしたり、情報をさがすために必要です。しかし、どちらも人の生活を忙しく変えました。私の考えとして、私達は時々ケータイもパソコンも消して、のんびりすることが必要だと思います。

a. Fill in the ( ) with the correct answer, either K for *keitai* or P for *pasokon*.

1. (　) 2. (　) 3. (　) 4. (　) 5. (　) 6. (　) 7. (　) 8. (　)

b. Write your original ideas. Then, discuss each point in more detail with your partner.

Three similarities/differences:

　1. _____
　2. _____
　3. _____

Your preference and give reasons:

_____
_____

10課

H. 会話「ビデオゲーム」：ペアワーク→クラスワーク

a. You will have a conversation with a Japanese boy, Kai. Identify and circle the different male and female informal speech forms in the following dialogues. See the examples marked with a ○.

Conversation between Kai, a Japanese boy and you, a boy:

カイ (男) ：やあ、久しぶり。元気？学校はどう？
私 (男) ：(やあ)、カイ、久しぶりだな。元気だよ。学校？学校は相変わらず忙しいよ。
カイ (男) ：あのう、この前から言おう言おうと思ってたことがあるんだ。君から借りたゲーム器のことなんだけどね。
私 (男) ：ああ、そう言えば、ゲーム器を貸していたね。すっかり忘れてた。どうした？
カイ (男) ：実はね、この前遊んでいた時に落としてしまって、壊れちゃったんだ。ごめんね。
私 (男) ：ええっ？壊しちゃった？もう使えない？どうしよう？
カイ (男) ：それで、弁償するから、ゲーム器いくらだったか教えて。
私 (男) ：弁償してくれる？それは有り難いけど、弁償しなくっていいよ。だって、いくらだったか覚えてないし、あのゲーム器、もう古かったから。

Conversation between Kai, a Japanese boy, and you, a girl:

カイ (男) ：やあ、久しぶり。元気？学校はどう？
私 (女) ：(ああ)、カイ君、久しぶり。元気よ。学校？学校は相変わらず忙しいよ。
カイ (男) ：あのう、この前から言おう言おうと思ってたことがあるんだ。君から借りたゲーム器のことなんだけどね。
私 (女) ：ああ、そう言えば、ゲーム器を貸していたね。すっかり忘れてた。どうしたの？
カイ (男) ：実はね、この前遊んでいた時に落としてしまって、壊れちゃったんだ。ごめんね。
私 (女) ：ええっ？壊しちゃったの？もう使えないの？どうしよう？
カイ (男) ：それで、弁償するから、ゲーム器いくらだったか教えて。
私 (女) ：弁償してくれるの？それは有り難いけど、弁償しなくていいわよ。だって、いくらだったか覚えてないし、あのゲーム器、もう古かったから。

b. Carry on an original conversation with Kai.

I. 文化発表「日本のテクノロジー」：ペアワーク→クラスワーク

　　Fill in the ( ) with the correct responses from the box.

1. 日本のテクノロジーは世界でもっとも（　　）している。
2. 日本は美しい工芸品を作る（　　）がある。
3. 新幹線の（　　）、デザイン、静かさは特に優れている。
4. 日本のハイブリッド車は、質が良くガソリンをたくさん使わないので、（　　）に良い。
5. 日本のロボット産業も発達している。日本は少子化により（　　）の介護をする人が足りなくなるので、ロボットのお手伝いさんが役に立つ。
6. 日本のビデオゲームも発達していて、日本だけでなく（　　）で人気がある。
7. 日本のケータイもすばらしく発達していて、いろいろな（　　）がついていて便利だ。
8. 日本人は通勤通学に（　　）やバスを利用する人が多く、学校や会社に行く途中の時間が長いので、ケータイがあるととても便利である。
9. 日本人は手が（　　）で、伝統的に美しい工芸品を作って来た。
10. 国として小さく資源の少ない日本は、テクノロジーによって（　　）を発達させることが出来たようだ。

| a. 発達 | b. 伝統 | c. 環境 | d. お年寄り | e. 機能 |
| f. 器用 | g. 電車 | h. 世界中 | i. 経済 | j. 速度 |

10課

<10課 - 聞く>

Listening: Technology

【You may take notes while listening. Do not look at the questions below before listening. You will have 12 seconds to answer each question. You may NOT move back and forth among questions.】

(Narrator) Now you will listen to an announcement once.

(Narrator) Now answer the questions for this selection.

1. What is NOT correct about the electronic dictionary Mai bought?
    (A) It has Japanese-English and English-Japanese dictionaries.
    (B) It has a Chinese character dictionary.
    (C) It allows you to hear the pronunciation of Japanese words.
    (D) It costs almost 40,000 yen.

2. What feature of the bullet trains did NOT surprise Ben?
    (A) The bullet trains were fast.
    (B) The bullet trains were on time.
    (C) The bullet trains were clean.
    (D) Several bullet trains were running every hour.

3. Which statement is NOT correct?
    (A) Mai thinks that Japanese people are smart.
    (B) Mai thinks that Japanese people have a better sense of beauty than Americans.
    (C) Mai thinks that Japanese people are good at making things with their hands because of activities they do as children.
    (D) Ben thinks that Japanese people are good at copying foreign products.

4. What did NOT surprise Ben about Japanese cellular phones?
    (A) There are many different colors.
    (B) There are many different designs.
    (C) There are many different functions.
    (D) The prices are low.

5. What statement is correct?
    (A) Ben made Mai realize how advanced Japanese technology is.
    (B) Mai likes Japanese high-tech products such as robots.
    (C) Mai likes Japanese cars and video games.
    (D) Mai had enough knowledge to discuss Japanese technology with Ben.

<10課 - 読む>
Reading: Robots
【You may move back and forth among all the questions.】

　日本はこれから少子高齢化社会を迎える。少子化というのは、子供がだんだん減るということで、高齢化とは、お年寄りがだんだん増えるということだ。もうすぐ日本の人口の２５％が６０歳以上のお年寄りになるそうだ。少子化によって、子供の数が少なくなるので、お年寄りを介護する人が必ず足りなくなる。東南アジアから若い移民を受け入れて、その移民達にお年寄りの介護を頼らなければならないかも知れない。

　そんな時に、お年寄りの介護をするためのロボットが役に立つだろう。うちの中で掃除や洗濯や料理をしてくれるロボット、話し相手になってくれるロボット、介護もしてくれるロボット、そんなロボットがいれば、きっとお年寄りのいいお手伝いさんになるに違いない。ロボットは掃除機や冷蔵庫やテレビのような電気製品の一つとして、電気屋さんで売られているかも知れない。

　ロボットの技術がどんどん発達して、質のいいロボットが作られることを期待している。そんな日が来るのも、遠い将来ではないような気がする。

<10課 - 読む (質問)>

Reading: Robots

(Narrator) Now answer the questions for this section.

1. What problem has Japan faced in recent years?
   (A) decreased number of children
   (B) increased number of elderly people
   (C) both (A) and (B)
   (D) none of the above

2. What role can immigrants from Southeast Asia play in Japan?
   (A) They can help to care for children.
   (B) They can help to build robots.
   (C) They can help to care for elderly people.
   (D) They can help with domestic work.

3. Among the possible capabilities of robots, which is NOT mentioned in the passage?
   (A) speaking and listening to a person
   (B) laundry
   (C) repair work
   (D) cooking

4. Where does the author think robots will be sold in the future?
   (A) electronic goods shops
   (B) computer shops
   (C) robot shops
   (D) department stores

5. What opinion does the author have about robots?
   (A) Robots will help with the problems that Japan will face in the future.
   (B) Robots will expand the problems that Japan will face in the future.
   (C) Robots will not replace people.
   (D) Robots will help only rich people who can afford them.

10課

<10課 - 書く (テキストチャット)>

Text Chat: Hybrid Cars

90秒×6

You will participate in a simulated exchange of text-chat messages. Each time it is your turn to write, you will have 90 seconds. You should respond as fully and as appropriately as possible.

You will have a conversation about recent technology with Satoshi Abe, a student at your sister school in Japan.

1. Respond. (90 seconds)
   こんにちは。阿部（あべ）です。どうぞよろしく。今日は車について意見を聞かせて下さい。

2. Give a specific example. (90 seconds)
   今、御家族はどんな車を運転しているんですか。

3. State and justify your preference. (90 seconds)
   日本の車とアメリカの車で、どちらの方が好きですか。

4. Explain your opinions. (90 seconds)
   そうですか。ハイブリッド車はどう思いますか。

5. Give a specific example. (90 seconds)
   将来（しょうらい）、自分の車が買えたら、どんな車を買うつもりですか。

6. Ask a specific question. (90 seconds)
   今日は有難うございました。僕はまだ車を運転していませんが、日本の車事情（じじょう）について何か質問がありますか。

<10課 - 書く (比較（ひかく）と対比（たいひ）)>

Compare and Contrast Article: Cellular Phones and Laptop Computers

20分

Directions: You are writing an article for the student newspaper of your sister school in Japan. Write an article in which you compare and contrast similarities and differences between cellular phones and laptop computers. Based on your personal experience, describe at least THREE aspects of each and highlight the similarities and differences between cellular phones and laptop computers. Also state your preference for either and give reasons for it.

Your article should be 300 to 400 characters or longer. Use the *desu/masu* or *da* (plain) style, but use one style consistently. Also, use *kanji* wherever *kanji* from the AP Japanese *kanji* list is appropriate. You have 20 minutes to write.

【NOTES/OUTLINE: 自分の作文のアウトラインを書こう！】

Introduction: _____

Three similarities/differences:

1. _____
2. _____
3. _____

Your preference and give reasons:
_____
_____

10課

<10課 - 話す (会話)>
Conversation: Video Game

20秒×4

You will participate in a simulated conversation. Each time it is your turn to speak, you will have 20 seconds to record. You should respond as fully and as appropriately as possible.

You will have a conversation with Kai, your Japanese friend, about a problem.

(Kai)
(20 seconds)
(Kai)
(20 seconds)
(Kai)
(20 seconds)
(Kai)
(20 seconds)

<10課 - 話す (日本文化)>
Cultural Perspective Presentation: Japanese Technology

4分+2分

Directions: Imagine you are making an oral presentation to your Japanese class. First, you will read and hear the topic for your presentation. You will have 4 minutes to prepare your presentation. Then you will have 2 minutes to record your presentation. Your presentation should be as complete as possible.

Present your own view or perspective of Japanese technology. Discuss at least FIVE aspects or examples of Japanese technology.

Begin with an appropriate introduction, give details, explain your own view or perspective, and end with a concluding remark.

【Let's take notes!】

1. Begin with an appropriate introduction.

_____

2. Discuss five aspects/examples of the topic.

    1.) _____
    2.) _____
    3.) _____
    4.) _____
    5.) _____

3. Explain your view or perspective.

_____

4. End with a concluding remark.

_____

10課

11課 仕事とキャリア
Work and Career

【AP® タスク：仕事とキャリア】
Discuss your college major preference(s). Discuss your post-high school plans. Discuss your college plans. Discuss your preferences for your future career. What is important as you decide on your occupation - high salary, contribution to the community, your passion, job location, etc.?

【文化】敬(けい)語：Honorific Language

A well-developed system of honorific language known as *keigo* (敬語) is a defining characteristic of the Japanese language. It is an excellent example of how a language reflects its society's values and structure.

The Japanese *keigo* system is built on two essential pillars. The first of these is the relationship between the listener and speaker in any given interaction. Depending on the degree of closeness between the listener and speaker, the speaker may choose to use the polite (formal) or plain (informal) verb forms. For example, when speaking with family and friends, one does not use the polite form, as polite forms are used between persons who are not familiar with one another.

The second pillar of the *keigo* system is the relative status of the person speaking and his/her perception of his/her relationship between him/her and the person being spoken about. The speaker will choose to elevate the person being spoken about by using honorific verb forms. The form used to elevate the person being spoken about is called *sonkeigo* (尊敬語). Besides elevating the person being spoken about, the speaker may lower himself/herself by using humble forms. These forms are called *kenjoogo* (謙譲語). Usually, the speaker will show respect by using *keigo* (*sonkeigo* and *kenjoogo*) to elevate the listener above his/her own position.

Sonkeigo and *kenjoogo* verbs each have a well-developed system of verb forms. There are special verb forms used in place of commonly used verbs such as います, 行きます, 食べます, します, etc. For example, instead of using the neutral します verb, one would use なさいます to show respect to a person doing something. When one speaks about oneself doing something, however, one would use the humble form いたします. Other verb systems also exist. For example, to say that one's teacher will read something, one would use お読みになります to show respect to the teacher. Yet another system is one that takes the verb and converts it into another variation of the verb. For example, when asking a teacher if she will read a book, the speaker may ask, 本を読まれますか.

Whenever one communicates in the honorific system using *sonkeigo* forms or *kenjoogo* forms, it is essential for the speaker to also use *teineigo* (polite) expressions. Most are nouns that are the polite equivalents of neutral terms. For example, for だれ (who), one would instead use どなた when one is using *keigo*. Other examples of *teineigo* are こちら for これ, かた (方) for ひと (人) or お水 for 水.

When is *keigo* used? *Keigo* is used often in situations where a customer or client is involved. The customer is treated with respect no matter what the actual status of the employee may be. For example, *keigo* is commonly heard at restaurants, stores and announcements in public transportation systems. It is also used within institutions where a definite hierarchy exists, i.e., companies, schools and school clubs. *Keigo* is first learned in high school clubs, where *koohai* (underclassmen) must speak and treat their elder *senpai* with respect. Because of this system, new workers at companies undergo special training on how to use *keigo* when they first join their companies.

The *keigo* system, though complicated, remains a part of the Japanese language, as it is still essential to maintaining good relationships among the Japanese. The *keigo* system reveals that Japanese still distinguish between 内 and 外 and still respect relative positions by status.

Questions to ponder: Is there a more subtle form of honorifics functioning in your own language? How and when do you think the keigo system first developed in Japan? Can you think of other situations when Japanese might use keigo besides situations named above?

11課 復習単語

トピック：仕事とキャリア

1. (お)仕事	(お)しごと	N	job
2. 会社	かいしゃ	N	company
3. 事務所	じむしょ	N	office
4. アルバイト(を)する		V3	(to) work part-time
5. 勤める	つとめる	V2	(to) be employed (at～)
6. 給料	きゅうりょう	N	salary; pay
7. 儲ける	もうける	V2	(to) earn/make (money)
8. 退職(を)する	たいしょく(を)する	V3	(to) retire (from a job)
9. 社長	しゃちょう	N	company president
10. 社員	しゃいん	N	company employee
11. 会社員	かいしゃいん	N	company employee
12. 弁護士	べんごし	N	lawyer
13. 医者	いしゃ	N	(medical) doctor [informal]
14. 御医者さん	おいしゃさん	N	(medical) doctor [polite form of いしゃ]
15. エンジニア		N	engineer
16. 建築家	けんちくか	N	architect
17. 農業	のうぎょう	N	agriculture; farming
18. 警官	けいかん	N	police officer
19. 軍人	ぐんじん	N	military personnel
20. 詩人	しじん	N	poet
21. 歌手	かしゅ	N	singer
22. 監督	かんとく	N	(movie) director; (baseball) manager
23. 俳優	はいゆう	N	actor
24. 女優	じょゆう	N	actress

| 11課 | ★★★ | 新しい単語 | ★★★ |

1. ～にとって　P+V　As for ～,
   私にとって好きな仕事をすることの方が、給料よりも大事だ。
   For me, it is more important to have I job that I like than a (good) salary.

2. げんだい＜現代＞　N　(the) present (age); modern age
   現代の技術で、海の水を飲料水に変えることが出来るそうだ。
   I understand that through modern technology, it is possible to convert sea water to fresh drinking water.

3. きかい＜機会＞　N　opportunity; chance
   機会があれば、日本に留学したい。　If I have a chance, I want to study abroad in Japan.

4. きぎょう＜企業＞　N　enterprise
   ホンダは日本の有名な企業だ。　Honda is a famous Japanese enterprise.

5. せいひん＜製品＞　N　manufactured goods
   現代の日本の製品は質がいいと思われている。　It is said that the quality of Japan's modern manufactured products is good.

6. としけいかく＜都市計画＞　N　urban planning
   都市計画の仕事に興味がある。　I have an interest in work in urban planning.

7. とりくみ＜取り組み＞　N　match; battle
   日本の環境への取り組みから習いたいことがたくさんある。　There are many things I want to learn from the environmental struggles in Japan.

8. がくれき＜学歴＞　N　academic background
   学歴がなくても、ビジネスに成功している人は多くいる。　Even without an academic background, there are many people who have succeeded in business.

9. じつりょく＜実力＞　N　ability; capability
   運も実力のうちだそうだ。　It is said that even luck is an ability.

10. のうりょく＜能力＞　N　ability; capacity; faculty
    すばらしい能力を持っている。　(He) has an amazing ability.

11. よてい＜予定＞　N　plan
    将来、博士号も取る予定だ。　In the future, I plan to get my doctoral degree too.

12. じゅけん＜受験＞　N　taking an entrance exam
    じゅけん＜受験＞(を)する／します　V3　to take an exam

| 11課 |

日本の高三は受験勉強で忙しい。 Seniors in Japanese high schools are busy with studies fo entrance exams.

13. るいじてん＜類似点＞　N　similar points
教師と医者の類似点は、教師も医者も人が相手だというところだ。 The common point between teachers and doctors is that they both interact with people.

14. そういてん＜相違点＞　N　difference
日本とアメリカの一番の相違点は、国の大きさだと思う。 I think the biggest difference between Japan and America is the size of the countries.

15. ちしき＜知識＞　N　knowledge
医者はいつも最新の知識が必要だ。 It is necessary for doctors to have the knowledge.

16. かんじゃ＜患者＞　N　(a) patient
医者の仕事は患者を治すことだ。 The job of the doctor is to heal the patient.

17. いのち＜命＞　N　life
命を大切にしてほしい。 I want you to cherish your life.

18. じきゅう＜時給＞　N　hourly salary
「時給はいくらですか。」 "How much is the hourly pay?"

19. はずかしい＜恥ずかしい＞　A　shy; bashful; shameful; embarrassing
知らないことは恥ずかしいことではない。 Not knowing something is not an embarrassment.

20. みぢか＜身近＞　Na　close (relationship); familiar
日本人はたいてい身近な人に丁寧語を使わない。 Japanese do not usually use polite language people they are close to.

21. かならず＜必ず＞　Adv　definitely; absolutely; surely
人が喜ぶ物を作れば、必ず売れる。 If one makes things that people are happy with, they will definitely be able to sell (them).

22. わざわざ　Adv　purposely; deliberately
「わざわざ来て下さり、有難うございました。」Thank you for making a special effort to come.

23. しょくぎょう(につく)＜職業(に就く)＞／就きます　V1　to find a job (occupation)
どんな職業に就きたい？　"What kind of job do you want?"

24. しゅうしょく＜就職＞(を)する／します　V3　to find employment
将来、日本で就職してみたい。 In the future, I want to try and find a job in Japan.

11課

25. すすむ＜進む＞／進みます　V1　to advance
    出来れば、大学院に進んで、修士号を取るつもりだ。　If I can, I plan to advance graduate school and earn a doctorate degree.

26. まなぶ＜学ぶ＞／学びます　V1　to learn
    日本のリサイクルをもっと学びたい。　I want to learn more about recycling in Japan.

27. やりがいがある／あります　V1　to be worth doing; to have a value
    人の役に立つやりがいのある仕事を探すつもりだ。　I plan to look for a job that will be of valuable use to people.

28. だいひょう＜代表＞(を)する／します　V3　to represent
    だいひょう＜代表＞　N　representative
    だいひょうてき＜代表的＞　Na　representative
    トヨタは日本を代表する企業だ。　Toyota is a representative Japanese enterprise.

29. ちょうせん＜挑戦＞(を)する／します　V3　to challenge
    私は新しいことに挑戦をすることが好きだ。　I like new challenges.

30. しっぱい＜失敗＞(を)する／します　V3　to fail; to make a mistake
    失敗は成功のもと。　Failure is the root of success.

31. おそれる＜恐れる＞／恐れます　V2　to be fearful of
    おそれ＜恐れ＞　N　fear
    失敗を恐れていては、何も出来ない。　If you are afraid of failure, you can't do anything.

32. すくう＜救う＞／救います　V3　to rescue; to save
    医者は人の命を救うことが出来る。　Doctors are able to save people's lives.

【もっと単語】
1. けいご＜敬語＞　　　　　　　　　　　　N　honorific language system
2. そんけいご＜尊敬語＞　　　　　　　　　N　honorific speech
3. けんじょうご＜謙譲語＞　　　　　　　　N　humble speech
4. ていねいご＜丁寧語＞　　　　　　　　　N　polite speech
5. にちじょうご＜日常語＞　　　　　　　　N　every day language; daily speech
6. めいし＜名詞＞　　　　　　　　　　　　N　noun
7. どうし＜動詞＞　　　　　　　　　　　　N　verb
8. れい＜例＞　　　　　　　　　　　　　　N　example
9. つき＜月＞　　　　　　　　　　　　　　N　moon

11課

10.	きゅうか＜休暇＞	N	a leave; a vacation
11.	こんいろ＜紺色＞	N	navy blue
12.	かみがた＜髪型＞	N	hairstyle
13.	ちゃぱつ＜茶髪＞	N	hair dyed blonde or reddish brown
14.	ぼうずあたま＜坊主頭＞	N	buzzed haircut; close cropped hair
15.	いれずみ＜入れ墨＞	N	tattoo
16.	もちあげる＜持ち上げる＞／持ち上げます	V2	to raise; to lift; to heave (up)
17.	さげる＜下げる＞／下げます	V2	to lower; to hang

11課 文法

> A. 飲まず(に)　　without/instead of drinking
> 　　食べず(に)　　without/instead of eating
> 　　勉強せず(に)　without/instead of studying
> 　　来〔こ〕ず(に)　without/instead of coming
>
> This form is the formal negative form of -ないで and is used most commonly in written form, but it is also occasionally used in more formal speaking situations.

Write the -ずに form of an appropriate verb in the blanks.

1. 大学に_____、働くつもりだ。
2. 今日試験があったので、ゆうべ_____、勉強した。
3. 感謝〔かんしゃ〕の気持ちを_____、生きて行きたい。
4. 花子はプロムに彼を_____、友達と来た。

> B. Usage of も
> 　　(Noun)も(Noun)も ＋ Affirmative predicate　　Both 〜 and 〜
> 　　(Noun)も(Noun)も ＋ Negative predicate　　Neither 〜 nor 〜

Complete the following sentences by choosing the correct responses from the choices below. Responses may be used several times.

```
父は一月に東京へ行った。母（　）一月（　）東京（　）行った。
父（　）一月（　）大阪〔さか〕（　）行った。
父（　）一月（　）東京（　）大阪〔さか〕（　）行った。
父（　）二月（　）東京（　）行った。
父（　）一月（　）二月（　）東京（　）行った。
父（　）母（　）一月（　）東京（　）行った。
父（　）母（　）一月（　）北海道（　）行かなかった。
新幹線〔かん〕はとても速かったそうだ。（　）便利〔べんり〕だったそうだ。
```

　　は　も　へ　へも　に　にも　で　でも　また

C. おいし＋そうだ。　　　　　　　　It looks delicious.
    おいしい＋そうだ。　　　　　　　I heard that it is delicious.
1a. 太郎君は頭が良〔よ〕さそうだ。　　Taro looks smart.
1b. 太郎君は頭がいいそうだ。　　　　I heard that Taro is smart.
2a. 太郎君はお金がなさそうだ。　　　Taro looks he does not have money.
2b. 太郎君はお金がないそうだ。　　　I heard that Taro does not have money.
3a. このレストランは静かそうだ。　　This restaurant looks quiet.
3b. このレストランは静かだそうだ。　I heard that this restaurant is quiet.
4a. 今日は雨が降りそうだ。　　　　　It looks like it will rain today.
4b. 今日は雨が降るそうだ。　　　　　I heard that it will rain today.

Restate in English.
1. 一番初めに作った物は「バタバタ」という製品だったそうだ。

2. 奥さんが買物に行く時の荷物は重そうだった。

3. 新製品はよく売れたそうです。
4. 本田氏はよく工員に「ばかやろう」とどなっていたそうです。

D. Someone＋に＋Verb (TE)＋もらう　　　ask someone to do ～
    Someone＋に＋Verb (TE)＋もらいたい　　want to ask someone to do ～
    Someone＋に＋Verb (TE)＋もらいたがっている
    　　　　　　　　　　　　　　　　(Third person) wants to ask someone to do ～

All of the above forms suggest that the subject of the sentence will or wants to have someone else do a favor for the subject. The person who is asked to do the favor, the indirect object, is followed by the particle に. The subject of the first two sentences are either first (I) or second (you) person, while the subject of the third sentence is always a third person (he/she/they).

Restate the following sentences in English.
1. 学歴がないから、人に教えてもらうことを恥ずかしいと思わなかった。

2. 君にこの本をぜひ読んでもらいたい。

3. 花子さんの両親は花子さんに早く結婚してもらいたがっている。

4. 人々にもっと協力してもらいたいと思っている。

| 11課 | | アクティビティー | |

A. 日本文化：一人か二人ワーク→クラスワーク

Divide the topics below among your classmates and research your topic on the Internet. Using visuals, present your findings with your classmates.

1. リクルートスーツ
2. 敬語(けい)、尊敬語(そんけい)、謙譲語(けんじょう)、ていねい語、目上の人、目下の人
3. 先輩〔せんぱい〕、後輩〔こうはい〕

B. 学部と職業〔しょくぎょう〕：ペアワーク→クラスワーク

a. What programs would you want to get into in college and what kind of job would you want in the future? Choose your top three choices by marking them 1〜3. Write the readings of the *kanji* in *hiragana* and write the English meanings of each word. Share them with your class.

ベスト 1〜3	学部名	読みがな	英訳	ベスト 1〜3	職業	読みがな	英訳
	1. 法学部	ほうがくぶ			1. 医者	いしゃ	
	2. 経済学部	けいざい がくぶ			2. 歯医者	はいしゃ	
	3. 文学部				3. 獣医	じゅうい	
	4. 理学部				4. 看護婦	かんごふ	
	5. 工学部	こうがくぶ			5. 弁護士	べんごし	
	6. 農学部	のうがくぶ			6. 会計士	かいけいし	
	7. 教育学部	きょういく がくぶ			7. 教師	きょうし	
	8. 医学部	いがくぶ			8. 教授	きょうじゅ	
	9. 薬学部	やくがくぶ			9. 建築家	けんちくか	
	10. 美術学部	びじゅつがくぶ			10. 警官	けいかん	
	11. 音楽学部				11. 消防士	しょうぼうし	
	12. 体育学部	たいいく がくぶ			12. ビジネスマン		
	13. 外国語学部				13. コック		
					14. 芸術家	げいじゅつか	
					15. 銀行家		
					16. エンジニア		

b. Circle the degree(s) you want to earn.

学士号（がくしごう）　修士号（しゅうしごう）　博士号（はかせごう）　MBA

c. What is most important to you when you search for a job? Indicate your top three choices by marking your choices 1～3.

ベスト1～3	仕事を選ぶ時、何が大事？
	給料〔きゅうりょう〕がいい仕事
	人や社会の役〔やく〕に立てる仕事
	情熱〔じょうねつ〕をかけられる仕事
	好きな場所で働ける仕事
	休暇〔きゅうか〕が多い仕事

C. 日本での面接の時のマナー：ペアワーク→クラスワーク

Complete each of the following sentences by circling the correct answer.

1. 面接の時の服装は（清潔　不潔）な服装にする。
2. 面接の時、着て行く服は（リクルートスーツ　ビジネススーツ）と呼ばれている。
3. 面接の時の服装は（派手　地味）な方がいい。
4. 面接の時の服の色は（グレーや紺色　黒や白　青や黄色）がいい。
5. 面接の時、男性はスーツとネクタイが（必要だ　必要ではない）。
6. 面接の時、女性は（派手なメーク　地味なメーク　ノーメーク）がいい。
7. 面接の時、男性は（長い髪　茶髪　短い髪　坊主頭）がいい。
8. 面接の時、男性はピアスを（していても問題はない　していない方がいい）。
9. 面接の時、入れ墨を（していても問題はない　していれば問題になる）。
10. 面接の時、（明るく元気に　暗く静かに）話す方がいい。

11課

D. 聞く Pre-Listening Activity 「面接」：ペアワーク→クラスワーク

Have a conversation with your partner in informal style using the following questions. Elaborate on your responses and speak at normal speed.

1. 大学では何を専攻（せんこう）するつもり？
2. 日本に留学したい？
3. もし将来（しょう）日本の有名企業（きぎょう）でインターンの機会（きかい）が与（あた）えられれば、どんな企業に行ってみたい？
4. 建築（けんちく）会社で働いてみたいと思う？
5. もう海の水を飲料水に変える技術（ぎじゅつ）はある？
6. もし月に行ける機会（き）があったら、行ってみたいと思う？なぜ？
7. 大学を卒（そつ）業した後、大学院に進（すす）んで修士号（しゅうしごう）や博士号（はかせごう）を取りたいと思う？
8. 都市計画（しけい）の勉強に興味（きょう）がある？
9. アメリカの環境（かんきょう）問題の取（と）り組（く）みは進（すす）んでいると思う？
10. アメリカは日本から環境（かんきょう）問題の取り組みについて、何を学ぶべきだと思う？
11. 将来（しょう）、どこで就職（しゅうしょく）したいと思う？
12. あなたにとって、やりがいのある仕事とはどんな仕事だと思う？

E. 聞く Post-Listening Activity 「面接」：ペアワーク→クラスワーク

Presentation: Ken

Present your view of Ken. Discuss at least FIVE aspects of Ken. Begin with an appropriate introduction, give details about the five aspects, explain your own view or perspective, and end with a concluding remark. You will have 4 minutes to prepare and 2 minutes to present. Your presentation should be as complete as possible.

【Let's take notes!】

1. Begin with an appropriate introduction.
   _____

2. Discuss five aspects/examples of the topic.
   1.) _____
   2.) _____
   3.) _____
   4.) _____
   5.) _____

3. Explain your view or perspective.
   _____

4. End with a concluding remark.
   _____

11課

F. 読む Pre-Reading Activity「ホンダ」：ペアワーク→クラスワーク

Discuss the following questions using informal forms with your partner.

1. HONDAの創業者の本田宗一郎さんは今も生きている？
2. 現代の日本を代表する企業として、HONDAのほかに、どんな企業がある？
3. HONDAは自動車の前に、どんな製品を作っていたと思う？
4. 戦後、本田宗一郎さんが町工場で仕事を始めた頃、日本は貧乏だった？
5. 本田宗一郎さんの学歴は小学校だけだったそうだけど、学歴は成功するために大切だと思う？
6. 本田宗一郎さんは挑戦することが好きな人だったと思う？

G. 読む Post-Reading Activity「ホンダ」：ペアワーク→クラスワーク

Restate Mr. Honda's quotes in English and express the message he wanted to convey using the 〜は大事だ ending.

例．「僕は学歴がないから、ほかの人に教えてもらうことを恥ずかしいと思わなかった。」

訳：“Because I don't have a degree, I didn't feel embarrassed to ask other people to teach (help) me,”

　　ほかの人に教えてもらうこと　　　　　　　　　　　は、大事だ。

1.「人が喜ぶ物を作れば、必ず売れる。」
   訳：＿＿＿＿＿＿＿＿＿＿＿＿＿＿＿＿＿＿＿＿＿＿＿＿＿＿＿＿＿＿＿＿＿＿
   ＿＿＿＿＿＿＿＿＿＿＿＿＿＿＿＿＿＿＿＿＿＿＿＿＿は、大事だ。

2.「一人では成功出来ない。人と協力出来なければ何事も成功出来ない。」
   訳：＿＿＿＿＿＿＿＿＿＿＿＿＿＿＿＿＿＿＿＿＿＿＿＿＿＿＿＿＿＿＿＿＿＿
   ＿＿＿＿＿＿＿＿＿＿＿＿＿＿＿＿＿＿＿＿＿＿＿＿＿は、大事だ。

3.「失敗をおそれるな。99％の失敗から１％の成功が産まれる。」
   訳：＿＿＿＿＿＿＿＿＿＿＿＿＿＿＿＿＿＿＿＿＿＿＿＿＿＿＿＿＿＿＿＿＿＿
   ＿＿＿＿＿＿＿＿＿＿＿＿＿＿＿＿＿＿＿＿＿＿＿＿＿は、大事だ。

4.「運も実力のうちだ。」
   訳：＿＿＿＿＿＿＿＿＿＿＿＿＿＿＿＿＿＿＿＿＿＿＿＿＿＿＿＿＿＿＿＿＿＿
   ＿＿＿＿＿＿＿＿＿＿＿＿＿＿＿＿＿＿＿＿＿＿＿＿＿は、大事だ。

11課

H. テキストチャット「将来の計画」：ペアワーク→クラスワーク

You will have a conversation about your future plans with Kaori, a student at a Japanese school. Each time, speak as fully as possible for 20 seconds. Take turns.

1. 今日はありがとうございます。ところで、進学先の大学はもう決まりましたか。どんな大学ですか。
2. 大学では何を専攻するつもりですか。
3. 大学を卒業したら、大学院に行って、修士号とか博士号も取る予定ですか。
4. 将来、どんな職業につきたいと希望していますか。
5. いい給料をもらうのと、好きな仕事をするのと、どちらの方が大事だと思いますか。
6. 私も今年は大学受験の年ですが、何か日本の受験について質問がありますか。

I. Compare & Contrast「教師の仕事と医者の仕事」：ペアワーク→クラスワーク

a. Fill in the blanks with the correct words from the box below.

　これから、教師の仕事と医者の仕事を比べてみましょう。教師の仕事と医者の仕事は類似点も相違点もあります。

　まず一つ目の（　）は、教師と医者の働く場所が違います。教師は（　）で生徒を教えますが、医者は（　）で病気の人を治します。

　二つ目の相違点は、教師は一度に３０人くらいの生徒を教えますが、医者は一度に一人の（　）を治します。教師は一クラスに多くの生徒がいるし、いろいろな能力の生徒が同じクラスにいるし、五つぐらいのクラスを教えるので、大変な仕事だと思います。しかし、医者は（　）の最新の知識が必要なので、いつも学び続けなくてはいけません。これも大変な仕事です。

　しかし、一つの（　）は、教師も医者も相手は人だというところです。教師は生徒を教えて、医者は患者を治します。教師の仕事も医者の仕事も人のための仕事なので、人に（　）されていて、人から「先生」と呼ばれています。

　（　）として、私は医者の仕事の方が教師の仕事より好きです。なぜなら、医者の仕事は人の命を救うことが出来る仕事だからです。病気の人は多いですから、私は病気の人を治してあげたいと思っています。

a. 尊敬　b. 専門　c. 学校　d. 相違点　e. 患者　f. 類似点　g. 病院　h. 結論

b. State your preference for a teacher's job or a doctor's job, and give reason(s) for your choice.

Preference: _____

Reason(s): _____

11課

J. 会話「アルバイト」：ペアワーク→クラスワーク

a. Answer each of the questions in the correct form in 20 seconds. Take turns.
   Situation: You will have a conversation with Mr. Harada, a store manager, about your job inquiry.

1. 質問：スマイリーシャツの山田ですが、うちの会社でアルバイトをしたいそうですね。
   答の例：ああ、スマイリーシャツの方ですか。お電話、わざわざ有難うございます。はい、私はぜひそちらのお店でアルバイトをしたいんです。お仕事がありますか。

2. 質問：うちの店は日本人観光客が多いんですよ。前に何か日本語を使ったアルバイトの経験がありますか。
   答の例：日本人観光客が多いんですか。大丈夫です。私は日本語をもう５年間も勉強していますから、日本語で日常会話ぐらいは話せます。日本語を使ってのアルバイトは経験ありませんが、以前観光相手のお店でアルバイトをしたことがあります。

3. 質問：私達は週末に働いてくれる人をさがしているんですが、働ける曜日と時間を教えて下さい。
   答の例：週末ですか。そうですねえ。土曜日はいつでも働けますが、日曜日は正午から午後六時ごろまでだったら、大丈夫です。

4. 質問：仕事について何か質問はありますか。
   答の例：そうですねえ。時給はいくらですか。それから、どんな仕事ですか。制服とかほかに何か知らなければいけないことがありますか。電話を下さいまして、どうも有難うございます。よろしくお願いいたします。

b. Now you give your original answers. Take turns. The person who answers must not look at the book.

K. 文化発表「敬語」：ペアワーク→クラスワーク

a. Fill in the blanks with the correct words from the box below.

　これから、日本語の敬語について話します。敬語の中に日本人の価値観を見ることが出来ます。
　まず第一に、敬語には丁寧語があります。日本人は知らない人には丁寧語を使います。しかし、（　　）や友人などの身近な人には、丁寧語を使わずに、日常語を使います。
　第二に、敬語には尊敬語も謙譲語もあります。（　　）は話している人を持ち上げる時に使い、（　　）は自分を下げる時に使います。
　第三に、よく使われる動詞には、特別な尊敬語と謙譲語があります。例えば、「します」という動詞の尊敬語は「（　　）」で、謙譲語は「（　　）」です。

11課

第四に、名詞に「御」か「御」をつけると、丁寧語になります。しかし、（　）のにではありません。

第五に、敬語がよく使われる場所は、（　）とかお店とかレストランなどで、お客さんによく使われます。学校の部活でも後輩は（　）に敬語を使わなければなりません。

（　）として、敬語は複雑ですが、日本人の価値観だと思います。日本人は人を尊敬することはとても大事だと思うようです。敬語は日本人の心の鏡でしょう。

> a. 会社　　b. 全部　　c. 謙譲語　　d. なさいます
> e. 結論　　f. 家族　　g. 尊敬語　　h. 先輩　　i. いたします

b. Explain your perspective about the Japanese honorific language.

_____

_____

11課

<11課 - 聞く>
Listening: Interview

12秒×5

【You may take notes while listening. Do not look at the questions below before listening. You will have 12 seconds to answer each question. You may NOT move back and forth among questions.】

(Narrator) Now you will listen once to a graduate school interview between Ken and a Japanese college professor.

(Narrator) Now answer the questions for this selection.

1. When did Ken study in Japan?
    (A) when he was in the 11th grade
    (B) after he graduated from high school
    (C) when he was a junior in college
    (D) after he graduated from college

2. Which one of the following choices is NOT related to Ken's study of interest?
    (A) environment
    (B) science
    (C) economics
    (D) city planning

3. What did Ken study while in Japan?
    (A) converting sea water to drinking water and city planning on the moon
    (B) drinking water and city planning in Japan
    (C) civil engineering and city planning on the moon
    (D) sea water and environmental consultation

4. Why does Ken want to study at a Japanese graduate school?
    (A) He wants to improve his Japanese.
    (B) He thinks that Japanese society is more advanced in dealing with environmental issues.
    (C) He made many friends while he studied in Japan.
    (D) He wants to pursue a career in international business.

5. Which one is NOT his dream for the future?
    (A) to get a job in an environmental consulting firm
    (B) to earn a higher salary and become rich
    (C) to solve environmental problems
    (D) to engage in an useful job

11課

<11課 - 読む>
Reading: Honda
【You may move back and forth among all the questions.】

Read this excerpt taken from a letter by a Japanese teacher to Ken.

　　本田宗一郎という方を知っていますか。現代の日本を代表する企業、世界のHONDAの創業者です。まず戦後、貧乏のどん底にあった日本で、本田氏は静岡の町工場で仕事を始めました。一番初めに作った物は、「バタバタ」という製品だったそうです。奥さんが買物に行く時の荷物が重そうで、自転車にモーターをつけたら楽になると思い、第一号を作りました。それがよく売れたそうです。本田氏はよく工員に「ばかやろう」とどなっていたそうです。しかし、彼のニックネームは「親父さん」で、工場の工員に「親父さん」「親父さん」と呼ばれて、「お父さん」のように慕われていたようです。このお話から、本田氏がこわいけど、温かい人だったことが分かります。

　　彼が生前言った言葉がたくさん残されていますから、君に紹介したいと思います。彼の学歴は小学校だけでした。でも、本田氏は言っています。「僕は学歴がないから、ほかの人に教えてもらうことを全然恥ずかしいと思わなかった。」「人が喜ぶ物を作れば必ず売れる。」「一人では成功出来ない。人と協力出来なければ、何事も成功しない。」「失敗をおそれるな。９９％の失敗から１％の成功が産まれる。」「運も実力のうちだ。」などです。

　　自分の能力に挑戦し続け、人をいつも信頼し、人の喜ぶ物を作り続けた彼の人生は、本当にすばらしいと思います。君にもぜひ彼について書かれた本を読んでもらいたいです。

<11課 - 読む (質問)>

Reading: Honda

(Narrator) Now answer the questions for this section.

1. What inspired Mr. Honda to invent his first product?
   (A) his love for his wife
   (B) his love for his product
   (C) poverty
   (D) speed

2. What kind of person was Mr. Honda?
   (A) Mr. Honda started his factory even before World War II.
   (B) Mr. Honda started his factory in a big city.
   (C) Mr. Honda yelled at his workers often.
   (D) Mr. Honda was called "Emperor" by his workers.

3. What was the highest level of education Mr. Honda completed?
   (A) college
   (B) high school
   (C) junior high school
   (D) elementary school

4. What value did Mr. Honda NOT insist on in his quotes?
   (A) Make products that please people.
   (B) Collaborate with people.
   (C) Don't worry about making mistakes.
   (D) Make products at a low cost.

5. What does the teacher want Ken to do?
   (A) He wants Ken to read many Japanese books to improve his Japanese.
   (B) He wants Ken to read books about Mr. Honda to learn from his life.
   (C) He wants Ken to study more to challenge himself further.
   (D) He wants Ken to become a resourceful person.

11課

<11課 - 書く (テキストチャット)>

Text Chat: Future Plans

90秒×6

You will participate in a simulated exchange of text-chat messages. Each time it is your turn to write, you will have 90 seconds. You should respond as fully and as appropriately as possible.

You will have a conversation about your future plans with Kaori, a student at a Japanese school.

1. Respond. (90 seconds)

   今日はありがとうございます。ところで、進学先の大学はもう決まりましたか。どんな大学ですか。

2. Respond. (90 seconds)

   大学では何を専攻するつもりですか。

3. State your plans. (90 seconds)

   大学を卒業したら、大学院に行って、修士号とか博士号も取る予定ですか。

4. Explain your preference. (90 seconds)

   将来、どんな職業につきたいと希望していますか。

5. State your opinion. (90 seconds)

   いい給料をもらうのと、好きな仕事をするのと、どちらの方が大事だと思いますか。

6. Ask a specific question. (90 seconds)

   私も今年は大学受験の年ですが、何か日本の受験について質問がありますか。

<11課 - 書く (比較と対比)>

Compare and Contrast Article: Teacher's Job and Doctor's Job

20分

Directions: You are writing an article for the student newspaper of your sister school in Japan. Write an article in which you compare and contrast similarities and differences between a teacher's job and a doctor's job. Based on your personal experience, describe at least THREE aspects of each and highlight the similarities and differences between a teacher's job and a doctor's job. Also state your preference for either and give reasons for it.

Your article should be 300 to 400 characters or longer. Use the *desu/masu* or *da* (plain) style, but use one style consistently. Also, use *kanji* wherever *kanji* from the AP Japanese *kanji* list is appropriate. You have 20 minutes to write.

【NOTES/OUTLINE: 自分の作文のアウトラインを書こう！】

Introduction:
_____

Three similarities/differences:

  1. _____
  2. _____
  3. _____

Your preference and give reasons:
_____
_____

11課

<11課 - 話す (会話)>
Conversation: Part-Time Job

20秒×4

You will participate in a simulated conversation. Each time it is your turn to speak, you will have 20 seconds to record. You should respond as fully and as appropriately as possible.

You will have a conversation with Mr. Harada, a store manager, about your job inquiry.

(Mr. Harada)
(20 seconds)
(Mr. Harada)
(20 seconds)
(Mr. Harada)
(20 seconds)
(Mr. Harada)
(20 seconds)

<11課 - 話す (日本文化)>
Cultural Perspective Presentation: Japanese Honorific Language

4分+2分

Directions: Imagine you are making an oral presentation to your Japanese class. First, you will read and hear the topic for your presentation. You will have 4 minutes to prepare your presentation. Then you will have 2 minutes to record your presentation. Your presentation should be as complete as possible.

Present your own view or perspective of Japanese honorific language. Discuss at least FIVE aspects or examples of Japanese honorific language.

Begin with an appropriate introduction, give details, explain your own view or perspective, and end with a concluding remark.

【Let's take notes!】

1. Begin with an appropriate introduction.

_____

2. Discuss five aspects/examples of the topic.

    1.) _____
    2.) _____
    3.) _____
    4.) _____
    5.) _____

3. Explain your view or perspective.

_____

4. End with a concluding remark.

_____

11課

12課 冠婚葬祭
Rites of Life

【AP® タスク：冠婚葬祭】

What would be a dream life for you? Discuss what your ideal college life, ideal career, ideal marriage, ideal partner, ideal place of residence, ideal family, ideal retirement life and ideal way of dying would be. Who do you respect most as a person and why? What is most important in your life? What are your favorite proverbs or sayings?

【文化】日本の式：Ceremonies in Japan

The Japanese enjoy marking milestones in their lives with rituals and ceremonies. These occasions provide a venue for Japanese to gather formally as groups to recognize life milestones.

Celebrations for children are plentiful in Japan. Special holidays such as *Shichi-Go-San*, *Hinamatsuri* and *Kodomo no Hi* celebrate the lives of children. It is a time to thank the gods for the children's good health and a time to pray for the children's good fortune and long life. *Shichi-Go-San*, held in November, is celebrated by taking *kimono* clad children aged 3, 5 and 7 to the shrine to be blessed as they enter a new life stage. In celebration of leaving childhood, Japanese observe *seijinshiki* (成人式), or the celebration of young persons as they approach adulthood at the age of twenty.

Every year, school children experience several school ceremonies that are marked with pomp and rituals. The entrance ceremony, *nyuugakushiki* (入学式) is held in April for students who are entering a new school. A *shuukai* (集会) is held on the first day of school to welcome back returning students. At the end of the school year, graduating students participate in *sotsugyooshiki* (卒業式). Students gather for these ceremonies in a large school hall in their uniforms, listen to speeches by the principal and other school officials, and sing the school song in the solemn ceremonies.

Just as schools mark the entrance of new students, traditional companies recognize the arrival of new employees with a *nyuushashiki* (入社式). These ceremonies are held in early April to welcome new employees to the "family," where the employers assume the role of "parent" to the young employees. Once hired, the new recruits undergo intensive training sessions for their new jobs.

Another major rite of passage is the wedding ceremony or *kekkonshiki* (結婚式). Although many options now exist, the traditional Shinto ceremony is still common. The traditional wedding is preceded by a formal ceremonial exchange of gifts between the families of the couple as a symbol of the couple's engagement. Wedding arrangements are presided over by a *nakoodo*, or a go-between person. In the traditional wedding, the bride and groom recite their vows to the gods of the Shinto shrine while exchanging cups of *sake* in a ritual called *san-san-ku-do*. Recently, wedding rings are exchanged at Shinto, Christian, Buddhist wedding ceremonies. Only close family members attend the ceremony. Receptions are expensive and elaborate affairs to which many guests are invited.

The final ceremony of one's life is the funeral or *osooshiki* (お葬式). Most funerals are Buddhist. The highly ritualistic ceremonies are officiated by a priest at a temple. The priest chants sutras and incense is burnt while family and friends gather to pay respects. The deceased lies in a coffin at the altar, and the temple altar holds a photo of the deceased, memorial tablets, flowers, votive lights, lamps and incense holders. Family and friends offer gifts of money called *kooden* (incense money) to the family. After the funeral services, the body is cremated, put in an urn and kept at home for about 49 days before it is placed in the family tomb in a cemetery.

Japanese value ceremonies to mark milestones throughout their lives. It is a way to share their lives with others, show respect to others, and create a bond among family and friends. Ceremonies are highly ritualistic and generally formal and solemn affairs, though informal celebrations usually follow.

Questions to ponder: Based on all of the ceremonies and celebrations mentioned above, what can you gather about what Japanese value as they journey through life? Why are these rites of passage so important in Japanese culture and society?

12課 復習単語

トピック：冠婚葬祭(かんこんそうさい)

1. 宗教（しゅうきょう）	しゅうきょう	N	religion
2. 仏教（ぶっきょう）	ぶっきょう	N	Buddhism
3. 仏壇（ぶつだん）	ぶつだん	N	a Buddhist (family) altar
4. 神道	しんとう	N	Shintoism
5. 教会	きょうかい	N	church
6. 祈る（いのる）	いのる	V1	(to) pray
7. 祝う（しゅく）	いわう	V1	(to) celebrate; congratulate
8. 花嫁（はなよめ）	はなよめ	N	a bride
9. 結婚(を)する（けっこん）	けっこん(を)する	V3	(to) be married (to〜)
10. 妊娠(を)する（にんしん）	にんしん(を)する	V3	(to) get pregnant
11. (御)葬式（お そうしき）	(お)そうしき	N	funeral
12. 死ぬ	しぬ	V1	(to) die
13. 天国	てんごく	N	heaven

12課　★★★　新しい単語　★★★

1. それでも　SI　nevertheless
   私は勉強しなかった。それでも、先生は励ましてくれた。 I didn't study. Nevertheless, my teacher encouraged me.

2. ～から～にかけて　P　from ～ through ～
   春学期から夏休みにかけて、日本に留学した。 From the summer term through the summer vacation, I stayed abroad (as a study abroad student.)

3. ～わけ＜訳＞ではない　E　I don't mean that ～
   日本語をあまり勉強しないけど、嫌いな訳じゃない。 I don't study Japanese very much, but it doesn't mean that I dislike it.

4. ただいま、ごしょうかいにあずかりました～ともうします
   ＜只今、ご紹介にあずかりました～と申します＞
   Exp　I am ～, and I am honored to have just been introduced.

5. (～を)おいのり＜祈り＞しています　Exp　to pray for; to wish for
   これからのお二人の幸せをお祈りしています。 I pray for the happiness of you two from here on.

6. こころよりかんしゃしております。＜心より感謝しております。＞
   Exp　I am deeply grateful (from the bottom of my heart.)

7. おげんきでおすごしください。＜お元気でお過ごし下さい。＞
   Exp　Please take good care of yourself.

8. おしえてくださり、ありがとうございました。＜教えて下さり、有難うございました。＞
   Exp　Thank you for teaching (telling) me about it.

9. にちべいりょうこく＜日米両国＞　N　both Japan and America
   将来は日米両国で仕事をしたい。 M In the future, I want to work in both Japan and America.

10. しんにゅうしゃいん＜新入社員＞　N　newly hired company worker
    日本の学校では新入生に入学式が、会社では新入社員に入社式がある。 At Japanese schools, there are entrance ceremonies for new students, but at companies, there are ceremonies for new employees.

11. しゅうかい＜集会＞　N　meeting; gathering; assembly
日本の学校では学期の初めと終わりに集会がある。　At Japanese schools, there are assemblies at the beginning and end of the school term.

12. ひろうえん＜披露宴＞　N　reception
日本の披露宴はたいてい豪華でとても高い。　Japanese receptions are generally luxurious and very expensive.

13. たからもの＜宝物＞　N　treasure
祖母のインタビューのビデオが貴重な宝物になった。　My grandmother's interview video became a valuable treasure (for me).

14. おきょう＜お経＞　N　(Buddhist) sutras
お葬式ではお坊さんがお経を詠んでいた。　The priest was chanting sutras at the funeral ceremonies.

15. しゃかいふくし＜社会福祉＞　N　social welfare
姉は大学で社会福祉を専攻した。　My older sister majored in social work in college.

16. ほうこう＜方向＞　N　direction
二人は違う方向に進んだ。　The two advanced toward different directions.

17. じき＜時期＞　N　time; season
そちらの高校での卒業式の時期はいつですか。　When is the time for graduations at high schools there (where you are)?

18. ふしめ＜節目＞　N　turning point; milestone
日本人は人生の節目にいろいろな式を行う。　Japanese mark life's milestones with various ceremonies.

19. すべて＜全て＞　N　all; every
日本の全ての式はとてもまじめだ。　All of the Japanese ceremonies are very serious.

20. まわり＜周り＞　N　surroundings
亡くなった人の写真の周りはお花で飾ってあった。　Flowers decorated the area around the deceased person's photo.

21. ちゅうとはんぱ＜中途半端＞　Na　by halves [negative]; unfinished
国際結婚で生まれた子供達の言語は中途半端になりやすい。　The language of children who are born to (couples of) international marriage tends to be less than perfect.

22. やっぱり　Adv　[informal word of やはり]　as expected; likewise; after all
やっぱり二人は愛し合っていたみたいだ。　It seems they were both in love after all.

12課

23. (〜を)おこなう＜行う＞／行います   V1   to do; to conduct [formal]

    卒業式は講堂で行われた。 The graduation ceremony was held at the assembly hall.

24. (〜に)しょぞく＜所属＞(を)する／します   V3   to belong to 〜

    兄は大学の柔道部に所属している。 My older brother belongs to the college judo club.

25. (〜に)もてる／もてます   V2   to be favored; to be welcomed

    僕は女の子に全然もてない。 I am not at all popular with girls.

26. より＜縒り＞をもどす＜戻す＞／戻します   V1   to become reconciled

    二人は縒りを戻したようだ。 It seems the two have reconciled.

27. (〜を)なつかしくおもう＜懐かしく思う＞   Exp   to miss 〜.; fondly reminisce

    去年のことを懐かしく思い出す。 I fondly recall last year's things.

28. (〜に)しゅっせき＜出席＞(を)する／します   V3   to attend

    いとこの結婚式に出席したことがある。 I have attended my cousin's wedding ceremony.

29. (〜を)けっせき＜欠席＞する／します   V3   to be absent from; to miss (an event)

    残念だったが、いとこの結婚式を欠席した。 It was unfortunate, but I missed my cousin's wedding ceremony.

30. よう(or きゅうよう)ができた＜用(or 急用)が出来た＞   Exp   have business to do

    用が出来て、パーティーに行けなくなった。 Some business arose, and I am now not able to go to the party.

【もっと単語】

1. かんこんそうさい＜冠婚葬祭＞   N   ceremonial occasions
2. にゅうしゃしき＜入社式＞   N   company entrance ceremony
3. おみやまいり＜お宮参り＞   N   shrine visitation
4. てんしょく＜転職＞(を)する   N   to change occupations
5. しゅっさん＜出産＞(を)する   N   to give birth to
6. やくどし＜厄年＞   N   a critical (bad luck) year
7. やくばらい＜厄払い＞   N   exorcism
8. かろう＜過労＞   N   overwork; over exertion
9. かんれき＜還暦＞   N   sixtieth birthday
10. きすう＜奇数＞   N   odd numbers
11. ぐうすう＜偶数＞   N   even numbers
12. おいわい＜お祝い＞   N   celebration
13. こうでん＜香典＞   N   monetary gift given to a bereaved family

12課 文法

> A-1. どういうわけですか。　　　　　What is the reason?
> 　　　そういうわけです。　　　　　That is the reason.
> 　　　私にはまったくわけが分からない。　I simply don't understand the reason.
> 　　　彼が来なかったわけを知らない。　I don't know the reason why he did not come.
> 　　　どういうわけか　　　　　　　for one reason or another
> 　　　わけのわからない人だ。　　　　He is an unreasonable man.
>
> The word わけ is defined as "reason." It is used in many expressions, but in most cases, can simply be translated as "reason" in any given context.

Restate the sentences into English.

1. 毎朝、学校に遅れるのは、どういうわけなんですか。

2. 私は学校が好きなんです。そのわけは、友達と会えるからです。

3. どうしてこんな事故を起こしたのか、そのわけを教えて下さい。

4. 彼はとてもおしゃべりなんです。こういうわけで、彼が嫌いなんです。

5. どういうわけか、私達はほとんどけんかをしたことがないんです。

> A-2.　1. Verb (plain)　　　　　　＋（という）わけではない　　　"It does not mean that ～"
> 　　　2. いadj.　　　　　　　　＋（という）わけではない
> 　　　3-1. なadj. [な／だった]　＋わけではない
> 　　　3-2. なadj. [(だ)／だった]　＋というわけではない
> 　　　4-1. Noun だった　　　　　＋わけではない
> 　　　4-2. Noun [(だ)／だった]　＋というわけではない
>
> This sentence final grammatical form usually denies another related remark or implied remark it follows. Since わけ is a noun, it is modified by plain forms as other nouns would be.
>
> 1. 日本語が分かる／分かった(という)わけではない。
>   It does not mean that I understand / understood Japanese.
> 2. 日本語が難しい／難しかった(という)わけではない。
>   It does not mean that Japanese is / was difficult.

12課

> 3-1. 読書が<u>嫌いな／嫌いだった</u>わけではない。
>   It does not mean that I dislike/disliked reading.
> 3-2. 読書が<u>嫌い(だ)／嫌いだった</u>というわけではない。
>   It does not mean that I dislike/disliked reading.
> 4-1. コンサートが<u>成功だった</u>わけではない。
>   It does not mean that the concert was a success.
> 4-2. コンサートが<u>成功(だ)／だった</u>というわけではない。
>   It does not mean that the concert is/was a success.

Circle the correct choice from the ( ) and restate the sentence into English.

1. 仕事をすることに反対（する　した）わけではないが、大学へ行った方がいいと思うよ。
   _____

2. 山田さんは決して高い車を買わないが、お金が（ない　なかった）というわけではない。
   _____

3. 私は日本語が上手（な　だ）わけではないけど、少し話せます。
   _____

4. テニスの試合に勝ったけど、簡単な試合（だ　だった）わけではない。
   _____

> A-3. 行く　　　＋わけにはいかない　　　I cannot go.
>
>   行かない＋わけにはいかない　　　There is no reason for me not to go. (I have to go.)
> Compare:
> a. 私は<u>歌えない</u>。　　　　　　　　　　I cannot sing.
> b. 私は<u>歌うわけにはいかない</u>。　　　　I cannot very well sing (owing to some circumstance).

Circle the correct choice from the ( ) and restate the sentence into English.

1. 母が病気なので、今、日本に旅行（する　しない）わけにはいかない。

2. 午後、友達が来るので、家を留守に（する　しない）わけにはいかない。

3. いとこの結婚式だから、結婚式に出席（する　しない）わけにはいかない。

4. 明日、大事な試験があるから、ちょっと熱があるけど、学校を（休む　休まない）わけにはいかない。_____

5. 今朝、交通事故を起こしたので、早く学校へ行かなければならなかったけど、警官を（呼ぶ　呼ばない）わけにはいかなかった。
   _____

12課

B. 敬語　　Honorific speech
a. 謙譲語：食べます/飲みます→いただきます, します→いたします, 行きます/来ます→まいります,
　　　　　います→おります, 言います→申します, 見ます→拝見します, 待ちます→お待ちします
b. 尊敬語：待って下さい→お待ちください, 見て下さい→ご覧下さい, 過ごして下さい→お過ごし下さい,
　　　　　書いてくれます→書いて下さいます, 教えてくれます→教えて下さいます;
　　　　　行きます/来ます→いらっしゃいます, 食べます→召し上がります, します→されます,
　　　　　帰ります→お帰りになります
c. 丁寧語：好きですか→お好きですか

The use of honorific (敬語) speech is based on the speaker's perception of the relative status of the person he/she is speaking about in relation to him/herself. To create distance is to show respect. One creates distance by elevating the person being spoken about, and/or lowering oneself when one speaks of oneself. The first category of verbs above is *kenjoogo*, that are used to demote oneself. The second category of verbs are those that elevate the person being spoken about (*sonkeigo*) and the third are polite forms of words that are usually also used when one is using honorific language.

Fill in the blanks with the correct honorific speech forms of the cues given in the (　).
1. 初めまして。田中と＿＿＿＿＿＿＿＿＿＿。（言います）
2. 私は現在は横浜で仕事をして＿＿＿＿＿＿＿＿＿＿。（います）
3. お二人の幸せを＿＿＿＿＿＿＿＿＿＿。（祈っています）
4. ＿＿＿＿＿＿＿＿＿＿です。（久しぶり）
5. ＿＿＿＿＿＿＿＿＿＿ですか。（元気）
6. 夏休みには、また日本に＿＿＿＿＿＿＿＿＿＿。（行きました）
7. 先生は僕を＿＿＿＿＿＿＿＿＿＿。（励ましました）
8. 先生は私の推薦状を＿＿＿＿＿＿＿＿＿＿。（書きました）
9. 僕は先生にいろいろ＿＿＿＿＿＿＿＿＿＿。（世話になりました）
10. いろいろ＿＿＿＿＿＿＿＿＿＿、有難うございました。（教えます）
11. 先生に心より感謝して＿＿＿＿＿＿＿＿＿＿。（います）
12. 先生、お元気で＿＿＿＿＿＿＿＿＿＿下さい。（過ごす）

C. 日本人みたいです。　　He is like a Japanese. [informal]
　　日本人のようです。　　He is like a Japanese. [formal]
1. 日本人みたいだ。　　　　日本人のようだ。　　　　(He) is like a Japanese.
2. 日本人みたいに話す。　　日本人のように話す。　　(He) speaks like a Japanese.
3. 日本に行ったみたいだ。　日本に行ったようだ。　　(He) seems to have gone to Japan.
4. 分かったみたいな気がする。　分かったような気がする。　I feel like he understood it.

みたい is a conversational equivalent of -よう (seems, is like...). Like -よう, it should also be treated as a な adjective. It is used to compare two nouns, behaviors or actions that are similar, but not identical.

12課

Circle the correct particle in the ( ) and restate the sentence in English. X means no particle needed.

1. 日本語を勉強して日本語が分かったみたい（の　**な**）気がする。
   _____

2. ケンは日本人（**の**　X）みたいに日本語がぺらぺら話せる。
   _____

3. まりの両親は結婚に反対している（の　**X**）ようだ。
   _____

4. アメリカの卒業式は日本（**の**　X）ように真面目ではない。
   _____

5. まりさんの着物はとても高い着物（**の**　X）ようだった。
   _____

D. 医者になった。　　　　　　(I) became a doctor.
　　上手になった。　　　　　　(He) became skillful.
　　おもしろくなった。　　　　(It) became interesting.
　　話せるようになった。　　　(I) became able to speak.
　　日本に行くことになった。　It has been decided that we go to Japan.

-に なる/-くなる is used to describe a noun, state or action that has changed, or become different in some way. Take special note that い adjectives that precede なる appear in the -く form.

Circle the correct particle in the ( ) and restate the sentence in English. X means no particle is needed.

1. 茶道や生け花や書道をしたこともいい経験（**に**　X）なりました。
   _____

2. 日本語を習ったおかげで、謙虚な人間（**に**　X）なったような気がします。
   _____

3. 日本語の歌が歌えるよう（**に**　X）なったし、日本語のテレビも見るよう（**に**　X）なりました。
   _____

4. 日本人と日本語で話せる自信が持てるよう（**に**　X）なりました。
   _____

5. 日本の文化が分かるよう（**に**　X）なりました。
   _____

6. 先生のおかげで、日本語がだんだんおもしろく（に　**X**）なって来ました。
   _____

7. 祖父をインタビューした時のビデオが、家族の宝物（**に**　X）なりました。

12課

> E. 日本に行く<u>ことになった</u>。　It has been decided that we go to Japan.
> 　　日本に行く<u>ことに決まった</u>。　It has been decided that we go to Japan.
> 　　日本に行く<u>ことにした</u>。　(I) decided to go to Japan.
> 　　日本に行く<u>ことに決めた</u>。　(I) decided to go to Japan.
>
> ことになる and ことに決まる are identical in meaning and are interchangeable. They are used when the speaker has had no control of the action. ことにする and ことに決める are likewise interchangeable and are used when the speaker has control over the action. The past tense form is used to indicate when the decision (not the action) has already been made.

Circle the correct word in the ( ) and restate the sentence in English.

1. 親友が日本で結婚式をすることにしたので、私も日本へ行くことに（した　なった）。

   _____

2. 夢はスタンフォード大学に入学することだったので、合格が決まった時、すぐスタンフォード大学に行くことに（決めた　決まった）。

   _____

3. 両親の仕事がユタ州に決まったので、子供達も引っ越すことに（した　なった）。

   _____

| 12課 | | アクティビティー | |

A. 人生すごろくゲーム：ペアーかグループワーク

a. ゲームの単語の勉強をしましょう。空白の中に単語の英訳を書きなさい。

単語	読み方	英訳	単語	読み方	英訳
1. 誕生	たんじょう		21. 成人式	せいじんしき	
2. お宮参り	おみやまいり	shrine visit	22. 就職	しゅうしょく	
3. 偶数	ぐうすう		23. 年末	ねんまつ	
4. 端午の節句	たんごのせっく	Boy's Day	24. 恋人	こいびと	
5. 奇数	きすう		25. 結婚	けっこん	
6. ひな祭り	ひなまつり		26. 長男出産	ちょうなんしゅっさん	
7. 幼稚園	ようちえん		27. 転職	てんしょく	
8. 入園式	にゅうえんしき		28. 長女出産	ちょうじょしゅっさん	
9. 遠足	えんそく		29. 厄年	やくどし	unlucky year
10. 忘れ物	わすれもの		30. 厄払い	やくばらい	exorcism
11. 祝い	いわい		31. 過労	かろう	overwork
12. 卒園式	そつえんしき		32. 入院	にゅういん	
13. 転校	てんこう		33. 退職	たいしょく	
14. 初恋	はつこい		34. 還暦	かんれき	60th birthday
15. 高校受験	こうこうじゅけん		35. 葬式	そうしき	
16. 橋を渡る	はしをわたる		36. 米寿	べいじゅ	88th birthday
17. 活躍	かつやく		37. 賞金	しょうきん	
18. 準備	じゅんび		38. 一等	いっとう	
19. 予備校	よびこう		39. すごろく	X	a child's dice game
20. 合格	ごうかく		40. さいころ	X	dice

b. ゲームで遊びましょう！　Necessary items: Dice and markers for each player.

Instructions:
1) Each player rolls the dice to determine the order of the players. Highest score goes first.
2) Each player rolls the dice and advances accordingly. Read instructions at each spot on which the player lands. Keep track of the amount of money gained/lost for each occasion.
3) Take turns. The first to reach the final destination earns 2,000 yen and the second to reach it receives 1,000 yen.
4) After all players are finished, count up the money each player has earned. The player with the most money wins the game.

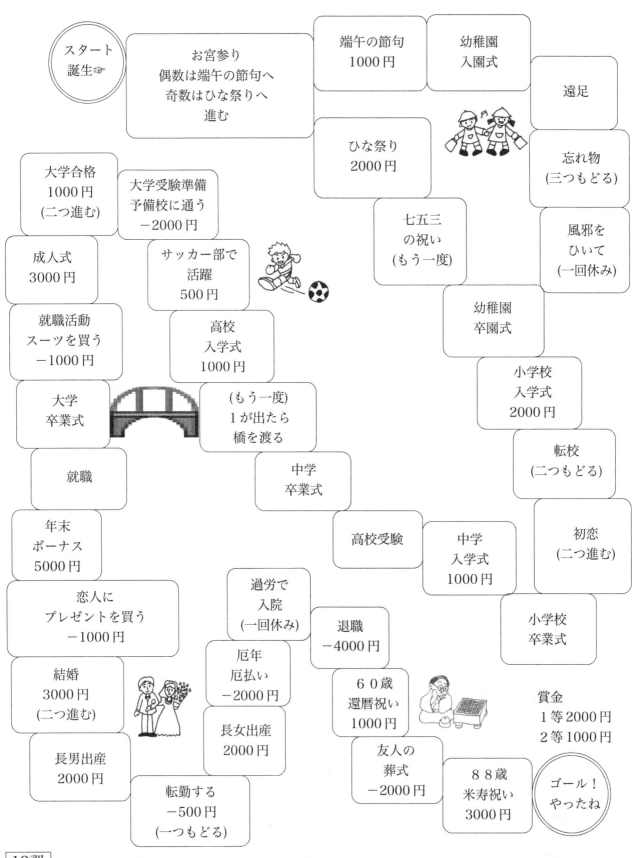

B. 聞く Pre-Listening Activity 「結婚スピーチ」：ペアワーク→クラスワーク

Have a conversation in informal style with your partner using the following questions. Use あいづち、elaborate and speak at normal speed.

1. エミとケンが仲が良かったのは、日本語のどのレベルのクラスだったか覚えてる？
2. まりがエミとケンの学校に留学して来たのは、日本語のどのレベルのクラスだったか覚えてる？
3. ケンは高二の時に日本に一年も留学してたけど、何のスポーツの部活に所属していたか覚えてる？
4. ケンはどこの大学に進学したか覚えてる？
5. ケンはエミとまりのどちらと結婚したと思う？

C. 聞く Post-Listening Activity 「結婚スピーチ」：一人→ペア→クラスワーク

Cultural Perspective Presentation: International Marriage

Imagine you are making an oral presentation to your Japanese class. You will have 4 minutes to prepare your presentation. Then you will have 2 minutes to present your presentation. Your presentation should be as complete as possible.

Present your own view or perspective of international marriage. Discuss at least FIVE aspects or examples of international marridge.

Begin with an appropriate introduction, give details, explain your own view or perspective, and end with a concluding remark.

【Let's take notes!】

1. Begin with an appropriate introduction.
_____

2. Discuss five aspects/examples of the topic.
   1.) _____
   2.) _____
   3.) _____
   4.) _____
   5.) _____

3. Explain your view or perspective.
_____

4. End with a concluding remark.
_____

12課

D. 読む Pre-Reading Activity「お礼状」：ペアワーク→クラスワーク

Underline words that are terms of respect or honorific speech and restate the sentences in English.

Ex. 先生は私を励まして下さいました。　　My teacher encouraged me.

1. おかげさまで、日本語はだんだんおもしろくなって来ました。
   _____

2. 日本語を習ったおかげで、少し謙虚な人間になったような気がします。
   _____

3. お世話になりました。　_____

4. いろいろ教えて下さり、本当に有難うございました。
   _____

5. 心より感謝しております。　_____

6. これからもお元気で、お過ごし下さい。　_____

E. 読む Post-Reading Activity「お礼状」：一人→ペア→クラスワーク

Write an outline of a thank you letter to your former Japanese teacher. Write an introduction, three things you appreciate about the teacher and close with an appropriate ending. Then neatly write a thank you letter by hand with a black pen.

Intro.: _____

1. _____

2. _____

3. _____

Ending: _____

F. テキストチャット「結婚式と葬式〔そうしき〕」：ペアワーク→クラスワーク

You will have a conversation about funerals in your country and in Japan with a student at your sister school in Japan. Each time, speak as fully as possible for 20 seconds. Take turns.

1. 川本です。どうぞよろしく。
2. アメリカのお葬式について教えて下さい。
3. お葬式に出席したことがありますか。
4. そちらのお葬式はどんな所で行われるんですか。
5. お葬式にはどんな服装で出席するんですか。
6. 日本にはお葬式にお金をあげる習慣がありますが、そちらもありますか。
7. どうも有難うございました。
8. 日本のお葬式について何か質問がありますか。

12課

G. Compare & Contrast「結婚と仕事」：ペア→クラスワーク

Discuss the following questions with your partner about marriage and career. Use the informal form. Then, form teams and debate the positive and negative features of each.

1. 結婚すると、どんな良いことがある？
2. 結婚すると、どんな悪いことがある？
3. 仕事をすると、どんな良いことがある？
4. 仕事をすると、どんな悪いことがある？
5. 結婚と仕事の似ている点は何？
6. 結婚と仕事の違う点は何？

H. 会話「お葬式〔そうしき〕」：ペアワーク→クラスワーク

a. Fill in the ( ) with the correct response from the box below.

1. 質問　：ごめん、パーティーへ行けなくなっちゃった。
   答の例：ええっ、パーティーに行けないって？どうして？何か急に用でも出来たの？
   　　　　ああ、（　　　　）だなあ。一緒に行けるのを（　　　　）にしていたのに。

2. 質問　：実は、昨日おじいちゃんが亡くなったんだ。
   答の例：ええっ、（　　　　）？おじいさんが亡くなったの？それは、（　　　　）に。
   　　　　病気だったの？それとも、（　　　　）に？

3. 質問　：それで、お葬式がこの日曜日にあるんだ。
   答の例：あっ、そう？お葬式が日曜日に？それじゃ、パーティーに行けなくても、
   　　　　（　　　　）ないね。お葬式は、どこで何時からあるの？

4. 質問　：それで、お願いがあるんだけど。
   答の例：お願い？私で出来ることだったら、（　　　　）するから、言って。どんなこと？

5. 質問　：マイクへのプレゼントをもう買ったから、渡してくれる？
   答の例：うん、（　　　　）いいよ。マイクにプレゼントを渡してあげるよ。
   　　　　もうプレゼントを買ったの？早いねえ。何にしたの？じゃ、またね。

   ┌───┐
   │ a. もちろん　 b. 本当　　c. 残念　　d. 気の毒 │
   │ e. 何でも　　 f. 楽しみ　 g. 仕方　　h. 急   │
   └───┘

b. Answer the questions from Part a. in 20 seconds. When you answer, do not rely on the book. Take turns. Situation: You will have a conversation with your close friend.

I. 文化発表「日本の式」：ペアワーク→クラスワーク

a. Fill in the blanks with the correct words from the box below.

　　日本人は人生の節目にいろいろな式を行います。そして、すべての式に日本人はとてもまじめです。
　　まず第一に、子供が生まれて（　　）になるまでにいろいろな式を行います。子供が生まれると、お宮参りに神社に行きます。女子は（　　）と七歳、男子は五歳の１１月に、七五三という行事があります。子供はきれいな服や着物を着て、（　　）に行きます。二十歳になると（　　）を行います。毎年３月（　　）にはひなまつり、５月（　　）には子供の日を祝います。日本の子供はとても大事に育てられているようです。
　　第二に、学校でもいろいろな式があります。４月には（　　）、学期が始まる時と終わる時には全生徒が集まる集会、そして、３月には（　　）があります。毎日の授業も「起立、（　　）」で始まり、終わります。
　　第三に、日本の会社の中でも、（　　）があります。新入社員は、この日から会社のファミリーの一員になります。
　　第四に、結婚式は人生で一番大事な式です。（　　）な結婚式は神社で挙げられますが、教会やお寺などで結婚式を挙げるカップルも多いです。披露宴はとても豪華で、家族や親戚や友人を（　　）します。
　　第五に、お葬式も人生の最後の大事な式です。伝統的なお葬式は（　　）で行われます。亡くなった人の（　　）を真ん中に、そのまわりをお花で飾ります。お坊さんのお経、線香の中で、家族や親戚や友人や近所の人達が亡くなった人にお別れをします。
　　結論として、日本人はアメリカ人より式を多くするようです。式は多分人々の気持ちを一つにすることが出来るので、「和」を大事にする日本人には（　　）なのかも知れません。

a. 神社	b. お寺	c. 成人式	d. 入学式	e. 入社式
f. 卒業式	g. ３日	h. ５日	i. 三歳	j. 礼
k. 招待	l. 写真	m. 大人	n. 大切	o. 伝統的

b. Write your own view or perspective on Japanese ceremonies.

_____
_____

12課

<12課 - 聞く>

Listening: Wedding Speech

  12秒×5

[You may take notes while listening. Do not look at the questions below before listening. You will have 12 seconds to answer each question. You may NOT move back and forth among questions.]

(Narrator) Now you will listen once to a speech at a wedding reception.

(Narrator) Now answer the questions for this selection.

1. What statement is true about Emi?
   (A) She is a fifth generation Japanese American.
   (B) She was in the same Japanese class as Ken during her senior year.
   (C) She is working in Hawaii now where she is using her Japanese.
   (D) Emi was a guest speaker at the wedding ceremony of Ken and Mari.

2. Where and when did Ken and Mari meet?
   (A) at high school in Hawaii when they were in the 9th grade
   (B) at high school in Japan when they were in the 9th grade
   (C) at high school in Hawaii when they were in the 10th grade
   (D) at high school in Japan when they were in the 10th grade

3. What is NOT true about Ken?
   (A) He was good at playing the piano.
   (B) He was a good athlete.
   (C) He was good looking.
   (D) He was popular with girls.

4. What is true about Ken's experience in Japan?
   (A) He stayed in Japan the summer after 10th grade.
   (B) He studied in Japan for one year during his junior year of college.
   (C) He received a Ph.D. in Japan.
   (D) He found a job in Japan.

5. What is true about Mari?
   (A) She studied in Hawaii for one year.
   (B) She graduated from high school in Hawaii.
   (C) She went to college in the U.S.
   (D) She studied earth science in college.

<12課 - 読む>
Reading: Letter
【You may move back and forth among all the questions.】

新緑の美しい今日この頃ですが、先生、お久しぶりです。お元気ですか。僕は先日、高校を卒業し、九月からミシガン大学に行くことになりました。

先生のクラスにいた去年のことを懐かしく思い出します。僕はあまりいい生徒ではありませんでしたね。宿題もせずに、勉強もしませんでしたが、日本語のクラスが嫌いだったわけではありません。それでも、先生はいつも励まして下さいましたね。おかげさまで日本語はだんだんおもしろくなってきました。今はだいたい日本人と日本語で話せるし、日本の文化が分かるようになりました。カラオケで日本語の歌が歌えるようになったし、日本語のテレビドラマも見るようになりました。そして、戦争体験のプロジェクトで祖父にインタビューしました。その後、その祖父が亡くなって、そのインタビューのビデオが家族の貴重な宝物になりました。茶道や生け花や書道をしたこともいい経験になりました。今、日本人と話せる自信があります。日本語を習ったおかげで、少し*謙虚な人間になったような気がします。それは一番大事なことですね。大学へ行っても日本語を続けるつもりです。そして、大学三年生の時に日本の大学に留学したいです。将来の夢は、環境工学を専攻して、日米両国で仕事をすることです。

いろいろ教えて下さり、本当にありがとうございました。心より感謝しております。これからも、お元気でお過ごし下さい。

六月一日

橋本町子先生

ケビン・ブラウン

新緑、この頃、懐かしく、嫌い、励まして、戦争、貴重、宝物、*謙虚、夢、環境、専攻、感謝

<12課 - 読む (質問)>

Reading: Letter

(Narrator) Now answer the questions for this section.

1. When are Kevin's plans?
   (A)　He plans to graduate from high school next month.
   (B)　He plans to major in earth sciences at the University of Michigan.
   (C)　He plans to study in Japan during his junior year.
   (D)　He plans to work in Japan in the future.

2. What kind of student was Kevin when he was in Ms. Hashimoto's class?
   (A)　He diligently did his homework.
   (B)　He often asked her questions.
   (C)　He studied hard.
   (D)　He was often encouraged by her.

3. What did Kevin remember from Ms. Hashimoto's class?
   (A)　He went to *karaoke* with his class.
   (B)　He interviewed his grandmother for his war project.
   (C)　The interview video he made for his war project has become a family treasure.
   (D)　He enjoyed his cultural experience at the Zen temple.

4. What was the biggest lesson Kevin learned from his Japanese studies?
   (A)　He became fluent in Japanese.
   (B)　He understands Japanese history well.
   (C)　He learned to enjoy *karaoke* and Japanese TV dramas.
   (D)　He learned to live life with humility.

5. Why did Kevin write this letter?
   (A)　He wanted to thank Ms. Hashimoto.
   (B)　He wanted to ask for a recommendation for a job.
   (C)　He wanted to invite Ms. Hashimoto to his graduation party.
   (D)　He wanted to ask some questions about the study abroad program at his university.

12課

<12課 - 書く (テキストチャット)>
Text Chat: Weddings and Funerals

90秒×6

You will participate in a simulated exchange of text-chat messages. Each time it is your turn to write, you will have 90 seconds. You should respond as fully and as appropriately as possible.

You will have a conversation about ceremonies with Maki Oda, a student at your sister school in Japan.

1. Respond. (90 seconds)
   小田です。どうぞよろしく。今日はアメリカの結婚式とお葬式(そう)について教えて下さい。
2. Respond. (90 seconds)
   最近、結婚式(そう)かお葬式(せき)に出席しましたか。
3. Describe. (90 seconds)
   そちらの結婚式やお葬式(そう)は、どこで行われるんですか。
4. Describe. (90 seconds)
   そちらではどんな服装(そうそう)でお葬式(せき)に出席するんですか。
5. Describe. (90 seconds)
   日本では結婚式やお葬式(そう)にお金をあげる習慣(かん)がありますが、そちらは何をしますか。
6. Ask a specific question. (90 seconds)
   有難うございます。日本の結婚式やお葬式(そう)について何か質問がありますか。

<12課 - 書く (比較(ひかく)と対比(たいひ))>
Compare and Contrast Article: Marriage and Career

20分

Directions: You are writing an article for the student newspaper of your sister school in Japan. Write an article in which you compare and contrast similarities and differences between marriage and career. Describe at least THREE aspects of each and highlight the similarities and differences between marriage and career. Also state your preference for either and give reasons for it.

Your article should be 300 to 400 characters or longer. Use the *desu/masu* or *da* style, but use one style consistently. Also, use *kanji* wherever *kanji* from the AP Japanese *kanji* list is appropriate. You have 20 minutes to write.

【NOTES/OUTLINE: 自分の作文のアウトラインを書こう！】

Introduction:
_____

Three similarities/differences:

1. _____
2. _____
3. _____

Your preference and give reasons:
_____
_____

12課

<12課 - 話す (会話)>
Conversation: Funeral

`20秒×4`

You will participate in a simulated conversation. Each time it is your turn to speak, you will have 20 seconds to record. You should respond as fully and as appropriately as possible.

You will have a conversation with Emi, your close friend, about her problem.

(Emi)
(20 seconds)
(Emi)
(20 seconds)
(Emi)
(20 seconds)
(Emi)
(20 seconds)

<12課 - 話す (日本文化)>
Cultural Perspective Presentation: Ceremonies in Japan

`4分+2分`

Directions: Imagine you are making an oral presentation to your Japanese class. First, you will read and hear the topic for your presentation. You will have 4 minutes to prepare your presentation. Then you will have 2 minutes to record your presentation. Your presentation should be as complete as possible.

Present your own view or perspective of ceremonies in Japan. Discuss at least FIVE aspects or examples of ceremonies in Japan.

Begin with an appropriate introduction, give details, explain your own view or perspective, and end with a concluding remark.

【Let's take notes!】

1. Begin with an appropriate introduction.

   _____

2. Discuss five aspects/examples of the topic.

   1.) _____
   2.) _____
   3.) _____
   4.) _____
   5.) _____

3. Explain your view or perspective.

   _____

4. End with a concluding remark.

   _____

13課　●●●　祭りと年中行事　●●●
Festivals and Annual Events

【AP® タスク：祭りと年中行事】
Select one annual event from the Japanese calendar and discuss three characteristics of the event. Discuss your thoughts and opinions about it. Compare and contrast them with characteristics of the same or a similar annual event on an American calendar.

【文化】 日本の年中行事： Japan's Annual Events

Japanese love celebrations. Holidays, festivals and special events honoring diverse aspects of Japanese culture fill their annual calendar.

The most celebrated holiday in Japan is *Oshoogatsu* (お正月), or New Year's. In late December, the Japanese begin cleaning their houses to rid them of dirt and evil spirits. They write New Year's cards, clear up financial obligations, purchase end of the year obligatory gifts called *oseibo*, and attend *boonenkai* (忘年会) parties to forget all of the year's troubles. Just before New Year's, they cook special foods called *osechi ryoori*. On New Year's Eve, Japanese watch the NHK *Koohaku Uta Gassen* (Red and White Song Contest), or go to a nearby temple to welcome the year with the ringing of the *Joya no Kane* 108 times, or eat hot *soba* noodles to ensure a long life. On New Year's morning, the family partakes of *ozooni*, a broth with vegetables, seafood and rice cakes. Donning *kimono*, many go out for *hatsumoode*, the first shrine visit. They also may relax at home, greet guests or visit family and friends. *Osechi ryoori* and *sake* are served. The home is decorated with *kadomatsu, shimenawa* and *kazarimochi*. Children may play traditional games such as *hanetsuki* (a badminton like game), kiteflying or top spinning, or watch special New Year's TV shows. Businesses and schools are closed for several days to a week to celebrate the New Year.

Children's festivals are common. They are *Hinamatsuri* (Girl's Day) on March 3, *Kodomo no Hi*, Children's Day (traditionally Boy's Day) on May 5, and *Shichi-Go-San*, on November 15. These celebrations are a time to thank the gods for the children's good health and to pray for continued blessings over them. Children may dress in their *kimono* and are served special foods.

Japanese revere age. Children become adults at age 20, and on January 15 (*Seijin no Hi*), young adults are recognized officially with special ceremonies at government offices. Young women don their brightly colored kimono, while young men dress in business suits. They later celebrate at parties. Around September 15 (*Keiro no Hi*), senior citizens are honored. It is a day to celebrate long life, pray for continued good health and recognize their contributions to the society. It is also used as a time to raise consciousness about issues that face the elderly.

Several holidays mark the change of seasons. Japanese celebrate *Setsubun* in early February. According to the lunar calendar, it marks the transition from winter to spring. It is now a celebration to chase off evil spirits and welcome in happiness. *Shunbun no Hi,* or Vernal Equinox Day, is a holiday held around March 21, the day when the length of daylight and night are exactly the same. Cherry blossoms begin to bloom at this time. The Autumnal Equinox Day or *Shuubun no Hi,* held around September 23, is the other day in the year when daylight and night are the same length. Both days are called *Ohigan,* when Japanese honor their ancestors' spirits by visiting their graves.

Another major celebration is *Obon*, a Buddhist festival held in mid-July or mid-August (depending on the region) to welcome back the spirits of one's ancestors. Lanterns are hung to guide the spirits back home, graves are visited, *bon* dances are held, and food offerings are made at family altars. Many urban dwellers flock home during the *obon* season to spend time with their families.

Festivals and celebrations reflect many of the values of any given culture. For the Japanese, marking the passage of time, celebrating children and the elderly, observing nature and its changes, and respecting ancestors are a few of the values visible in their special annual events.

Questions to ponder: Are there any other values you observe in these and other Japanese holidays? What values are evident in the holidays and events you celebrate in your culture?

13課

13課 復習単語

トピック：祭りと年中行事

1. (御)正月	(お)しょうがつ	N	New Year
2. 明けましておめでとう（ございます） あけましておめでとう（ございます）		Exp	[New Year's greeting]
3. 御年玉	おとしだま	N	money received mainly by children from adults at New Year's
4. 神社	じんじゃ	N	shrine (Shinto)
5. 御守り	おまもり	N	good-luck charm
6. 万歳	ばんざい	Exp	Hurray!
7. 二十歳	はたち	N	twenty years old
8. (御)花見	(お)はなみ	N	cherry blossom viewing
9. 母の日	ははのひ	N	Mother's Day

| 13課 | ★★★ | 新しい単語 | ★★★ |

1. しょちゅうみまい＜暑中見舞い＞　N　summer correspondence inquiring about the receiver's health during the hot summer
   しょちゅうおみまいもうしあげます＜暑中お見舞い申し上げます＞　Exp　I express my greetings to you during this hot summer season.
   日本にはお正月に年賀状を、夏には暑中見舞いのはがきを送る。In Japan, one sends *nengajoo* at New Year's and *shochuumimai* cards during the summer.

2. よいおとしをおむかえください。＜良いお年をお迎えください。＞
   Exp　Wishing you a good year.

3. どちらかというと　SI　If I had to choose... [Used to vaguely express one's opinion.]
   どちらかというと私はお正月の方がクリスマスより好きだ。 If I had to choose, I would have to say I like New Year's better than Christmas.

4. ～のかわりに　P　instead of ; in place of～
   日本では着物を着ると、くつのかわりにぞうりを履く。 If I wear *kimono* in Japan, I wear slippers instead of shoes.

5. (お)まつり＜お祭り＞　N　festival(s)
   夏に東北地方で三つの大きなお祭りがある。 In the Toohoku region, there are three big festivals during the summer.

6. ねんちゅうぎょうじ＜年中行事＞　N　annual event(s)
   日本の年中行事の中で、やはりお正月が一番大事な行事だろう。 Among Japan's annual events, New Years is probably the biggest event, after all.

7. しゅくじつ＜祝日＞　N　(national) holiday
   日本の祝日から日本人の価値観が見える。 You are able to see the values of the Japanese people from the holidays of Japan.

8. がんたん＜元旦＞　N　the first day of the year
   日本人は元旦に神社へ初詣に出かける。 On the first day of the year, Japanese go to shrines for the first shrine visit of the year.

9. (お)ぼん＜お盆＞　N　Bon Festival (celebration of the return of ancestors' spirits)
   たいてい日本人はお正月とお盆に自分の故郷に帰る。 Japanese usually return home to their hometowns at New Year's and at *Obon*.

10. れんきゅう＜連休＞　N　consecutive vacation holidays
アメリカでは感謝祭の時にたいてい四日間の連休になる。 In America, there are usually four consecutive days off for Thanksgiving.

11. しゅうかん＜習慣＞　N　custom
日本には伝統的な習慣が多く残っている。 Many traditional customs remain in Japan.

12. おくりもの＜贈り物＞　N　present(s)
日本には夏と冬にお世話になった人に贈り物をあげる習慣がある。 In Japan, there is a custom of giving gifts during the summer and winter to persons who have taken care of you.

13. しょうひんけん＜商品券＞　N　gift certificate
日本ではお中元やお歳暮に商品券をあげる人が多い。 In Japan, there are many people who give gift certificates during the *ochuugen* and *oseibo* seasons in Japan.

14. げんきん＜現金＞　N　cash
日本の結婚式とお葬式では、現金をあげる習慣がある。 In Japan, there is a custom of giving cash for weddings and funerals.

15. かみさま＜神様＞　N　God; gods
神様にいい人が見つかりますようにとお祈りした。 I prayed to god that I would be able to find a good person.

16. キリストきょうと＜キリスト教徒＞　N　Christian believers
日本にはキリスト教徒が少ない。 There are (only) a few Christian believers in Japan.

17. どくしん＜独身＞　N　single; unmarried
兄はまだ独身だ。 My older brother is still single.

18. (ご)かぞくづれ＜(御)家族連れ＞　N　to have a family; with a family
家族連れの旅行者が多い。 There are many travellers who are with families.

19. しゅうかく＜収穫＞　N　harvest
秋には食べ物の収穫に感謝して、お祭りをする。 In the autumn, we express thanks for the harvest of food and celebrate it.

20. せいちょう＜成長＞　N　growth
日本では子供の成長を祈るいろいろな日がある。 In Japan, there are many days when one prays for the growth of the chlidren.

21. やたい＜屋台＞　N　stand; booth
日本のお祭りにはたくさんの屋台が出ている。 Many booths appear at Japanese festivals.

22. はながら＜花柄＞　N　flower design
    花柄の浴衣を着て、花火大会へ行った。　I wore a *yukata* with a flower design and went to the fireworks display.

23. あせ＜汗＞びっしょり　N　soaked in perspiration
    日本の夏は本当に暑いので、汗びっしょりになった。　Since Japan's summers are so hot, I was soaked in perspiration.

24. きょうみぶかい＜興味深い＞　A　interesting [formal equivalent of おもしろい]
    日本の歴史はとても興味深い。The history of Japan is very interesting.

25. ぶじ＜無事＞　Na　safe
    親はいつも子供の無事を祈っている。　Parents always pray for the safety of their children.

26. けっこう＜結構＞　Adv　quite; not so bad
    日本人はけっこういい服を着て、外出する。　Japanese wear quite good clothing and go out.

27. ちょくせつ＜直接＞(に)⇔かんせつ＜間接＞(に)　Adv　directly ⇔ indirectly
    日本ではお中元やお歳暮はたいていデパートから直接送ってもらう。　Japanese usually have their *ochuugen* and *oseibo* gifts sent directly from the department store.

28. (〜を)いわう＜祝う＞／祝います　V1　to celebrate
    (〜の)おいわい＜お祝い＞(を)する／します　V3　to celebrate 〜
    大学合格を祝って、パーティーをしよう。　Let's celebrate (my) acceptance to college and have a party.

29. こうかん＜交換＞(を)する／します　V3　to exchange
    パーティーでプレゼントを交換した。　We exchanged gifts at the party.

30. ちょきん＜貯金＞(を)する／します　V3　to save money
    両親は私の大学教育のために貯金してくれている。　My parents are saving money for my college education.

31. すます＜済ます＞／済まします　V2　to finish [= 終わらせる or 終える]
    仕事を済ませて、食事に行こう。　Let's finish up the work and go to eat (a meal).

32. てをつなぐ＜手をつなぐ＞／つなぎます　V1　to hold hands
    二人は手をつないで歩いている。　The two of them are holding hands and walking.

13課

【もっと単語】

1. じたく＜自宅＞	N	private residence
2. じっか＜実家＞	N	one's family home
3. おちゅうげん＜お中元＞	N	mid-summer gift giving season
4. おせいぼ＜お歳暮＞	N	end of the year gift giving season
5. としのくれ＜年の暮れ＞	N	end of the year
6. おいわい＜お祝い＞	N	celebration
7. おかえし＜お返し＞	N	a gift that is given in return after receiving a gift
8. のしぶくろ＜のし袋＞	N	special gift envelope
9. ゆかた＜浴衣＞	N	summer cotton *kimono*
10. げた＜下駄＞	N	wooden clogs
11. おび＜帯＞	N	*kimono* sash
12. たこやき＜たこ焼き＞	N	cooked octopus dumplings
13. ラムネ	N	citrus flavored carbonated drink in a special bottle
14. きんぎょすくい＜金魚すくい＞	N	gold fish scooping game

13課 　　文法

> A. Noun＋の＋かわりに　　　　　　in place of ～
> Verb (plain form)＋かわりに　　　instead of ～
> この/その/あの＋かわりに　　　　instead of this/that
>
> This expression names a different alternative that one has taken or will take.
> 1. 先生のかわりに、私が教えた。　　　I taught in place of my teacher.
> 2. 大学へ行くかわりに、仕事をする。　I will work instead of going to college.
> 3. そのかわりに、映画に行こう。　　　Instead of that, let's go to a movie.

Circle the correct particle in the ( ) and translate the sentences into English.

1. 今日いつもの先生(の　X)かわりに、若い男性が先生としてやって来た。
   _____

2. 祖母は早く亡くなった母(の　X)かわりに、僕を育ててくれた。
   _____

3. 弟は近所のおばさんからハロウィーンでお菓子(の　X)かわりに、歯ブラシを
   もらったそうだ。_____

4. 「卒業パーティーをする？」「いや、その(の　X)かわりに、海外旅行をしたい。」
   _____

5. キャンプを中止する(の　X)かわりに、何か思い出に残ることを計画しよう。
   _____

> B. 「(Someone ＋ が) -ますように。」　　　"I pray ～."
> This is an expression one uses when one wishes for, prays for, or requests a certain outcome.
> 1. 「いい人に会えますように。」　　　"I pray that you will be able to meet a good person."
> 2. 「おばあちゃんが元気になりますように。」　"I pray that your grandmother will get well."

Translate into English.
1. 「希望の大学に合格出来ますように。」 _____
2. 「子供が無事でありますように。」 _____
3. 「今年も健康でいられますように。」 _____
4. 「交通事故を起こしませんように。」 _____
5. 「将来お金持ちになれますように。」 _____

> C. 〜たり 〜たり する/です　　do things like 〜 and 〜; sometimes 〜 and sometimes 〜
> 　〜たり する/です　　　　　such things as 〜
>
> The -たり form is created by using the -た forms of verbs, い adjectives, な adjectives, and nouns and adding り. When more than one -たり form is used, it suggests that those mentioned are representative actions or descriptions. It might also suggest that the actions or descriptions are sometimes one or more of those described. If only one -たり is mentioned, it carries the meaning of "such things as..."
>
> 1. パーティーで食べたり、飲んだりした。　I did such things as eat and drink at the party.
> 2. 成績は良かったり、悪かったりする。　My grades are sometimes good and sometimes bad.
> 3. 生徒は上手だったり、下手だったりする。
> 　　Some students are skillful and some students are unskillful.
> 4. 先生は日本人だったり、アメリカ人だったりする。
> 　　Teachers are sometimes Japanese and sometimes are Americans.
> 5. 日曜に美術館に行ったりしたい。　I want to do such things as go to the museum on Sundays.

Fill in the ( ) with appropriate words using the - TARI form.

1. 私は週末に（　　　　　　　　）、（　　　　　　　　　）する。
2. 日本人はお正月に（　　　　　　　）、（　　　　　　　　）する。
3. アメリカ人はクリスマスに（　　　　　　　）、（　　　　　　　　　）する。
4. 私は昼食を（　　　　　　　）、（　　　　　　　　）する。
5. 私は車に乗っている時、（　　　　　　　　）、（　　　　　　　　　）する。
6. 大学へ行ったら、（　　　　　　　　　　）したいと思っている。

> D. Dictionary/Nai form + ように　　do something in such a way that 〜; so that
> When followed by the dictionary form or -ない form of a verb, ように expresses how or what one must do for the action that follows.
> 1. 分かるようにゆっくり話してください。Please speak slowly so that I can understand you.
> 2. 風邪をひかないように気をつけよう。Let's take care of ourselves so that we don't catch a cold.

Fill in the the underlined space by modifying the verb in the ( ) to the appropriate dictionary or -nai form. Some of the verbs must be changed to the potential form.

1. ＿＿＿＿＿＿＿＿＿＿＿＿＿ように字をきれいに書いて下さい。（読む）
2. 日本人とぺらぺら＿＿＿＿＿＿＿＿＿＿ように今日本語を勉強している。（話す）
3. 運転しながら＿＿＿＿＿＿＿＿＿＿＿ようにコーヒーを飲んだ。（寝る）
4. 希望の大学に＿＿＿＿＿＿＿＿＿＿ように一生懸命勉強してきた。（合格する）
5. ＿＿＿＿＿＿＿＿＿＿ように手をつないで歩いた。（迷子になる）
6. 交通事故を＿＿＿＿＿＿＿＿＿＿ように運転しよう。（起こす）
7. 元気に＿＿＿＿＿＿＿＿＿＿＿ように健康な物を食べている。（生きる）

13課

E. Greetings and Expressions

Match the correct context with the appropriate expression.

1. ____ 「よいお年を（お迎えください）。」
2. ____ 「明けましておめでとうございます。」
3. ____ 「本年もどうぞよろしくお願いいたします。」
4. ____ 「暑中お見舞い申し上げます。」
5. ____ 「残暑お見舞い申し上げます。」
6. ____ 「お元気でお過ごしください。」
7. ____ 「お体を大切に。」

   a. "Happy New Year" greeting used beginning New Year's Day.
   b. "Happy New Year!" greeting used before New Year's Day.
   c. Summer seasonal greeting used in writing during the mid-summer.
   d. Summer seasonal greeting used in writing toward the end of summer.
   e. Expression used to say, "Please take good care of yourself."
   f. Expression used to wish someone a healthy life.
   g. Expression used at the New Year to ask for a continued good relationship throughout the new year.

F. 敬語 Honorifics

Write the polite neutral form of the underlined humble or respect forms.

1. 「只今、京都よりレポートをしております。」（　　　　　　　）
2. 「雪も少し降っております。」（　　　　　　　）
3. 「着物を着ていらっしゃる若い女性にインタビューさせていただきましょう。」
    （　　　　　　　）　　　　　　　　　（　　　　　　　）
4. 「今日は神社で何をお祈りされましたか。」（　　　　　　　）
5. 「それでは、これでレポートを終了させていただきます。」（　　　　　　　）

| 13課 | | アクティビティー | |

A. 日本の年中行事：ペアーワーク→クラスワーク　　　◎ 祝日 National holidays

何の日か下のリストから選んで、書きなさい。

◎ 1月1日		New Year's Day
◎ 1月第二月曜日		Coming-of-Age-Day [20 years old = adult]
2月3日		Bean-Throwing Ceremony
◎ 2月11日		National Founding Day
3月3日		Girl's Day
◎ 3月21日		Vernal Equinox Day
4月8日		Buddha's Birthday Festival
◎ 4月29日		Showa Day (*Showa* Emperor's Birthday)
◎ 5月3日		Constitution Memorial Day
◎ 5月4日		Green Day
◎ 5月5日		Children's Day
7月7日		Star Festival
◎ 7月第三月曜日		Marine Day
8月11日		Mountain Day
8月15日		Bon Festival
◎ 9月第三月曜日		Respect-for-the-Aged Day
◎ 9月23日		Autumnal Equinox Day
◎ 10月第二月曜日		Health-Sports Day
◎ 11月3日		Culture Day (*Meiji* Emperor's Birthday)
11月15日		Festival Day for 3, 5, 7 Year Old Children
◎ 11月23日		Labor Thanksgiving Day
◎ 12月23日		The *Heisei* Emperor's Birthday
12月31日		New Year's Eve

> 大晦日、節分、勤労感謝の日、春分の日、(お)正月　昭和の日、敬老の日、七夕、
> みどりの日、建国記念日、文化の日、子供の日、海の日、お盆、体育の日、山の日、
> ひな祭り、成人の日、七五三、天皇誕生日、花祭り、秋分の日、憲法記念日

13課

B. 日本の四季〔しき〕：ペアーワーク→クラスワーク

a. 日本の季節の言葉の読みと英訳と季節を書きなさい。

春：３月〜５月　夏：６月〜８月　秋：９月〜１１月　冬：１２月〜２月

風物〔ふうぶつ〕	読み	英訳	季節	風物〔ふうぶつ〕	読み	英訳	季節
1. 七五三				20. ひな祭り	ひなまつり		
2. 引っ越し	ひっこし			21. せみ	X	cicada	夏
3. お花見				22. どんぐり	X	acorn	
4. バラ	X		春	23. 梅雨	つゆ/ばいう		
5. 朝顔	あさがお			24. こたつ	X		
6. ひまわり	X			25. 門松	かどまつ		
7. 獅子舞	ししまい		冬	26. 運動会	うんどうかい		
8. 秋祭り	あきまつり			27. 卒業式	そつぎょうしき		
9. 芸術	げいじゅつ			28. 紅葉	もみじ/こうよう		
10. とんぼ	X	dragonfly		29. あやめ	X	iris	夏
11. 桜	さくら			30. 羽子板	はごいた		
12. 海水浴	かいすいよく			31. お月見			
13. 花火大会				32. 入学式	にゅうがくしき		
14. カブト虫	かぶとむし	beetle		33. すいか	X		
15. サンタクロース	X			34. いちょう	X	ginkgo	
16. クリスマスツリー	X			35. 風鈴	ふうりん		
17. 七夕				36. 雪だるま			
18. 鯉のぼり	こいのぼり			37. 初日の出	はつひので		
19. 読書				38. 凧揚げ	たこあげ	kite flying	

13課

b. それぞれの絵は何ですか。前のページのリストから選んで、（　）の中に書きなさい。
そして、日本の季節についての意見と感想を書きなさい。

四季	季節の行事と風物〔ふうぶつ〕と花	意見と感想
春	（　）（　）（　）（　）（　） （　）（　）（　）（　）	
夏	（　）（　）（　）（　）（　） （　）（　）（　）（　）（　）	
秋	（　）（　）（　）（　）（　） （　）（　）（　）（　）（　）	
冬	（　）（　）（　）（　）（　） （　）（　）（　）（　）	

13課

C. 贈り物の習慣：ペアワーク→クラスワーク
a. 日本にはいろいろな贈り物の習慣があります。（　）の中に下から適当な言葉を選んで書きなさい。
1. だれかのうちを訪問する時、お菓子とかの（　　　　）を持って行く習慣がある。
2. 旅行から帰って来ると、家族や友人に旅行へ行った場所の（　　　　）をあげる習慣がある。
3. お世話になった両親やおじいさんおばあさんや会社の上司などに、夏のお盆の頃に、
（　　　　）を、年の暮れに（　　　　）をあげる習慣がある。贈り物は
（　　　　）とかコーヒーなどが多く、（　　　　）から直接送ってもらうことが一般的だ。
4. ２月１４日の（　　　　）に女性は好きな男性にチョコレートをあげて、一カ月後の３月１４日には男性が女性に（　　　　）としてホワイトチョコレートをあげる日がある。これを（　　　　）と言う。
5. 結婚式に（　　　　）として、お葬式に（　　　　）として、（　　　　）をのし袋に入れてあげる習慣がある。祝う時は（　　　　）と白ののし袋を、お葬式には（　　　　）と白ののし袋を使う。

> お土産　御中元　現金　ホワイトデー　香典　御歳暮　手土産
> お返し　黒　商品券　赤　バレンタインデー　お祝い　デパート

b. 日本の贈り物の習慣についての意見、感想を述べなさい。
_____
_____
_____

D. 聞く Pre-Listening Activity「新年のレポート」：ペアワーク→クラスワーク
When people visit shrines on New Year's Day, what do they pray for? Write a prayer that each person described below might say using the 「～ますように。」pattern.
1. 若い独身女性はどんなお祈りをすると思う？ _____
2. 子供はどんなお祈りをすると思う？ _____
3. 受験生はどんなお祈りをすると思う？ _____
4. 親はどんなお祈りをすると思う？ _____
5. お年寄りはどんなお祈りをすると思う？ _____

13課

E. 聞く Post-Listening Activity「新年のレポート」：ペアワーク→クラスワーク

Compare and Contrast: Japanese New Year's Day and American New Year's Day

Prepare an outline on this topic within 4 minutes and do a 2 minute presentation on it with your partner.

Introduction:
_____

Three similarities/differences:

1. _____
2. _____
3. _____

Your preference and reasons for it:
_____
_____

F. 読む Pre-Reading Activity「暑中見舞い」：ペアワーク→クラスワーク

Fill in the ( ) with the correct word from the list below for items 1-5 and circle the correct word for items 6 - 9.

1. 日本でお正月には年賀状(ねんがじょう)を送りますが、夏には（　　　　　　）をはがきで送ります。
2. 浴衣(ゆかた)の上から締(し)めるベルトのような物を（　　　　　　）と言います。
3. 浴衣(ゆかた)を着る時に、足に（　　　　　　）を履(は)きます。
4. 浴衣(ゆかた)を着る時に、女性はハンドバッグのかわりに（　　　　　　）を持ちます。
5. 日本の夏は暑いので、日本人はよく団扇(うちわ)を使いますが、（　　　　　　）形をしています。
6. たこ焼(や)きは、（食べ物　飲み物　ゲーム）です。
7. ラムネは、（食べ物　飲み物　ゲーム）です。
8. 金魚すくいは、（食べ物　飲み物　ゲーム）です。
9. 夏の花火大会は日本で（６月　７月　８月）に多く、アメリカで（６月　７月　８月）に多いです。

> 下駄(げた)　帯(おび)　袋(ふくろ)　暑中見舞い　丸(まる)い　四角(かく)

G. 読む Post-Reading Activity「暑中見舞い」：ペアワーク→クラスワーク

Presentation: Summer in Japan

Present your views on summer in Japan. Discuss at least FIVE aspects of summer in Japan. Begin with an appropriate introduction, give details about the five aspects, explain your own view or perspective, and end with a concluding remark. You will have 4 minutes to prepare and 2 minutes to present. Your presentation should be as complete as possible. Work with your partner.

【Let's take notes!】

1. Begin with an appropriate introduction.
   _____

2. Discuss five aspects/examples of the topic.
   1.) _____
   2.) _____
   3.) _____
   4.) _____
   5.) _____

3. Explain your view or perspective.
   _____

4. End with a concluding remark.
   _____

H. テキストチャット「冬休み」：ペアワーク→クラスワーク

You will have a conversation about winter vacation with Hiroe Hori, your Japanese host sister who is about your age. She is visiting you this coming winter.

First, read this text chat conversation with your partner. Next, read the questions and your partner will respond without looking at the book. Give your original answers to the questions. For each question, use 20 seconds to answer. Take turns asking and answering questions.

1. 質問：こんにちは。裕恵よ。冬休みにそっちに行くから、今からわくわくしているの。

   答：裕恵さん、お久しぶり。元気？冬休みにこっちに来るそうだけど、何日に来るの？後、何日？一緒に何をしようかな。早く来てね。

2. 質問：クリスマスの日には、どんなことをしてお祝いするの？

   答：そうだねえ。。。クリスマスの日の朝は早く起きて、プレゼントを開けるよ。前の日から待てないよ。朝、皆で教会に行って、お昼からターキーを焼いて、いろいろなご馳走を作って、晩ご飯に親戚がたくさん集まって、とっても楽しいよ。

3. 質問：家族の間でプレゼントを交換したりする？家族の全員にプレゼントをあげるの？

   答：もちろん、皆にプレゼントをあげるし、皆からプレゼントをもらうよ。特に、おじいさんとおばあさんはいつもお金をくれるから、毎年楽しみにしてる。でも、私はあまりお金がないから、悲しい。

4. 質問：教会にも行くの？私もちゃんとした服を持って行った方がいいかなあ。

   答：教会に行く時は、いつもちょっときれいな服を着た方がいいよ。特にクリスマスの時は、皆けっこういい服を着ているよ。

5. 質問：クリスマスとお正月と、どっちの方が好き？それは、なぜ？

13課

答： そうだねえ。。。私はもちろんクリスマスの方が好き。だって、たくさんプレゼントをもらえるからね。

6. 質問：日本から何かほしい物があったら、教えてね。遠慮しないで。じゃ、会える日を楽しみにしているね。

答： 日本からのお土産ねえ、ありがとう、ちょっと考えてから、またメールで知らせるね。じゃ、私も裕恵さんが来るのを楽しみにしているね。いろんなことをして楽しもうね。そっちの皆さんによろしくね。

I. Compare & Contrast「感謝祭とクリスマス」：ペアワーク→クラスワーク

First, read this compare and contrast passage with your partner. Next, work with your partner and together, list three similarities and/or differences, your preference and the reason. Give your original opinions. Then, share your presentation with your class.

　　これから感謝祭とクリスマスを比べてみます。感謝祭とクリスマスは同じことも違うこともあります。
　　まず、同じことは、感謝祭もクリスマスもアメリカの大事な祝日です。感謝祭は１１月の最後の週の木曜日で、学校は四日間の連休になります。そして、クリスマスは、１２月２５日で、冬休みの間にあります。両方ともお休みなので、皆、感謝祭もクリスマスも大好きです。
　　しかし、一つ目の大きな違いは、その感謝祭とクリスマスの目的です。感謝祭はアメリカに来た家族達が食べ物の収穫に感謝して祝ったことから始まりました。だから、その目的は物や人に感謝することです。しかし、クリスマスはイエスの誕生日なので、その目的はイエスの誕生を祝うことです。キリスト教徒には特に大事な日です。
　　二つ目の大きな違いは、人達はたいてい、感謝祭にはプレゼントをあげませんが、クリスマスには家族や友達などにたくさんプレゼントをあげます。
　　結論として、私はどちらかと言うと、感謝祭の方がクリスマスより好きです。なぜなら、クリスマスにはたくさんのプレゼントを買って、家族や友人にあげますが、感謝祭には感謝の気持ちをあげるからです。たくさんの人がクリスマスの本当の意味を忘れていると思います。しかし、感謝祭もクリスマスも家族が集まるので、私は大好きです。

13課

J. 会話「宗教」：ペアワーク→クラスワーク

You will have a conversation with Mrs. Tamura, a visitor from Japan, about your religious practices. First, read this conversation with your partner. Next, read the questions; your partner will respond without looking at the book. Give your original answers to the questions. For each question, use 20 seconds to answer. Take turns asking and answering questions.

田村：初めまして。田村です。ちょっと個人的なことを質問してもいいですか。

私　：初めまして。(Name)です。こちらこそ、どうぞよろしくお願いします。個人的な質問ですか。どのような質問でしょうか。聞いてみてください。

田村：日曜日にはいつも教会に行ってるんですか。

私　：ああ、教会ですか。私の両親は熱心なキリスト教徒なので、毎週日曜日、家族で教会に行っています。私はサンデースクールで子供達を教えています。田村さんも教会に行きますか。

田村：宗教についてどんな考えを持っていますか。ちょっと教えて下さい。

私　：宗教ですか。そうですねえ。私は宗教を信じることは、いいことだと思っていますが、どの宗教を信じるかは、個人の自由ですよね。人がどの宗教を信じても、尊敬すべきだと思っています。

田村：どうも有難う。とても興味深かったです。私にも何か質問がありますか。

私　：質問ですか。そうですねえ。田村さんは、何の宗教を信じていますか。日本にもキリスト教徒は多いですか。今日は私に質問して下さって有難うございました。楽しかったです。

K. 文化発表「日本の年中行事」：ペアワーク→クラスワーク

First, read the cultural presenation about Japanese annual events with your partner. Then, together, write your original outline in 4 minutes and present it to your class within 2 minutes.

　　これから日本の年中行事について発表します。日本ではたくさんの伝統的な年中行事を祝いますが、アメリカの年中行事ととても違います。

　　まず第一に、日本のお正月は日本人にとって一年で一番大事な年中行事です。日本人はお正月の前から家を大掃除したり、おせち料理を作ったり、鏡餅を飾ったり、門松を玄関のそばに立てたりして、お正月の準備をします。そして、お正月には神社に初詣に出かけて、一年の幸福を祈ります。

　　第二に、日本には子供を祝う年中行事がたくさんあります。３月３日のひな祭り、５月５日の子供の日、１１月１５日には七五三があって、それぞれ子供の無事な成長を祈ります。

　　第三に、日本には人生の節目を祝う年中行事もあります。１月の成人式では二十歳に

なった人達を祝い、9月の敬老の日ではお年寄りを祝います。
　第四に、日本では季節の変わり目を祝う年中行事も多いです。2月初めの節分の日は、春の初めを祝います。3月21日の春分の日と9月23日の秋分の日は、昼と夜の時間が同じ長さになります。農業が大事な日本では、季節と生活はとても深い関係があるようです。
　第五に、もう一つの大事な年中行事は夏のお盆です。亡くなった先祖がうちに帰って来ると言われています。お盆には都会に住んでいる多くの人達が故郷に帰ります。
　結論として、日本人の年中行事を見ると、日本人が大切にしている価値観が見えて来ます。日本人の価値観は人生の節目の年、子供やお年寄り、自然の変化、先祖などを大切にすることなどのようです。

1. Begin with an appropriate introduction.
   _____

2. Discuss five aspects/examples of the topic.
   1.) _____
   2.) _____
   3.) _____
   4.) _____
   5.) _____

3. Explain your view or perspective.
   _____

4. End with a concluding remark.
   _____

13課

<13課 - 聞く>

Listening: Report

12秒×5

【You may take notes while listening. Do not look at the questions below before listening. You will have 12 seconds to answer each question. You may NOT move back and forth among questions.】

(Narrator) Now you will listen to a report once.

(Narrator) Now answer the questions for this selection.

1. What season was being described?
   (A) spring
   (B) summer
   (C) fall
   (D) winter

2. Under what conditions is this reporter giving his report?
   (A) He is giving a report on New Year's Eve.
   (B) He is giving a report from a temple in Kyoto.
   (C) He is giving a report in heavy snow.
   (D) He is giving a report in the afternoon.

3. What kind of people were NOT visiting the temple?
   (A) many young ladies wearing kimono
   (B) many young men wearing kimono
   (C) families
   (D) couples

4. What did the young lady who was interviewed pray for?
   (A) to find a partner to marry
   (B) to become rich
   (C) to find a good job
   (D) to find a boyfriend

5. A boy was expecting monetary gifts from his family. Which information is correct?
   (A) He was expecting to receive 5,000 yen from each of his grandparents and his parents.
   (B) He was expecting to receive 3,000 yen from his uncle and 1,000 yen from his aunt.
   (C) He wanted to save all the money he received.
   (D) He wanted to buy a game and save the rest.

<13課 - 読む>

Reading: Letter

【You may move back and forth among all the questions.】

暑中お見舞い申し上げます。

先生、お元気ですか。今日はホストファミリーのお姉さんと一緒に浴衣を着て、花火大会に行きました。お母さんとおばあさんが私達にお揃いの花柄のきれいな浴衣を着せて下さいました。お姉さんのは青の浴衣にみどりの帯、私のは赤い浴衣に黄色の帯でした。帯はとてもきつくて死ぬかと思いました。下駄をはいて、手には袋とうちわを持って、まるで日本人みたいでしたよ。写真をたくさん撮ったので、同封しますね。私達は浴衣を着て、地下鉄に乗りましたが、とても混んでいたので、帯の形がくずれてしまいました。川のそばまで歩いて行きましたが、その道は人がいっぱい。迷子にならないように手をつないで歩きました。花火は百発ぐらいあったかも知れません。ものすごく大きいのや、有名なアニメの花火もあり、すごかったです。花火は一時間ぐらいで終わり、その後、道のそばに出ていた屋台のお店で、たこ焼きを食べたり、ラムネを飲んだり、金魚すくいをしたりして、とっても楽しい一日でした。でも、本当に暑かったので、汗びっしょりでした。では、お元気で。

八月九日

マリア

お見舞い　申し　浴衣　お揃い　花柄　帯　下駄　袋
撮った　同封　混んで　迷子　汗

<13課 - 読む (質問)>
Reading: Letter

(Narrator) Now answer the questions for this section.

1. What did Maria wear on this day?
    - (A) a red *yukata* with a yellow sash
    - (B) a blue *yukata* with a yellow sash
    - (C) a red *yukata* with a green sash
    - (D) a green *yukata* and a red sash

2. Who dressed Maria in the *yukata* and sash?
    - (A) her host older sister
    - (B) her host mother and grandmother
    - (C) her host mother
    - (D) her host grandmother

3. What did Maria experience on this day?
    - (A) She saw fireworks from the park.
    - (B) She tasted a Japanese traditional *bento*.
    - (C) She drank a can of Japanese soda.
    - (D) She played a fish game.

4. What problem did Maria experience on that day?
    - (A) The streets were a little crowded.
    - (B) The subways were a little crowded.
    - (C) It was a little hot.
    - (D) Maria perspired a lot.

5. What did Maria want to do by sending this postcard?
    - (A) to report about life in Japan to her mother
    - (B) to let her sister know that she wore a *yukata* for the first time
    - (C) to send a mid-summer greeting card to her teacher
    - (D) to let her teacher know about school life in Japan

<13課 - 書く (テキストチャット)>

90秒×6

Text Chat: Winter Vacation

You will participate in a simulated exchange of text-chat messages. Each time it is your turn to write, you will have 90 seconds. You should respond as fully and as appropriately as possible.

You will have a conversation about winter vacation with Hiroe Hori, your Japanese host sister who is about your age. She is visiting you this coming winter.

1. Respond. (90 seconds)
   こんにちは。裕恵よ。冬休みにそっちに行くから、今からわくわくしているの。
2. Give a specific example. (90 seconds)
   クリスマスの日には、どんなことをしてお祝いするの？
3. Respond. (90 seconds)
   家族の間でプレゼントを交換したりする？家族の全員にプレゼントをあげるの？
4. Respond and suggest. (90 seconds)
   教会にも行くの？私もフォーマルな服を持って行った方がいいかなあ。
5. Explain your preference and justify your opinion. (90 seconds)
   クリスマスとお正月と、どっちの方が好き？それは、なぜ？
6. Request a specific item. (90 seconds)
   日本から何かほしい物があったら、教えてね。遠慮しないで。じゃ、会える日を楽しみにしているね。

<13課 - 書く (比較と対比)>

20分

Compare and Contrast Article: Thanksgiving and Christmas in the U.S.

Directions: You are writing an article for the student newspaper of your sister school in Japan. Write an article in which you compare and contrast similarities and differences between Thanksgiving and Christmas in the U. S. Based on your personal experience, describe at least THREE aspects of each and highlight the similarities and differences between Thanksgiving and Christmas in the U. S. Also state your preference for either and give reasons for it.

Your article should be 300 to 400 characters or longer. Use the *desu/masu* or *da* (plain) style, but use one style consistently. Also, use *kanji* wherever *kanji* from the AP Japanese *kanji* list is appropriate. You have 20 minutes to write.

【NOTES/OUTLINE: 自分の作文のアウトラインを書こう！】

Introduction:
_____

Three similarities/differences:

1. _____
2. _____
3. _____

Your preference and reasons for it:
_____
_____

13課

<13課 - 話す (会話)>
Conversation: Religion

`20秒×4`

You will participate in a simulated conversation. Each time it is your turn to speak, you will have 20 seconds to record. You should respond as fully and as appropriately as possible.

You will have a conversation with Mrs. Tamura, a visitor from Japan, about your religious practices.

(Female)
(20 seconds)
(Female)
(20 seconds)
(Female)
(20 seconds)
(Female)
(20 seconds)

<13課 - 話す (日本文化)>
Cultural Perspective Presentation: Japanese Annual Events

`4分+2分`

Directions: Imagine you are making an oral presentation to your Japanese class. First, you will be given the topic of your presentation. You will have 4 minutes to prepare your presentation. Then you will have 2 minutes to record your presentation. Your presentation should be as complete as possible.

Present your own view or perspective of Japanese annual events. Discuss at least FIVE aspects or examples of Japanese annual events.

Begin with an appropriate introduction, give details, explain your own view or perspective, and end with a concluding remark.

【Let's take notes!】

1. Begin with an appropriate introduction.

   _____

2. Discuss five aspects/examples of the topic.

   1.) _____
   2.) _____
   3.) _____
   4.) _____
   5.) _____

3. Explain your view or perspective.

   _____

4. End with a concluding remark.

   _____

`13課`

14課 　　交通
Transportation

【AP® タスク：交通】
Discuss dangerous driving in your daily life. Share an experience of a car accident that you have been involved in or have seen. How can we change our commuting lifestyle in order to improve sustainability? Discuss the pros and cons of mass transit systems.

【文化】日本の交通機関：Japan's Transportation System

Japan's transportation system is one of the most advanced and efficient in the world. Because of Japan's limited land area, transportation systems play a vital role in maintaining efficient use of time and space, particularly in the urbanized areas of Japan.

The train system in Japan is extensive, efficient and convenient. Railways are found in nearly all parts of Japan. Japan Railways (JR), now operated and owned by a conglomerate of six passenger railway companies, was formerly operated by the Japanese government. It now operates about 70% of all of the railways in Japan. The remaining 30% is owned by smaller private companies. At last count, over 22 billion trips were taken by train in Japan in one year. Because of their reliability, trains are one of the most favored modes of transportation for those living in the cities.

As efficient as the train systems are, so are the subway systems that are found in most of the major cities of Japan. Many subway stops intersect with train lines for easy transfer. One of the largest and most widely used subway systems in the world is the Tokyo Metro along with the Toei Subway. More than a dozen lines crisscross below the streets of Tokyo. Each line (like the trains) is color coded for easy identification.

The bullet train, or *shinkansen,* demonstrates transportation technology at its best. The *shinkansen* now extends from Hokkaido to Kyushu and from the Pacific to the Japan Sea. Some *shinkansen* may travel as quickly as 300 miles per hour. The most heavily used and oldest route, the Tokaido-Sanyo Line, runs from Fukuoka through Hiroshima, Osaka, Kyoto, Nagoya and Tokyo. The three kinds of bullet trains on this line are the Nozomi, the speediest that makes the fewest stops, the Hikari, and finally, the Kodama, which stops at all of the smaller *shinkansen* stations.

Ships, boats and ferries are still a common means of transportation in Japan. Ships and boats provide a good alternative for transporting goods from port to port in this island country. Fishing vessels are still common, though restrictions on the fishing industry have narrowed the amount of fishing boats out at sea. Domestic ferries are a natural part of life for those who live and work on many of the hundreds of islands off mainland Japan. They carry people, vehicles and cargo to and from the islands. Ferries are also used for traveling and sightseeing.

Finally, cars, buses and taxis are all viable forms of transportation. In cities where train and subway systems are extensive, some Japanese do not own cars. In less populated areas, however, Japanese depend on cars for transportation. Other than main streets, most roads in Japan are narrow. Japanese cars are small, highly dependable and well maintained. Japanese tend not to keep their cars for a long time. Hybrid cars and electric cars are now popular as the cost of fuel is high. Buses are also commonly used by Japanese. In cities with good train and subway systems, buses are used as means to get to stations, but in other cities, buses are used much more extensively. Taxis are also an important part of the transportation picture in Japan. When all other means of transportation are not available, people catch cabs. At midnight, many train and bus services stop, and taxis are in high demand.

In a country as densely populated and limited in space as Japan, efficient, reliable and convenient transportation is essential. Coupled with Japan's advanced technology, Japan boasts one of the most well developed transportation systems in the world.

Questions to ponder: How does the highly developed transportation system correlate to limited space in Japan? Does the value of "group" make it easier to use public transportation for Japanese than for those in cultures where individuality and independence are more highly valued?

14課 復習単語

トピック：交通

#	語	かな	品詞	意味
1.	電車	でんしゃ	N	electric train
2.	JR [ジェイアール]		N	Japan Railway
3.	地下鉄	ちかてつ	N	subway
4.	中央線	ちゅうおうせん	N	Chuo(Central) Line [orange colored train line in Tokyo]
5.	～番線	～ばんせん	N	track number ～
6.	地図	ちず	N	map
7.	入口	いりぐち	N	entrance
8.	出口	でぐち	N	exit
9.	駅	えき	N	train station
10.	駅員	えきいん	N	station employee
11.	バス		N	bus
12.	バス停	バスてい	N	bus stop
13.	自動車	じどうしゃ	N	car; vehicle
14.	運転(を)する	うんてん(を)する	V3	(to) drive
15.	運転免許	うんてんめんきょ	N	driver's license
16.	運転手	うんてんしゅ	N	driver
17.	ドライバー		N	driver
18.	駐車(を)する	ちゅうしゃ(を)する	V	(to) park
19.	駐車場	ちゅうしゃじょう	N	parking lot
20.	交差点	こうさてん	N	intersection
21.	信号	しんごう	N	traffic lights
22.	安全	あんぜん	Na	(is) safe
23.	交通事故	こうつうじこ	N	traffic accident
24.	シートベルトをする		V3	(to) wear a seat belt
25.	スピードを出す	スピードをだす	V1	(to) speed
26.	止まれ	とまれ	V1	Stop. [command form]
27.	自転車	じてんしゃ	N	bicycle
28.	歩く	あるく	V1	(to) walk
29.	迷子になる	まいごになる	V1	(to) get lost
30.	通り	とおり	N	street; avenue
31.	突き当たり	つきあたり	N	end (of a street; hallway)

| 14課 | ★★★ | 新しい単語 | ★★★ |

1. たすかる＜助かる＞よ。　Exp　It is of great help (to me). [informal]
   たすかります＜助かります＞。　Exp　It is of great help to me. [formal]
2. ほこうしゃ＜歩行者＞　N　pedestrian
   銀座は日曜日になると歩行者天国になる。　On Sundays, Ginza becomes a pedestrian's heaven.
3. おうだんほどう＜横断歩道＞　N　crosswalk
   歩行者は横断歩道を渡るべきだ。　Pedestrians should cross at crossswalks.
4. ちゅうこしゃ＜中古車＞　N　used car
   両親に中古車を買ってもらった。　I had my parents buy me a used car.
5. あんぜんうんてん＜安全運転＞　N　safe driving
   安全運転をして、事故をゼロにしよう。　Let's drive carefully and have no accidents.
6. いんしゅうんてん＜飲酒運転＞　N　drunk driving
   けっして飲酒運転をしてはいけない。　You must never drive drunk.
7. いねむりうんてん＜居眠り運転＞　N　sleeping while driving
   父は居眠り運転をして事故を起こした。　My dad fell asleep while driving and caused an accident.
8. ちゅうしゃいはん＜駐車違反＞　N　parking violation
   駐車違反をしてチケットをもらってしまった。　I ended up receiving a ticket for a parking violation.
9. でんしんばしら＜電信柱＞　N　electric pole
   時々、電信柱にぶつかって死ぬ人がいる。　There are sometimes people who hit electric poles and die.
10. しまぐに＜島国＞　N　island country
    日本は島国なので、船はなくてはならない物だ。　Since Japan is an island country, ships are necessary things.
11. じじょう＜事情＞　N　circumstances; conditions
    アメリカの交通事情を調べている。　I am investigating the traffic conditions in America.
12. こじんしゅぎ＜個人主義＞　individualism
    アメリカは個人主義の国なので、人の考えがもっと自由なようだ。　Since America is a country of individualism, it seems people's thinking is more liberal.

13. こうきょうこうつうきかん＜公共交通機関＞　N　public transportation system
    日本は公共交通機関が発達している。Japan's public transportation system is well developed.

14. (〜が)すすんでいる＜進んでいる＞　V1　is advanced [進む=to advance]
    日本の技術は進んでいる。Japan's technology is advanced.

15. (タイヤが)パンク(を)する／します　V3　to have a flat (tire)
    今朝タイヤがパンクしてしまった。This morning, I had a flat tire.

16. しゅうり＜修理＞(を)する／します　V3　to repair
    パンクを修理してもらいに、ガソリンスタンドに寄った。I stopped by a service station to have my flat tire repaired.

17. じゅうたい＜渋滞＞する／します　V3　(traffic) becomes congested
    最近の道路の渋滞はひどい。Recently, the traffic on the streets has become terrible.

18. (〜に)ぶつかる／ぶつかります　V1　to hit [informal]
    今朝、前の車にぶつかってしまった。This morning, I ended up hitting the car in front (of me.)

19. (〜に)しょうとつ＜衝突＞(を)する／します　V3　to collide
    しょうとつじこ＜衝突事故＞　N　collision (accident)
    今朝、前の車に衝突してしまった。This morning, I ended up colliding with the car in front (of me).

20. (〜を)ひく＜轢く＞／轢きます　V1　to run over
    今朝、犬を轢くところだった。This morning, I almost ran over a dog.

21. ひやっとする／ひやっとします　V3　to have a chilling scare
    犬を轢きそうになって、ひやっとした。I almost ran over a dog and had a chilling scare.

22. よっぱらう＜酔っぱらう＞／酔っぱらいます　V1　to get drunk
    よっぱらい＜酔っぱらい＞　N　a drunk
    よっぱらいうんてん＜酔っぱらい運転＞　N　drunken driving
    酔っぱらい運転は、とても危ないです。Drunken driving is very dangerous.

23. (〜に)おくれる＜遅れる＞／遅れます　V2　to be late
    今朝、渋滞があり、学校に遅れるところだった。This morning, I was about to be late for school because of the traffic congestion.

24. じこ＜事故＞にあう＜遭う＞／遭います　V1　to get into an accident
    ゆうべ事故に遭って、パーティーに遅れてしまった。Last night, I got into an accident and was late to the party.

14課

25. そくし＜即死＞する／します　V3　to die instantly
   山田君はオートバイの事故で即死した。　Mr. Yamada died instantly in a motorcycle accident.

26. じゅうしょう＜重傷＞をおう＜負う＞／負います　V1　to get seriously injured
   事故で五人が重傷を負った。　Five people were seriously injured in the accident.

27. ギブスをする／します　V3　to have a cast
   バスケットの試合でケガをして、今ギブスをしている。　I was injured during a basketball game and now have a cast on.

28. ちりょう＜治療＞をうける＜受ける＞／受けます　V2　to be treated
   母は治療を受けるために、毎朝、病院に通っている。　In order to receive treatment, my mother goes to the hospital every day.

29. (～が)つかまる＜捕まる＞／捕まります　V1　～ is caught [intransitive]
   (～を)つかまえる＜捕まえる＞／捕まえます　V2　to catch ～; to capture [transitive]
   どろぼうが警官に捕まった。　The thief was caught by the police.

30. きんし＜禁止＞(を)する／します　V3　to prohibit
   ちゅうしゃきんし＜駐車禁止＞　N　no parking
   ケータイを使いながらの運転は禁止すべきだ。　Driving while using cell phones should be prohibited.

31. かんげい＜歓迎＞(を)する／します　V3　to welcome
   かんげいかい＜歓迎会＞　N　welcome party
   高校を卒業してすぐバスケット部のOBの歓迎会に出席した。　After graduating from high school, I attended a welcome party for the basketball alumni group.

32. せいかく＜正確＞　Na　accurate
   日本の交通機関は時間に正確だ。　Japan's traffic system always operates on time.

【もっと単語】

1. こうそくどうろ＜高速道路＞　　　　　　　N　highway
2. ほうりつ＜法律＞　　　　　　　　　　　　N　law
3. ほけん＜保険＞　　　　　　　　　　　　　N　insurance
4. ばっきん＜罰金＞　　　　　　　　　　　　N　a fine
5. うで＜腕＞　　　　　　　　　　　　　　　N　arm
6. OB　　　　　　　　　　　　　　　　　　　N　alumni group
7. しゃせん＜車線＞　　　　　　　　　　　　N　(highway) lane

14課

8. ろせん＜路線＞　　　　　　　　　　　　N　rail line(s)
9. たいほ＜逮捕＞する　　　　　　　　　　V3　to arrest
10. おいこす＜追い越す＞／追い越します　　V2　to pass; to overtake
　　おいこし＜追い越し＞　　　　　　　　N　passing; overtaking
11. きゅうていしゃ＜急停車＞(を)する／します　V3　to stop suddenly
12. のろのろうんてん＜のろのろ運転＞　　　N　slow driving
13. ききいっぱつ＜危機一髪＞　　　　　　　Exp　In the nick of time; a close call
14. ふこうちゅうのさいわい＜不幸中の幸い＞　Exp　Unfortunate happening in the midst of happiness.
15. みずくさい＜水くさい＞　　　　　　　　A　not frank; reserved; distant
16. おたがいさま＜お互い様＞　　　　　　　Exp　It is mutually so!

14課　文法

A. Space＋を　　through 〜; along 〜; across 〜

When using a verb that suggests traversing through a street or any space, the particle that follows is an を, as it considered a direct object. Using particles such as で or に gives the sentence a different interpretation.

1. この道をまっすぐ行って。　　　　Go straight along this street.
2. この橋を渡ろう。　　　　　　　　Let's cross this bridge.
3. この交差点を右に曲がって。　　　Turn right along this intersection.
4. 山道をよく歩いた。　　　　　　　I often walked along the mountain path.
5. 公園を通って帰ろう。　　　　　　Let's go home through the park. (lit. passing through the park.)
6. 鳥が海の上を飛んでいる。　　　　The birds are flying over the ocean.

Circle the correct particle in the ( ).

1. 父は朝うち（に　で）いたが、午後うち（を　に）出て、散歩（を　に）出かけた。
2. 姉は朝うち（を　で）掃除をして、午後友達（を　と）美術館（へ　で）行った。
3. 私（は　が）道（に　を）渡っていた時に、交通事故（が　を）起きた。
4. その角（を　に）左（に　で）曲がって、その道（を　で）まっすぐ行って下さい。
5. 舟（で　を）この川（で　を）渡ろう。

B. Verb (stem)＋そうになる　　almost happens

This construction is used when one describes something that is about to happen. The verb is restricted to use with non-volitional verbs, that is, verbs that express something that is beyond one's control, such as 風邪を引く "to catch a cold" or おぼれる "to drown." Since passive and potential forms are considered non-volitional verbs, they can be also used with そうになる. Volitional verbs cannot be used if the subject is the speaker.

1. 昨日、雨にぬれて、風邪を引きそうになった。

   I got wet in the cold rain yesterday and I almost caught a cold. [non-volitional verb]

2. 昨日、もうちょっとで車にひかれそうになった。

   Yesterday I almost got run over by a car. [passive = non-volitional verb]

3. やっと日本へ行けそうになった時に、母が病気になってしまった。

   When I was finally about to go to Japan, my mother got ill. [potential = non-volitional verb]

4. X 私がお昼ご飯を食べそうになった時、友達から電話がかかって来た。

   When I was about to eat my lunch, I received a call from my friend. [volitional verb]

   → 私がお昼ご飯を食べようとした時、友達から電話がかかって来た。

Using the verb cue in the ( ), complete each sentence to mean "almost happened," and translate the entire sentence into English.

1. 前の車に_____。（衝突する）
   英訳：_____

2. 今朝、犬を_____。（ひく）
   英訳：_____

3. 今朝、前の車に_____。（ぶつかる）
   英訳：_____

4. 人を_____、ひやりとした。（ひく）
   英訳：_____

5. ゆうべ悲しい映画を見て、_____。（泣く）
   英訳：_____

> C. Verb (Dic. form)＋ところだった。　almost happened
>
> 　＝ Verb (Stem form)＋そうになった。　almost happened
>
> These structures both carry the meaning of "about to happen." As mentioned in Note A, the verb used in the そうになった pattern must be a non-volitional verb. However, するところだった does not carry this restriction.

Convert the underlined portions of each of the following to a sentence ending in ところだった, then translate the entire sentence into English.

1. 前の車に衝突しそうになった。
   ＝_____　英訳：_____

2. ゆうべ運転していた時に、人をひきそうになった。
   ＝_____　英訳：_____

3. もう少しで車にひかれそうになった。
   ＝_____　英訳：_____

4. 前の車が急に止まったので、事故を起こしそうになった。
   ＝_____　英訳：_____

5. 地震が起きた時、家が壊れそうになった。
   ＝_____　英訳：_____

> D. する/しない＋ように＋する　　to make an effort to/not to do
>
> This structure is used when the subject makes a conscious effort to do or not to do something. The sentence ending may take any form (past, *-te kudasai*, *-mashoo*, etc.)

14課

Complete the sentences with the verb in the (　), using this structure. Use the affirmative or negative ending depending on the context.

1. 日本語のクラスでは日本語を_____。（話す）
2. 先生と出来るだけ英語を_____。（話す）
3. 高いから、ケータイを出来るだけ_____。（使う）
4. 車を運転している時、食べたり_____。（飲む）
5. 道が渋滞していても、あまり_____。（いらいらする）

E.　Noun ＋ ばかり　　　　　　　　only 〜

　　Verb (TE form)＋ばかり＋いる　　be just doing 〜

　　Verb (TA form)＋ばかり＋だ　　have just done 〜

When ばかり follows a noun, it means "only," with a suggestion that there is also a large or frequent quantity of that particular object. When ばかり follows a verb in its -て form, it also suggests that the action described is done often, and seemingly exclusively of other things. It is followed by the verb いる. However, when ばかり follows a verb in the -た form, it is a description of an action that has just been completed.

1. 父はビールばかり飲んでいる。　　　My father is drinking only (and lots of) beer.
2. 弟はゲームで遊んでばかりいる。　　My younger brother is doing nothing but playing games.
3. 私は昼食を食べたばかりだ。　　　　I have just eaten my lunch.

Complete the following sentences using the cue words in the (　) and the appropriate sentence endings.

1. 姉は先月_____ばかり_____。（結婚する）
2. 兄は来月のマラソンに出るので、毎日_____ばかり_____。（練習する）
3. 妹は読書が好きで、本ばかり_____。（読む）
4. 兄は去年大学を_____ばかり_____。（卒業する）
5. 妹は疲れているようで、毎日_____ばかり_____。（寝る）

14課

14課 アクティビティー

A. 文化ノート：ペアワーク→クラスワーク

What are the following car parts in English? Write the English definitions.

1. ハンドル _____   7. タイヤ _____   13. リヤバンパー _____
2. ボディー _____   8. バックミラー _____   14. サイドミラー _____
3. アクセル _____   9. トランク _____   15. フロントガラス _____
4. エンジン _____   10. ライト _____   16. ガソリンタンク _____
5. ボンネット _____   11. ブレーキ _____   17. シートベルト _____
6. ウィンカー _____   12. メーター _____   18. ナンバープレート _____

B. 聞く Pre-Listening Activity「運転」：ペアワーク→クラスワーク

Circle True or False depending on what you consider to be safe driving.

1. (T   F) 歩行者は横断歩道じゃないところを渡ってもいい。
2. (T   F) 信号が赤でも、交差点を渡ってもいい。
3. (T   F) スピードを出さない方がいい。
4. (T   F) 中古車でも、よく修理すれば大丈夫だ。
5. (T   F) 飲酒運転は危ない。
6. (T   F) 居眠り運転は危ない。
7. (T   F) 壊れている自動車を運転しても大丈夫だ。
8. (T   F) パンクしたタイアは修理すべきだ。
9. (T   F) ケータイを使いながら運転するのは、法律で禁止すべきだ。
10. (T   F) 運転している時、前を見なくてもいい。
11. (T   F) 食べたり飲んだりしながら、運転してもいい。
12. (T   F) オートバイを運転する時、ヘルメットをかぶった方がいい。
13. (T   F) オートバイは歩道で乗ってもいい。
14. (T   F) 前の車に衝突してもいい。
15. (T   F) 道路が渋滞していて、いらいらしている時も、おこらないようにする。
16. (T   F) 自動車保険があるから、事故を起こしてもいい。
17. (T   F) 警官を見たら、捕まらないようにスピードを出して逃げる。
18. (T   F) 人をひかないように、安全運転をする。
19. (T   F) 駐車禁止の所でも、自動車を駐車する。
20. (T   F) 駐車違反をしてもいい。

14課

C. 聞く Post-Listening Activity 「運転」：ペアワーク→クラスワーク

Compare & Contrast: Driving to school and Riding a Bus to School

Prepare an outline in 4 minutes and present it to your partner in 2 minutes.

Introduction: _____

Three similarities/differences:

   1. _____
   2. _____
   3. _____

Your preference and reasons:

_____
_____

D. 読む Pre-Reading Activity 「交通事故」：ペアワーク→クラスワーク

Fill in the ( ) with the correct readings of the *kanji* and the [ ] with their English translations.

1. 事故死　　（　　　）[　　　　]　　8. 重傷　　　（　　　）[　　　　]
2. 国道　　　（　　　）[　　　　]　　9. 飲酒運転　（　　　）[　　　　]
3. 軽自動車　（　　　）[　　　　]　　10. OB歓迎会　（　　　）[　　　　]
4. 電信柱　　（　　　）[　　　　]　　11. 先輩　　　（　　　）[　　　　]
5. 横転　　　（　　　）[　　　　]　　12. 二次会　　（　　　）[　　　　]
6. 助手席　　（　　　）[　　　　]　　13. 途中　　　（　　　）[　　　　]
7. 両足骨折　（　　　）[　　　　]　　14. 警察　　　　　　　[　　　　]

E. 読む Post-Reading Activity 「交通事故」：ペアワーク→クラスワーク

Describe a car accident you or someone you know has experienced, or that you have seen or heard on the news. You may also choose to make up your own story. Complete the questions below, then begin describing the accident to your partner.

1. いつ？　　　　　_____
2. どこで？　　　　_____
3. だれが？　　　　_____
4. 何を？　　　　　_____
5. どうした？　　　_____

F. テキストチャット 「運転免許〔うんてんめんきょ〕」：ペアワーク→クラスワーク

You will have a conversation with Daisuke, a student at a Japanese school, about obtaining driver's licenses. First, read this text chat conversation with your partner. Next, read the questions and your partner will respond without looking at the book. Use the underlined parts in your response, but give

14課

your original answers to the questions. Take 20 seconds to answer each question. Take turns asking and answering questions.

1. 質問：こんにちは。今運転についてアメリカの事情を調べているんですが、御協力を御願いします。もう運転免許を持っていますか。

    答 (例)：Respond.
    こんにちは。運転についてですか。分かりました。出来るだけ、協力しましょう。運転免許なら、私はもう持っています。去年の夏に取りました。私の運転はとても安全ですよ。

2. 質問：アメリカでは運転免許が何歳で取れるんですか。

    答 (例)：Respond. (90 seconds)
    運転免許が取れる年ですか。州によって違うらしいですが、私の州では１６歳です。若すぎると言う人もいますが、アメリカは車社会なので、車を運転できなければ、どこへも行けません。日本では、何歳で取れるんですか。

3. 質問：ところで、町で交通事故は多いですか。交通事故を見たことがありますか。

    答 (例)：Describe a specific example. (90 seconds)
    交通事故ですか。交通事故は毎日町のどこかで起きているようです。ニュースでいつも見ます。私は一度事故が起きた後を見たことがあります。二台の車が衝突して、前の車の前と後ろの車の前が壊れていました。でも、運転手は無事だったようです。

4. 質問：日本では運転しながらケータイを使うとつかまってしまいますが、そちらでも同じ法律があるんですか。

    答 (例)：Describe a situation. (90 seconds)
    ケータイですか。最近、運転しながらケータイを使ってはいけないという法律が出来ました。私はいい法律だと思います。ケータイを使っている運転手は運転に集中できないから、危ないですよ。

5. 質問：僕はもう十八歳ですが、まだ運転免許を持っていません。アメリカで運転免許を取った方がいいと思いますか。

    答 (例)：Suggest. (90 seconds)
    運転免許をまだ持っていないんですか。十八歳なら、運転免許を取った方がいいと思いますよ。日本人がアメリカに来て、すぐ運転免許が取れるかどうか知りませんが。アメリカでは運転免許を取るのはあまり難しくないです。

6. 質問：どうも有難うございました。日本の交通について何か質問があったらして下さい。

    答 (例)：Ask a specific question. (90 seconds)

14課

<u>日本の交通</u>ですか。たくさんの日本人は学校や仕事に電車で行くと聞きましたが、日本で自動車を運転している人は多いですか。道路は混んでいますか。このテキストチャットは楽しかったです。またしましょう。お元気で。

G. Compare & Contrast「公共交通機関は必要か」：ペアワーク→クラスワーク

a. 公共交通機関に賛成意見：

1. 公共交通機関の良い点　　1) _____
　　　　　　　　　　　　　　2) _____

2. 自家用車の悪い点　　　　1) _____
　　　　　　　　　　　　　　2) _____

3. 公共交通機関が必要だと思う理由
_____

b. 公共交通機関に反対意見：

1. 自家用車の良い点　　　　1) _____
　　　　　　　　　　　　　　2) _____

2. 公共交通機関の悪い点　　1) _____
　　　　　　　　　　　　　　2) _____

3. 公共交通機関は必要ではないと思う理由
_____

H. 会話「交通事故」：ペアワーク→クラスワーク

You will have a telephone conversation with Ichiro, a close Japanese friend, about his problem. First, read this conversation with your partner using the correct male/female speech style. Take turns. Next, read the Ichiro's parts and your partner will respond without looking at the book. The answers should be your original. For each question, use 20 seconds to answer. Take turns asking and answering questions.

1. 一郎：「もしもし、一郎だけど、実は、今病院にいるんだ。」
　答(男)：「ええっ、病院に？どうした？何かあったのか？大丈夫か？」
　答(女)：「ええっ、病院に？どうしたの？何かあったの？大丈夫？」

2. 一郎：「交通事故に遭って、治療を受けたところなんだ。」
　答(男)：「交通事故？怪我はひどいのか？どこを怪我したんだい？」
　答(女)：「交通事故？怪我はひどいの？どこを怪我したの？」

3. 一郎：「あまり心配いらないよ。ひどい怪我じゃないから。」
　答(男)：「ああ、それを聞いて安心した。でも、どんな怪我？うちへ帰れるのか？」

14課

それとも、入院しなきゃいけないのか？」

答(女)：「ああ、それを聞いて安心した。でも、でも、どんな怪我なの？うちへ帰れるの？それとも、入院しなきゃいけないの？」

4. 一郎：「でも、左の腕にギブスをしているよ。」

答(男)：「ギブス？左の腕？痛むのか？じゃ、歩けるんだ。不幸中の幸いだったな。」

答(女)：「ギブス？左の腕？痛む？じゃ、歩けるのね。不幸中の幸いだったね。」

5. 一郎：「歩けるけど、うちに一人で帰る自信がないんだ。ちょっと手伝ってくれないかな。」

答(男)：「もちろん、手伝ってやるよ。病院の名前と場所を教えて。すぐ車で迎えに行くから。」

答(女)：「もちろん、手伝ってあげるよ。病院の名前と場所を教えて。すぐ車で迎えに行くから。」

6. 一郎：「ありがとう。助かるよ。」

答(男)：「水くさいことは言うなよ。困った時は、おたがい様だ。よく僕に電話してくれたな。嬉しいよ。」

答(女)：「水くさいことは言わないでよ。困った時は、おたがい様よ。よく私に電話してくれたね。嬉しいよ。」

7. 一郎：「じゃ、病院の待合室で待ってるね。」

答(男)：「分かった。出来るだけ早く行くから、待ってて。じゃな。」

答(女)：「分かった。出来るだけ早く行くから、待っててね。じゃね。」

I. 文化発表「日本の公共交通機関」：ペアワーク→クラスワーク

a. Choose the correct word from below and write the correct letter in the (　) below the passage.

　　これから日本の交通機関について発表します。日本の交通機関は世界で最も進んでいるようです。

　まず第一に、日本の電車は日本のどこへでも行けて、とても便利です。そして、時間にとても正確です。だいたいはＪＲという会社によって運営されています。

　第二に、日本の都会にはだいたい地下鉄があって、とても便利です。東京の地下鉄は世界でも路線の多さと時間の正確さで有名です。路線によって色が違うので、分かりやすいです。

　第三に、新幹線はその速さと安全性と(1.)さで有名です。南は九州から北は北海道まで、新幹線で行くことが出来ます。(2.)によって、のぞみとひかりとこだまの三つの種類があります。日本人は(3.)や旅行に新幹線をよく使います。

14課

第四に、島国の日本には、船やフェリーがなくてはならない乗物です。毎日の生活にも (4.) にも日本人はよく船やフェリーを利用します。

第五に、車やバスやタクシーも日本で大事な乗物です。日本の道はせまいし、ガソリンも高いので、車を持っている日本人はアメリカ人と比べて (5.) です。その分、日本ではタクシーがアメリカより多く走っています。

私の意見として、個人主義のアメリカでは車をよく利用しますが、せまくて (6.) が多い日本では、車より公共の交通機関が発達しているようです。そして、(7.) が進んでいる日本は、すばらしい交通システムを作り上げて来たと思います。

1. (　) 2. (　) 3. (　) 4. (　) 5. (　) 6. (　) 7. (　)

a. 速さ　b. 人口　c. 旅行　d. 少ない　e. 正確　f. ビジネス　g. 技術

b. Discuss three differences between transportation in Japan and America, and state your own view or perspective.

Three differences:

1. _____

2. _____

3. _____

Explain your view or perspective.

_____

14課

<14課 - 聞く>

Listening: Driving

12秒×5

【You may take notes while listening. Do not look at the questions below before listening. You will have 12 seconds to answer each question. You may NOT move back and forth among questions.】

(Narrator) Now you will listen once to a prerecorded message.

(Narrator) Now answer the questions for this selection.

1. What happened to this person today?
    (A) He got into a major accident.
    (B) He hit a person with his car.
    (C) He was hit by a car.
    (D) He almost got into an accident.

2. Why did this person go to the university?
    (A) He had to take his economics exam.
    (B) He had to turn in his report.
    (C) The exam started at 9:00 a.m.
    (D) He had to attend his literature lecture.

3. What happened to this person while driving his car in the morning?
    (A) A pedestrian started walking in front of his car.
    (B) A pedestrian didn't use the pedestrian crossing.
    (C) The truck in front of him stopped suddenly.
    (D) He stopped for a pedestrian.

4. What happened to this person after arriving at the university?
    (A) The parking lot was full.
    (B) He could not park his car on the street.
    (C) He did not receive a parking violation ticket.
    (D) He was late to his exam.

5. Which one of the following is correct about the traffic violation this person committed?
    (A) He has never had a parking violation.
    (B) He has never driven while drunk.
    (C) He has never exceeded the speed limit.
    (D) He once fell asleep while driving.

<14課 - 読む>

Reading: Car Accident

【You may move back and forth among all the questions.】

高三事故死

3月3日午前2時ごろ京都市の国道一号で奈良県奈良市在住Aさん(18)の軽自動車が鴨川手前の電信柱に衝突した。車はその後、横転し鴨川に転落した。この事故でAさんは即死。助手席に乗っていた友人のB子さんは両足骨折などの重傷を負った。原因は飲酒運転と考えられている。B子さんの話によると、二人は3月1日に奈良市内の高校を卒業したばかりで、翌3月2日は夕方6時から二人が所属していたバスケット部のOB会歓迎会に出席した。Aさんは先輩のすすめでビールや酒を飲み、その後、二次会のカラオケ店でもビールやウイスキーを4～5杯飲んでかなり酔っぱらっていたらしい。カラオケ店からB子さんを家へ送り届ける途中、Aさんはこの事故を起こした。この事故で、歓迎会に参加していた20人全員が明日警察で調べを受ける。

<14課 - 読む (質問)>

Reading: Car Accident

(Narrator) Now answer the questions for this section.

1. When and where did this car accident happen?
   (A) About 2:00 a.m. on March 3rd in Kyoto
   (B) About 2:00 p.m. on March 3rd in Kyoto
   (C) About 2:00 a.m. on March 3rd in Nara
   (D) About 2:00 p.m. on March 3rd in Nara

2. What happened to the passengers?
   (A) Persons A and B died.
   (B) Person A died and Person B fractured her two legs.
   (C) Person A fractured two arms and Person B died.
   (D) Person A fractured two legs and Person B died.

3. What happened to the car?
   (A) The car hit a tree.
   (B) The car hit a telephone pole and stopped.
   (C) The car hit a telephone pole and rolled sideways into the river.
   (D) The driver lost control and the car was tossed into the river.

4. What activities did the passengers have on the day of the accident?
   (A) They attended a graduation ceremony.
   (B) They attended a basketball club welcoming party.
   (C) They went to a *karaoke* room with their classmates.
   (D) They went to a graduation party.

5. What was the main reason for the accident?
   (A) speed
   (B) carelessness
   (C) sleeping while driving
   (D) drunkenness

<14課 - 書く (テキストチャット)>
Text Chat: Driver's Licenses

[90秒×6]

You will participate in a simulated exchange of text-chat messages. Each time it is your turn to write, you will have 90 seconds. You should respond as fully and as appropriately as possible.

You will have a conversation with Daisuke, a student at a Japanese school, about driver's licenses.

1. Respond. (90 seconds)
   こんにちは。今運転についてアメリカの事情(じょう)を調べているんですが、御協力(きょう)を御願いします。もう運転免許(めんきょ)を持っていますか。

2. Respond. (90 seconds)
   アメリカでは運転免許(めんきょ)が何歳で取れるんですか。

3. Provide a specific example. (90 seconds)
   ところで、町で交通事故(こ)は多いですか。交通事故(こ)を見たことがありますか。

4. Describe a situation. (90 seconds)
   日本では運転しながらケータイを使うとつかまってしまいますが、そちらでも同じ法律(りつ)があるんですか。

5. Suggest. (90 seconds)
   僕はもう十八歳ですが、まだ運転免許(めんきょ)を持っていません。アメリカで運転免許(めんきょ)を取った方がいいと思いますか。

6. Ask a specific question. (90 seconds)
   どうも有難うございました。日本の交通について何か質問があったらしてください。

<14課 - 書く (比較(ひかく)と対比(たいひ))>
Compare and Contrast Article: Buses and Cars

[20分]

Directions: You are writing an article for the student newspaper of your sister school in Japan. Write an article in which you compare and contrast similarities and differences between taking buses and cars as means of transportation. Based on your personal experience, describe at least THREE aspects of each and highlight the similarities and differences between commuting by bus and car. Also state your preference for either and give reasons for it.

Your article should be 300 to 400 characters or longer. Use the *desu/masu* or *da* (plain) style, but use one style consistently. Also, use *kanji* wherever *kanji* from the AP Japanese *kanji* list is appropriate. You have 20 minutes to write.

【NOTES/OUTLINE: 自分の作文のアウトラインを書こう！】

Introduction: _____

Three similarities/differences:
1. _____
2. _____
3. _____

Your preference and give reasons: _____
_____
_____

[14課]

<14課 - 話す (会話)>
Conversation: Accident

20秒×4

You will participate in a simulated conversation. Each time it is your turn to speak, you will have 20 seconds to record. You should respond as fully and as appropriately as possible.

You will have a telephone conversation with Ichiro, your close Japanese friend, about his problem.

(Ichiro)
(20 seconds)
(Ichiro)
(20 seconds)
(Ichiro)
(20 seconds)
(Ichiro)
(20 seconds)

<14課 - 話す (日本文化)>
Cultural Perspective Presentation: Public Transportation in Japan

4分+2分

Directions: Imagine you are making an oral presentation to your Japanese class. First, you will read and hear the topic for your presentation. You will have 4 minutes to prepare your presentation. Then you will have 2 minutes to record your presentation. Your presentation should be as complete as possible.

Present your own view or perspective of public transportation in Japan. Discuss at least FIVE aspects or examples of public transportation in Japan.

Begin with an appropriate introduction, give details, explain your own view or perspective, and end with a concluding remark.

【Let's take notes!】

1. Begin with an appropriate introduction.
   _____

2. Discuss five aspects/examples of the topic.
   1.) _____
   2.) _____
   3.) _____
   4.) _____
   5.) _____

3. Explain your view or perspective.
   _____

4. End with a concluding remark.
   _____

14課

15課　天気と気候
Weather and Climate

【AP® タスク：天気と気候】

Predict tomorrow's weather by forecasting information such as average temperatures in centigrade and the probability of rain or other kinds of weather. How can we change our daily lives in order to save energy even in very hot or cold climates?

【文化】 日本の季節：Japan's Seasons

Japan's four seasons are each distinctly unique and have influenced many of the ways in which Japanese live. The dramatic seasonal changes in Japan are caused by its geographical location which brings cold winters from the north and warm, humid climate from the Pacific. A fifth "season" is the monsoon season that precedes the hot summer. Japanese sensitivity to the seasons is best represented in the arts.

Winter in the mountainous central ridges of Japan, along the Western coastal regions and in Hokkaido bring frequent and heavy snowfall. Winters are cold and dry. The cold winds that blow from continental Asia in the winter months of December, January and February are particularly harsh. Traditionally, the people living in these areas were snowbound, but today these areas host many who arrive at ski and hot spring resorts to enjoy the snow or respite from the snow.

Spring, which arrives in March, April and May, brings a profusion of flowers. The most famous is the *sakura* (桜) or cherry blossom, the flower symbolic of Japan. Cherry blossoms begin blooming in late March in southern Japan and continue to bloom through April as the *sakura-zensen* (桜前線), or cherry blossom front moves north. Japanese enjoy gathering together under the cherry trees to party with friends for 花見 (*hanami*, flower viewing). It is a joyous time of celebrating the arrival of spring, but cherry blossoms also remind Japanese of the transience of life, as the cherry blossom enjoys a very short life before scattering to the ground. Other flowers, such as plum, azalea, wisteria and iris also draw throngs of *hanami* viewers.

Before the arrival of summer, Japan experiences the "fifth season" known as *tsuyu* or *baiu* (梅雨), the rainy monsoon season that begins in mid-June and continues for about a month. Constant rain is characteristic of the monsoon season, and Japanese don their raincoats and carry their umbrellas as they enjoy the various hues of huge blue balls of hydrangea blossoms that thrive in the rainy weather.

The end of the rainy season marks the true beginning of summer in Japan. The months of July, August and early September are extremely hot and humid. Only Hokkaido and the alpine peaks of central Honshu escape this unbearably uncomfortable weather. The Japanese however, do look forward to the many summer festivals and the *Obon* season when they are able to wander outdoors in the cooler evenings. The Japanese enjoy fireworks displays along riversides during the summer festivals.

The autumn months are September, October and November. During September, Japan is often inundated by typhoons which are tropical storms originating in the Pacific Ocean. Typhoons that have hit land have wreaked havoc in many cities and villages, sometimes killing thousands in their path from southern Japan to the more northern reaches of the island chain. October and November, however bring peaceful and calm days, and as the temperature dips, the autumn foliage turns the mountains into a brilliant array of red, orange and gold. Just as Japanese enjoy the spring flowers, during the autumn, many venture outdoors to admire the richly colored maple leaves in nearby temple grounds, famous parks and gardens, and mountainsides.

The Japanese love of nature is rooted in their admiration of each of the distinct seasons and the dramatic changes they bring to their daily lives. The unique beauty of each season is depicted in all traditional genres of their art, literature, foods, fashion and architecture.

Questions to ponder: Can you think of how seasons are depicted in specific Japanese examples of art, literature, food preparation, fashion and architecture? How was the daily lifestyle of the Japanese affected by the seasonal changes long ago? How are they affected today?

15課 復習単語

トピック：天気と気候

1. (お)天気	(お)てんき	N	weather
2. 天気予報	てんきよほう	N	weather forecast
3. 春	はる	N	spring
4. 夏	なつ	N	summer
5. 秋	あき	N	autumn
6. 冬	ふゆ	N	winter
7. 晴れ	はれ	N	clear (weather)
8. 雨	あめ	N	rain
9. 雨が止んだ	あめがやんだ	V1	It stopped raining.
10. 曇り	くもり	N	cloudy
11. 曇り一時晴れ	くもりいちじはれ	N	cloudy and occasionally clear
12. 雪	ゆき	N	snow
13. 温度	おんど	N	(weather) temperature
14. 暑い	あつい	A	(is) hot [temperature]
15. 暖かい	あたたかい	A	warm
16. 寒い	さむい	A	is cold (temperature)
17. 雲	くも	N	cloud
18. 桜	さくら	N	cherry blossom

| 15課 | ★★★ | 新しい単語 | ★★★ |

1. ごぶさたしています。＜ご無沙汰しています。＞　Exp　Excuse me for not keeping in touch. (Used in formal communication.)

2. みなさん＜皆さん＞によろしく。　Exp　Please give my best regards to everyone.

3. おやくにたてて、うれしいです。＜お役に立てて、嬉しいです。＞
Exp　I am happy to have been of some use.

4. さいこうきおん＜最高気温＞　N　highest temperature
さいていきおん＜最低気温＞　N　lowest temperature
天気予報によると今日の最高気温は30度で、最低気温は25度だそうだ。　According to the weather forecast, I understand that the high temperature today is 30 degrees and the low is 25 degrees.

5. こうすいかくりつ＜降水確率＞　N　probability of rain
天気予報によると今日の降水確率は10%だから、傘は持って行かない。　According to the weather forecast, the probability of rain today is 10%, so I will not take an umbrella.

6. かし＜華氏＞　N　fahrenheit (°F)
アメリカでは温度に華氏を使うが、日本人には分からない。　In America, Fahrenheit is used for temperature, but Japanese don't understand it.

7. せっし＜摂氏＞　N　centigrade (°C)
日本では気温に摂氏を使う。　In Japan, centigrade is used for temperature.

8. しつど＜湿度＞　N　humidity
日本の夏は湿度がとても高くて、蒸し暑い。　The humidity in Japan is very high in the summers and it is very muggy.

9. おおがた＜大型＞　N　large size
ちゅうがた＜中型＞　N　medium size
こがた＜小型＞　N　small size
大型台風が沖縄に近づいているそうだ。　I understand that a very large typhoon is approaching Okinawa.

10. ふうそく＜風速＞　N　wind speed
最大風速40キロの台風だった。　It was a typhoon with a maximum wind speed of 40 km (per hour).

11. しんろ＜進路＞　N　course; path
台風は進路を変えて、日本海の方へ行った。　The typhoon changed its course and went toward the Sea of Japan.

12. ちゅういほう＜注意報＞　N　warning
    今日十時ごろ大雨注意報が出た。　At about 10:00 today, a flash flood warning was put in effect.
13. ほくとう＜北東＞　N　northeast
    台風は北東に向かっている。　The typhoon is heading toward the northeast.
14. きんきちほう＜近畿地方＞　N　Kinki region [including Hyogo, Kyoto, Shiga, Osaka, Nara, Wakayama and Mie prefectures]
    近畿地方は今日雨が一日中降っていた。　Today, it was raining the whole day in the Kinki region.
15. ぼんち＜盆地＞　N　basin
    京都は山に囲まれている盆地なので、夏暑く、冬寒い。　Kyoto is a basin area surrounded by mountains so it is hot during the summer and cold in the winter.
16. いちねんじゅう＜一年中＞　N　all year long
    ハワイは一年中暖かい。　Hawaii is warm all year long.
17. つゆ/ばいう＜梅雨/梅雨＞　N　rainy (monsoon) season [mid June - mid July]
    日本は六月の中旬頃から梅雨に入って、毎日雨が降る。　In Japan, the rainy season begins from about mid-June and it rains every day.
18. しとしと＜しとしと＞　N　drizzle (rain)
    日本の梅雨にはしとしと雨が降る。　During the rainy season in Japan, it drizzles.
19. かえる＜蛙＞　N　frog
    日本の梅雨の頃、田んぼでは小さい緑色の蛙がうるさく鳴いている。　During the rainy season in Japan, small green frogs cry loudly in the rice fields.
20. こたつ＜炬燵＞　N　portable foot warmer
    日本人は冬に炬燵に入る。　During the winter, Japanese go into the portable foot warmer.
21. なべもの＜鍋物＞　N　one pot food (dish)
    日本人は冬になると、よく鍋物を食べる。　When it is winter, the Japanese often eat one pot dishes.
22. はんそで＜半袖＞　N　short sleeve
    秋になると、半袖のTシャツでは寒すぎる。　In the autumn, short sleeve t-shirts are too cold.
23. おくない＜屋内＞　N　indoor
    冬は、屋内プールで泳ぐ。　During the winter, we swim in indoor pools.
24. おくがい＜屋外＞　N　outdoor
    夏は、屋外プールで泳ぐ。　During the summer, we swim in outdoor pools.

15課

25. きじ＜記事＞　N　article

今、世界の気候について記事を書いている。　Now, (information about) the temperature worldwide is written in articles.

26. さわやか＜爽やか＞　Na　refreshing

秋が来ると、爽やかな風が吹く。　When it is autumn, the refreshing breezes blow.

27. できるだけ＜出来るだけ＞　Adv　as much as possible

出来るだけ答えてみた。　I tried to answer as much as I could.

28. すごす＜過ごす＞／過ごします　V1　to spend time

秋は涼しくて、過ごしやすい。　Autumn is cool, and it is easy to spend the time. (It is comfortable.)

29. めをだす＜芽を出す＞／出します　V1　to sprout

春になると、植物が芽を出す。　When it is spring, the plants all begin to sprout.

30. かれる＜枯れる＞／枯れます　V2　(plants) die

冬になると、植物が枯れる。　When it is winter, the plants all dry up.

【もっと単語】

A. 方角 (Directions)

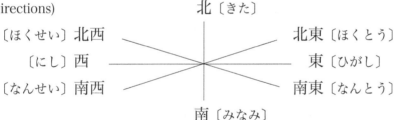

B. 地方

北海道地方　ほっかいどうちほう
東北地方　とうほくちほう
関東地方　かんとうちほう
中部地方　ちゅうぶちほう
近畿地方　きんきちほう
中国地方　ちゅうごくちほう
四国地方　しこくちほう
九州地方　きゅうしゅうちほう
沖縄地方　おきなわちほう

15課

15課 　文法

> **A. 降り出すでしょう**　　It will probably start to rain.
>
> There are several expressions that may be used to indicate the beginning of an action. In this case, when a verb stem is attached to a form of *-dasu*, there is a suggestion that the action occurred suddenly and unexpectedly.
> Compare:
>
> 1. 雨が急に降り出した。　　　　　　　　It started to rain suddenly.
> 2. 雨が止んだ。　　　　　　　　　　　　It stopped raining.
> 3. 本を読み始めた。　　　　　　　　　　I started to read a book.
> 4. 本を読み終えた or 読み終わった。　　I finished reading the book.
> 5. 本を読み続けた。　　　　　　　　　　I continued to read the book.

Write the correct form of the verb in the (　), then circle the appropriate verb ending in the < >.

1. 赤ちゃんが急に＿＿＿＿＿＿＿＿＿〈始めた　出した〉。（泣く）
2. 急に雪が＿＿＿＿＿＿＿＿＿〈始めた　出した〉。（降る）
3. 母は二時間前から本を＿＿＿＿＿＿＿＿＿〈始めて　出して〉、まだ読んでいる。（読む）
4. 父は５年前からマラソンに＿＿＿＿＿＿＿＿＿〈始めた　出した〉と思う。（参加する）
5. やっと雨が＿＿＿＿＿＿＿＿＿、晴れて来た。（止む）
6. 梅雨になると、毎日雨が＿＿＿＿＿＿＿＿＿〈止む　始める　続ける〉。（降る）
7. 大学でも日本語を＿＿＿＿＿＿＿＿＿〈始める　続ける　終わる〉つもりだ。（勉強する）
8. 最後の大学願書を＿＿＿＿＿＿＿＿＿〈始めて　続けて　終わって〉、ほっとしている。（書く）

> **B. 書き＋やすい**　　easy to write
> 　　**書き＋にくい**　　hard to write
>
> To express that an action is easy or difficult to do, take the verb stem of the verb and attach *-yasui* or *-nikui*. Remember that the suffixes *-yasui* and *-nikui* only mean easy and difficult when attached to a verb stem. Once *-yasui* and *-nikui* are attached, the word becomes an i-adjective, and conjugates as such. The subject of the sentence should befollowed by the particle は.
> Compare:
>
> 1. この大学は、合格しにくい。　　　　This college is difficult to get into.
> 2. この大学に合格するのは、大変だ。　It's difficult to get into this college.

Write the correct form of the verb given in the (　), then circle the correct verb ending in the < >.

1. 日本の夏はとても蒸し暑くて、＿＿＿＿＿＿＿＿＿（やすい　にくい）。〈過ごす〉
2. この靴は高かったのに、とても＿＿＿＿＿＿＿＿＿（やすい　にくい）。〈履く〉

3. 去年の先生は優しかったので、とても_____（やすかった　にくかった）。〈話す〉
4. この漢字の辞書はあまり_____（やすくない　にくくない）。〈使う〉
5. 日本の大学は_____（やすくて　にくくて）、_____（やすい　にくい）と聞いた。〈入学する〉〈卒業する〉

C. 何もしなくても、〜　　　　Even though/if I don't do anything, 〜
　　高くても、〜　　　　　　Even though/if it's expensive, 〜
　　静かでも、〜　　　　　　Even though/if it is quiet, 〜
　　明日でも、〜　　　　　　Even though/if it's tomorrow, 〜

Using the -ても form of verbs, いadjectives, なadjectives and nouns at the beginning of a sentence creates the meaning of "even though/even if." In the case of negatives, use the -なくても form of each.

Change the form of the verb given in the (　) to mean "Even though/if 〜."

1. 日本語を四年_____、まだあまり上手に話せない。（勉強する）
2. 漢字の勉強は_____、おもしろいと思う。（難しい）
3. パーティーが日曜日の_____、田中さんは来るだろう。（夜）
4. 山本君は_____、成績がいい。（勉強しない）
5. この本は_____、読まなければならない。（おもしろくない）
6. ダンスが_____、ダンスパーティーに行こう。（好きじゃない）
7. いい_____、キャンプに行こう。（天気じゃない）

D. 暑くもなく寒くもない or 暑くも寒くもない　　　It's neither hot nor cold.
　　食べもしないし、飲みもしない　　　　　　　　He neither eats nor drinks it.
　　好きでもなく嫌いでもない or 好きでも嫌いでもない　I neither like it nor dislike it.
　　犬でもなく猫でもない or 犬でも猫でもない　　It's neither a dog nor a cat.

There are several possible ways of expressing the same meaning of the "neither...nor" meaning of this new grammatical form. What is required, however, is that も follow the -く form for contrasting forms of いadjectives, contrasting verb stems, or the で forms of contrasting なadjectives or nouns.

Write the correct forms of the cues given in the (　).

1. 日本の秋は暑くも_____、とても過ごしやすい。（寒い）
2. この授業は易しくもなく_____、ちょうどいい。（難しい）
3. この店の物は安くも_____ない。（高い）
4. ゴルフは上手でも、_____ない。（下手）
5. このドアは壊れていて、開けられもしないし、_____ない。（閉める）
6. 私の好きな人は山田君でもなく、_____ない。（川中君）

15課

> E. <u>どこかに</u>＋旅行したい　　　　　　　　I want to travel somewhere.
> 　<u>どこか</u>おもしろい所<u>に</u>＋旅行したい　I want to travel somewhere interesting.
> 　<u>だれかと</u>＋話したい　　　　　　　　　I want to talk to someone.
> 　<u>だれか</u>やさしい人<u>と</u>＋話したい　　　I want to talk to someone nice.
>
> When a question word is followed by か and an affirmative form, the resulting word carries the meaning of "some- ..." as shown in the examples above. When followed by a negative form (see below), it takes on the meaning of "any- ..."
> Compare:
> 1. <u>だれも</u>パーティーに来なかった。　　　No one came to the party.
> 2. <u>だれか</u>いない？　　　　　　　　　　　Isn't anyone here?
> 3. <u>だれでも</u>使える。　　　　　　　　　　Anyone can use it.
> 4. <u>だれも</u>死ぬ。　　　　　　　　　　　　Everyone dies.

Circle the correct response from the choices in the (　).

1. 大学を卒業したら、（いつも　いつか　いつでも）世界旅行をしたい。
2. 冬になると、（だれも　だれか　だれでも）寒そうな格好をしている。
3. （だれも　だれか　だれでも）優しい人（は　に　と）結婚したい。
4. 梅雨の時は雨が多いから、（どこも　どこか　どこでも　どこへも）出かけたくない。
5. 寒い冬には（何も　何か　何でも）温かい物（は　が　を）食べたい。
6. 「どのシャツが好き？」「（どれも　どれか　どれでも）好きじゃないよ。」
7. 「卒業しても、（いつも　いつか　いつでも　いつまでも）友達でいようね。」

15課

| 15課 | | アクティビティー | |

A. 日本文化：一人か二人ワーク→クラスワーク

Divide the topics below among your classmates and research your topic on the Internet. Using visuals, present your findings with your classmates.

1. 梅雨（つゆ）、雨靴（あまぐつ）、雨傘（あまがさ）、田んぼ、蛙（かえる）、梅雨前線（ばいうぜんせん）
2. うちわ、ハンカチ、蝉（せみ）
3. こたつ、鍋物（なべもの）
4. 桜（さくら）、お花見、桜前線（さくらぜんせん）
5. 紅葉（もみじ）、紅葉（こうよう）、紅葉前線（こうようぜんせん）
6. クールビズ、ウォームビズ

B. 聞く Pre-Listening Activity「天気予報」：ペアワーク→クラスワーク

a. Based on the weather forecast chart below, fill in the blanks with the correct responses.

各地	きょう	あす	あさって
札幌	☃→☁	☃→☁	☁｜☃
仙台	☁｜☃	☁	☁｜☂
東京	☀	☀	☁
新潟	☃	☂｜☁	☁｜☂
名古屋	☁→☀	☁→☀	☁
大阪	☁→☀	☀→☁	☁
松江	☂→☁	☀→☂	☁｜☂
広島	☁→☀	☀→☁	☁
高松	☁→☀	☀→☁	☁
福岡	☁→☀	☀→☁	☁
那覇	☁	☁	☁｜☂

→ ＝ のち　　｜ ＝ 時々

1. ＿＿＿＿は今日＿＿雪のち曇り＿＿でしょう。
2. 名古屋（なごや）は今日＿＿＿＿＿＿＿＿でしょう。
3. 松江（まつえ）は今日＿＿＿＿＿＿＿＿でしょう。
4. 新潟（にいがた）は明日＿＿＿＿＿＿＿＿でしょう。
5. 福岡（ふくおか）は明日＿＿＿＿＿＿＿＿でしょう。
6. 松江（まつえ）は明日＿＿＿＿＿＿＿＿でしょう。
7. 札幌（さっぽろ）は明後日（あさって）＿＿＿＿＿＿＿＿でしょう。
8. 仙台（せんだい）は明後日（あさって）＿＿＿＿＿＿＿＿でしょう。
9. 今日私の住んでいる所の天気は

　　＿＿＿＿＿＿＿＿でしょう。

b. Based on the Tokyo weather forecast below, fill in the blanks with the correct responses.

東京	12/5 (水)	12/6 (木)	12/7 (金)	12/8 (土)	12/9 (日)	12/10 (月)	12/11 (火)
天気	☀	☀｜☁	☁	☁｜☀	☁｜☀	☀｜☁	☀｜☁
最高気温　最低気温	11℃　4℃	12℃　4℃	14℃　7℃	13℃　8℃	11℃　6℃	12℃　6℃	13℃　6℃
降水確率〔こうすいかくりつ〕	0%	10%	40%	20%	30%	20%	20%

華氏（かし）Fahrenheit °F ＝ 摂氏（せっし）Centigrade ℃ × 9 ÷ 5 + 32

1. １２月５日水曜日の東京のお天気は＿＿＿＿＿＿＿＿でしょう。
2. １２月８日土曜日の＿＿＿＿＿＿＿＿＿＿＿は摂氏１３度(＝華氏＿＿＿)でしょう。
3. １２月８日土曜日の＿＿＿＿＿＿＿＿＿＿＿は摂氏８度(＝華氏＿＿＿)でしょう。
4. １２月＿＿＿日＿＿＿曜日に東京は雨が降らないでしょう。

C. 聞く Post-Listening Activity「天気予報」：ペアワーク→クラスワーク

Compare and Contrast: Summer Weather and Winter Weather

Compare summer weather and winter weather where you live. Prepare an outline on this topic within four minutes and do a two minute presentation of it with your partner.

Introduction:
_____

Three similarities/differences:
  1. _____
  2. _____
  3. _____

Your preference and reasons for it:
_____
_____

D. 読む Pre-Reading Activity「日本の気候」：ペアワーク→クラスワーク

a. Fill in the ( ) with the correct Japanese season from among the following: 春, 梅雨, 夏, 秋, 冬.

1. しとしと　　　(　)　　6. 汗　　　　(　)　　11. 蛙　　　　　(　)
2. 雪　　　　　　(　)　　7. 鍋物　　　(　)　　12. こたつ　　　(　)
3. 雨靴　　　　　(　)　　8. 紅葉　　　(　)　　13. うちわ　　　(　)
4. 桜　　　　　　(　)　　9. お花見　　(　)　　14. 蒸し暑い　　(　)
5. 雨傘　　　　　(　)　　10. 寒い　　　(　)　　15. ハイキング　(　)/(　)

b. Fill in each ( ) with the number of the matching word above. Some drawings have more than one match.

Ex. (15)　　(　)　　(　)　　(　)　　(　)　　(　)(　)(　)

(　)　　(　)(　)　　(　)(　)　　(　)　　(　)

15課

E. 読む Post-Reading Activity 「日本の気候」：ペアワーク→クラスワーク

Compare and Contrast: Climate in Kyoto and Climate Where I Live

Prepare an outline on this topic within 4 minutes and do a 2 minute presentation on it with your partner.

Introduction:
_____

Three similarities/differences:

1. _____
2. _____
3. _____

Your preference and reasons for it:
_____
_____

F. テキストチャット「お天気」：ペアワーク→クラスワーク

You will have a conversation about weather with Kaori Anzai, your Japanese host mother who may be visiting you soon.

First, read this text chat conversation with your partner. Next, read the questions and your partner will respond without looking at the book. Give your original answers to the questions. For each question, use 20 seconds to answer. Take turns asking and answering questions.

1. 安斉：お久しぶり。安斉です。元気？いつかそちらに旅行したいと思ってるんだけど。

   私　：ご無沙汰しています。私は元気ですが、皆さんお元気ですか。こちらに旅行ですか。いつですか。御家族皆で来るんですか。

2. 安斉：今、８月にそっちへの旅行を計画しているんだけど、その頃のお天気はどう？

   私　：８月ですか。こっちの８月の天気は、暑いけど、とてもいいですよ。空は青いし、海も青いし、毎日泳ぎに行けますよ。でも、私は８月にどこかに旅行しているかも知れません。

3. 安斉：今日のお天気は？気温は？過ごしやすい？

   私　：今日のお天気は、あまり良くないです。曇っていて、時々雨が降っていますよ。気温は華氏８０度ぐらいですが、摂氏では２５度ぐらいですよね。ちょっと涼しくなって、過ごしやすくなりました。

4. 安斉：一年中で旅行に一番いい季節って、いつ？どうして？

   私　：ここの一番いい季節は多分５月ごろだと思いますね。寒くも暑くもなくて、気持ちのいい季節です。花がたくさん咲いてとってもきれいですよ。

5. 安斉：今の季節は、そちらでどんな格好をすればいいか教えてくれる？

   私　：今ですか。今お昼は暖かいんですが、朝夕少し涼しくなりますから、セーターか

15課

ジャケットがあるといいですよ。お昼は半袖(そで)のシャツと長いパンツで大丈夫(じょうぶ)です。

6. 安斉(ざい)：いろいろ教えてくれて有難(がと)う。じゃ、もう少し考えてからまた連絡(れんらく)するね。日本に旅行する予定(よてい)はないの？

　　私：残念(ざんねん)ながら、今のところ、その予定(よてい)はありません。でも、日本に行きたいから、ぜったいまた行きますね。ぜひ御家族(ごか)でこちらに来て下さい。楽しみにしています。では、お元気で。皆さんによろしく。

G. Compare & Contrast「二つの季節」：ペアワーク→クラスワーク

a. First, read this compare and contrast passage with your partner.

　一年には春夏秋冬いろいろな季節(きせつ)がありますが、これから、春と秋の季節を比(くら)べてみます。春と秋は同じことも違うこともあります。

　まず、一つ目の違いは、春には植物(しょく)が新しい新しい芽(め)を出しますが、秋には植物(しょく)が枯(か)れて行きます。だから、春には何か希望(きぼう)を感(かん)じることができますが、秋には寂(さび)しさを感(かん)じます。

　しかし、同じこともあります。春も秋も暑くもなく、寒くもなく、とても過(す)ごしやすい季節(きせつ)です。だいたい春は暖(あたた)かく、秋は涼(すず)しく感(かん)じます。

　そして、二つ目の同じところは、春も秋も朝と昼の時間がだいたい同じくらいです。夏にはお昼が夜より長いですが、冬には夜が昼より長いです。ですから、昼と夜が同じくらいの春と秋は、屋内でも屋外でもいろいろな活動(かつ)が出来る季節(きせつ)です。

　結論(けつろん)として、私は秋の方が春より好きです。なぜなら、秋に私の心はもっと落(お)ち着くからです。春はなぜか忙(いそが)しく感(かん)じて、ストレスが多いです。

---

b. Next, work with your partner and together compare and contrast two seasons. List three similarities and/or differences, your preference and the reason. Give your original opinions. Then, share your presentation with your class.

Introduction:
_____

Three similarities/differences:

1. _____
2. _____
3. _____

Your preference and give reasons:
_____
_____

15課

H. 会話「気候」：ペアワーク→クラスワーク

First, read this conversation with your partner. Next, read the questions; your partner will respond without looking at the book. Repeat the underlined parts and give your original answers to the questions. For each question, use 20 seconds to answer. Take turns asking and answering questions.

1. 質問：初めまして。山岡高校新聞部の中田です。今日は世界のいろいろな所の気候について記事を書いています。どうぞ御協力を御願いします。

    答(例)：<u>初めまして。(Last name) です。こちらこそどうぞよろしくお願いします。気候についての質問ですか。</u>何でも聞いて下さい。出来るだけ答えてみます。

2. そちらの一年の気候はどうですか。教えて下さい。

    答(例)：<u>一年の気候ですか。</u>そうですねえ。<u>こちらは</u>一年中暖かいですが、冬には涼しくなって雨が多くなります。

3. 一年で一番過ごしやすい季節はいつですか。

    答(例)：<u>一番過ごしやすい季節ですか。</u>私は秋だと思いますね。こちらの秋は暑くもなく寒くもなく、とてもさわやかでいい気持です。

4. 今日は御協力ありがとうございました。日本の気候について、何か質問がありますか。

    答(例)：<u>日本の気候についての質問ですか。</u>そうですねえ。日本に旅行したいんですが、どの季節が一番いいか教えて下さい。では、いい記事を書いて下さい。<u>お役に立てて、嬉しいです。</u>

I. 文化発表「日本の気候」：ペアワーク→クラスワーク

a. Choose the correct answers for each season from the choices below.

季節	1. 読み方 (ひらがなで)	2. いつからいつまで	3. どんな気候	4. 季節の植物	5. 季節を感じる物や活動
春					
梅雨					
夏					
秋					
冬					

1. 季節の読み方：あき、つゆ、なつ、ばいう、ふゆ、はる
2. いつからいつまで？：３月～５月、７月～８月、９月～１１月、１２月～２月、６月中旬～７月中旬

15課

3. どんな気候？：寒い、台風が多い、蒸し暑い、湿度が高い、暖かい、涼しい
4. 季節の植物：菊 chrysanthemum、梅 plum、紅葉 maple、あやめ iris、つつじ azalea、藤 wisteria、桜 cherry blossom
5. 季節を感じる物や活動：傘、お盆、田植え rice planting、お花見、雨靴、スキー、レインコート、夏祭り、花火

 b. Write how Japanese seasons are depicted in specific Japanese examples of art, literature, food preparation, fashion and architecture.

1. 美術：_____
2. 文学：_____
3. 食物/料理：_____
4. 服装：_____
5. 建築：_____

15課

<15課 - 聞く>
Listening: Weather Forecast

【You may take notes while listening. Do not look at the questions below before listening. You will have 12 seconds to answer each question. You may NOT move back and forth among questions.】

(Narrator) Now you will listen twice to a prerecorded message.

(Narrator) Now answer the questions for this selection.

1. What is the date today?
   (A) Today is Thursday, the 4th.
   (B) Today is Friday, the 4th.
   (C) Today is Thursday, the 8th.
   (D) Today is Friday, the 8th.

2. What is today's weather forecast?
   (A) Sunny → cloudy
   (B) Cloudy → rainy → cloudy
   (C) Sunny → cloudy → rainy
   (D) Rainy → cloudy → sunny

3. What is NOT correct about today's weather forecast?
   (A) The highest temperature will be 24°C.
   (B) The lowest temperature will be 19°C.
   (C) The chance of rain is 50%.
   (D) There is a warning of a typhoon.

4. Which description is NOT correct about the typhoon?
   (A) The typhoon is a large scale typhoon.
   (B) The typhoon is the eighth of this year.
   (C) The typhoon is approaching the south of Okinawa.
   (D) The wind speed is 20 kilometers per hour.

5. What will happen to the typhoon?
   (A) The typhoon will land in Shikoku and the Kansai (Kinki) area.
   (B) The typhoon will land in the Kanto area.
   (C) The typhoon will move away to the Sea of Japan.
   (D) The typhoon will move away from Okinawa on Sunday morning.

<15課 - 読む>

Reading: Report

【You may move back and forth among all the questions.】

日本の気候

　私は日本の大学に留学して、一年京都に住んでいたので、その時の経験を書く。

　日本に着いたのは、梅雨の季節で毎日朝から晩まで雨がしとしと降っていたのを覚えている。私の住んでいた寮は田舎にあったので、田んぼに小さい緑色の蛙がたくさんいてうるさかった。毎日、雨靴をはいて、傘をさして、大学へ通っていた。

　梅雨が終わって夏になると、京都はとても暑くなった。京都は盆地で山に囲まれているので、夏は暑く冬は寒い。風がなくて、蒸し暑かったので、夜なかなか寝られなかった。何もしなくても汗が出て来て、いつもうちわとハンカチを使っていた。

　秋になると、とても気持ちがいい天気が続いた。京都の秋が大好きだった。特に晩秋は紅葉が美しかった。週末になると、仲間とよくハイキングに行ったり、京都の寺を訪れたりした。

　冬になると、京都は寒い。雪は多くなかったが、気温が低かった。夕方になると、寮の仲間とよく集まって、こたつに入って、鍋物を食べていたのを思い出す。

　春になると、少しずつ暖かくなって、気持ちも明るくなった。桜が咲くころには、弁当を持って、仲間とよく花見に出かけた。満開の桜の下で、食べたり、飲んだり、歌ったり、踊ったりした。懐かしい思い出だ。

　とにかく京都の一年は季節によっていろいろな景色があり、楽しめた。季節の中で、秋が一番好きだ。また、あの紅葉で赤く染まった晩秋の寺を訪れたい。

<15課 - 読む (質問)>

Reading: Report

(Narrator) Now answer the questions for this section.

1. Where was this person living while in Japan?
    - (A) in Tokyo
    - (B) in an apartment
    - (C) in the countryside
    - (D) in the city of Kyoto

2. According to this person, what was the rainy season like?
    - (A) It rained heavily all day long every day.
    - (B) There were many big frogs in the rice fields.
    - (C) This person did not use rain boots.
    - (D) This person sometimes used an umbrella.

3. According to this person, what was summer like?
    - (A) It was windy.
    - (B) The temperature was just right.
    - (C) This person used an air conditioner all day long.
    - (D) This person perspired a lot.

4. How did this person enjoy nature?
    - (A) She went hiking often in the summer.
    - (B) She enjoyed eating out with her friends in the winter.
    - (C) She enjoyed viewing the cherry blossoms from her room in the spring.
    - (D) She often visited temples in the fall.

5. What impression does this person have of Japan?
    - (A) She enjoyed the different scenery of each season in Japan.
    - (B) She liked the cherry blossom season the most.
    - (C) She enjoyed hiking with her boyfriend in the mountains of Japan.
    - (D) She wants to visit Japan again and experience the festivals in Japan.

<15課 - 書く (テキストチャット)>

`90秒×6`

Text Chat: Weather

You will participate in a simulated exchange of text-chat messages. Each time it is your turn to write, you will have 90 seconds. You should respond as fully and as appropriately as possible.

You will have a conversation about weather with Kaori Anzai, your Japanese host mother who may be visiting you soon.

1. Respond. (90 seconds)
 お久しぶり。安斉です。元気？いつかそちらに旅行したいと思ってるんだけど。
2. Describe a specific example. (90 seconds)
 今、8月にそっちへの旅行を計画しているんだけど、その頃のお天気はどう？
3. Respond. (90 seconds)
 今日のお天気は？気温は？過ごしやすい？
4. Give a preference and justify your opinion. (90 seconds)
 一年中で旅行に一番いい季節って、いつ？どうして？
5. Suggest. (90 seconds)
 今の季節はそちらでどんな格好をすればいいか教えてくれる？
6. Respond and greet. (90 seconds)
 いろいろ教えてくれて有難う。じゃ、もう少し考えてから、また連絡するね。日本に旅行する予定はないの？

<15課 - 書く (比較と対比)>

`20分`

Compare and Contrast Article: Two Seasons in Japan

Directions: You are writing an article for the student newspaper of your sister school in Japan. Write an article in which you compare and contrast similarities and differences between two seasons in Japan. Based on your personal experience, describe at least THREE aspects of each and highlight the similarities and differences between two seasons in Japan. Also state your preference for either and give reasons for it.

Your article should be 300 to 400 characters or longer. Use the *desu/masu* or *da* (plain) style, but use one style consistently. Also, use *kanji* wherever *kanji* from the AP Japanese *kanji* list is appropriate. You have 20 minutes to write.

【NOTES/OUTLINE: 自分の作文のアウトラインを書こう！】

Introduction:
_____

Three similarities/differences:

1. _____
2. _____
3. _____

Your preference and give reasons:
_____
_____

15課

<15課 - 話す (会話)>
Conversation: Climate

`20秒×4`

You will participate in a simulated conversation. Each time it is your turn to speak, you will have 20 seconds to record. You should respond as fully and as appropriately as possible.

You will have a conversation with Mr. Nakata, a Japanese journalist, about the climate.

(Man)
(20 seconds)
(Man)
(20 seconds)
(Man)
(20 seconds)
(Man)
(20 seconds)

<15課 - 話す (日本文化)>
Cultural Perspective Presentation: Climate in Japan

`4分+2分`

Directions: Imagine you are making an oral presentation to your Japanese class. First, you will read and hear the topic for your presentation. You will have 4 minutes to prepare your presentation. Then you will have 2 minutes to record your presentation. Your presentation should be as complete as possible.

Present your own view or perspective of climate in Japan. Discuss at least FIVE aspects or examples of climate in Japan.

Begin with an appropriate introduction, give details, explain your own view or perspective, and end with a concluding remark.

【Let's take notes!】

1. Begin with an appropriate introduction.

_____

2. Discuss five aspects/examples of the topic.

    1.) _____
    2.) _____
    3.) _____
    4.) _____
    5.) _____

3. Explain your view or perspective.

_____

4. End with a concluding remark.

_____

`15課`

16課 ●●● 食物 ●●●
Food

【AP® タスク：食物】

Discuss three differences between Japanese foods and American foods and give your preference and opinions. Discuss five characteristics of Japanese table manners such as utensils, tableware, preparation of Japanese foods, etc. State your opinions.

【文化】 日本の食事マナー：Japanese Table Manners

Japanese enjoy their meals for their nutrition, taste and appeal. They are also always conscious of expressing their gratitude for a meal, and carefully observing rules of etiquette to show respect to those who host them, and those who enjoy their meals with them.

Most Japanese begin their meal with expressions of thanks for the food by holding their hands together as in prayer, bowing slightly, and saying, "*Itadakimasu.*" After the meal, one again expresses one's appreciation by saying "*Gochisoosama deshita*." When one is treated to a meal at a restaurant, for example, one may say "*Gochisoo ni narimashita*" to the host. As with all Japanese greetings, these expressions are uttered with a slight bow.

When one sits down for a traditional Japanese meal in a Japanese style room, one is expected to sit *seiza* (正座), which is the traditional manner of sitting on one's knees on *tatami* flooring. One sits on a floor cushion called *zabuton* (ざぶとん) with one's back straight. These days, Japanese are also less accustomed to sitting this way, and women are allowed to rest their legs to the side while men may sit cross-legged. If one is lucky, the restaurant may have openings below the table where one may sink one's legs. They may also have legless chairs (ざいす) with backs to rest on while sitting around a low table on *tatami* mat flooring.

When eating Japanese meals, one will of course, use chopsticks. While there are perhaps more than a dozen rules about chopstick etiquette, several will be mentioned here. If one is using disposable wooden chopsticks, one must never roll them together or cross them back and forth as if to remove splinters. When using any kind of chopsticks, one should not ever leave them standing in rice or other containers, as it reminds Japanese of a custom practiced at services for the dead. Another is to never allow chopsticks to "wander" over dishes of food as if in indecision about what food to take. One should also never spear food, or use chopsticks to move dishes on the table.

All containers, such as soup bowls and rice bowls, are to be held with the left hand and brought up to the height of one's chest. The food or soup is then consumed using chopsticks held in the right hand. Because they are hand held, Japanese bowls are constructed more deeply and smaller than Western soup bowls.

Another commonly shared rule is one to observe when having noodles. In Japan, it is acceptable, and even expected, that one slurp while eating noodles from a broth. This is an indication that one is enjoying the noodles. Noodle bowls are left on the table and one must bend forward to consume the noodles with chopsticks. At the end, it is acceptable to drink the broth directly from the bowl by lifting it with both hands.

Japanese observe many rules of etiquette when eating. It represents the Japanese sense of appreciating foods they eat, as well as respecting others who share the meal with them. It emphasizes the fact that meals were traditionally consumed in the company of others, and that meals should be a communal event.

Questions to ponder: How are table manners different in Japan and your culture? Why? Are there other Japanese rules of etiquette that you know of? Do they also represent some of the traditional values of Japanese culture?

16課　復習単語

トピック：食物

#	漢字	かな	品詞	意味
1	食べ物	たべもの	N	food
2	食事	しょくじ	N	meal; dining
3	食事(を)する	しょくじ(を)する	V3	(to) dine; have a meal
4	日本料理	にほんりょうり	N	Japanese-style cooking
5	西洋料理	せいようりょうり	N	Western-style cooking
6	和食	わしょく	N	Japanese meal
7	洋食	ようしょく	N	Western style meal
8	御馳走	ごちそう	N	feast; a big meal
9	御馳走(を)する	ごちそう(を)する	V3	(to) treat (someone)
10	弁当	べんとう	N	box lunch
11	材料	ざいりょう	N	ingredients
12	調味料	ちょうみりょう	N	seasonings
13	塩	しお	N	salt
14	砂糖	さとう	N	sugar
15	胡椒	こしょう	N	pepper
16	酢	す	N	vinegar
17	味	あじ	N	taste; flavor
18	味わう	あじわう	V1	to taste
19	甘い	あまい	A	(is) sweet
20	塩辛い	しおからい	A	is salty
21	すっぱい		A	is sour
22	油	あぶら	N	oil
23	小麦粉	こむぎこ	N	(wheat) flour
24	御飯	ごはん	N	(cooked) rice
25	玄米	げんまい	N	brown rice
26	(お)むすび		N	riceball
27	(お)にぎり		N	riceball
28	(御)味噌汁	(お)みそしる	N	soup flavored with *miso* (soy bean paste)
29	(お)茶漬け	(お)ちゃづけ	N	tea poured over a bowl of rice, eaten with garnishes
30	納豆	なっとう	N	fermented soybeans
31	寿司	すし	N	*sushi*

16課

32. にぎり寿司	にぎりずし	N	*sushi* rice shaped in bite-sized rectangles topped with fish, roe, shellfish, vegetables, egg, etc.
33. ざるそば		N	buckwheat noodle dish
34. 親子丼	おやこどんぶり	N	cooked chicken and egg over a bowl of steamed rice
35. すき焼き	すきやき	N	*sukiyaki*
36. 糸こんにゃく	いとこんにゃく	N	shredded *konnyaku* [grey or transparent tube root gelatin]
37. 卵	たまご	N	egg
38. 生卵	なまたまご	N	raw egg
39. 牛肉	ぎゅうにく	N	beef
40. 豚肉	ぶたにく	N	pork
41. 魚	さかな	N	fish
42. 焼き肉	やきにく	N	meat grilled on a fire
43. 焼き鳥	やきとり	N	grilled skewered chicken
44. 焼き魚	やきざかな	N	grilled fish
45. 煮物	にもの	N	boiled (in broth) foods
46. 酢の物	すのもの	N	vinegared vegetables
47. 漬け物	つけもの	N	pickled vegetables
48. 沢庵	たくあん	N	pickled turnip
49. 豚カツ	とんかつ	N	pork cutlet
50. うどん		N	thick white noodles in broth
51. 肉うどん	にくうどん	N	*udon* topped with beef
52. ハンバーガー		N	hamburger
53. カレーライス		N	curry rice
54. ピザ		N	pizza
55. ラーメン		N	Chinese noodle soup
56. サンドイッチ		N	sandwich
57. パン		N	bread
58. フライドポテト		N	french fries
59. ポテトチップ		N	potato chips
60. サラダ		N	salad
61. 野菜	やさい	N	vegetable
62. 人参	にんじん	N	carrot
63. 竹の子	たけのこ	N	bamboo shoot

16課

64. 果物	くだもの		N	fruit
65. 苺	いちご		N	strawberry
66. 飲み物	のみもの		N	a drink
67. (お)水	(お)みず		N	water
68. お茶	おちゃ		N	(green) tea
69. 抹茶	まっちゃ		N	powdered green tea
70. 紅茶	こうちゃ		N	black tea
71. コーヒー			N	coffee
72. ジュース			N	juice
73. 牛乳	ぎゅうにゅう		N	(cow's) milk
74. ミルク			N	(cow's) milk
75. コーラ			N	cola (drink)
76. (御)酒	(お)さけ		N	rice wine; liquor in general
77. ビール			N	beer
78. デザート			N	dessert
79. おやつ			N	snacks
80. 和菓子	わがし		N	Japanese sweets
81. 煎餅	せんべい		N	Japanese crackers
82. アイスクリーム			N	ice cream
83. チョコレート			N	chocolate
84. 飴	あめ		N	candy
85. キャンディ			N	candy (hard)

16課

| 16課 | ★★★ | 新しい単語 | ★★★ |

1. **どちらかというと＜どちらかと言うと＞**　Exp　if I have to make a choice,
   どちらかと言うと、私は中華料理の方が好きだ。　If I have to make a choice, I like Chinese food better.

2. **ざいりょう＜材料＞**　N　ingredients
   日本料理は季節の材料を使って料理することが大切だ。　When cooking Japanese food, it is important to use seasonal foods as ingredients.

3. **ちょうみりょう＜調味料＞**　N　seasonings; spices
   塩や砂糖などの調味料は、使いすぎない方がいい。　It is better not to use too much of seasonings such as salt and sugar.

4. **ゆうきやさい＜有機野菜＞**　N　organic vegetables
   有機野菜を食べるのは体にいいらしい。　It seems to be better for your body to eat organic vegetables.

5. **しょうみきげん＜賞味期限＞**　N　expiration date
   この食物は賞味期限が切れている。　The expiration date of this food has passed.

6. **えいようがある＜栄養がある＞／あります**　V1　nutritious
   栄養がある物を食べるように。　You should eat things that are nutritious.

7. **インスタントしょくひん＜インスタント食品＞**　N　instant foods
   インスタント食品は便利だけど、健康的じゃないと思う。　I think that although instant foods are convenient, they are not healthy.

8. **れいとうしょくひん＜冷凍食品＞**　N　frozen foods
   冷凍食品でも冷蔵庫に長く置いておかない方がいい。　It is better not to leave even frozen foods in the refrigerator for a long time.

9. **ちゅうかりょうり＜中華料理＞**　N　Chinese food
   中華料理では野菜を生で食べないらしい。　It seems that raw vegetables are not eaten in Chinese cooking.

10. **りょう＜量＞**　N　quantity; amount (↔質 quality)
    アメリカの料理は日本の料理より量が多い。　The quantity (portion size) of food in American cooking is larger than in Japanese food.

11. さいしょくしゅぎしゃ＜菜食主義者＞　N　vegetarian
姉は菜食主義者なので、肉を全然食べない。　Since my older sister is a vegetarian, she does not eat meat at all.

12. えいぎょうじかん＜営業時間＞　N　business hours
このレストランの営業時間は午後５時から１１時までだ。　The business hours for this restaurant are 5:00 p.m. to 11:00 p.m.

13. かいせんりょうり＜海鮮料理＞　N　seafood (dishes)
このレストランの海鮮料理は有名だ。　This restaurant is famous for its seafood.

14. かに＜蟹＞　N　crab
父は蟹が大好きだ。　My dad loves crab.

15. えび＜海老＞　N　shrimp
海老の天ぷらを食べたい。　I want to eat shrimp tenpura.

16. やきめし＜焼き飯＞　N　fried rice
ご飯が残っているから、焼き飯を作ろう。　Since there is leftover rice, let's make fried rice.

17. こんかい＜今回＞　N　this time
日本へ行くのは、今回が初めてだ。　This time is the first time I am going to Japan.

18. にんずう＜人数＞　N　number of people
パーティーに来る人数は何人ぐらいか知っている？　Do you know the number of people coming to the party?

19. おこのみ＜お好み＞　N　liking; preference
お好みの料理は何ですか。　What food is to your liking?

20. せいしき＜正式＞　Na　formal
畳の上に正式に座る時は、正座するはずだ。　When sitting on tatami (straw) mats, you should sit properly (Japanese style).

21. しょっき＜食器＞　N　tableware
日本料理はいろいろなデザインが違う食器を使う。　For (serving) Japanese foods, tableware in various designs is used.

22. わりばし＜割り箸＞　N　wooden (disposable) chopsticks
割り箸を使う時、マナーに気をつけなければならない。　One must be careful with etiquette when using wooden chopsticks.

23. おわん＜お椀＞　N　soup bowl
みそ汁をいただく時、お椀は手に持つはずだ。　When having soup, one should hold the bowl in one's hands.

24. めんるい＜麺類＞　N　noodles
日本の麺類には、そばやうどんなどがある。　Within (the category of) Japanese noodles, there are soba (buckwheat noodles) and udon.

25. そうべつかい＜送別会＞　N　farewell party
来週の土曜日に山田君の送別会をしよう。　Let's have a farewell party for Yamada on Saturday of next week.

26. どうきゅうせい＜同級生＞　N　classmate(s)
私は彼と中学で同級生だった。　In middle school, he and I were classmates.

27. つごう＜都合＞　N　convenience
つごう＜都合＞がいい/わるい＜悪い＞　A　convenient/inconvenient
土曜日の午後はちょっと都合が悪い。　Saturday afternoon will be slightly inconvenient.

28. くわしい＜詳しい＞　A　detailed
くわしく＜詳しく＞　Adv　in detail
誕生日のパーティーについてもっと詳しく教えて下さい。　Please give me more details about the birthday party.

29. しんせん＜新鮮＞　Na　fresh
地元の新鮮な野菜や果物を食べよう。　Let's eat fresh local vegetables and fruits.

30. あきらか＜明らか＞　Na　clear; obvious
あきらかに＜明らかに＞　Adv　clearly; obviously
日本の料理の方がアメリカの料理より量が少ないことは、明らかだ。　It is clear that the quantity (portion size) of Japanese food is less than American food.

31. いまのところ＜今のところ＞　Adv　so far ; as of now
今のところパーティーに来るのは、五人だけだ。　As of now, there are only 5 people who are coming to the party.

32. -めい＜-名＞　Nd　counter for people [formal]
ウェイター：「何名様ですか。」　Waiter: "How many in your party?"

33. ながいき＜長生き＞(を)する／します　V3　to live a long life
日本人は世界で一番長生きをするそうだ。　I understand that Japanese live the longest lives (of all the people) in the world.

16課

34. おとをたてる＜音を立てる＞／立てます　V2　to make noise
　　日本ではそばやうどんを食べる時、音を立ててもいい。　In Japan, it is alright to slurp (make sounds) when eating *soba* and *udon*.

35. わりびき＜割引＞(を)する／します　V3　to discount
　　にわりびき＜二割引＞　N　20% discount
　　たいてい割引のあるお店で買物をする。　I usually shop at stores that have discounts.

【もっと単語】

A. 野菜の名前
1. きゅうり　　　　　　　　　cucumber
2. レタス　　　　　　　　　　lettuce
3. にんじん＜人参＞　　　　　carrots
4. たまねぎ＜玉葱＞　　　　　(round) onion
5. ねぎ＜葱＞　　　　　　　　green onions
6. じゃがいも　　　　　　　　potatoes
7. れんこん　　　　　　　　　lotus root
8. だいこん＜大根＞　　　　　Japanese turnip
9. なす　　　　　　　　　　　eggplant
10. ほうれんそう＜ほうれん草＞　spinach
11. キャベツ　　　　　　　　　cabbage
12. えだまめ＜枝豆＞　　　　　soy beans

B. 果物の名前
1. いちご＜苺＞　　　　　　　strawberry
2. りんご＜林檎＞　　　　　　apple
3. なし＜梨＞　　　　　　　　pear
4. みかん　　　　　　　　　　tangerine orange
5. すいか　　　　　　　　　　watermelon
6. もも＜桃＞　　　　　　　　peach
7. かき＜柿＞　　　　　　　　persimmon
8. バナナ　　　　　　　　　　banana
9. ぶどう　　　　　　　　　　grapes
10. レモン　　　　　　　　　　lemon
11. トマト　　　　　　　　　　tomato
12. メロン　　　　　　　　　　melon

C. すしの材料
1. まぐろ＜鮪＞　　　　　　　tuna
2. いか　　　　　　　　　　　squid
3. たこ　　　　　　　　　　　octopus
4. うなぎ＜鰻＞　　　　　　　eel
5. わさび　　　　　　　　　　horseradish
6. のり　　　　　　　　　　　seaweed

16課 文法(ぶんぽう)

A. Comparison using nouns:

In Japanese, comparative grammatical structures differ according to whether one is comparing nouns or verbs, and also according to the number of things or actions being compared. When comparing verbs, the nominalizer の must be attached to the verb. When comparing three or more objects or actions, or comparing choices in an entire category, one must use the superlative 一番, which is NOT used when comparing two alternatives. The question word used for comparing two things or three or more things is also different. Note the differences in the examples below.

1. 赤と青(と)で、どちら(or どっち)の方が好き？　　Which do you like more, red or blue?
2. 赤の方が、青より好きだ。　　　　　　I like red more than blue.
3. 青は、赤ほど好きじゃない。　　　　　I don't like blue as much as red.
4. 赤と青と白で、何が一番好き？　　　　Among red, blue and white, what do you like best?
5. 色の中で、何が一番好き？　　　　　　Among the colors, what do you like best?

Comparison using verbs:

1. 料理を作るのと、皿(さら)を洗うのと、どちらの方が好き？
   Which do you like better, cooking or washing dishes?
2. 料理を作る方が、皿(さら)を洗う(の)より、好きだ。
   I like cooking more than washing dishes.
3. 皿(さら)を洗うのは、料理を作るほど、好きじゃない。
   I don't like washing dishes as much as cooking.

Circle the correct responses below.

1. a. 世界の料理の中（に　で　と）、（どちら　どれ）が（もっと　一番）好き？
   b. 日本料理と中華(ちゅうか)料理と韓国(かんこく)料理（で　に）、（どちら　どれ）が（もっと　一番）好き？
   c. この中（に　で　と）、日本料理（は　が）（もっと　一番）好きだ。
2. a. 日本料理と中華料理（に　で）、（どっち　どれ）の方が好き？
   b. 日本料理（の　X）方が、中華料理（の　X）より（もっと　一番）好きだ。
   c. 中華料理は、日本料理（の　X）ほど、好き（だ　ではない）。
3. a. レストランで食べる（の　X）と、うちで食べる（の　X）と、（どっち　どれ）の方が好き？
   b. うちで食べる（の　X）方が、レストランで食べる（の　X）より、好きだ。
   c. レストランで食べる（の　X）は、うちで食べる（の　X）ほど、好きではない。

> B. お客が多い/少ない   many/few customers
>
> The adjectives 多い and 少ない do not behave as most い-adjectives do. They do not appear before the noun they modify as い-adjectives, but may appear in other positions, or in the -く form with a の before the noun they modify. See below. When たくさん and 大勢〔おおぜい〕 are used before a noun, they too, should be followed by a の.
>
> X 1. 多い客が来る。
> ○ 2. 客が多い。　　　　　　　　There are many customers.
> ○ 3. 多くの客が来る。　　　　　There are many customers.
> ○ 4. 大勢の客が来る。　　　　　There are many customers.
> ○ 5. 客が大勢来る。　　　　　　There are many customers.

Circle the correct choices.

1. アメリカ料理は（量が多い　多い量だ）。
2. アメリカ料理は（多い　多くの）油を使う。
3. （大勢　大勢の）人が、料理をするのは好きじゃないらしい。
4. おすしには（たくさんの　多い）種類の魚を使う。
5. まだ（少ない　少しの）アメリカ人だけが健康に気をつけている。
6. もっと（多い　多くの）健康食品を食べるようにしたい。
7. 塩は（少し　少ない）だけ食べる方がいいらしい。

> C. 食べる前に、〜　　Before (I) eat, 〜
>
> 　食べた後に/で、〜　After (I) eat, 〜
>
> 　食べながら、〜　　While (I) eat, 〜
>
> 　食べる時に、〜　　When (I) eat, 〜
>
> 　食べてから、　　　(Immediately) after (I) eat,
>
> Note the distinctions above in the forms (dictionary, -た, verb stem, or -て forms) used with each structure and also the differences in meaning.

Circle the correct choices.

1. 日本人は食べ（始める　始め　始めた）前に、「いただきます」と言う。
2. 日本人は食べ（終わる　終わり　終わった）後に、「ごちそうさま」と言う。
3. 日本ではうどんやそばなどの麺類を（食べる　食べ　食べた）時に、音を立ててもいい。
4. 日本では片手で茶碗やお椀を（持つ　持ち　持った）ながら、食べてもいい。
5. お箸を使っていない（前に　後に　時に）、そのお箸を茶碗のご飯に立ててはいけない。
6. 食べる（前に　後に　から）、二本の割り箸をくるくる回してはいけない。
7. 皆が座って（前に　後に　ながら　から）、食事を始める。

16課

16課　アクティビティー

A. 日本文化：一人か二人ワーク→クラスワーク
Divide the topics below among your classmates and research your topic on the Internet. Using visuals, present your findings with your classmates.

1. 丼、うどん、そば
2. 納豆、枝豆、豆腐
3. 酢の物、おでん、煮物、焼き物、盛り合わせ
4. にぎり寿司、巻き寿司

B. 健康な食生活：一人か二人ワーク→クラスワーク
Answer with the response that best promotes a healthy lifestyle.

1. 健康な体のために有機野菜を食べることは（a. いい　b. 悪い）。
2. 私の町にある健康食品のスーパーの名前は（　　　　　　　）だ。
3. 料理の材料は、出来るだけ地元の（a. 新鮮な　b. 古い）野菜などを使う方が健康的だ。
4. 塩などの調味料は、取り過ぎると、（a. 病気　b. 健康）になる。
5. 賞味期限が切れている食物は（a. 食べた方がいい　b. 食べない方がいい）。
6. 栄養のある食物を食べることは体に（a. いい　b. 悪い）。
7. インスタント食品は体に（a. いい　b. 悪い）。
8. 冷凍食品の方が新鮮な食物より体に（a. いい　b. 悪い）。
9. 残り物を捨てるのはもったいない（a. から、全部食べる方が体にいい
   b. が、全部食べるのは体に良くない）。

C. 聞く Pre-Listening Activity「パーティーの食事」：ペアワーク→クラスワーク
With the following questions, initiate a conversation with your partner using the informal style.

1. 世界のいろいろな料理の中で、どこの国の料理が一番好き？そして、その理由は？
2. 中華料理と韓国料理と日本料理で、一番好きなのはどれ？その理由は？
3. レストランを選ぶ時、質と量で、どちらの方が大事？
4. 牛肉と豚肉と鳥肉と魚で、何が一番好き？
5. 辛い料理が好き？
6. 酸っぱい物はどう？塩辛い物は？
7. 甘い物が好き？例えば、どんな物？
8. 菜食主義者はどんな人のこと？
9. この土曜日のお昼、一緒にお昼を食べて映画に行かない？都合はどう？

D. 読む Pre-Reading Activity「レストランガイド」：ペアワーク→クラスワーク

Fill in the ( ) with the letter of a word with a corresponding meaning from the box on the right.

1. 営業時間　（ ）　9. 牛肉　　（ ）
2. 料金　　　（ ）　10. 卵　　　（ ）
3. 個室　　　（ ）　11. そば　　（ ）
4. 駐車場　　（ ）　12. 焼き飯　（ ）
5. 海鮮料理　（ ）　13. 果物　　（ ）
6. かに　　　（ ）　14. 野菜　　（ ）
7. えび　　　（ ）　15. 飲み物　（ ）
8. 魚　　　　（ ）　16. 酒　　　（ ）

a. シーフード	i. チャーハン
b. フィッシュ	j. シュリンプ
c. プライベートルーム	k. フルーツ
d. ビジネスアワー	l. アルコール
e. プライス	m. パーキング
f. ドリンク	n. ビーフ
g. エッグ	o. ベジタブル
h. クラブ	p. ヌードル

E. 読む Post-Reading Activity「日本料理」：ペアワーク→クラスワーク

a. Based on information you are given on the menu, write five observations you can make about Japanese food.

1.) _____
2.) _____
3.) _____
4.) _____
5.) _____

b. Explain your view or perspective about the Japanese food. Why do you think one or more of the characteristics above is true?

_____

日本料理　　あじひな

一品料理		すし	
豆腐	¥ 300	にぎり盛り合わせ	¥ 3,500
納豆	¥ 350	巻きずし	¥ 1,500
枝豆	¥ 400	うどん、そば	
きゅうり酢の物	¥ 450	肉うどん	¥ 800
野菜サラダ	¥ 400	月見うどん	¥ 700
天ぷら盛り合わせ	¥ 1,000	天ぷらうどん	¥ 850
えび天ぷら	¥ 1,000	なべ焼きうどん	¥ 1,200
野菜天ぷら	¥ 700	天ぷらそば	¥ 850
刺身盛り合わせ	¥ 2,000	ざるそば	¥ 700
まぐろ刺身	¥ 2,500	どんぶり	
焼き魚	¥ 1,000	みそ汁・漬物付き	
焼き鳥	¥ 1,000	天丼	¥ 1,500
おでん	¥ 1,000	親子丼	¥ 1,200
鳥照焼き	¥ 800	牛丼	¥ 1,500
野菜煮物	¥ 500	うな丼	¥ 2,000

16課

F. テキストチャット「食事」：ペアワーク→クラスワーク

You will have a conversation about meals with Mrs. Matsushita, who will be your host mother when you stay in Japan this coming summer vacation.

First, read this text chat conversation with your partner. Next, read the questions and your partner will respond without looking at the book. Give original answers to the questions. For each question, answer in 20 seconds. Take turns asking and answering questions.

1. 松下：初めまして。松下です。夏にうちにホームステイするそうですね。どうぞよろしく。

　私　：初めまして。(my full name)と申します。こちらこそ、どうぞよろしくお願いいたします。私は今回日本へ行くのが初めてなので、とても楽しみにしています。これからお世話になります。

2. 松下：毎朝、どんな食事をしているか教えて。

　私　：朝食ですか。朝はだいたいフルーツとシリアルで済ませています。でも、だいたい何でも食べられますから、私のために特別に作らないで下さい。皆さんと同じものを食べてみたいです。

3. 松下：じゃ、夕食はだいたい何を食べているか教えて。

　私　：夕食ですか。そうですねえ、私の家族はいろいろな物を食べています。例えば、ゆうべはスパゲティーでした。そして、その前の日は皆でタイ料理を食べに行きました。でも、私は何でも食べられますから、皆さんが食べている物でいいです。

4. 松下：お肉とお魚と、どちらの方が好きですか。

　私　：肉も魚も両方好きですが、どちらかと言うと、肉の方が好きです。でも、日本のお魚はとても新鮮でおいしいらしいですから、ぜひ、いろいろな物を食べてみたいです。

5. 松下：野菜や果物も好きですか。何か食べられない物がありますか。

　私　：私はピーナッツのアレルギーがあります。ピーナッツを食べると苦しくなるんです。野菜はあまり好きな方ではありませんが、ほかには何でも食べられます。母はいつも野菜を食べなさいと私をしかります。果物は何でも大好きです。

6. 松下：だいたい分かりました。夏に日本で会える日を楽しみにしていますね。何か私達について質問がありますか。

　私　：何かこちらの物でほしい物がありませんか。あったら、ぜひ知らせて下さい。いろいろ私の好きな物を聞いて下さって、有難うございます。今、どきどきわくわくしています。お会いできる日を楽しみにしています。

16課

G. Compare & Contrast 「日本の料理とアメリカの料理」：ペアワーク→クラスワーク

a. First, read this compare and contrast passage with your partner.

> これから日本の料理とアメリカの料理を比べてみます。日本の料理とアメリカの料理は、同じ食物でも、たくさんの違う点があります。
>
> まず、一つ目の違いは、日本の料理はアメリカの料理ほど油を使いません。アメリカ料理は、フライドチキンやフライドポテトなどのように、油をたくさん使う料理が多いです。しかし、日本料理で油料理はてんぷらぐらいです。
>
> そして、二つ目の違いは、日本の料理はアメリカの料理ほど量が多くないです。肉料理を比べると、それは明らかです。アメリカのステーキは本当に大きいですが、日本の焼き肉もすき焼きも、肉はとても薄く切ってあります。
>
> 最後に、三つ目の違いは、日本人はお米を主に食べますが、アメリカ人はポテトやパスタを主に食べます。ご飯はそのまま食べますが、ポテトやパスタはだいたいバターを使ったりして、コレステロールが多いです。
>
> 結論として、私は日本の料理の方がアメリカの料理より好きです。なぜなら、日本の料理の方が健康的で、もっと長生きできそうですから。

b. Next, work with your partner and together compare and contrast Japanese food and American food. List three similarities and/or differences, your preference and the reason for your preference. Give your own opinions. Then, share your presentation with your class.

Introduction:
_____

Three similarities/differences:

1. _____
2. _____
3. _____

Your preference and reasons:
_____
_____

H. 会話「レストランの予約」：ペアワーク→クラスワーク

First, read this conversation with your partner. Next, read the questions and your partner will respond without looking at the book. Repeat the underlined parts and give your own answers to the questions. For each question, answer in 20 seconds. Take turns asking and answering questions. You will have a conversation with Mrs. Kimura, a manager at a restaurant, about plans for your friend's birthday party.

16課

1. 質問： 東京レストランの木村です。毎度有難うございます。
   答(例)： スミスと申します。友達の誕生会をそちらのレストランでしたいと思っているんですが、ちょっと相談にのってください。
2. 質問： 誕生日会についてもう少し詳しく教えて下さい。
   答(例)： はい、会は今月の３０日土曜日のお昼、１２時から２時にしたいんですが、空いていますか。人数は今のところ１２人ぐらいです。
3. 質問： そうですか。食べ物は和食と洋食とどちらにしましょうか。お友達のお好みは？
   答(例)： そうですねえ、皆好みがいろいろ違うから、メニューを見てから、注文してもいいですか。メニューはウェブページにありますよね。
4. 質問： 分かりました。何か値段についてご質問がありますか。
   答(例)： 値段はメニューを見れば分かりますから、大丈夫です。でも、バースデーケーキを持って行ってもいいですか。では、また連絡させて下さい。よろしくお願いします。

I. 文化発表「日本の食事のマナー」：ペアワーク→クラスワーク

a. Mark the following statements about Japanese table manners True or False.

1. (T　F) 西洋料理は食事の時にナプキンを使うが、日本料理の時は使わない。
2. (T　F) 日本料理は西洋料理より食器をたくさん使う。
3. (T　F) 日本人は食べ始める前に「いただきます」と言って、食べ終わった時に「ごちそうさま」と言う。
4. (T　F) 日本人は「いただきます」や「ごちそうさま」と言う時に、少し頭を下げる。
5. (T　F) 畳の上で日本食を食べる時、正式には座布団に正座して食べるはずだ。
6. (T　F) 日本食は、だいたいお箸だけで食べる。
7. (T　F) 食べる前に、割り箸二本を合わせて両手でくるくる回す。
8. (T　F) お箸は、使っていない時に、ご飯に立てる。
9. (T　F) 日本食を食べる時、ご飯の入ったお茶碗やみそ汁の入ったお椀を片手で持ちながら、食べてもいい。
10. (T　F) 日本のうどんやそばなどのめん類を食べる時、音を立てて食べてもいい。

b. Respond to the following questions on Japanese table manners.

1. なぜ日本料理を食べる時に箸を使って、西洋料理を食べる時にナイフ、フォーク、スプーンを使うのだろうか。

　_____

2. なぜ日本のうどんやそばを食べる時に音を立ててもいいのに、西洋料理のスープを飲む時に、静かに飲まなければいけないというマナーがあるのだろうか。

　_____

3. なぜ日本人は食前に「いただきます」と言って、食後に「ごちそうさま」と言うんだろうか。

　_____

4. なぜ日本人は茶碗やお椀を片手で持ちながら、食べるのだろうか。

　_____

5. 食事の時に西洋料理はナプキンを使うのに、日本料理はなぜ使わないのだろうか。

　_____

<16課 - 聞く>

Listening: Party Food

12秒×5

【You may take notes while listening. Do not look at the questions below before listening. You will have 12 seconds to answer each question. You may NOT move back and forth among questions.】

(Narrator) Now you will listen to a conversation once.

(Narrator) Now answer the questions for this selection.

1. When is the party?
   (A) on March 8th
   (B) on Saturday
   (C) at lunch time
   (D) at dinner time

2. Where is the party?
   (A) at a restaurant owned by this student's uncle
   (B) at a restaurant owned by a classmate's father
   (C) at a Chinese restaurant across from the school
   (D) at a Chinese restaurant on the right side of the school

3. What kind of place is this restaurant?
   (A) spacious
   (B) serves large portions
   (C) clean
   (D) expensive

4. What does this teacher NOT eat?
   (A) beef
   (B) fish
   (C) seafood
   (D) spicy food

5. What is the occasion of this party?
   (A) A group of students is planning to have a retirement party for their teacher.
   (B) The whole class is planning a farewell party for their teacher.
   (C) The whole class is planning to have a class party before graduation.
   (D) A group of students is planning to have a class party after graduation.

16課

<16課 - 読む>

Reading: Restaurant Guide

【You may move back and forth among all the questions.】

レストラン東風　国際ホテル内2階　電話：240-0558

新鮮な海鮮と国内産中国野菜をふんだんに使った体にやさしい、あっさりとしたコクのある中華料理

営業時間：11:30〜15:00、17:30〜22:00

席数：テーブル40（個室5）

セットメニュー料金：季節のおすすめコース 3,150円、5,250円、
　　　　　　　　　料理長特選 8,400円

単品メニュー料金：五目焼きそば 940円、
　　　　　　　　カニと卵入りフカヒレスープ 1,200円、
　　　　　　　　えびチャーハン 1,300円

飲物料金：生ビール（中）550円、ビンビール（中）650円、酒 600円、
　　　　　ソフトドリンク（ジュース）330円

定休日：月曜日

カード利用：UC, VISA, JCB, DC 他

駐車場：50台（有料）

＜16課 - 読む (質問)＞

Reading: Restaurant Guide

(Narrator) Now answer the questions for this section.

1. What kind of food is served at this restaurant?
   - (A) Italian
   - (B) French
   - (C) Chinese
   - (D) Japanese

2. What information is correct about this restaurant?
   - (A) It is inside of a hotel.
   - (B) It is on the third floor.
   - (C) It is not open for lunch.
   - (D) It is open from 11:30 a.m. to 10:00 p.m.

3. According to the advertisement, what kind of food does the restaurant NOT serve?
   - (A) fresh seafood
   - (B) domestic vegetables
   - (C) healthy
   - (D) spicy dishes

4. What is NOT correct about the restaurant menu?
   - (A) There are some dishes recommended by the chef.
   - (B) The fried noodles are the cheapest.
   - (C) The fried rice has crab meat in it.
   - (D) They sell soft drinks.

5. What is correct about this restaurant?
   - (A) It has private rooms.
   - (B) It is open every day.
   - (C) The customers must pay in cash only.
   - (D) It has free parking.

<16課 - 書く (テキストチャット)>

Text Chat: Meals

90秒×6

You will participate in a simulated exchange of text-chat messages. Each time it is your turn to write, you will have 90 seconds. You should respond as fully and as appropriately as possible.

You will have a conversation about meals with Mrs. Matsushita, who will be your host mother when you visit Japan this coming summer vacation.

1. Respond. (90 seconds)

   初めまして。松下です。夏にうちにホームステイするそうですね。どうぞよろしく。ちょっと質問があります。

2. Give a specific example. (90 seconds)

   毎朝、どんな食事をしているか教えて。

3. Respond and describe. (90 seconds)

   じゃ、夕食はだいたい何を食べているか教えて。

4. Explain your preference. (90 seconds)

   お肉とお魚と、どちらの方が好きですか。

5. Respond. (90 seconds)

   野菜や果物も好きですか。何か食べられない物がありますか。

6. Ask a specific question and greet. (90 seconds)

   だいたい分かりました。夏に日本で会える日を楽しみにしていますね。何か私達について質問がありますか。

<16課 - 書く (比較と対比)>

Compare and Contrast: Japanese Food and American Food

20分

Directions: You are writing an article for the student newspaper of your sister school in Japan. Write an article in which you compare and contrast similarities and differences between Japanese food and American food. Based on your personal experience, describe at least THREE aspects of each and highlight the similarities and differences between Japanese food and American food. Also state your preference for either and give reasons for it.

Your article should be 300 to 400 characters or longer. Use the *desu/masu* or *da* (plain) style, but use one style consistently. Also, use *kanji* wherever *kanji* from the AP Japanese *kanji* list is appropriate. You have 20 minutes to write

【NOTES/OUTLINE: 自分の作文のアウトラインを書こう！】

Introduction:
_____

Three similarities/differences:

   1._____
   2._____
   3._____

Your preference and give reasons:
_____
_____

16課

＜16課 - 話す (会話)＞
Conversation: Restaurant Reservations

20秒×4

You will participate in a simulated conversation. Each time it is your turn to speak, you will have 20 seconds to record. You should respond as fully and as appropriately as possible.

You will have a conversation with Mrs. Kimura, a manager at a restaurant, about plans for your friend's birthday party.

(Female)
(20 seconds)
(Female)
(20 seconds)
(Female)
(20 seconds)
(Female)
(20 seconds)

＜16課 - 話す (日本文化)＞
Cultural Perspective Presentation: Table Manners in Japan

4分+2分

Directions: Imagine you are making an oral presentation to your Japanese class. First, you will read and hear the topic for your presentation. You will have 4 minutes to prepare your presentation. Then you will have 2 minutes to record your presentation. Your presentation should be as complete as possible.

Present your own view or perspective of table manners in Japan. Discuss at least FIVE aspects or examples of table manners in Japan.

Begin with an appropriate introduction, give details, explain your own view or perspective, and end with a concluding remark.

【Let's take notes!】

1. Begin with an appropriate introduction.
   _____

2. Discuss five aspects/examples of the topic.
   1.) _____
   2.) _____
   3.) _____
   4.) _____
   5.) _____

3. Explain your view or perspective.
   _____

4. End with a concluding remark.
   _____

| 17課 | | 買物 | |

Shopping

【AP® タスク：買物】

Discuss three differences between Japanese department stores and American department stores and give your opinions and preferences regarding various differences.

【文化】 日本のデパート：Japanese Department Stores

Japanese department stores are a microcosm of the contemporary Japanese lifestyle, as they uphold many cherished Japanese traditions while keeping up with some of the most modern trends. Some of the unique features of Japanese department stores combine both aspects as the stores attempt to maintain customer service at its best, even in challenging economic times.

One of the most noticeable features of Japanese department stores is their remarkable customer service. Clerks are always available, and display the utmost politeness in manner and language. Store employees are always dressed in crisp uniforms, so they are easily identifiable by customers who need assistance. At the beginning of each work day, clerks swing open the doors of the department store, and a line of uniformly dressed employees greets the first customers of the day. Elevator girls may ride up and down elevators all day in their uniforms and white gloves. They control the elevator buttons, hold open doors and announce each stop and the items sold on each of the floors. Although not present at most department stores these days, some also have uniform clad escalator girls who stand at the bottom of escalators. Their job is to remind customers to step carefully onto the escalators.

Another aspect of customer service is wrapping. Japanese clerks wrap gifts efficiently and with precision in special wrapping paper designed for the department store. They use very little paper when wrapping, as they are wrapped diagonally. Very little tape is used to hold the paper together. All purchases are wrapped, whether they are purchased as gifts or not. All wrapping is done at the sales counter while the customer waits.

The basement houses several floors of groceries and prepared foods. Since many department stores are located near train stations, these floors are convenient stops for working commuters to purchase their dinners or ingredients to prepare dinners. Some types of foods sold here are traditional Japanese dishes, sushi, cooked rice, main dishes, pickled vegetables, salads, side dishes, baked goods, Japanese and Western sweets, and juices.

The top floors of department stores offer a diverse variety of dining options, with restaurants featuring cafeteria style dining to classier dining. There is almost always at least a choice of Japanese food, Chinese food and Western food. Most large department stores offer a wide variety of food selections from all parts of the world.

For the convenience of young families, some major department stores have playgrounds on the rooftops of the department stores. This offers children and mothers a perfect recreational and rest spot during the day. It is common to see children having snacks or *bento* at this location. There are also nurseries for infants where diaper changing or feeding is accommodated.

Department stores also offer those who enjoy the arts many opportunities. Special art or craft exhibits are often shown in the galleries that occupy the upper floors of most department stores. Tickets to concerts, theater productions and other art shows are sold at ticket outlets in the department stores.

Other services at department stores include areas where foreign currency can be exchanged and travel reservations may be arranged.

Although the popularity of department stores has declined in recent years, they still serve as pillars against which all shopping experiences are measured in Japan.

Questions to ponder: Why is customer service of utmost importance to the Japanese? What might apanese find lacking as they shop in stores abroad? Why might there be a decline in department store popularity in recent years?

| 17課 | | 復習単語 | |

トピック：買物

1. スーパー		N	supermarket
2. コンビニ		N	convenience store
3. レジ		N	cash register
4. セール(中)	セール(ちゅう)	N	(on) sale
5. 店員	てんいん	N	store clerk
6. 客	きゃく	N	customer; guest
7. 御客様	おきゃくさま	N	customer; guest [polite]
8. (御)値段	(お)ねだん	N	price
9. お釣	おつり	N	change (from a larger unit of money)
10. 税金	ぜいきん	N	tax
11. 案内所	あんないじょ	N	information booth

| 17課 | ★★★ | 新しい単語 (たん) | ★★★ |

1. **ねえねえ**　Exp　Say; Hey; Look... [informal]
「ねえねえ、明日一緒に映画を見に行かない？」 "Say, won't to come with me to see a movie tomorrow?"

2. **な〜んだ**　Exp　What!?! [informal]
「試験は今日じゃないの？な〜んだ。」 "The test is not today? What!?!"

3. **ばかみたい**　Exp　It is so stupid! [informal]
「試験は今日じゃないの？一生懸命勉強したのに。ばかみたい。」 "The test is not today? I studied so hard for it! I'm so stupid!"

4. **やっきょく＜薬局＞**　N　pharmacy
薬局にアスピリンを買いに行く。 I am going to the pharmacy to buy some aspirin.

5. **デパちか＜デパ地下＞**　N　department store basement
デパ地下に寄って、今晩のおかずを買う。 I will stop by the department store basement and buy some side dishes for tonight's dinner.

6. **けしょうしつ＜化粧室＞**　N　restroom [lit. powder room]
「ちょっと化粧室へ行って来るね。」 "I will go to the restroom for a little while."

7. **しょくりょうひんうりば＜食料品売り場＞**　N　grocery section (of a store)
デパ地下はデパートの地下にある食料品売り場だ。 The department store basement is where the grocery/food section is.

8. **おくじょう＜屋上＞**　N　rooftop
日本のデパートの屋上にたいてい遊び場がある。 There is usually a play area on the rooftops of Japanese department stores.

9. **しなもの＜品物＞**　N　goods
デパートの品物の種類は多い。 There is a large variety of goods at department stores.

10. **だいどころようひん＜台所用品＞**　N　kitchenware
デパートにはいろいろなおもしろい台所用品がある。 There are various interesting kinds of kitchenware in department stores.

11. **おもちゃ**　N　toy
子供はおもちゃ売り場へ行くと、帰りたがらない。 When children go to the toy section (of a store), they don't want to leave.

12. わがし＜和菓子＞　N　Japanese sweets
　　ようがし＜洋菓子＞　N　Western sweets
　　和菓子にはおいしさだけでなく、季節や自然の美しさもある。　Japanese sweets are not only delicious, they also possess the beauty of the seasons and of nature.

13. ふじんふく＜婦人服＞　N　women's wear
　　しんしふく＜紳士服＞　N　men's wear
　　デパートには婦人服の売り場は多いのに、紳士服の売り場は少ししかない。　Department stores have many women's wear sections, but only have a limited amount of men's wear sections.

14. ししょく＜試食＞　N　food samples
　　デパ地下の食料品売り場ではたいてい試食させてくれる。　You are usually allowed to sample foods in the food section of the department store basement.

15. びじゅつてん＜美術展＞　N　art exhibition
　　デパートではいろいろな美術展も開催されている。　There are also various kinds of art shows on exhibit at the department stores.

16. たっきゅうびん＜宅急便＞　N　home delivery service
　　お中元やお歳暮などの贈り物をデパートから宅急便で送ってもらうことが出来る。　You are able to request delivery of mid-year and end-of-the-year gifts through the home delivery service at the department stores.

17. るすばんでんわ＜留守番電話＞　N　voice mail [also known as 留守電]
　　母に電話しても、たいてい電話に出ないので、留守番電話にメッセージを残しておく。　Even if I call my mother, she usually does not answer, so I leave a message on her voice mail.

18. (お)こづかい＜(お)小遣い＞　N　allowance ; spending money
　　両親はお小遣いを少ししかくれない。　My parents only give me a little allowance.

19. クレジットカード　N　credit card
　　クレジットカードは便利だが、使いすぎてしまうのがこわい。　Credit cards are convenient but it is scary when they are overused.

20. かいぎ＜会議＞　N　conference; meeting
　　大事な会議があるので、出席しなければならない。　Since there is an important conference, I have to attend.

21. ちょうしょ＜長所＞　N　good point; strong point; advantage
　　ネットの買物の長所はいつでもうちから買物出来ることだろう。　The advantage of shopping on the Internet is that you can shop anytime from home.

22. たんしょ＜短所＞　N　weak point; disadvantage
  父の短所はすぐおこることだ。　My father's weakness is that he becomes upset easily.
23. よなか＜夜中＞　N　midnight
  ネットでは夜中でも買物が出来る。　You can even shop at midnight on the Internet.
24. うまく　Adv　skillfully [informal]
  うまい　A　tasty; skillful [informal]
  ネットでの買物もお店での買物も両方うまく使うことが大事だ。　It is important to shop skillfully both on the Internet and in stores.
25. たりる＜足りる＞／足ります　V2　to be enough; sufficient
  お金が足りない。　I don't have enough money.
26. てにとってみる＜手に取って見る＞／手に取って見ます　V2　to take in one's hand; to touch
  ネットの買物は品物を手に取って見ることが出来ない。　When shopping on the Internet, one cannot take it (the item) in one's hand and look at it.
27. ためす＜試す＞／試します　V1　to try out; to test out
  新しいコンピューターを試してみたい。　I want to to try out the new computer.
28. あきれる＜呆れる＞／呆れます　V2　to be surprised [negative meaning]; to be shocked
  私がたくさん買物して帰った時、親は私に呆れていた。　When I came home with all of my shopping, my parents were shocked.
29. ほうそう＜包装＞(を)する／します　V3　to wrap
  ほうそうし＜包装紙＞　N　wrapping paper
  デパートの店員はとても速く美しく包装してくれる。　The department store clerk wraps (the gift) very quickly and beautifully for me.
30. したく＜支度＞(を)する／します　V3　to make preparations (for a meal, for an outing, etc.)
  夕食の支度に間に合わない。　We will not have time to make preparations for dinner.
31. メモをとる＜取る＞／取ります　V3　to take notes
  「メモを取って下さい。」　"Please take notes."

【もっと単語】
1. にわりびき＜２割引＞　　　　　　　　　　N　20% off (discount)
2. はんがくセール＜半額セール＞　　　　　　N　half price sale

17課

3. あんないしょ＜案内所＞	N	information booth; information desk
4. えいぎょうじかん＜営業時間＞	N	business hours
5. ねんじゅうむきゅう＜年中無休＞	N	open all year round
6. しゅげい＜手芸＞	N	handicrafts
7. ぶっさんてん＜物産展＞	N	product fair
8. ごふく＜呉服＞	N	*kimono*
9. しんぐ＜寝具＞	N	bedding
10. ふじんはだぎ＜婦人肌着＞	N	women's lingerie [formal]
11. ふじんぐつ＜婦人靴＞	N	women's shoes
12. こもの＜小物＞	N	accessories; belongings
13. おかず	N	side dish
14. いちば＜市場＞	N	market; marketplace
15. つけもの＜漬物＞	N	pickles
16. れんらくつうろ＜連絡通路＞	N	access road
17. はくさい＜白菜＞	N	Chinese cabbage
18. なましいたけ＜生椎茸＞	N	fresh mushroom

17課　文法

A. あればあるほど、いい　　the more ～, the better

This sentence structure is used to express " the more... the more/better....: The verb, いadjective or なadjective in the first position appears in the －ば form, followed by the plain form (+な after な-adjectives) of the same word + ほど and the concluding remark.

1. 練習<u>すればするほど</u>、上手になる。　　The more you practice, the more skillful you will be.
2. 物は<u>安ければ安いほど</u>、いい。　　The cheaper goods are, the better.
3. 字は<u>きれいならきれいなほど</u>、いい。　The neater the writing, the better.

Fill in the blanks with the correct BA form and circle the correct particle in the (　).

1. 日本語は、＿＿＿＿＿＿＿＿話す（の　な　X）ほど、上手になる。
2. 漢字が＿＿＿＿＿＿＿＿読める（の　な　X）ほど、新聞が分かる。
3. 物が＿＿＿＿＿＿＿＿高い（の　な　X）ほど、人はもっと安い物をさがす。
4. 野菜や果物は＿＿＿＿＿＿＿＿新鮮（の　な　X）ほど、おいしい。
5. レストランは料理が＿＿＿＿＿＿＿＿おいしい（の　な　X）ほど、お客が増える。
6. ＿＿＿＿＿＿＿＿食べる（の　な　X）ほど、太るから、あまり食べないようにしている。

B. もし千ドルもらったら、～　　If I received $1,000, ～

The conditional -たら forms of verbs, いadjectives and なadjectives and nouns are usually translated as "If...", but can sometimes be translated as "when...". The main clause following -たら is usually a statement that is personal in nature.

1. もし日本に留学<u>出来たら</u>、～。　　If I could study in Japan, ～.
2. もし服がとても<u>安かったら</u>、～。　　If the clothing is very cheap, ～.
3. もし彼女がとても<u>上手だったら</u>、～。　If she was very skillful, ～.
4. もし私が<u>医者だったら</u>、～。　　If I was a doctor, ～.

Fill in each blank with the correct form of the cue given in the (　).

1. もし誰かが千ドル＿＿＿＿＿＿＿＿、どうしようかなあ。（くれる）
2. もし大学の奨学金が＿＿＿＿＿＿＿＿、私は大学に行けない。（もらえない）
3. もしこのテレビが三割引＿＿＿＿＿＿＿＿、絶対に買う。（だ）
4. もしもっと背が＿＿＿＿＿＿＿＿、バスケットをしていたかも知れない。（高い）
5. もしクレジットカードを＿＿＿＿＿＿＿＿、すぐ銀行に知らせるはずだ。（なくす）

> C. 店が<u>開いて</u>いる　　　The store is open.
> This sentence structure is used to describe a state. A verb given in the て form is always followed by some form of いる. The subject of the intransitive sentence is almost always followed by the particle が.
>
> a. Intransitive verbs:　　　　　　　Transitive verbs:
>
> 1. ドアが<u>開く</u>。　　The door opens.　　　1. ドアを<u>開ける</u>。　　I will open the door.
> 2. ドアが<u>閉まる</u>。　The door closes.　　　2. ドアを<u>閉める</u>。　I will close the door.
> 3. 電気が<u>つく</u>。　　The lights turn on.　　3. テレビを<u>つける</u>。　I will turn on the TV.
> 4. 電気が<u>消える</u>。　The lights turn off.　　4. テレビを<u>消す</u>。　　I will turn off the TV.
> 5. 車が<u>壊れる</u>。　　The car breaks.　　　　5. 車を<u>壊す</u>。　　　I will damage the car.
>
> b. Intransitive verb + いる　　　　Transitive verb + いる
>
> 1. テレビが<u>ついている</u>。The TV is on.　　1. テレビを<u>つけている</u>。He/she is turning on the TV.
> 2. テレビが<u>消えている</u>。The TV is off.　2. テレビを<u>消している</u>。He/she is turning off the TV.

Circle the correct verb in the (　).

1. 午後九時に買物に行ったら、お店は（閉めて　閉まって）いた。
2. この時計は買ったばかりなのに、（壊して　壊れて）いるようだ。
3. ネットのお店は２４時間（開けて　開いて）いるので、とても便利だ。
4. このお店は電気が（つけて　ついて）いるから、入ってみよう。
5. このお店の電気はもう（消えて　消して）いるから、また明日来てみよう。

> D. 帰ろうとしたら、〜　　　When I was about to go home, 〜
> To express that something occurred at the moment when one was about to do something else, one uses this sentence structure. The action that one was about to do appears in the verb OO form. It is followed by とした and an extension.
>
> a. Verb OO form
>
>   Group 1 verbs: 行く→行<u>こう</u>、送る→送<u>ろう</u>、買う→買<u>おう</u>
>
>   Group 2 verbs: 食べる→食べ<u>よう</u>
>
>   Group 3 verbs: 買物(を)する→買物(を)<u>しよう</u>
>
> b. Verb OO form + とする
>
> 1. <u>帰ろう</u>としたところだった。　　　　　I was about to go home.
> 2. <u>出かけよう</u>とした時、友達が来た。　　When I was about to leave, my friend came.
> 3. <u>寝よう</u>としたら、電話がかかって来た。When I was about to sleep, the telephone rang.

Fill in each blank with the correct form of the cue in the (　).

1. お金を＿＿＿＿＿＿＿＿としたら、お金を持っていないことに気がついた。（払う）

17課

2. どろぼうが車を＿＿＿＿＿＿＿としていたところを見た。（盗む）
3. 車を＿＿＿＿＿＿＿としたら、エンジンがかからなかった。（運転する）
4. エレベーターに＿＿＿＿＿＿＿とした時に、ばったり昔の友達に会った。（乗る）
5. 今テレビを＿＿＿＿＿＿＿としたところだ。（見る）

E. 店員にさがしてもらう　　I will have the store clerk find it.

This sentence structure is used when the subject requests, or wishes for someone (indirect object) to do something for the subject. When the subject is equal or lower in status than the indirect object, the verb もらう is used as the extender. If the indirect object is superior in status, the verb いただく is used instead.

1. 両親に車を買ってもらいたい。　　I want my parents to buy a car for me.
2. 先生に推薦状を書いていただいた。　　I asked my teacher to write a recommendation for me.

Fill in each blank with the correct form of the verb cue in the ( ), then circle the correct verb in the [ ].

1. 昨日、友達に５ドル＿＿＿＿＿＿＿［もらった　いただいた］。（貸す）
2. 母に新しい服を＿＿＿＿＿＿＿［もらいたい　いただきたい］。（買う）
3. お中元をデパートから宅急便で＿＿＿＿＿＿＿［もらえる　いただける］。（送る）
4. 店員：「すみませんが、証明書を＿＿＿＿＿＿＿［もらえませんか　いただけませんか。］」（見せる）

F. 親におこられた　　I was scolded by my parents.

The passive construction is a commonly used form in Japanese. The subject is the object or person to which the action has been committed, while the indirect object is the causer of the action.

a. Verb Passive form

　Group 1 verbs: 売る→売られる、書く→書かれる、言う→言われる

　Group 2 verbs: 見る→見られる

　Group 3 verbs: 相談(を)する→相談(を)される、来る→来られる

b. Passive sentence

1. お金が盗まれた。　　　　　　　My money was stolen.
2. さいふはどろぼうに盗まれた。　　My wallet was stolen by a thief.
3. 兄はどろぼうに車を盗まれた。　　My older brother had his car stolen by a thief.
4. 母は父に死なれて、苦労した。　　After my father died my mother suffered.

Fill in the [ ] with the correct particle and write the passive form of the verb cues in the blanks.

1. 僕はショッピングセンターで車［　］＿＿＿＿＿＿＿。（盗む）
2. 悪い成績を見せたら、すごく親［　］＿＿＿＿＿＿＿。（しかる）

17課

17課　アクティビティー

A. 日本文化：一人か二人ワーク→クラスワーク

Divide the following words among the students in your class and research the topics on the Internet. Report your findings to your class using visuals.

1. デパ地下、試食（ししょく）
2. 包装（ほうそう）
3. デパートの店員、サービス
4. 物産展（ぶっさんてん）
5. 宅急便（たっきゅうびん）

B. 聞く Pre-Listening Activity「留守番電話」：ペアワーク→クラスワーク

The following telephone conversations are between a family member at home and a family member on his/her way home. Fill in the blanks with the correct answer from the box.

1. 「ちょっと帰りに、すき焼（や）きの材料（ざい）を買って来てくれない？」
   「今日デパートへ行くから、＿＿＿＿＿＿に寄って買って来るね。」

2. 「ちょっと熱（ねつ）があるから、アスピリンを買って来てくれない？」
   「大丈夫（じょうぶ）？じゃ、＿＿＿＿＿＿に寄（よ）って買って来るね。」

3. 「ねえねえ、野菜のセールがあるはずだから、帰りに、サラダの材料（ざい）、買って来て。」
   「うちの近くの＿＿＿＿＿＿だよね。分かった。」

4. 「明日の朝食べるパンがないんだけど、帰りに買って来て。」
   「分かった。駅の近くの＿＿＿＿＿＿だね。あの店、高いけどおいしいよね。」

5. 「コンピューターのインクがなくなっちゃったんだ。帰りに買って来てくれないかな。」
   「それなら、＿＿＿＿＿＿のコンピューターのコーナーに行くと、売っているね。」

> パン屋
> 電気屋
> 薬局（やっきょく）
> スーパー
> デパ地下

C. 聞く Post-Listening Activity「留守番電話」：ペアワーク→クラスワーク

Compare and Contrast Article: Supermarket and Convenience Store

Compare and contrast supermarkets and convenience stores. List three differences or similarities, your preference and the reason for your choice.

Introduction:
_____

Three similarities/differences:

1. _____
2. _____
3. _____

Your preference and give reasons:
_____
_____

D. 読む Pre-Reading Activity「日本のデパート案内」：ペアワーク→クラスワーク

Circle the choices that are not found in American department stores.

a. レストラン	d. 宝石(ほう)	g. 化粧品(しょうひん)	j. 化粧室(しょう)	m. 婦人服(ふふく)
b. 酒(さけ)	e. 喫茶店(きっ)	h. 遊び場(あそ)	k. 工芸品(こうげいひん)	n. ビューティーサロン
c. 台所用品(ようひん)	f. ペット	i. おもちゃ	l. 和菓子(が)	o. ベーカリー

E. 読む Post-Reading Activity「日本のデパート案内」：ペアワーク→クラスワーク

Compare and Contrast Article: Department Stores in Japan and the U.S.

Compare and contrast department stores in Japan and the U.S. List three similarities and/or differences, your preference and the reason for your choice.

Introduction:
_____

Three similarities/differences:

1. _____
2. _____
3. _____

Your preference and give reasons:
_____
_____

F. テキストチャット「お小遣い〔おこづかい〕」：ペアワーク→クラスワーク

You will have a conversation about spending money with Kazuki Tamura, a student at a Japanese school. First, read this text chat conversation with your partner. Next, read the questions and your partner will respond without looking at the book. Give your own answers to the questions. For each question, use 20 seconds to answer. Take turns asking and answering questions.

1. 田村：こんにちは。今、お小遣(づか)いについて調(しら)べています。御協力(ごきょうりょく)よろしくお願(ねが)いします。

   私　：こんにちは。はい、協力(きょうりょく)しますので、何でも聞いて下さい。お小遣(づか)いは、おもしろそうなテーマですね。

2. 田村：お小遣(づか)いは一か月にいくらぐらいもらっていますか。それで十分ですか。

   私　：私はお小遣いを一か月に５０ドルもらっていますが、全然(ぜん)足りません。もちろんもっとほしいけど、両親(りょうしん)はだめだと言います。アルバイトをしようと思って

17課

います。

3. 田村：だいたいお小遣いを何に使っていますか。
   私　：そうですねえ。映画とか食事とかシャツとかに使っています。でも、靴とかもっと高い物は両親が払ってくれています。

4. 田村：もし今千ドルもらったら、貯金しますか。それとも、ほしい物を買いますか。
   私　：千ドルですか。すごいですねえ。誰もそんな大金を私にくれませんよ。でも、もし、誰かが私に千ドルくれたら、まず今ほしい物を買って、残りを貯金します。自分の車がほしいんです。

5. 田村：貯金することは大事だと思いますか。なぜですか。
   私　：はい、貯金は大事だと思います。大学の授業料は高いし、自分の車もほしいし、お金がなければ、何も出来ません。お金があればあるほど、生活は楽になると思います。

6. 田村：御協力有難うございました。僕達のお金の使い方について何か質問がありますか。
   私　：一つ質問があります。日本の高校生はだいたい一か月にいくらぐらいお小遣いをもらっているんですか。楽しいチャットを有難うございました。またしましょう。

G. Compare & Contrast「ネットの買物とお店の買物」：ペアワーク→クラスワーク

a. First, read this compare and contrast passage with your partner.

　　これからネットの買物とお店の買物を比べてみます。両方とも買物ですが、良いところも悪いところもあります。三つの違いについて述べます。

　　まず一つ目の違いは、ネットの買物はうちでひまな時に出来るのに、お店の買物はお店が開いている時だけ出来ます。ネットでは夜中でも買物が出来ます。一年中、２４時間開いているお店です。しかし、お店はだいたい午前１０ごろに開いて、平日は９時ごろに閉まります。日曜日は４時ごろに閉めてしまいます。

　　次に二つ目の違いは、ネットの買物はクレジットカードで払いますが、お店ではクレジットカードや現金で払います。クレジットカードをネットで使うのは、時々問題があります。ネットの買物では買う人の顔を見ないので、だれか悪い人がほかの人の情報を使って買物をする問題が起きます。

　　最後に三つ目の違いは、お店では品物を手に取って見ることが出来ますが、ネットの買物は品物を手に取って見ることが出来ません。服などは試着が出来なければ、自分の体に本当に合っているかどうか分かりません。

　　結論として、私はネットの買物もお店の買物も両方うまく使うことが大事だと思いま

17課

す。両方に長所と短所があります。私はチケットや音楽や本などのよく知っている物はネットで買って、服や靴などの試してみないと分からない物はお店で買います。

b. Next, work with your partner and together compare and contrast Japanese food and American food. List three similarities and/or differences, your preference and the reason for your preference. Give your own opinions. Then, share your presentation with your class.

Introduction:
_____

Three similarities/differences:
1. _____
2. _____
3. _____

Your preference and reasons:
_____
_____

H. 会話「買物」：ペアワーク→クラスワーク

You will have a conversation with Akira, your Japanese friend, about yesterday's shopping experience. First, read this conversation with your partner. Next, read the questions and your partner will respond without looking at the book. Repeat the underlined sections and give your own answers to the questions. For each question, answer within 20 seconds. Take turns asking and answering questions.

1. あきら　　：ちょっと聞いて。昨日、買物に行って、大変なことがあったんだ。
　 私(男/女)：ええっ、どんな大変なこと？さいふを落としたとか、盗まれたとか？

2. あきら　　：ショッピングセンターで買物をした後で、帰ろうとしたら、車が見つからなかったんだ。
　 私(男/女)：へえ〜。どうして？車を盗まれたとか？すぐ警察を呼んだ？

3. あきら　　：セキュリティーの人に電話をして探してもらったら、2階だと思ったのに1階にあったんだよ。
　 私(男)　　：な〜んだ。ばかみたい。頭、大丈夫？まだ若いのに、何でそんな間違いをするのか、僕には分からないよ。
　 私(女)　　：な〜んだ。ばかみたい。頭、大丈夫？まだ若いのに、何でそんな間違いをするのか、私には分からないよ。

4. あきら　　：うちに帰って親に話したら、すごくおこられたよ。こんな経験ない？
　 私(男)　　：もちろん、ないよ。親も君にあきれてたんじゃない？もう車を貸してくれないよ。僕はそんなばかなこと、絶対にしないね。
　 私(女)　　：もちろん、ないわよ。親もあなたにあきれてたんじゃない？もう車を

17課

貸してくれない<u>わ</u>よ。<u>私</u>はそんなばかなこと、絶対にしないね。

I. 文化発表「日本のデパート」：ペアワーク→クラスワーク

a. Circle True or False based on your opinions.

1. (T　F) 日本のデパートの店員は包装が速くて上手だ。
2. (T　F) 日本のデパートの店員はとても丁寧だ。
3. (T　F) 日本のデパートは食料品売り場が地下にあって試食出来る。
4. (T　F) 日本のデパートは品物の種類が豊富だ。
5. (T　F) 日本のデパートは子供が遊ぶ所が屋上にあって、家族で楽しめる。
6. (T　F) 日本のデパートにはレストランや喫茶店があって楽しい。
7. (T　F) 日本のデパートには美術展や催し物があって、楽しめる。
8. (T　F) 日本のデパートから宅急便で贈り物を送ってもらうことが出来る。

b. Answer the questions about Japanese department stores.

1. なぜ日本のデパートでカスタマーサービスが大事なのでしょうか。
　_____

2. 日本のデパートは、なぜアメリカのデパートより大きいのでしょうか。
　_____

3. 最近、日本のデパートは以前のように客が来なくなりました。なぜでしょうか。
　_____

17課

<17課 - 聞く>
Listening: Telephone Message

12秒×5

【You may take notes while listening. Do not look at the questions below before listening. You will have 12 seconds to answer each question. You may NOT move back and forth among questions.】

(Narrator) Now you will listen to a telephone message twice.

(Narrator) Now answer the questions for this selection.

1. Why did this person leave this message?
    (A) to ask the other person to shop for a takeout dinner
    (B) to ask the other person to shop for groceries for dinner
    (C) to ask the other person to cook dinner
    (D) to ask the other person to cook rice

2. Why will this person be late for dinner?
    (A) Her friends wanted to consult with her immediately.
    (B) She was called to an urgent conference.
    (C) She was requested to replace her co-worker on the night shift.
    (D) She wanted to finish her work at the company.

3. What did she NOT ask the other person to buy?
    (A) beef
    (B) eggs
    (C) vegetables for salad
    (D) mushrooms

4. Where does she suggest that the other person go to shop?
    (A) at the supermarket
    (B) at the grocery store
    (C) at the department store
    (D) at the convenience store

5. What is the relationship between the caller and the person who received this call?
    (A) a married couple who support one another
    (B) a mother and her daughter who support one another
    (C) a married couple who do not support one another
    (D) a mother and her daughter who do not support one another

17課

<17課 - 読む>
Reading: Department Store
【You may move back and forth among all the questions.】

あじひなデパート　全館のご案内　■営業時間　午前10時〜午後8時　年中無休
　　　　　　　　　　　　　　　　■10階レストラン街営業時間　午前11時〜午後10時

アイコン		階	フロア	設備
☎	公衆電話	R	屋上プレイランド	🚻
🚻	化粧室	10階	レストラン街	☎ 🚻 👩 ♿ 👶 👨‍👩 💺
👩	婦人用化粧室	9階	手芸/ペット/ビューティー&ヘルシー/京都物産展/贈り物コーナー	☎ 🚻 💺
👨	紳士用化粧室	8階	宝石/時計/メガネ/美術/工芸品/呉服/旅行サロン	☎ 🚻 💺
👨‍👩‍👧	家族用化粧室	7階	インテリア用品（食器・台所用品・寝具・タオルほか）ギフトサロン　ブライダルサロン	🚻 💺
♿	車いす用化粧室	6階	ベビー洋品・こども服　おもちゃ	☎ 🚻 👩 ♿ 👶 👨‍👩 💺
👨‍👩	ベビーキープ付き化粧室	5階	婦人服（ミセス）/エレガンスサロン/サイズ/フォーマル	👩 💺 ☕
👶	ベビーベッド	4階	婦人服（ミッシー・ミセス）/婦人肌着/ナイティー	☎ 👩 💺 ☕
🚼	ベビーカー貸し出し	3階	バスセンター	🚌 👩
ℹ	総合案内所	2階	婦人靴・婦人服（ミッシーカジュアル）	☎ 👩 ℹ 🚼 💺 ☕
💺	休憩所	1階 正面入口	化粧品/洋品小物/ハンドバッグ/商品券	☎ 👨 👶 ℹ 🚼 💺 ☕
☕	喫茶	B1階	和菓子/洋菓子/酒/茶	☎ 👨 💺 ☕
🚌	バスのりば	B2階	おかず市場/漬物/ベーカリー	☎ 👨 👩

← 地下街連絡通路

<17課 - 読む (質問)>

Reading: Department Store

(Narrator) Now answer the questions for this section.

1. When is the department store open?
   (A)   The department is closed every Monday.
   (B)   The whole store is open from 10:00 a.m. to 8:00 p.m.
   (C)   The restaurant floor is open from 10:00 a.m. to 8:00 p.m.
   (D)   The restaurant floor is open from 11:00 a.m. to 10:00 p.m.

2. What floor sells Japanese sweets?
   (A)   1st basement floor
   (B)   2nd basement floor
   (C)   9th floor
   (D)   10th floor

3. Which floor should you go to for children's clothing?
   (A)   1st floor
   (B)   6th floor
   (C)   7th floor
   (D)   8th floor

4. Which information is NOT correct about the department store?
   (A)   There is a bus station on the 3rd floor.
   (B)   You can go to the underground shopping mall from the 1st basement floor.
   (C)   You can find a coffee shop on the 6th floor.
   (D)   You can find a men's bathroom on the 4th and 5th floor.

5. Which information is correct about the department store?
   (A)   There is more than one floor of women's clothing.
   (B) ˙ There is a product fair on the 8th floor.
   (C)   There is a playground on the top floor.
   (D)   There is a restroom for handicapped people on every floor.

<17課 - 書く (テキストチャット)>

`90秒×6`

Text Chat: Spending Money

You will participate in a simulated exchange of text-chat messages. Each time it is your turn to write, you will have 90 seconds. You should respond as fully and as appropriately as possible.

You will have a conversation about spending money with Kazuki Tamura, a student at your sister school who is doing some research on American high school students.

1. Respond. (90 seconds)
   こんにちは。今、お小遣いについて調べています。御協力よろしくお願いします。
2. Give a specific example and respond. (90 seconds)
   お小遣いは一か月にいくらぐらいもらっていますか。それで十分ですか。
3. Give specific examples. (90 seconds)
   だいたいお小遣いを何に使っていますか。
4. Respond and explain your preference. (90 seconds)
   もし今千ドルもらったら、貯金しますか。それとも、ほしい物を買いますか。
5. Express your opinion. (90 seconds)
   貯金することは大事だと思いますか。なぜですか。
6. Ask a specific question. (90 seconds)
   御協力有難うございました。僕達のお金の使い方について何か質問がありますか。

<17課 - 書く (比較と対比)>

`20分`

Compare and Contrast Article: Online Shopping and Store Shopping

Directions: You are writing an article for the student newspaper of your sister school in Japan. Write an article in which you compare and contrast similarities and differences between online shopping and store shopping. Based on your personal experience, describe at least THREE aspects of each and highlight the similarities and differences between online shopping and store shopping. Also state your preference for either and give reasons for it.

Your article should be 300 to 400 characters or longer. Use the *desu/masu* or *da* (plain) style, but use one style consistently. Also, use *kanji* wherever *kanji* from the AP Japanese *kanji* list is appropriate. You have 20 minutes to write.

【NOTES/OUTLINE: 自分の作文のアウトラインを書こう！】

Introduction:
_____

Three similarities/differences:

1. _____
2. _____
3. _____

Your preference and give reasons:
_____
_____

17課

<17課 - 話す (会話)>
Conversation: Shopping

`20秒×4`

You will participate in a simulated conversation. Each time it is your turn to speak, you will have 20 seconds to record. You should respond as fully and as appropriately as possible.

You will have a conversation with Akira, your Japanese friend, about yesterday's shopping experience.

(Akira)
(20 seconds)
(Akira)
(20 seconds)
(Akira)
(20 seconds)
(Akira)
(20 seconds)

<17課 - 話す (日本文化)>
Cultural Perspective Presentation: Japanese Department Stores

`4分+2分`

Directions: Imagine you are making an oral presentation to your Japanese class. First, you will read and hear the topic for your presentation. You will have 4 minutes to prepare your presentation. Then you will have 2 minutes to record your presentation. Your presentation should be as complete as possible.

Present your own view or perspective of Japanese department stores. Discuss at least FIVE aspects or examples of Japanese department stores.

Begin with an appropriate introduction, give details, explain your own view or perspective, and end with a concluding remark.

【Let's take notes!】

1. Begin with an appropriate introduction.
   _____

2. Discuss five aspects/examples of the topic.
   1.) _____
   2.) _____
   3.) _____
   4.) _____
   5.) _____

3. Explain your view or perspective.
   _____

4. End with a concluding remark.
   _____

17課

18課   体と健康
Body and Health

【AP® タスク：体と健康】
Discuss one unhealthy practice and one healthy practice in your daily lifestyle. Discuss what you have to be careful about to maintain your health when you are in college. Discuss Americans' health problems related to their diet, and explain your opinions.

【文化】 日本人の健康生活：Healthy Lifestyle of Japanese

The Japanese boast the longest lifespans in the world. According to a recent survey, the average lifespan of a Japanese man is 80 years old, while the average Japanese woman lives to be 87 years old. This is easily attributable to the daily lifestyle of the Japanese.

Traditionally and today, fish is the main source of protein for Japanese meals, and is naturally a healthier choice than beef. Beef is very expensive in Japan, due to lack of space for raising cattle. At home, beef is prepared in small amounts and cooked with vegetables.

Japanese cooking requires far less oil and fats than Western cooking. Although foods are now cooked in oil (frying and deep frying), these styles of cooking have been adopted from other cultures. Traditional styles of cooking are grilling, poaching, boiling, and steaming.

Japanese eat many soy based foods. Unlike meats and dairy products that are high in cholesterol and saturated fat, soy is a healthy source of protein. Foods made from soybeans are essential to the traditional Japanese diet. They include *tofu* (豆腐), *shoyu* (soy sauce), *natto* (fermented soy beans) and *abura-age* (deep fried *tofu*). Japanese have enjoyed eating soybeans, or *edamame* (枝豆) long before they became popular in Western foods.

Another practice that contributes to the good health of Japanese is their conscious effort to eat fresh foods. Traditionally, women of the household went shopping daily to purchase fresh fish, meat, *tofu*, vegetables and fruits for the family's meal. They did not rely on frozen foods or canned foods for their meals. Specialty food stores and supermarkets sell their products in small portions. Japanese kitchens need only a small refrigerator and freezer and do not have large pantries to store large amounts of foods. This value is consistent with the Japanese need to conserve space.

Japanese also eat smaller portions of foods than Westerners. Their main staple, rice, is supplemented with several small portions of side dishes served in small dishes.

The one other significant point is that many Japanese lead less sedentary lifestyles. Streets in cities and towns are narrow and parking spaces are very limited, so it is far more convenient to walk, ride a bike, or take public transportation, which requires one to walk to and from stations, bus stops and other pick up points. The fast pace of city life also encourages Japanese to walk at a brisk pace. These commuting habits contribute to the healthy lifestyle of the Japanese.

Traditionally, Japanese have placed an emphasis on physical fitness. Whether at a school or a workplace, all are gathered in an open space outside the buildings in the mornings for early morning ラジオ体操 (*rajio taiso*), calisthenics done to music that is blared out through a public address system. It is not unusual to see scores of children, factory or company workers outdoors standing in neat lines diligently doing their morning exercises before starting their day. It is also not uncommon to see senior citizens meeting in parks to do *tai chi* or other exercises. Lifelong physical fitness has long been an established value for the Japanese.

In recent years, the fast food craze has affected the diet of Japanese, and there are now more health problems because of the higher fat intake and the younger generation's preference for Western foods. Obesity has become a major health issue. Japanese are working hard to address these growing health issues.

Questions to ponder: How has the physical environment affected the traditional dietary habits of the Japanese? What dietary habits similar to the Japanese do you practice or want to practice? Why?

18課 ◆◆◆ 復習単語 ◆◆◆

トピック：体と健康

#	語	読み	品詞	意味
1.	体	からだ	N	body
2.	頭	あたま	N	head
3.	髪(の毛)	かみ(のけ)	N	hair
4.	顔	かお	N	face
5.	鼻	はな	N	nose
6.	髭	ひげ	N	beard; moustache
7.	口	くち	N	mouth
8.	歯	は	N	tooth
9.	喉	のど	N	throat
10.	首	くび	N	neck
11.	指	ゆび	N	finger; toe
12.	脚	あし	N	leg
13.	足	あし	N	foot
14.	健康	けんこう	N	health
15.	健康的	けんこうてき	Na	healthy
16.	病院	びょういん	N	hospital
17.	病気	びょうき	N	illness; sickness
18.	薬	くすり	N	medicine
19.	裸	はだか	N	naked; nude
20.	骨	ほね	N	bone
21.	筋肉	きんにく	N	muscles
22.	背	せ	N	height
23.	風邪	かぜ	N	a cold
24.	風邪を引く	かぜをひく	V1	(to) catch a cold
25.	血	ち	N	blood
26.	血が出る	ちがでる	V2	(to) bleed
27.	白血病	はっけつびょう	N	leukemia
28.	目が不自由な人	めがふじゆうなひと	N	a blind person
29.	痛い	いたい	A	is painful; sore
30.	看病(を)する	かんびょう(を)する	V3	(to) take care of (a sick person)
31.	救急車	きゅうきゅうしゃ	N	ambulance
32.	亡くなる	なくなる	V1	(to) pass away; die [polite form of 死ぬ]

18課

| 18課 | ★★★ | 新しい単語 | ★★★ |

1. (〜に)かんする＜関する＞〜　　PN　on 〜, about 〜, relating to〜
   (〜に)かんして＜関して＞　　P+V　about 〜
   セミナーに参加したら、健康に関する情報をたくさんもらった。 When I participated in the seminar about health, I received a lot of information about it.

2. のど＜喉＞　　N　throat
   喉が痛くて、話したくない。 My throat hurts and I don't want to talk.

3. むね＜胸＞　　N　chest, breast
   祖父の胸が苦しくなったので、祖母はすぐ救急車を呼んだ。 My grandfather started to have chest pains, so my grandmother called the ambulance immediately.

4. せなか＜背中＞　　N　back
   背中が痛くて、まっすぐ座れない。 My back hurts and I can't sit straight.

5. きんにく＜筋肉＞　　N　muscle
   毎日ジムで筋肉トレーニングをしている。 I go to the gym everyday and do muscle training (weightlifting).

6. はい＜肺＞　　N　lung
   たばこを吸っていると、肺が悪くなるそうだ。 If you smoke cigarettes, I understand that your lungs will get bad.

7. しんぞう＜心臓＞　　N　heart (cardiac)
   しんぞうびょう＜心臓病＞　　N　heart disease
   コレステロールが高いと、心臓病になりやすい。 If you have high cholesterol, you are susceptible to heart disease.

8. がん＜癌＞　　N　cancer
   にゅうがん＜乳癌＞　　N　breast cancer
   癌にかかる人が多い。 There are many people who get cancer.

9. ひまん＜肥満＞　　N　obesity, excess weight
   子供の肥満が問題になっている。 Childhood obesity has become a problem.

10. かんじゃ＜患者＞　　N　patient
    病院へ行ったら、たくさんインフルエンザの患者がいた。 When I went to the hospital, there were many patients with the flu.

11. しょうじょう＜症状＞　　N　symptom
「どんな症状がありますか。」What kind of symptoms do you have?
「熱が高くて、喉が痛いです。」I have a high fever and my throat hurts.

12. ずつう＜頭痛＞　　N　headache
今朝から頭痛がして、よく考えられない。 I've had a headache since this morning and I can't think well.

13. すいみんぶそく＜睡眠不足＞　　N　lack of sleep
すいみんやく＜睡眠薬＞　　N　sleeping pill
最近、試験やレポートが多くて、睡眠不足だ。 Recently, I have had many exams and papers, and have not had enough sleep.

14. けつあつ＜血圧＞　　N　blood pressure
こうけつあつ＜高血圧＞　　N　high blood pressure
ていけつあつ＜低血圧＞　　N　low blood pressure
父は血圧が高いので、薬で血圧を下げている。 My dad has high blood pressure, so he lowers his blood pressure with medication.

15. ちりょう＜治療＞　　N　treatment
母は治療のために入院している。 My mother has been hospitalized for a (medical) treatment.

16. ほうほう＜方法＞　　N　method, way
どうしたらすぐ寝られるかいい方法を教えてほしい。 Please tell me how (the way) I can get to sleep quickly.

17. こうせいぶっしつ＜抗生物質＞　　N　antibiotic
抗生物質を飲んだら、熱が下がった。 When I took the antibiotics, my temperature went down.

18. えいよう＜栄養＞　　N　nutrition
病気の時は栄養のある物を食べて、よく休むことだ。 When you are ill, you should eat nutritious foods and get lots of rest.

19. しゅじゅつ＜手術＞　　N　surgery
父は癌の手術を二回も受けた。 My father had surgery twice for his cancer.

20. ちゅうしゃ＜注射＞　　N　injection
インフルエンザの予防注射を受けた。 I took a flu shot.

21. だいず＜大豆＞　　N　soy beans
大豆は植物なので、コレステロールがない。 Since soy beans are vegetables, they have no cholesterol.

18課

22. せきがでる＜咳が出る＞／出ます　V2　to cough
    咳が出て、止まらない。 My coughing does not stop.

23. しょくよく＜食欲＞がある／あります　V1　to have an appetite
    風邪を引いて、あまり食欲がない。 I have a cold, and don't have much of an appetite.

24. さむけがする＜寒気がする＞／します　V3　to have the chills
    寒気がするから、風邪を引いたかも知れない。 I have the chills, so I might have caught a cold.

25. （〜を）さげる＜下げる＞／下げます　V2　to lower (〜) [transitive]
    （〜が）さがる＜下がる＞／下がります　V1　(〜) to hang ; fall; suspend [intransitive]
    熱を下げる薬を飲んだら、下がった。 I took medication to lower my temperature, so my fever dropped.

26. （〜を）あげる＜上げる＞／上げます　V2　to raise (〜) [transitive]
    （〜が）あがる＜上がる＞／上がります　V1　(〜) rise [intransitive]
    薬の値段を上げてはいけないと思うけど、薬の値段は上がっている。 I don't think we should raise the price of medications, but the prices of medications are rising.

27. きたえる＜鍛える＞／鍛えます　V2　to train
    体を鍛えるために、プールで泳いでいる。 In order to train my body, I swim at the pool.

28. かいしょう＜解消＞する／します　V3　to reduce; to resolve
    ストレスを解消するために、カラオケに行く。 In order to relieve my stress, I go to *karaoke*.

29. (病気に)かかる／かかります　V1　to contract (an illness); to get (sick, etc.)
    インフルエンザにかかって、死にそうになった。 I caught the flu and I felt like dying.

30. よぼう＜予防＞(を)する／します　V3　to prevent
    虫歯を予防するために、コーラを止めた。 In order to prevent cavities, I quit (drinking) cola.

31. ながいき＜長生き＞(を)する／します　V3　to live a long life
    日本人は長生きで有名だ。 Japanese are famous for their longevity (long lives).

【もっと単語】

1. インフルエンザ　　　　　　　N　influenza, flu
2. アレルギー　　　　　　　　　N　allergy
3. ビタミン　　　　　　　　　　N　vitamins
4. カルシウム　　　　　　　　　N　calcium
5. すいぶん＜水分＞　　　　　　N　water; moisture
6. ほけんしつ＜保健室＞　　　　N　health room

18課 　文法

> A. 一日に三回　　　　　　　　　　　three times a day
> 食後〔しょくご〕、食前〔しょくぜん〕　after meals, before meals
> 2時間毎〔ごと〕に　　　　　　　　　every two hours
> 2日置〔お〕きに　　　　　　　　　　every third day, every three days
>
> The expressions above are used to communicate frequency, or given times within a specified duration of time.

Fill in the blanks with the proper Japanese responses using cues in the ( ).

1. 医者：「この薬を_____飲みなさい。」 (after every meal)
2. 医者：「この抗生物質を_____飲みなさい。」 (three times a day)
3. 医者：「この薬を_____飲みなさい。」 (before you go to bed)
4. 看護師：「これから、_____来て下さい。」 (once a month)
5. 看護師：「この薬は_____飲んで下さい。」 (every four hours)
　　or 「この薬は_____飲んで下さい。」 (every five hours)

> B. 「よく寝るように。」　　　　"Sleep well." Advice, suggestion [informal]
> 「よく寝るようにして下さい。」"Please sleep well." Advice, suggestion [polite]
> 「よく寝ること。」　　　　　"Sleep well." Instruction, direction, resolution [informal]
> 「よく寝ることです。」"Please sleep well." Instruction, direction, resolution [polite]

Translate the sentences into English.

1. 医者：「水分を十分取るように。」 _____
2. 医者：「少しずつ栄養のある食べ物を食べるように。」 _____
3. 医者：「よく休むことです。」 _____
4. 医者：「一日に三回食後に飲むように。」 _____
5. 私：「毎日、宿題をすること。」 _____
6. 私：「毎日二十分運動をすること。」 _____
7. 母：「早く寝るようにしなさい。」 _____
8. 看護師：「この薬を一日に三回食事の前に飲むようにして下さい。」 _____
9. 医者：「元気になるまで会社へ行かないことです。」 _____

18課

C.
食べ<u>すぎ</u>は、悪い。	Eating too much is bad.
食べ<u>すぎた</u>。	(I) ate too much.
食べ<u>すぎて</u>はいけない。	(I) should not eat too much.
食べ<u>すぎないで</u>。	Do not eat too much.
高<u>すぎる</u>。	It's too high/expensive.
静か<u>すぎる</u>。	It's too quiet.

To express that there is an excess, one uses the extender -すぎる when forming a verb and -すぎ when forming a noun. The extender, which means "too much," is attached to the verb stem, adjective base or -な adjective.

Fill in the blanks with the correct すぎる form using the cues in the ( ).

1. お酒の_____は、体に良くない。（飲む）
2. _____と、肥満になる。（食べる）
3. コンピューターを_____て、目が悪くなった。（使う）
4. 熱が_____ので、アスピリンを飲んだ。（高い）
5. 風邪で喉が_____て、話せない。（痛い）

D. せいで   because (with an undesirable result)

The word せい is a dependent noun expressing a cause which brings about an undesirable result beyond the speaker's control.

1. 交通事故<u>のせいで</u>、学校に遅れてしまった。
   I was late to school because of a car accident.
2. 先生にしかられたのは、あなた<u>のせいだ</u>。
   It's because of you that I was scolded by my teacher.
3. お酒を飲ん<u>だせいで</u>、事故を起こしてしまった。
   I caused a car accident because I drank (alcohol).

Compare: おかげで because (with a desirable result and appreciation)
  おかげ and せい are similar in that both express a cause. The difference is that おかげ is used when the result is desirable, while せい is used when the result is undesirable. Note also that おかげ implies that the person who attained the result is thankful for the cause.

4. 先生<u>のおかげで</u>、クラスはとても楽しかったです。
   Thanks (to the teacher), the class was enjoyable.
5. 日本語を勉強した<u>おかげで</u>、日本へ行ってもあまり困らなかった。
   Because I studied Japanese, I didn't have too many problems in Japan.

Compare: ために "sake; purpose or reason"

6. 将来<u>のために</u>、今がんばる。 I will do my best now for the sake of my future.
7. 両親は子供を育てる<u>ために</u>、朝から晩まで働いている。
   The parents are working from morning until night in order to raise their children.

18課

Circle the correct response.

1. 友達の（おかげで　せいで　ために）宿題を終わることが出来た。
2. 弟の（おかげで　せいで　ために）宿題が出来なかった。
3. 友達が遅く起きた（おかげで　せいで　ために）私も学校に遅れた。
4. 先生の（おかげで　せいで　ために）いい大学に合格出来ました。
5. 私の（おかげで　せいで　ために）祖母は早く起きて私の弁当を作ってくれる。
6. 週末を楽しむ（おかげで　せいで　ために）宿題を全部しておくつもりだ。
7. コーチの（おかげで　せいで　ために）テニスが上手になった。
8. 友達の（おかげで　せいで　ために）誕生ケーキを作るつもりだ。

E. 風邪のようだ　　　seems to be a cold [formal]
　　風邪みたいだ　　　seems to be a cold [informal]
　　元気そうだ　　　　looks healthy
　　悪そうだ　　　　　looks bad
　　良〔よ〕さそうだ　looks good
　　悪くなさそうだ　　does not look bad
　　元気だそうだ　　　I heard that he/she is healthy.

Using the cues in the ( ), complete the following statements by the speaker.

1. A doctor tells the patient that he seems to have caught a bad flu.
医者：「悪い風邪を_____。」（引く）

2. A doctor tells the patient after an examination that his lungs seem fine.
医者：「肺は_____。」（大丈夫）

3. A doctor reports to a patient that the patient seems to have cancer.
医者：「癌が_____。」

4. Your friend reports to you that it seems that your classmate Taro will be absent from school tomorrow.
友達：「太郎は病気で明日学校を_____。」（休む）

5. A doctor reports to the patient's wife that her husband looks healthy, but he seems to have diabetes.
医者：「ご主人は_____が、糖尿病が_____。」
　　　（元気、ある）

F. Informal style and formal style:

Informal style	Formal style
1. なんで？	なぜ？
2. 風邪でも引いたんじゃない？	風邪でも引いたのではありませんか。
3. 発表が出来なくなっちゃって、ごめん。	発表が出来なくなってしまって、すみません。
4. 仕方がないじゃない。	仕方がないではありませんか。
5. 何も心配するなよ。	何も心配しないでくださいよ。

18課　アクティビティー

A. 文化ノート：ペアワーク→クラスワーク

Divide the topics below among your classmates and research your topic on the Internet. Using visuals, present your findings with your classmates.

1. 東洋医学、指圧、鍼治療
2. 大豆、味噌、醤油、豆腐、納豆、枝豆
3. 諺：「風邪は万病のもと」

B. 聞く Pre-Listening Activity「病気」：ペアワーク→クラスワーク

Circle two answers for each question.

1. 風邪を引いた時、どんな症状はないでしょうか。
   a. 熱が低い　b. 喉が痛い　c. 頭痛がする　d. 咳が出る　e. 鼻水が出る　f. 食欲がある
2. 患者が風邪を引いた時、お医者さんがふつう言わないことは、どれですか。
   a. 学校を休まないこと。
   b. よく寝ること。
   c. 栄養のある物を食べること。
   d. 熱を下げる薬を飲むこと。
   e. 水分を十分に摂ること。
   f. よく運動をすること。

C. 聞く Post-Listening Activity「病気」：ペアワーク→クラスワーク

Role play the following scenarios.

例.＜病院で＞
　医者：どうしましたか。
　患者：熱があって、喉が痛くて、食欲がないんです。それに、睡眠不足で。
　医者：そうですか。たくさん水分をとって、一日に三回食後に薬を飲んで下さい。よく寝た方がいいですよ。
　患者：はい、分かりました。どうも有難うございました。
　医者：では、お大事に。

1. ＜病院で＞
   患者：Symptoms: high fever, sore throat, no appetite.
   医者：Recommendation: Take Tylenol every six hours, drink enough water, sleep well.
2. ＜うちで＞
   娘：Symptoms: stomachache, headache, lack of sleep.
   母：Give advice.

3. ＜学校の保健室で＞
　　生徒：Description of current dietary practice: No food, lots of supplements such as vitamins and calcium, etc., lost too much weight.
　　看護婦：Make a recommendation.
4. ＜カウンセラー室で＞
　　生徒：Discussion of your problems: You cannot stop drinking alcohol and smoking.
　　カウンセラー：Give advice.
5. ＜病院で＞
　　姉：　Description of your diet: You eat too many sweets such as cake and ice cream, and worry about your weight.
　　医者：Make a recommendation.

D. 読む Pre-Reading Activity「健康〔けんこう〕」：ペアワーク→クラスワーク

　Circle the correct response from the ( ).
1. アメリカ人は日本人より（癌　心臓病）で死ぬ人が多い。
2. （癌　心臓病）の治療を受けると、髪の毛がなくなったりする。
3. 地元の有機野菜は、健康的（だ　ではない）。
4. インスタント食品や冷凍食品は、健康的（だ　ではない）。
5. 賞味期限が切れている食べ物は、（食べた　食べない）方がいい。
6. 血圧が高い人は塩分が（多い　少ない）食べ物を食べた方がいい。
7. 肥満の問題は、アメリカに（多い　少ない）。
8. たばこやお酒の飲みすぎは、体に（いい　悪い）。

E. 読む Post-Reading Activity「健康〔けんこう〕」：ペアワーク→クラスワーク

Compare and Contrast: American Healthy Habits and Asian Healthy Habits

　Prepare an outline on this topic within 4 minutes and do a 2 minute presentation of it with your partner.

Introduction:
_____

Three similarities/differences:
　1. _____
　2. _____
　3. _____

Your preference and give reasons:
_____
_____

18課

F. テキストチャット「健康〔けんこう〕」：ペアワーク→クラスワーク

You will have a conversation with Akiko, a student at a Japanese school, about health. First, read this text chat conversation with your partner. Next, read the questions and your partner will respond without looking at the book. Give your original answers to the questions. For each question, use 30 seconds to answer. Take turns asking and answering questions.

1. 明子：初めまして。今日は健康に関するアンケートに御協力、有難うございます。

   私　：初めまして。(Last name) です。こちらこそ、どうぞよろしくお願いします。健康はとても大事なテーマですね。出来るだけ、答えてみます。

2. 明子：何か特別なダイエットをしていますか。

   私　：私は特別なダイエットはしていませんが、あまり体に悪い物は食べないようにしています。例えば、ファーストフードは食べませんし、ステーキとか油の多い食べ物は食べません。

3. 明子：そうですか。では、アメリカ人の食事と日本人の食事と、どちらの方が健康的だと思いますか。なぜですか。

   私　：もちろん、日本人の食事の方がアメリカ人の食事より健康的だと思います。日本人の食事はあまり油を使いませんね。それに、日本人は肉より魚をもっと食べます。

4. 明子：ところで、体をきたえるために、どんな運動をしていますか。

   私　：私は毎日2マイルぐらい走っていますし、学校のジムで筋トレをしています。夏に泳いだり、冬にスキーに行ったりします。私はスポーツが大好きです。

5. 明子：そうですか。私はストレスが多くて困っています。ストレス解消のいい方法を教えて下さい。

   私　：ストレスは体に良くないですね。ストレスがある時は、外に行って歩いたり、走ったりすると、気持ちが良くなりますよ。友達とおしゃべりするのもいいです。でも、宿題や試験が多いとストレスでいっぱいになります。

6. 明子：ありがとうございました。ところで、東洋の指圧とか鍼治療について何か知っていますか。

   私　：指圧や鍼は、テレビで見たことはありますが、本当にしてもらったことはありません。指圧は気持ち良さそうですが、鍼は痛そうですね。このチャットは楽しかったです。また、しましょう。

18課

G. Compare & Contrast 「テレビと運動」：ペアワーク→クラスワーク

a. First, read this compare and contrast passage with your partner.

> これから、うちでテレビを見ることと外で運動をすることを比べてみます。
>
> まず一つ目の違いは、うちでテレビを見ることは、体に良くありませんが、外で運動することは、体にとてもいいです。それに、テレビを見ながら、食べたり飲んだりするので、もっと体に悪いです。
>
> そして、二つ目の違いは、うちでテレビを見ることは、努力しなくても出来ますが、外で運動することは、努力しなければ出来ません。だから、外で運動をしている人は、心が強い人かもしれません。
>
> しかし、一つの同じことは、どちらも時間がかかることです。テレビを見るとすぐ時間が経ってしまいますし、外で運動しても時間がかかります。忙しい人は、両方出来ないので、テレビを見るだけか、運動をするだけかの二つのタイプに分かれるようです。
>
> 結論として、私は外で運動することの方が、うちでテレビを見るより好きです。もちろん、テレビを見ることが大好きですが、平日は時間がないので、週末に見るようにしています。外で運動をすると、体だけでなく気持ちも良くなるので、運動は大事だと思います。

b. Next, work with your partner and compare and contrast watching TV at home and doing exercise outdoors. List three similarities and/or differences, your preference of which you would rather have and the reasons. Give your original opinions. Then, share your presentation with your class.

Introduction:
_____

Three similarities/differences:
1. _____
2. _____
3. _____

Your preference and give reasons:
_____
_____

H. 会話「風邪〔かぜ〕」：ペアワーク→クラスワーク

You will have a telephone conversation with Mari, your classmate, about her problem.
First, read this conversation with your partner using the correct male/female speech style. Take turns. Next, read Mari's parts and your partner will respond without looking at the book. The answers should be your original. For each question, use 20 seconds to answer. Take turns asking and answering questions.

18課

1. まり： 「もしもし、まりだけど、今日学校を休むことにしたの。」
   答(男/女)：「ええっ、なんで？病気？大丈夫？」
2. まり： 「熱もあるし、頭痛もするし、寒気もするし。」
   答(男)： 「本当？可哀想に。風邪でも引いたんじゃない？学校は休めばいいよ。よく寝たら、元気になるよ。」
   答(女)： 「本当？可哀想に。風邪でも引いたんじゃない<u>の</u>？学校は休めばいい<u>わよ</u>。よく寝たら、元気になる<u>わよ</u>。」
3. まり： 「それで、今日の社会科の授業で一緒にするはずだったプロジェクトの発表が出来なくなっちゃって。ごめん。」
   答(男)： 「ああ、そんなことを心配してる<u>のか</u>。病気なら、仕方ないじゃない。先生も分かってくれるよ。」
   答(女)： 「ああ、そんなことを心配してる<u>の</u>？病気なら、仕方ないじゃない。先生も分かってくれる<u>わよ</u>。」
4. まり： 「じゃ、何か大事なことがあったら、電話してくれる？今から風邪薬を飲んで、寝るつもり。じゃね。」
   答(男)： 「分かった。何かあったら、電話する<u>よ</u>。でも、何も心配する<u>なよ</u>。よく寝るのが一番の薬だから、学校のことなんか忘れて、寝てたらいいよ。」
   答(女)： 「分かった。何かあったら、電話する<u>ね</u>。でも、何も心配し<u>ないで</u>。よく寝るのが一番の薬だから、学校のことなんか忘れて、寝てたらいい<u>わよ</u>。」

I. 文化発表「日本人の健康生活」：ペアワーク→クラスワーク

a. Choose the correct word from below and write the correct letter in the ( ) below the passage.

　これから、日本人の健康生活について発表します。日本人は世界で最も長生きすることで有名です。それは、(1.　) な生活をしているからです。
　まず第一に、日本人は牛肉より魚の方をよく食べます。牛肉はコレステロールが高く、(2.　) ほど健康的ではありません。
　第二に、日本人は料理にあまり油を使いません。アメリカ人は料理に油をよく使うので、(3.　) が高くなります。
　第三に、日本人はよく大豆を料理に使います。豆腐、(4.　)、味噌、納豆などは大豆から作られています。大豆は (5.　) なので、コレステロールはありません。
　第四に、日本人は新鮮な食べ物を食べます。日本で売っている魚も (6.　) も果物もとても新鮮です。

18課

第五に、日本人はよく歩きます。日本人は自動車より(7.　)やバスをよく使うので、よく歩かなければなりません。そして、歩くことは(8.　)にとてもいいです。

結論として、日本人は健康的な食べ物を食べ、よく歩くので、(9.　)することが出来ると思います。アメリカ人は(10.　)に乗ってあまり運動しないし、コレステロールの多い食べ物を食べているので、日本人ほど長生き出来ないのでしょう。

> a. コレステロール　b. 体　c. 野菜　d. 魚　e. 植物
> f. 健康的　g. 醤油　h. 車　i. 長生き　j. 電車

b. Write three things you can improve in your own lifestyle in order to live a healthy, long life.

1. _____
2. _____
3. _____

18課

<18課 - 聞く>

Listening: Illness

12秒×5

【You may take notes while listening. Do not look at the questions below before listening. You will have 12 seconds to answer each question. You may NOT move back and forth among questions.】

(Narrator) Now you will listen once to a conversation.

(Narrator) Now answer the questions for this selection.

1. What symptom does this patient NOT have?
    (A) High fever
    (B) Stomachache
    (C) Frequent coughing
    (D) Headache

2. What did the doctor NOT check?
    (A) The patient's chest
    (B) The patient's back
    (C) The patient's throat
    (D) The patient's ears

3. What did the doctor find out after examining the patient?
    (A) The patient's lungs are normal.
    (B) The patient's stomach is normal.
    (C) The patient's throat is normal.
    (D) The patient has the flu.

4. What did the doctor NOT recommend to the patient?
    (A) To eat well
    (B) To drink enough liquids
    (C) To begin eating nutritious food
    (D) To rest well

5. What medicines did the doctor prescribe to the patient?
    (A) Fever medicine to be taken two times a day after meals.
    (B) Antibiotics to be taken three times a day before meals.
    (C) Fever medicine and antibiotics to be taken three times before meals.
    (D) Fever medicine and antibiotics to be taken three times after meals.

18課

＜18課 - 読む＞
Reading: Health
【You may move back and forth among all the questions.】

去年、母は乳癌の手術をした。治療のせいで髪の毛がなくなったりしたが、いつも明るく、暗い顔を全然見せなかった。現在は普通の生活が出来るまで元気になった。その後、食事にとても気をつけるようになった。まず、地元の有機野菜しか食べなくなり、町にある健康食品のスーパーで毎日の買い物をしている。買い物に行っても、野菜や果物の新鮮さや賞味期限などを注意深く調べている。インスタント食品とか冷凍食品は全然食べなくなった。残り物も全然食べない。そして、毎日健康のためによく歩くようになった。

また父は血圧が高くて心臓が少し弱いので、塩分の少ない食事をしている。好きな漬物などの塩辛い物はあまり食べないようにしている。たばこはかなり前にやめたが、お酒は現在もまだ少し飲んでいる。

来年結婚を予定している姉は肥満を気にして、最近ダイエットを始めた。カロリー計算をして、低カロリーの物ばかり食べている。甘い物が大好きだったのに、おやつもやめた。今ビタミンなどのサプリメントに凝っている。毎日プールに泳ぎに行って、短い間に3キロも痩せたと自慢している。

私の家族はそれぞれ違う健康上の問題を持っているが、皆で協力して健康的な食生活をするようにしている。

＜18課 - 読む (質問)＞

Reading: Health

(Narrator) Now answer the questions for this section.

1. What kind of health problem did the mother have?
   (A) She had breast cancer and had surgery last year.
   (B) She lost quite a lot of weight and feels weak now.
   (C) She had a heart attack and recovered.
   (D) She has bad headaches once in a while.

2. What description is NOT correct about the mother?
   (A) The mother can eat any kind of food now.
   (B) The mother only shops at the health food store.
   (C) The mother checks the freshness, expiration date and additives of food she buys.
   (D) The mother quit eating instant foods and frozen foods.

3. What description is NOT correct about the father?
   (A) The father has a heart problem.
   (B) The father has high blood pressure.
   (C) The father eats salty food.
   (D) The father quit smoking, but is drinking a little alcohol.

4. What description is NOT correct about the older sister?
   (A) The older sister is on a diet now.
   (B) The older sister eats only a few sweets.
   (C) The older sister loves to take supplements.
   (D) The older sister is happy about losing 3 kilograms in such a short time.

5. What is this family trying to accomplish?
   (A) They try to eat together.
   (B) They try to eat healthy food.
   (C) They are trying to lose weight.
   (D) They try to communicate more effectively.

<18課 - 書く (テキストチャット)>
Text Chat: Health

90秒×6

You will participate in a simulated exchange of text-chat messages. Each time it is your turn to write, you will have 90 seconds. You should respond as fully and as appropriately as possible.

You will have a conversation with Akiko, a student at a Japanese school, about health.

1. Respond. (90 seconds)

   初めまして。今日は健康(けんこう)に関するアンケートに御協力して下さり、有難うございます。

2. Respond. (90 seconds)

   何か特別なダイエットをしていますか。

3. Compare and justify your opinion. (90 seconds)

   そうですか。では、アメリカ人の食事と日本人の食事と、どちらの方が健康的(けんこう)だと思いますか。なぜですか。

4. Respond. (90 seconds)

   ところで、体をきたえるために、どんな運動をしていますか。

5. Suggest. (90 seconds)

   そうですか。私はストレスが多くて困っています。ストレス解消(かいしょう)のいい方法を教えて下さい。

6. Ask a specific question. (90 seconds)

   ありがとうございました。ところで、東洋の指圧(あつ)とか鍼治療(はりちりょう)について何か知っていますか。

<18課 - 書く (比較(ひかく)と対比(たいひ))>
Compare and Contrast Article: Cold and Cancer

20分

Directions: You are writing an article for the student newspaper of your sister school in Japan. Write an article in which you compare and contrast similarities and differences between having a cold and having cancer. Based on your personal experience, describe at least THREE aspects of each and highlight the similarities and differences between cold and cancer. Also state your preference for either and give reasons for it.

Your article should be 300 to 400 characters or longer. Use the *desu/masu* or *da* (plain) style, but use one style consistently. Also, use *kanji* wherever *kanji* from the AP Japanese *kanji* list is appropriate. You have 20 minutes to write.

【NOTES/OUTLINE: 自分の作文のアウトラインを書こう！】

Introduction:
_____

Three similarities/differences:

1. _____
2. _____
3. _____

Your preference and give reasons:
_____
_____

18課

<18課 - 話す (会話)>
Conversation: A Cold

20秒×4

You will participate in a simulated conversation. Each time it is your turn to speak, you will have 20 seconds to record. You should respond as fully and as appropriately as possible.

You will have a telephone conversation with Mari, your classmate, about her problem.

(Mari)
(20 seconds)
(Mari)
(20 seconds)
(Mari)
(20 seconds)
(Mari)
(20 seconds)

<18課 - 話す (日本文化)>
Cultural Perspective Presentation: Japanese Healthy Life

4分+2分

Directions: Imagine you are making an oral presentation to your Japanese class. First, you will read and hear the topic for your presentation. You will have 4 minutes to prepare your presentation. Then you will have 2 minutes to record your presentation. Your presentation should be as complete as possible.

Present your own view or perspective of Japanese healthy life. Discuss at least FIVE aspects or examples of Japanese healthy life.

Begin with an appropriate introduction, give details, explain your own view or perspective, and end with a concluding remark.

【Let's take notes!】

1. Begin with an appropriate introduction.

_____

2. Discuss five aspects/examples of the topic.

    1.) _____
    2.) _____
    3.) _____
    4.) _____
    5.) _____

3. Explain your view or perspective.

_____

4. End with a concluding remark.

_____

19課 旅行
Travel

【AP® タスク：旅行】
Think about your travel experiences to a foreign country or another state. What did you learn? How did travel change your way of thinking? What is the biggest difference between where you traveled and where you live? Describe your inner change. Why is travel to another country significant? If you could live in Japan, what would you want to experience most? Why?

【文化】 旅館：Japanese Inns

The Japanese inn, or *ryokan* (旅館), treats a traveler to an experience quite different from a hotel. For the modern Japanese, a visit to a *ryokan* offers a comfortable and nostalgic escape to a bit of traditional Japan.

A *ryokan* is usually located in the mountains or by ocean resorts. One is greeted warmly by the staff and even possibly by the proprietress of the *ryokan* when one arrives. The Japanese style rooms are given names such as "plum blossom," "pine" or "bamboo." They are complete with a small entranceway, *tatami* flooring, *tokonoma*, *shoji* and *fusuma*. Rooms are furnished simply with low tables, and often offer views of the ocean, mountains or well-manicured gardens. There is also a toilet area, and a small bath area. Upon settling in, one is served tea and a sweet in one's room.

Meals may be served in a large dining area if one is visiting in a large group, such as with working colleagues. Traditionally, however, dinner and breakfast are served in one's own room. The food at *ryokan* is Japanese style and is elaborately presented in trays and served on low tables surrounded by cushions or foldable legless chairs for the guests. *Sake* and tea are also served. Often the meals feature the specialty foods of the region and of the season.

After dinner, it is customary to take a leisurely stroll in the neighborhood. In resort areas, it is acceptable to walk about outdoors in one's *yukata*, or simple *kimono*. The *yukata* is furnished by the *ryokan*, and one wears the signature *ryokan's yukata* with the sash tied around one's waist, and slippers on one's feet. During the summer, the *yukata* is a light cotton garment. During the colder seasons, the *yukata* is made of thicker material, and may also come with a warm Japanese overcoat. The *yukata* may also be worn indoors to relax in the *ryokan*, or to bed as nightclothes.

One of the favorite activities of *ryokan* guests is taking a bath. Although all rooms have their own small bathing rooms, *ryokan* have at least one large communal bathing area. The bathing areas may be very luxurious, giving the guests a feeling of being immersed in nature. Often, *ryokan* also offer outdoor baths in secluded areas. *Ryokan* are plentiful near hot spring resorts and these *ryokan* offer many different *onsen* experiences to their guests.

When one returns to one's room in the evening, it will have been transformed to a bedroom. The meal table, chairs and cushions have been magically stored away. The maids have carefully laid out the *futon* bedding on the floors, one *futon* set per guest. After a comfortable night's rest, the maids return in the morning to put away all of the bedding in the *oshiire*, or closet that is designed especially to store the *futon*.

The Japanese *ryokan* caters to its guests with excellent service. They perform all services one would expect from a hotel concierge, plus more. For example, the special express delivery service known as *takkyuubin* is handled here. Despite extra amenities and services, tips are not accepted at *ryokan*.

The *ryokan* has adopted many modern luxuries, but it has also retained many of the traditions of Japanese hospitality and impeccable service that Japanese enjoy. The *ryokan* fosters the Japanese preference for group travel and encourages bonding among members of the group throughout its services and venues. The *ryokan* will always remain a favorite haven for the Japanese.

Questions to ponder: Why do Japanese crave ways to escape? How is the ryokan an expression of the traditional values of Japan? How does the ryokan differ from a hotel?

19課 ◆◆◆ 復習単語 ◆◆◆

トピック：旅行

1. 旅行	りょこう	N	trip; traveling
2. 旅行(を)する	りょこう(を)する	V3	(to) travel
3. 海外旅行	かいがいりょこう	N	overseas travel
4. 観光旅行	かんこうりょこう	N	sightseeing tour
5. 観光客	かんこうきゃく	N	tourist
6. 観光バス	かんこうバス	N	tour bus
7. タクシー		N	taxi
8. 乗り場	のりば	N	place of embarkment; place one gets on a vehicle
9. 料金	りょうきん	N	fare
10. 有料	ゆうりょう	N	a charge
11. 地図	ちず	N	map
12. パスポート		N	passport
13. トラベラーズチェック		N	traveler's checks
14. レールパス		N	JR railpass (for foreigners)
15. 旅館	りょかん	N	Japanese inn
16. 泊まる	とまる	V1	(to) stay overnight
17. 一泊二日	いっぱくふつか	N	one night, two days
18. 出発(を)する	しゅっぱつ(を)する	V3	depart
19. 出発時間	しゅっぱつじかん	N	departure time
20. 到着(を)する	とうちゃく(を)する	V3	(to) arrive
21. 到着時間	とうちゃくじかん	N	arrival time
22. 飛行機	ひこうき	N	airplane
23. 空港	くうこう	N	airport
24. 関西空港	かんさいくうこう	N	Kansai Airport
25. 船	ふね	N	boat; ship
26. 港	みなと	N	port; harbor
27. 駅	えき	N	train station
28. 駅弁	えきべん	N	a box lunch sold at stations
29. 新幹線	しんかんせん	N	bullet train
30. 日程表	にっていひょう	N	intinerary; daily schedule
31. 時刻表	じこくひょう	N	time table

19課

32. みどりの窓口	みどりのまどぐち	N	JR ticket window
33. 自由席	じゆうせき	N	non reserved seat
34. 指定席	していせき	N	reserved seat
35. グリーン車	グリーンしゃ	N	green car [JR first class car]
36. 禁煙車	きんえんしゃ	N	non-smoking car
37. ホーム		N	platform
38. 券売機	けんばいき	N	ticket vending machine
39. 切符	きっぷ	N	ticket
40. 改札口	かいさつぐち	N	ticket gate
41. 〜方面	〜ほうめん	N	〜direction
42. 北口	きたぐち	N	north entrance/exit
43. 南口	みなみぐち	N	south entrance/exit
44. 西口	にしぐち	N	west entrance/exit
45. 本土	ほんど	N	mainland
46. 東海岸	ひがしかいがん	N	east coast
47. 西海岸	にしかいがん	N	west coast
48. 関東	かんとう	N	Kanto area [region of eastern Honshu including Tokyo]
49. 関西	かんさい	N	Kansai area [region of western Honshu including Osaka and Kyoto]
50. 北海道	ほっかいどう	N	Hokkaido
51. 本州	ほんしゅう	N	Honshu
52. 四国	しこく	N	Shikoku
53. 九州	きゅうしゅう	N	Kyushu
54. 札幌	さっぽろ	N	Sapporo
55. 仙台	せんだい	N	Sendai
56. 東京	とうきょう	N	Tokyo
57. 東京駅	とうきょうえき	N	Tokyo Station
58. 山手線	やまのてせん	N	Yamanote Line [green colored train line in Tokyo]
59. 総武線	そうぶせん	N	Sobu Line [yellow colored train line in Tokyo]
60. 秋葉原	あきはばら	N	Akihabara [a city in Tokyo]
61. 池袋	いけぶくろ	N	Ikebukuro [a city in Tokyo]
62. 銀座	ぎんざ	N	Ginza [a city in Tokyo]

19課

63.	原宿	はらじゅく	N	Harajuku [a city in Tokyo]
64.	神田	かんだ	N	Kanda [a city in Tokyo]
65.	皇居	こうきょ	N	Imperial Palace
66.	お茶の水	おちゃのみず	N	Ochanomizu [a city in Tokyo]
67.	渋谷	しぶや	N	Shibuya [a city in Tokyo]
68.	品川	しながわ	N	Shinagawa [a city in Tokyo]
69.	新宿	しんじゅく	N	Shinjuku [a city in Tokyo]
70.	上野	うえの	N	Ueno [city in Tokyo]
71.	名古屋	なごや	N	Nagoya
72.	京都	きょうと	N	Kyoto
73.	奈良	なら	N	Nara
74.	大阪	おおさか	N	Osaka
75.	神戸	こうべ	N	Kobe
76.	広島	ひろしま	N	Hiroshima
77.	福岡	ふくおか	N	Fukuoka
78.	沖縄	おきなわ	N	Okinawa
79.	那覇	なは	N	Naha [a city in Okinawa]
80.	見物(を)する	けんぶつ(を)する	V3	(to) sightsee
81.	自然	しぜん	N	nature
82.	海	うみ	N	beach; ocean; sea
83.	山	やま	N	mountain
84.	島	しま	N	island
85.	景色	けしき	N	view; scenery
86.	温泉	おんせん	N	hot springs
87.	城	しろ	N	castle
88.	庭園	ていえん	N	garden [formal]
89.	歌舞伎座	かぶきざ	N	*kabuki* theater
90.	名物	めいぶつ	N	well-known product (of a given area)
91.	(御)土産	(お)みやげ	N	souvenir gift

19課

| 19課 | ★★★ | 新しい単語 | ★★★ |

1. こくないりょこう＜国内旅行＞　N　domestic travel
国内旅行より海外旅行の方がおもしろい。　Travelling abroad is more interesting than domestic travel.

2. よていひょう＜予定表＞　N　itinerary
旅行の予定表によると、東京には三泊するらしい。　According to the travel itinerary, it seems we are staying three nights in Tokyo.

3. みぶんしょうめいしょ＜身分証明書＞　N　identification
海外を旅行している時、パスポートは身分証明書になる。　When travelling abroad, your passport becomes your identification document.

4. かんこうち＜観光地＞　N　sightseeing spot; tourist attraction
日本の有名な観光地を教えて下さい。　Please tell me where the famous tourist attractions are in Japan.

5. おおさかじょう＜大阪城＞　N　Osaka Castle
大阪城は豊臣秀吉によって建てられたお城だ。　Osaka Castle is the castle that was built by Toyotomi Hideyoshi.

6. ヨーロッパ　N　Europe
ヨーロッパを旅行して、いろいろな国の人に会った。　I travelled through Europe and met people from many different countries.

7. なかい＜仲居＞さん　N　maid
旅館に泊まると、仲居さんがとてもよく世話してくれる。　When you stay at a Japanese inn, the maids take very good care of you.

8. こじん＜個人＞　N　private; individual; personal
個人で旅行する人が増えている。　The number of people who travel on their own is increasing.

9. だんたいりょこう＜団体旅行＞　N　group travel
日本人は団体旅行によく行く。　Japanese often go on group tours.

10. ちほう＜地方＞　N　district; region; countryside
この地方は冬によく雪が降る。　Snow often falls in this region in the winter.

11. とくさんひん＜特産品＞　N　specialty product
旅館ではよく地方の特産品を食べさせてくれる。　At Japanese inns, they often let you eat the specialty products of the region.

12. まんかい＜満開＞　N　full bloom
    京都の桜は満開だった。　The cherry blossoms in Kyoto were in full bloom.
13. こくさいご＜国際語＞　N　international language
    最近、英語が国際語になっているようだ。　Recently, it seems that English has become the international language (of the world.)
14. しょうご＜正午＞　N　noon
    ホテルのチャックインは正午だった。　The hotel check-in was at noon.
15. なんぱくなんにち＜何泊何日＞　N　How many days and nights?
    四泊五日のハワイ旅行は日本人に人気があるようだ。　Four day, five night trips to Hawaii seem to be popular among the Japanese.
16. チップ　N　tip
    日本にはチップをあげる習慣がない。　There is no custom of giving tips in Japan.
17. かくやす＜格安＞　N　cheap; reasonable
    シーズンオフに旅行すると、格安の飛行機のチケットが買える。　If you travel during the off-season, you can buy reasonable airline tickets.
18. こうかんレート＜交換レート＞　N　exchange rate
    今のドルと円の交換レートによると、一ドルは何円ですか。According to the dollar and yen exchange rate, how many yen is a dollar now?
19. ドルだか＜ドル高＞　N　high dollar exchange rate
    ドル高の時は、アメリカ人にとって海外旅行をしやすい。　When the value of the dollar is high, it is easy for Americans to travel abroad.
20. 〜いない＜以内＞　Nd　within 〜
    三か月以内の日本旅行には、ビザが要らない。　You don't need a visa for travel in Japan within a period of three months.
21. 〜つき＜〜付き＞　Nd　included
    日本の旅館に泊まると、朝食夕食付きだ。　When staying at a Japanese inn, breakfast and dinner are included.
22. しゅくはく＜宿泊＞する　V3　to stay over in accommodation
    しゅくはくだい＜宿泊代＞　N　hotel/lodging charge
    奈良で二日宿泊した。　We stayed at accommodation in Nara for two days.

23. りよう＜利用＞する／します　V3　to utilize; to use
日本を旅行した時に、新幹線をよく利用した。 When we travelled in Japan, we used the bullet train often.

24. もうしこむ＜申し込む＞／申し込みます　V1　to apply; reserve
春の桜ツアーがおもしろそうなので、家族で申し込んだ。 The spring cherry blossom tour seems interesting so we made reservations as a family.

25. むかう＜向かう＞／向かいます　V1　to face; to go towards
京都で桜を見物した後、観光バスで奈良に向かった。 After viewing the cherry blossoms in Kyoto, we headed toward Nara in a tour bus.

26. わくわくどきどき (する／します)　V3　to become excited
夏休みに日本に行けると思うと、わくわくどきどきする。 When I think I can travel to Japan this summer, I get very excited.

27. なくす／なくします　V1　to lose
海外旅行中にパスポートをなくすと、大変なことになる。 If you lose your passport while travelling abroad, it will be a terrible thing.

28. とく＜得＞をする／します　V3　to profit; benefit; gain
買った物がセールだったので、得をした。 Since the things I bought were on sale, I benefitted (saved money) from it.

29. (〜が)つうじる＜通じる＞／通じます　V2　to convey; to communicate
アメリカ人はどこへ行っても英語が通じると思っているようだ。 Americans seem to think that they can communicate in English wherever they go.

30. (〜に)せっする＜接する＞／接します　V2　to come in contact with
海外旅行をすると、いろいろな国の文化や人に接することが出来る。 When you travel abroad, you can come in contact with people and cultures of many countries.

【復習単語】
1. -はつ＜-発＞　　　　　　　　　Nd　　- departure
2. -ちゃく＜-着＞　　　　　　　　Nd　　- arrival

19課 文法

> **A. どこかに行こう**   Let's go somewhere.
>
> When a question word is followed by か, the question word carries a meaning of "some 〜." For example, だれか means "someone", どこか means "somewhere," etc.

Write the correct word from the list at the right.

1. (　　　　) 質問がありますか。
2. 将来 (　　　　) 歌手になるのが夢だ。
3. 彼女は突然 (　　　　) 遠くの町に行ってしまった。
4. 日本か韓国か (　　　　) 旅行しよう。
5. 美術館はどこかな。(　　　　) 聞いてみよう。

a. どちらかに
b. 何か
c. どこか
d. だれかに
e. いつか

> **B.** (もし) あなたが行ければ、   If you can go,
>   (もし) 切符が安ければ、   If the ticket is cheap,
>   (もし) 魚が好きなら、   If you like fish,
>   (もし) 四月なら、   If it's in April,
>
> Verb BA form:
>   Group 1   買う→買えば、書く→書けば、泳ぐ→泳げば、話す→話せば、立つ→立てば、
>   死ぬ→死ねば、あそぶ→あそべば、飲む→飲めば、帰る→帰れば
>   Group 2   食べる→食べれば、いる→いれば
>   Group 3   する→すれば、来〔く〕る→来〔く〕れば
>
> The verb -ば form is the conditional form that means, "If and only if...." It appears at the beginning ot the sentence as a subordinate clause.

Fill in the blanks with the BA form of the word in the ( ).

1. 何かこちらから持って行ける物が_____、知らせて下さい。（ある）
2. もし、_____、電車で行こう。（遠い）
3. もし、この週末に桜が_____、日曜日にお花見に行こう。（満開）
4. 旅館に_____、ぜったい温泉に入ってみるといい。（泊まる）
5. 旅行中にパスポートを_____、問題になる。（なくす）
6. 日本旅行が三か月_____、ビザはいらないそうだ。（以内）
7. 日本語が_____、日本の電車に乗るのは大変だ。（分からない）

19課

> C. 日本へ行ける日　　　　　　　　the day I can go to Japan
> Verb Potential form:
> 　Group 1　買う→買える、書く→書ける、泳ぐ→泳げる、話す→話せる、立つ→立てる、
> 　　　　　　死ぬ→死ねる、あそぶ→あそべる、飲む→飲める、帰る→帰れる
> 　Group 2　食べる→食べられる (or 食べれる)、いる→いられる (or いれる)
> 　Group 3　する→出来る、来る→来られる(or 来れる)
> The potential verb form indicates that the subject of the sentence can do 〜. All verbs that are converted to the potential form become Group 2 verbs. The particle following the word that appears to be the direct object may be followed by を or が. The potential form of the verb "can see" (visible) is 見える, and the verb "can hear" (audible) is 聞こえる. The word that precedes these verbs as the object that one can see or hear is always followed by the particle が.

Fill in the blanks with the appropriate potential form of the verb in the ( ).

1. こちらから何か持って＿＿＿＿＿＿物があれば、知らせて下さい。（行く）
2. 日本でどこか安く＿＿＿＿＿＿所を知らない？（泊まる）
3. もし＿＿＿＿＿＿、北海道や沖縄にも行ってみたい。（する）
4. 漢字を二千ぐらい知っていれば、日本の新聞は＿＿＿＿＿＿はずだ。（読む）
5. もし、日本語が＿＿＿＿＿＿、日本旅行はもっと楽しい。（話す）
6. そんなニュースは、＿＿＿＿＿＿。（信じない）

> D. 英語を話されますか。　　　　　Do you speak English? [honorific]
> The honorific and humble forms of verbs are used to show respect by raising the status of the superior subject or lowering the status of the inferior (in most cases, oneself or someone in one's in-group) subject.

Change the underlined word to the non-honorific (neutral) desu/masu form.

1. 教えていただけませんか。→教えて＿＿＿＿＿＿。
2. どうぞよろしくお願いいたします。→どうぞよろしくお願い＿＿＿＿＿＿。
3. 田中と申します。→田中と＿＿＿＿＿＿。

19課

E. Review of informal speech style and formal speech style:

	Informal male	Informal female	Polite
1.	コンテストがあっただろう？	コンテストがあったわよね。	コンテストがあったでしょう？
2.	信じられないけど、	信じられないけど、	信じられませんが、
3.	ゆうしょうしたんだよ。	ゆうしょうしたのよ。	ゆうしょうしたんですよ。
4.	すごいじゃないか。	すごいじゃない。	すごいじゃありませんか。
5.	一週間の旅行なんだよ。	一週間の旅行なのよ。	一週間の旅行なんですよ。
6.	一人で行かなきゃいけないのか。	一人で行かなきゃいけないの？	一人で行かなければいけないんですか。
7.	一人で行かなくちゃいけないんだ。	一人で行かなくちゃいけないの。	一人で行かなければいけないんです。
8.	どうしよう？	どうしよう？	どうしましょうか。
9.	大変だね。	大変ね。	大変ですね。
10.	いいんじゃないかなあ。	いいんじゃないかなあ。	いいんじゃないですか。
11.	そうだね。	そうよね。	そうですよね。
12.	だいじょうぶだよね。	だいじょうぶよね。	だいじょうぶですよね。
13.	だいじょうぶだよ。	だいじょうぶよ。	だいじょうぶですよ。
14.	いつ日本に行くの？	いつ日本に行くの？	いつ日本に行きますか。
15.	おみやげ、買って来てくれよ。	おみやげ、買って来てよ。	おみやげを買って来て下さいよ。 [Inappropriate to say this sentence.]
16.	ほしい物があるんだ。	ほしい物があるの。	ほしい物があります。
17.	おめでとう。	おめでとう。	おめでとうございます。

19課

19課		アクティビティー	

A. 日本文化：一人か二人ワーク→クラスワーク

Divide the topics below among your classmates and research your topic on the Internet. Using visuals, present your findings with your classmates.

1. 豊臣秀吉、大坂城
2. お花見、吉野山
3. 旅館、温泉、浴衣
4. 日本間、畳、障子、襖、玄関、床の間、お風呂、座布団、布団、押入れ
5. 新幹線、のぞみ
6. 成田空港、関西空港
7. 宮島、お好み焼き、広島平和公園
8. 平安神宮、三十三間堂、清水寺、二条城、金閣寺、竜安寺
9. 東大寺、奈良公園

B. ホテル：ペアワーク→クラスワーク

Answer the following questions in English about this hotel.

ホテルセンチュリー２１名古屋

名古屋駅南口より徒歩３分。ビジネスに観光に幅広く御利用いただける本格的なホテルです。便利で優れた２１世紀という名のホテルです。

シングル	¥9,240〜
ツイン	¥16,170〜
ダブル	¥15,015
和室	¥16,170〜
和洋室	¥20,790〜
ロイヤルスイート	¥34,650〜
インペリアルスイート	¥57,750〜

（税*・サービス料込み*）

チェックイン	正午
チェックアウト	午前11:00

● 駐車場　３４台（有料）
● 名古屋駅南口より徒歩３分

宿泊予約・婚礼・レストラン各種のご案内
ご予約・お問い合わせは (0568)263-3111
http://www.hotelcentury21nagoya.com

税* tax、込み* included

1. Where is this hotel? _____
2. Why is this hotel convenient? _____
3. When traveling alone, which room should you choose? _____
   What is the cost of this room in dollars? _____
4. When are the check-in and the check-out times? _____
5. Is parking free? _____
6. What other facilities does this hotel have? _____

C. 聞く Pre-Listening Activity「旅行レポート」：ペアワーク→クラスワーク

Have a conversation with your partner using the following questions in informal form.

1. 日本に旅行したことある？
2. 京都と奈良と大阪の有名な観光地を知っている？
3. 満開の桜を見たことがある？
4. 日本に旅行をしたら、ホテルと旅館とどっちの方に泊まりたい？その理由は？
5. 東京から京都へ行く時、新幹線と飛行機でどちらの方が便利だと思う？その理由は？
6. 日本のお城を見たことがある？
7. 日本のお城とヨーロッパのお城は、何が違うと思う？

D. 聞く Post-Listening Activity「旅行レポート」：ペアワーク→クラスワーク

Compare and Contrast Article: Hotels and Japanese Inns

Compare and contrast hotels and Japanese inns. List three similarities/differences, your preference and the reason. Prepare with your partner in four minutes and present it in class for two minutes.

Introduction:
_____

Three similarities/differences:
1. _____
2. _____
3. _____

Your preference and give reasons:
_____
_____

E. 読む Pre-Reading Activity「日本旅行予定表」：ペアワーク→クラスワーク

Have a conversation with your partner using the following questions in informal form.

1. 一番最近旅行した所は、どこ？そして、だれといつ旅行をした？
2. 何泊何日の旅行だった？
3. どこに宿泊した？それは良かった？
4. 飛行機に乗った？そのほかにもどんな乗物を利用した？
5. 朝食、昼食、夕食はどうした？
6. 観光した中で一番良かったと思う所は、どんな所だった？その理由は？

F. 読む Post-Reading Activity「日本旅行予定表」：ペアワーク→クラスワーク

Cultural Perspective Presentation: Famous Sightseeing Spots in Japan

Present your own view or perspective of famous sightseeing spots in Japan. Discuss at least FIVE aspects or examples of trip to Japan. Begin with an appropriate introduction, give details, explain your own view or perspective, and end with a concluding remark. You will have 4 minutes to prepare your presentation with your partner. Then you will have 2 minutes for your presentation.

1. Begin with an appropriate introduction.
   _____

2. Discuss five aspects/examples of the topic.
   1.) _____
   2.) _____
   3.) _____
   4.) _____
   5.) _____

3. Explain your view or perspective.
   _____

4. End with a concluding remark.
   _____

G. テキストチャット「日本旅行」：ペアワーク→クラスワーク

You will have a conversation about a trip to Japan with Mrs. Nonaka, who will be your host mother in Tokyo for this summer.

First, read this text chat conversation with your partner. Next, read the questions; your partner will respond without looking at the book. Give original answers to the questions. For each question, answer in 20 seconds. Take turns asking and answering questions.

1. 野中：初めまして。野中です。日本行きも、もうすぐですね。

   私　：初めまして。(Last name)と申します。どうぞよろしくお願いします。日本に行くのをとても楽しみにしています。

19課

2. 野中：前、日本に来たことがありますか。
   私　：いいえ、日本へ行ったことはありません。今回が初めてなので、今からわくわくどきどきしています。日本について日本語のクラスでいろいろ習いましたが、本当にこの目でいろいろな物を見てみたいです。
3. 野中：日本に来たら、私達家族と一緒にどこかに旅行しませんか。温泉に興味がありますか。
   私　：わあ、皆さんと一緒に旅行ですか。嬉しいですねえ。有難うございます。日本での旅行は、本当に楽しそうです。温泉ももちろん入ってみたいです。何でも体験したいです。
4. 野中：じゃ、日本で行ってみたい所はどこですか。なぜですか。
   私　：そうですねえ。日本では京都とか奈良のように日本の歴史が残っている伝統的なお寺とか神社を見てみたいです。お城にもぜひ行ってみたいです。でも、もしうちから遠ければ、近くでいいです。
5. 野中：そうですか。ホテルと旅館とどっちの方が好きかしら。
   私　：もちろん旅館の方がホテルよりおもしろそうです。アメリカには旅館はありませんし、旅館は初めての体験なので、ぜひ行ってみたいです。日本語のクラスでも旅館について習いました。ゆかたも着てみたいです。
6. 野中：日本に来ることについて何か質問があったら、聞いて下さい。じゃ、会えるのを楽しみにしていますね。
   私　：すみません、御家族についてもっと教えていただけませんか。皆さんは英語を話されますか。私も日本に行ける日を本当に楽しみにしています。もし、私がそちらに持って行ける物があれば、ぜひ知らせて下さい。では、どうぞよろしくお願いいたします。

G. Compare & Contrast「国内旅行と海外旅行」：ペアワーク→クラスワーク
   a. First, read this compare and contrast passage with your partner.

　これから国内旅行と海外旅行を比べてみます。国内旅行も海外旅行も旅行なので、どちらも楽しいですが、違う点もあります。
　まず一つ目の違いは、海外旅行に行く時には、パスポートとビザが必要ですが、国内旅行に行く時には、パスポートもビザも必要ありません。パスポートは身分証明書になるので、旅行中なくせば、問題になります。ビザは日本に観光で行く時、三か月以内なら、要らないそうです。

19課

次に、二つ目の違いは、海外に旅行すると、その国のお金が必要ですが、国内旅行は、同じお金が使えます。お金の交換レートは毎日変わるので、アメリカ人にはドル高の時に、旅行する方が得です。

　最後に、三つ目の違いは、海外旅行ではその国の言葉を話すはずですが、国内旅行は外国語を話さなくてもいいです。しかし、最近英語が国際語のようになっているので、だいたいどこの国へ行っても、英語が通じます。

　結論として、私は海外旅行の方が国内旅行より好きです。なぜなら、海外旅行へ行くと、いろいろな違う国の人達や文化に接することが出来るからです。海外旅行をして、いろいろな国の人と友達になれば、世界はもっと平和になるはずです。

b. Next, work with your partner and together compare and contrast overseas travel and domestic travel. List three similarities and/or differences, your preference and the reason for your preference. Give your own opinions. Then, share your presentation with your class.

Introduction:
___

Three similarities/differences:
1. ___
2. ___
3. ___

Your preference and reasons:
___
___

H. 会話「スピーチコンテスト」：ペアワーク→クラスワーク

First, read this conversation with your partner. Next, read the questions; your partner will respond without looking at the book. Repeat the underlined parts and give your own answers to the questions. For each question, answer in 20 seconds. Take turns asking and answering questions. You will have a conversation with Masashi, your Japanese friend, about his speech contest.

1. 質問：今日スピーチコンテストがあっただろう？信じられないけど、優勝したんだよ。

　答 (例-女)：優勝？本当？すごいじゃない。おめでとう！やったね。優勝した感想はどう？

　答 (例-男)：優勝？本当？すごいじゃないか。おめでとう！やったね。優勝した感想はどう？

2. 質問：それで、賞が一週間の日本旅行なんだよ。

　答 (例-女)：ええっ、日本旅行？わあ、いいなあ。うらやましい。でも、いつ日本に行くの？一人で行かなきゃいけないの？

19課

答(例-男)：ええっ、日本旅行？わあ、いいなあ。うらやましい。でも、いつ日本に行くの？一人で行かなきゃいけないのか。
3. 質問：でも、困ったことに、先生と一緒に行かなくちゃいけないんだ。どうしよう？
   答(例-女/男)：へえ、先生と二人で？それはちょっと大変だね。でも、先生と一緒だったら、心配することはないから、いいんじゃないかなあ。
4. 質問：そうだね。大丈夫だよね。
   答(例-女)：もちろん、大丈夫よ。それで、いつ日本に行くの？日本に行ったら、おみやげ、買って来てね。ほしい物があるの。とにかく、おめでとう！
   答(例-男)：もちろん、大丈夫だよ。それで、いつ日本に行くの？日本に行ったら、おみやげ、買って来てくれよ。ほしい物があるんだ。とにかく、おめでとう！

I. 文化発表「日本の旅館」：ペアワーク→クラスワーク

a. Choose the correct word from below and write the correct letter in the ( ) below the passage.

これから日本の旅館について発表します。日本の旅館はホテルのようですが、ホテルととても違います。旅館の五つの(1.)について話します。
　まず第一に、旅館はとても(2.)です。部屋はたいてい畳の日本間で、障子や襖もあり、玄関や床の間などもあります。部屋に案内してくれる仲居さんは着物を着ていて、とてもていねいです。
　第二に、旅館に泊まると、朝食と夕食が付いています。個人で泊まると、食事はたいてい自分の部屋で食べます。仲居さんが部屋に食事を持って来てくれます。食事は(3.)で、いろいろな食べ物が出されますが、その地方の特産物を味わうことが出来ます。
　第三に、旅館では(4.)を着て、食事をしたり、外に散歩に行ったり、寝たりします。夏の浴衣は涼しいですが、寒い季節の浴衣は、温かいです。
　第四に、旅館での一番の楽しみは、(5.)です。部屋にもお風呂がありますが、旅館にはいろいろな健康にいい温泉も外にある温泉もあります。
　第五に、旅館では(6.)に寝ます。夕方、外から部屋に帰ると、部屋には布団が敷いてあります。朝になると、仲居さんが来て布団を押入れに片付けてくれます。
　結論として、旅館は日本のいろいろな伝統的な(7.)を体験出来る所です。旅館での客へのサービスは特別です。それに、チップをあげる習慣もありません。外国からの観光客はぜひ旅館に泊まって、日本を体験するといいです。
　私の発表を聞いて下さいまして、有難うございました。以上です。

19課

1. (　)　2. (　)　3. (　)　4. (　)　5. (　)　6. (　)　7. (　)

a. 和食　b. 布団（ふとん）　c. 浴衣（ゆかた）　d. 特徴（ちょう）　e. 温泉（おんせん）　f. 文化　g. 日本的

b. Discuss the following questions with your partner and classmates.

1. なぜ日本にはチップをあげる習慣(かん)がないのでしょうか。
_____

2. なぜ旅館では浴衣(ゆかた)を着て、食事をしたり、外を散歩(さん)したり、寝たりするのでしょうか。
_____

3. なぜ日本人は温泉(おんせん)やお風呂が好きなのでしょうか。
_____

19課

<19課 - 聞く>
Listening: Travel Report

12秒×5

【You may take notes while listening. Do not look at the questions below before listening. You will have 12 seconds to answer each question. You may NOT move back and forth among questions.】

(Narrator) Now you will listen to a presentation of trip in Japan once.

(Narrator) Now answer the questions for this selection.

1. What tour did he plan?
   (A) a tour to see the cherry blossoms in Kyoto
   (B) a three night, four day tour
   (C) a weekend tour
   (D) a bus tour from Tokyo

2. What information did he get from the Internet?
   (A) Mt. Yoshino has more than one hundred cherry trees.
   (B) Mt. Yoshino is in Kyoto.
   (C) Mt. Yoshino turns red during the cherry blossom season.
   (D) Mt. Yoshino is historically famous for cherry blossoms.

3. What kind of tour did he join?
   (A) The tour was by bus.
   (B) The price was very cheap.
   (C) The tour price included two nights lodging fee.
   (D) The tour was from Osaka Station.

4. Where did he stay during his trip?
   (A) in Kyoto and Nara
   (B) in Kyoto and Osaka
   (C) in Nara and Osaka
   (D) in Kyoto for two nights

5. What was his impression of the tour?
   (A) Taking photos of the cherry blossoms at night was fun.
   (B) The cherry blossom viewers were well mannered.
   (C) Viewing the cherry blossoms at Osaka Castle was the best.
   (D) Viewing the cherry blossoms from the hot spring was the best.

<19課 - 読む>
Reading: Travel Brochure
【You may move back and forth among all the questions.】

		日本旅行予定表
7月11日（火）	12:20	ホノルル発 Jalways 77 便
7月12日（水）	16:05	関西空港着
		英語通訳の出迎え、バスで広島へ（荷物持参）
		夕食：バス内（幕の内弁当）
		宿泊：ニュー広電ホテル
7月13日（木）		朝食：ホテルにて
	08:30	一日観光：宮島（英語ガイド付き）
		昼食：弁当
		夕食：お好み焼き（ホテルグランビアにて）
		宿泊：ニュー広電ホテル
7月14日（金）		＊＊荷物は京都へトラックで搬送＊＊
		朝食：ホテルにて
	08:30	広島平和公園と資料館（英語ガイド付き）
	12:00	広島発　新幹線のぞみ20号
		昼食：新幹線で弁当
	13:45	京都着、英語ガイドの出迎え
		市内観光：平安神宮、三十三間堂、清水寺
		夕食：ホテルにて
		宿泊：京都リーガロイヤルホテル
7月15日（土）		朝食：ホテルにて
	08:00	京都観光：二条城、金閣寺、竜安寺（英語ガイド）
		昼食：京料理
		奈良観光：東大寺、奈良公園で鹿見学
		夕食：ステーキハウス
		宿泊：京都リーガロイヤルホテル
7月16日（日）		朝食：ホテルにて
	09:32	京都発　新幹線のぞみ122号
	11:53	東京着、バスで慶応高校へ
7月16日（日）〜8月3日（木）：慶応高校にて夏期講座（午前日本語授業、午後社会見学）、国際交流、ホームステイ		
8月03日（木）	16:00	慶応高校集合、成田国際空港へバスで
	20:25	成田国際空港発 Jalways76 便
8月03日（木）	08:30	ホノルル空港到着

19課

<19課 - 読む (質問)>

Reading: Travel Brochure

(Narrator) Now answer the questions for this section.

1. When this group arrives in Japan, how will they be transported from the airport to Hiroshima?
   (A) bus
   (B) bullet train
   (C) airplane
   (D) electric car

2. In Hiroshima, what is NOT planned?
   (A) sightseeing with an English speaking guide
   (B) stay at a Japanese inn
   (C) visiting the Peace Park
   (D) eating *bento* for lunch

3. What activities are included while staying in Kyoto and Nara?
   (A) staying at a Japanese inn in Kyoto.
   (B) visiting a castle in Nara.
   (C) visiting temples and shrines for two days.
   (D) eating Japanese style dinner for two days.

4. What is NOT scheduled while they are in Tokyo?
   (A) homestay
   (B) Japanese language study
   (C) field trips
   (D) community service

5. Which is NOT correct?
   (A) They arrive at Kansai Airport.
   (B) They ride the bullet train once.
   (C) They leave Japan from Narita Airport on the departure day.
   (D) They gather at school and go to the airport on the day they depart from Japan.

<19課 - 書く (テキストチャット)>

Text Chat: Trip to Japan

90秒×6

You will participate in a simulated exchange of text-chat messages. Each time it is your turn to write, you will have 90 seconds. You should respond as fully and as appropriately as possible.

You will have a conversation with Mrs. Nonaka, your host mother in Tokyo for this summer, about your plans.

1. Respond. (90 seconds)

   初めまして。野中です。日本行きも、もうすぐですね。

2. Describe your experience. (90 seconds)

   前、日本に来たことがありますか。

3. Respond. (90 seconds)

   日本に来たら、私達家族と一緒にどこかに旅行しませんか。温泉(おんせん)に興味(きょう)がありますか。

4. State your opinion. (90 seconds)

   じゃ、日本で行ってみたい所はどこですか。なぜですか。

5. Give your preference. (90 seconds)

   そうですか。ホテルと旅館とどっちの方が好きかしら。

6. Ask a specific question. (90 seconds)

   日本に来ることについて何か質問があったら、聞いて下さい。じゃ、会えるのを楽しみにしていますね。

<19課 - 書く (比較(ひかく)と対比(たいひ))>

Compare & Contrast Article: Hotels & Japanese Inns

20分

Directions: You are writing an article for the student newspaper of your sister school in Japan. Write an article in which you compare and contrast similarities and differences between hotels and Japanese inns. Based on your personal experience, describe at least THREE aspects of each and highlight the similarities and/or differences between hotels and Japanese inns. Also state your preference for either and give reasons for it.

Your article should be 300 to 400 characters or longer. Use the *desu/masu* or *da* (plain) style, but use one style consistently. Also, use *kanji* wherever *kanji* from the AP Japanese *kanji* list is appropriate. You have 20 minutes to write.

【NOTES/OUTLINE: 自分の作文のアウトラインを書こう！】

Introduction:
_____

Three similarities/differences:

　1. _____
　2. _____
　3. _____

Your preference and give reasons:
_____
_____

19課

＜19課 - 話す(会話)＞
Conversation: Speech Contest

`20秒×4`

You will participate in a simulated conversation. Each time it is your turn to speak, you will have 20 seconds to record. You should respond as fully and as appropriately as possible.

You will have a conversation with Masashi, your Japanese friend, about his speech contest.

(Masashi)
(20 seconds)
(Masashi)
(20 seconds)
(Masashi)
(20 seconds)
(Masashi)
(20 seconds)

＜19課 - 話す(日本文化)＞
Cultural Perspective Presentation: Japanese Inns

`4分+2分`

Directions: Imagine that you are making an oral presentation to your Japanese class. First, you will read and hear the topic for your presentation. You will have 4 minutes to prepare your presentation. Then you will have 2 minutes to record your presentation. Your presentation should be as complete as possible.

Present your own view or perspective of Japanese inns. Discuss at least FIVE aspects or examples of Japanese inns.

Begin with an appropriate introduction, give details, explain your own view or perspective, and end with a concluding remark.

【Let's take notes!】

1. Begin with an appropriate introduction.

_____

2. Discuss five aspects/examples of the topic.

    1.) _____
    2.) _____
    3.) _____
    4.) _____
    5.) _____

3. Explain your view or perspective.

_____

4. End with a concluding remark.

_____

20課　日本と世界
Japan and the World

【AP® タスク：世界】
What kind of global citizen do you want to become? How would you like to incorporate Japan and/or the Japanese language into your life? How would you want to contribute to the global community using the Japanese language?

【文化】 日本への外国からの影響（えいきょう）：Foreign Influences in Japan

Almost every aspect of the modern day Japanese lifestyle has in some way been touched by foreign influence at some time in Japan's history.

One of the most powerful influences came from China during several major points in Japan's history. Before 200 CE, Japan did not possess its own writing system, but thereafter adopted Chinese characters, and even created *hiragana* and *katakana* from *kanji*. The teachings of Confucianism melded well with the values of the native Japanese and continue to guide the lives of the Japanese. The bureaucratic governmental structure of China, featuring the Imperial Court, was adopted by the Japanese. Chinese city planning models, built around the imperial center, were used when designing the cities of Kyoto and Nara. The even, rectangular layout of fields and irrigation systems and construction of roads in Japanese cities were also patterned after cities in China. Some of Japan's architecture reflects Han Dynasty influences. Traditional women's *kimono* is modeled after Han dynasty robes worn by women of wealth or status.

Asian continental neighbors influenced Japan through Korea, which served as a conduit to Japan. Artifacts that traveled along the Silk Road through China and Korea are said to have made their way to Japan. Buddhism, which originated in India, evolved in form as it spread through China, Korea and finally to Japan. Chinese court music and dance also found their way to Japan through Korea and many traditional Japanese instruments have counterparts in China and Korea. Some of Japan's oldest temples in Nara were designed and built by Koreans. Japan's handicrafts, particularly those made of wood, lacquer, gilt bronze and metal, are said to be Korean influenced.

One of the first of Japan's encounters with the West was with Portuguese Basque Jesuit missionaries who arrived in Kyuushuu in the mid-1500's. Along with Christianity, the Portuguese introduced firearms, the printing press and Western musical instruments. Portuguese words such as *pan*, *tabako*, *botan* (button) and *bisuketto*, entered the Japanese language at this time.

After the Portuguese, the Dutch enjoyed trading privileges in isolated Japan for several centuries during the Edo Period. Although the Japanese developed a somewhat cautious relationship with them, they learned from the Dutch about Western medicine, geography, various sciences, military arts and the fine arts. Many words of Dutch origin remain in the Japanese vocabulary today. The words *biiru*, *koohii* and *garasu* are some examples.

Since the opening of Japan toward the end of the Edo Period by Commodore Perry, Japan has been influenced significantly by the West, particularly the U. S. In 1871, the Iwakura Mission was sent abroad by Meiji leaders on an extended tour of the U. S. and Europe to learn as much as it could from the West. From the Americans and French, they adopted a Western educational system and introduced many new American agricultural practices. Since then, and particularly after World War II, Americans have had considerable influence on the daily lives of the Japanese in government, pop culture, education, politics and economics. English has become the primary second language of the Japanese.

Over the course of its history, Japan has been fascinated by the cultures of foreign countries. It has embraced them with vigor, while also cleverly adapting what was best suited to them with a constant desire to improve, refine and perfect.

Questions to ponder: Can you think of other foreign-conceived products that Japan has adapted and improved? What characteristics of the Japanese make them so successful at this?

20課　復習単語

トピック：日本と世界

1. 地球	ちきゅう	N	the earth
2. 世界	せかい	N	world
3. 国	くに	N	country; nation
4. 州	しゅう	N	state
5. 移民	いみん	N	immigrant
6. 人種	じんしゅ	N	ethnic race
7. 人種差別	じんしゅさべつ	N	racial discrimination
8. 何人	なにじん	Ni	what nationality?
9. 何語	なにご	Ni	what language?
10. 通訳(を)する	つうやく(を)する	V3	(to) interpret
11. 戦争	せんそう	N	war; warfare
12. 軍	ぐん	N	military
13. 日本軍	にほんぐん	N	Japanese military
14. 敵	てき	N	enemy
15. 敵国人	てきこくじん	Na	citizen of a hostile (an enemy) country
16. 召集(を)する	しょうしゅう(を)する	V3	(to) draft (for military service)
17. 第二次世界大戦	だいにじせかいたいせん	N	World War II
18. 真珠湾	しんじゅわん	N	Pearl Harbor
19. 収容所	しゅうようじょ	N	internment camp; concentration camp
20. 原爆	げんばく	N	atomic bomb
21. 平和	へいわ	N/Na	peace; peaceful
22. 大統領	だいとうりょう	N	president (of country)
23. 経済	けいざい	N	economics
24. 米国	べいこく	N	U.S.
25. 日米	にちべい	N	Japan-U.S.
26. 日本	にほん	N	Japan
27. 日本人	にほんじん	N	Japanese citizen
28. 日系(人)	にっけい(じん)	N	person of Japanese descent
29. - 世	せい	Nd	(counter for) generation
30. アメリカ		N	U.S.
31. アメリカ人	アメリカじん	N	U.S. citizen
32. 中国	ちゅうごく	N	China

33. 韓国　　　　　かんこく　　　　　　N　　　South Korea
34. ドイツ　　　　　　　　　　　　　N　　　Germany
35. フランス　　　　　　　　　　　　N　　　France
36. スペイン　　　　　　　　　　　　N　　　Spain

20課

20課　★★★　新しい単語　★★★

1. (お)みまい＜(御)見舞い＞　N　visit to someone who is ill
   みまう＜見舞う＞／見舞います　V1　to visit someone who is ill
   母は祖母の見舞いに病院へ行った。My mom went to the hospital to visit my grandmother.

2. おもいやり＜思いやり＞　N　empathetic thoughtfulness
   友人はとても思いやりがある。My friend is very thoughtful (and empathetic).

3. やまのぼり＜山登り＞　N　mountain climbing
   とざん＜登山＞　N　mountain climbing
   とざんか＜登山家＞　N　mountain climber
   山登りは好きだが、エベレストのような山は特別な登山家しか登らない。I like mountain climbing, but only special mountain climbers climb mountains like Everest.

4. おちこぼれ＜落ちこぼれ＞　N　dropout
   父は子供の時、落ちこぼれだったそうだ。When my father was a child, I understand he was a dropout.

5. さんちょう＜山頂＞　N　mountain top; summit
   元旦に富士山の山頂から朝日を見た。On New Year's Day, we saw the sunrise from the summit of Mt. Fuji.

6. たいりょう＜大量＞　N　large quantity
   山にゴミが大量に捨てられている。There is a large amount of trash strewn about the mountain.

7. いちりゅう＜一流＞　first class; foremost
   日本人のマナーが一流かどうか知らない。I don't know if Japanese manners are top notch or not.

8. えんぜつ＜演説＞　N　speech
   大統領は演説が上手だ。The president is skilled at speech making.

9. せだい＜世代＞　N　generation
   次の世代に美しい自然を残そう。Let's leave some natural beauty for the next generation.

10. せいひん＜製品＞　N　manufactured products
    にほんせい＜日本製＞　N　made in Japan
    日本製の携帯はいろいろな機能が入っている。Japanese cell phones have many different functions.

11. たじんしゅ＜多人種＞　N　multi-ethnic
    アメリカは多人種の国だ。　America is a multi-ethnic country.

12. せんきょ＜選挙＞　N　election
    大統領も知事も市長も選挙で選ばれる。　The president, governor and mayor are all chosen by elections.

13. せいじ＜政治＞　N　politics
    若者も政治に参加することが大事だ。　It is important that the young people also participate in politics.

14. そうりだいじん＜総理大臣＞　N　prime minister
    日本の総理大臣がだれか知らない。　I don't know who the prime minister of Japan is.

15. かけがえのない　A　irreplaceable; precious
    かけがえのない自然を守ろう。　Let's protect our precious nature.

16. どうか　Adv　please; somehow
    どうかもう一度考えてみてください。　Please somehow try and think about it once more.

17. おる＜折る＞／折ります　V1　to fold
    おりがみ＜折り紙＞　N　*origami* paper
    おりづる＜折り鶴＞　N　*origami* crane
    千羽鶴を折ったことがある。　I have folded a thousand cranes before.

18. ひろげる＜広げる＞／広げます　V2　to spread; extend; widen
    思いやりの心を周りに広げよう。　Let's extend our thoughtfulness to those around us.

19. ねがい＜願い＞を＜込める＞／込めます　V2　to put into; to include
    折り鶴に願いを込めて折って下さい。　Please include your hopes in your folded cranes as you fold the origami cranes.

20. (〜に)しんぱい＜心配＞をかける／かけます　V2　to worry (someone)
    家族に心配をかけたくない。　I don't want to worry my family.

21. ゆにゅう＜輸入＞(を)する／します　V3　to import
    ゆにゅうひん＜輸入品＞　N　imported goods
    日本は外国から多くの資源を輸入している。　Japan imports many resources from foreign countries.

22. ゆしゅつ＜輸出＞(を)する／します　V3　to export
    ゆしゅつひん＜輸出品＞　N　exported goods
    日本は多くの製品を海外に輸出している。　Japan exports many manufactured goods abroad.

20課

23. とりもどす＜取り戻す＞／取り戻します　V1　to take back; regain
　　山登りを始めて、自信を取り戻すことが出来た。　I began mountain climbing and regained self-confidence.

24. N1にN2をかける／かけます　V2　to stake; to take a gamble (on)
　　青春を山にかけた。　He staked his youth on the mountain.

25. くふう＜工夫＞(を)する／します　V3　to devise; scheme, figure out
　　日本人は物を工夫して、より良い物を作ることが上手だ。　Japanese are skilled at taking something and devising it into something even better.

26. きょうぞん＜共存＞(を)する／します　V3　to co-exist
　　違う文化が共存出来ることが大事だ。　It is important for different cultures to be able to co-exist together.

27. とうひょう＜投票＞(を)する／します　V3　to vote
　　私も今の大統領に投票したい。　I want to vote for the current president too.

28. とりいれる＜取り入れる＞／取り入れます　V2　to take in; to adopt (something)
　　日本は歴史的に海外からいろいろなものを取り入れた。　Historically, Japan has adopted many things from abroad.

29. まねる＜真似る＞／真似ます　V2　to imitate; to mimic
　　真似ることは、学ぶことだ。　To mimic (others) is to learn (from others).

30. いんさつ＜印刷＞(を)する／します　V3　to print
　　レポートは印刷して提出して下さい。　Please print the report and turn it in.

31. きよう＜器用＞　Na　dextrous, skillful
　　きようさ＜器用さ＞　N　dexterity; skill
　　日本人は手が器用だ。　Japanese are skilled with their hands.

【もっと単語】
1. たいりく＜大陸＞　　　　　　　　　　N　continent
2. きぼう＜希望＞　　　　　　　　　　　N　hope
3. しゅくじつ＜祝日＞　　　　　　　　　N　national holiday
4. だいとうりょう＜大統領＞　　　　　　N　president (of a country)
5. こうし＜孔子＞　　　　　　　　　　　N　Confucius
6. れいぎ＜礼儀＞　　　　　　　　　　　N　manners; etiquette
7. ポルトガル　　　　　　　　　　　　　N　Portugal

20課

8. オランダ		N	Netherlands; Holland
9. さこく＜鎖国＞		N	isolation (of country)
10. ちり＜地理＞		N	geography
11. ぐんじ＜軍事＞		N	military
12. くろふね＜黒船＞		N	black ship
13. せんきょうし＜宣教師＞		N	missionary
14. みんしゅとう＜民主党＞		N	Democratic Party
15. きょうわとう＜共和党＞		N	Republican Party
16. きちょう＜貴重＞		Na	valuable
17. のべる＜述べる＞／述べます		V2	to describe
18. さんせい＜賛成＞(を) する／します		V3	to agree
19. はんたい＜反対＞(を) する／します		V3	to disagree
20. ぼうえき＜貿易＞(を) する／します		V3	to trade
21. きょか＜許可＞(を) する／します		V3	to permit

20課 文法

> A. 分からない<u>ように</u>、泣いた。　　cry in such a way ～
>
> When －ように follows a verb in a plain form in a subordinate clause, it carries the meaning of the subject doing a subsequent action in a similar way suggested by that verb, or in consideration of the action suggested by that verb.

Circle the most appropriate response from within the (　).

1. 日本語は（読む　読まない　読める　読めない）ように、きれいに書いて下さい。
2. 風邪を（引く　引かない）ように、気をつけよう。
3. アジアの人と（話す　話さない　話せる　話せない）ように、大学へ行ったら、日本語も中国語も韓国語も勉強したいんです。
4. 周りに心配を（かける　かけない）ように、誰にも言わなかった。
5. 富士山が（登る　登らない　登れる　登れない）ように、毎日4マイル歩いている。
6. 去年姉が日本の大学に（留学する　留学しない　留学した　留学しなかった）ように、私も大学へ行ってから、日本の大学に留学したい。
7. 日本が外国からいろいろな事を（習う　習わない　習った　習わなかった）ように、私達も新しい事を習い続ける方がいい。
8. 祖母が生前決して動物の肉を（食べる　食べない　食べた　食べなかった）ように、私も野菜しか食べない。

> B. <u>だれも</u>知らない。　　　　No one knows.
>   <u>だれも(が)</u>知っている。　Everyone knows.
>   <u>だれか</u>知っている？　　　Does anyone know it?
>
> When a question word such as だれ, どこ, いつ, etc. is followed by も and an negative sentence ending it means "no ～," as in "no one." When it is followed by an affirmative ending, it means "every ～," such as "everyone." When -か follows a question word, it means "any ～," as in "anyone."

Circle the most appropriate response from within the (　).

1. ゴミは（何か　何も）しなければいけないと思う。
2. 家族に心配をかけたくなかったので、（だれか　だれにも）言わなかった。
3. 世界平和は（だれか　だれも）希望している。
4. 戦争は（だれか　だれも）ほしくない。
5. （だれか　だれも）富士山へゴミ拾いに行きたい人は、いない？
6. （だれか　だれも）富士山へゴミ拾いに行きたい人は、いない。

C. 痛い→痛さ　　　　　　　pain
　いい→良〔よ〕さ　　　　　good point
　静か→静かさ　　　　　　　quietness
　教える→教え　　　　　　　teaching

Certain いadjectives, なadjectives and verbs can be converted to nouns. For いadjectives, add -さ after dropping the final い of the adjective. For なadjectives, add -さ to the -な adjective. For verbs, use the verb stem.

Fill in the blanks with the noun form of the word in the (　).

1. 船に乗って、太平洋の_____に驚いた。（広い）
2. 入院していた時に、多くの友人が_____に来てくれた。（見舞う）
3. 貧しい人の生活の_____は、金持ちには分からないようだ。（苦しい）
4. 日本人の_____は、いい点だと思う。（まじめ）
5. _____がある時には、だれかに話した方がいい。（悩む）
6. 日本製品の_____は、よく作られていることだ。（いい）

D. Causative form　　make/let someone do ～

Group 1:　買う→買わせる、書く→書かせる、話す→話させる、立つ→立たせる、
　　　　　死ぬ→死なせる、遊ぶ→遊ばせる、読む→読ませる、帰る→帰らせる
Group 2:　食べる→食べさせる、見る→見させる
Group 3:　する→させる、来〔く〕る→来〔こ〕させる

The causative form is used when a person or thing (causee) is caused, made, allowed or forced to do an action by the subject or implied subject (causer). The subject is followed by は (sometimes が) and the person or thing caused to do something is followed by を or に. When the verb is transitive, the causee is followed by に, as a direct object (followed by を) already exists. When the verb is intransitive, the causee may be followed by を or に. Usually, when it is followed by を, the sentence suggests that the causee is being forced, rather than allowed, to do the action. If, however, a verb extender that is a verb of giving (あげる, やる, くれる, etc.), the sentence suggests that the causee is being allowed to do the action, regardless of the particle following the causee.

Fill in the blanks with the appropriate causative form of the word in the (　) and circle the correct word from the [　].

1. 富士山登山を_____たい。（成功する）
2. 家族に_____たくない。（心配する）
3. ペリーの黒船は日本に鎖国を_____た。（やめる）
4. 先生は生徒に教室のごみを_____た。（拾う）
5. 両親は私にピアノを_____た。（続ける）
6. 両親は夏に私を日本へ_____［あげる　くれる　もらう］。（行く）
7. 私は夏に両親に日本へ_____［あげ　くれ　もらい］たい。（旅行する）

20課

8. 私は弟に私のゲームを＿＿＿＿＿＿［やる　くれる　もらう］。（使う）
9. 祖母に私のバイオリンを＿＿＿＿＿＿［あげ　くれ　もらい］たい。（聞く）

E. Verb Passive form

Group 1：買う→買われる、書く→書かれる、話す→話される、待つ→待たれる、
　　　　　死ぬ→死なれる、呼ぶ→呼ばれる、読む→読まれる、帰る→帰られる

Group 2：食べる→食べられる、見る→見られる

Group 3：する→される、来〔く〕る→来〔こ〕られる

The passive form is identical in form to the *sonkeigo* irregular verb forms, though they are not related in usage. Passive forms are used more frequently in Japanese than in English as they are perceived as less direct. In passive constructions, the subject (usually followed by は) is the object or party that is the receiver of the action. The party or object that is the agent is followed by に. In the case of an active transitive sentence that is converted to a passive, the direct object becomes the subject (as in many English sentences) and the original subject becomes the agent. Japanese also has indirect passives. In these cases, the subject (receiver of the action) is often the victim or the one negatively affected by the action.

Fill in the blanks with the appropriate passive form of the word in the ( ).

1. 私は日本の大学に留学すべきだと先生に＿＿＿＿＿＿た。（言う）
2. 私は友達に誕生パーティーに＿＿＿＿＿＿た。（さそう）
3. エベレストにも富士山にもゴミが多く＿＿＿＿＿＿いるそうだ。（捨てる）
4. 漢字は中国で＿＿＿＿＿＿た。（作る）
5. １９４５年に原爆が広島と長崎に＿＿＿＿＿＿た。（落とす）
6. 日本が江戸時代に鎖国していた時にも、オランダは日本との貿易を＿＿＿＿＿＿いた。（許可する）
7. 鉄砲はポルトガル人によって日本に＿＿＿＿＿＿た。（伝える）

F. ～だけでなく、～も　　　not only ～, but also ～

1. 日本だけでなく、中国もオリンピックに参加した。
　　It was not only Japan, but also China that participated in the Olympics.
2. 日本は小さいだけでなく、資源も少ない。
　　Japan is not only small, but also has scarce resources.
3. 日本料理が好きなだけでなく中国料理も好きだ。
　　I like not only Japanese food, but also Chinese food.
4. 日本へ行っただけでなく中国へも行った。
　　I went to not only Japan, but also to China.

To mention one statement about the subject and add another supporting piece of information about that subject in one sentence, one uses the だけでなく form. Usage of this form strongly emphasizes that two important points are being made.

20課

Fill in the ( ) with one particle from the list below. You may use the same particle more than once.

1. 柔道をして、体（　）だけでなく、心（　）大事だと習った。
2. 日本の歴史は中国から（　）だけでなく、韓国から（　）強い影響（　）受けた。
3. 富士山は日本一高い（　）だけではなく、形（　）非常に美しい。
4. ケンさんは日本で仕事をする（　）だけでなく、中国で（　）仕事（　）する。
5. 日本人は手が器用（　）だけでなく、とてもまじめに仕事（　）するので、いい物（　）作る。
6. 野口さんは山登りによって、自信を取り戻した（　）だけでなく、山（　）ゴミ拾いの運動（　）始めることにした。

| を | の | な | も | X |

20課

20課　アクティビティー

A. 日本文化：一人か二人ワーク→クラスワーク

Divide the topics below among your classmates and research your topic on the Internet. Using visuals, present your findings with your classmates.

1. 佐々木禎子、千羽鶴、白血病、原爆
2. 富士山、野口健
3. 茶道、書道、生け花、俳句、柔道、剣道
4. 孔子
5. 鎖国
6. ペリー、黒船

B. 聞く Pre-Listening Activity「世界平和」：ペアワーク→クラスワーク

Have a conversation with your partner with the following prompts, using the informal style.

1. 原爆が日本のどの都市に落とされたか知っている？
2. 禎子という女の子のお話の本を読んだことがある？それはいつのことだった？
3. 禎子が何の病気で亡くなったか、何才で亡くなったか、知っている？
4. 千羽鶴が何か知っている？
5. 禎子がなぜ千羽鶴を折っていたか知っている？

C. 聞く Post-Listening Activity「世界平和」：ペアワーク→クラスワーク

Cultural Perspective Presentation: Sadako

You will have 4 minutes to prepare your presentation. Then you will have 2 minutes to do your presentation. Your presentation should be as complete as possible.

Present your own view or perspective on Sadako. Discuss at least FIVE aspects or examples.

Begin with an appropriate introduction, give details, explain your own view or perspective, and end with a concluding remark.

1. Begin with an appropriate introduction.
   _____

2. Discuss five aspects/examples of the topic.
   1.) _____
   2.) _____
   3.) _____
   4.) _____
   5.) _____

3. Explain your view or perspective.
   _____

4. End with a concluding remark.
   _____

D. 読む Pre-Reading Activity 「環境〔かんきょう〕」：ペアワーク→クラスワーク

With the following questions, have a conversation with your partner using the informal style.

1. 山登りが好き？
2. チャンスがあれば、エベレストに登りたいと思う？
3. 冒険することが好き？
4. 青春をかけている何か特別なものがある？
5. 落ちこぼれの人が山登りをすると、自信を取り戻せると思う？
6. 富士山やエベレストの山頂にゴミが大量に捨てられていることを知っている？
7. 富士山にゴミ拾いに登りたいと思う？
8. 日本人のマナーは一流だと思う？

E. 読む Post-Reading Activity 「環境〔かんきょう〕」：ペアワーク→クラスワーク

Cultural Perspective Presentation: A Famous Historical Figure of Japan

You will have 4 minutes to prepare your presentation. Then you will have 2 minutes to do your presentation. Your presentation should be as complete as possible.

Present your own view or perspective of a famous historical figure of Japan. Discuss at least FIVE aspects or examples.

Begin with an appropriate introduction, give details, explain your own view or perspective, and end with a concluding remark.

1. Begin with an appropriate introduction.
   _____

2. Discuss five aspects/examples of the topic.
   1.) _____
   2.) _____
   3.) _____
   4.) _____
   5.) _____

3. Explain your view or perspective.
   _____

4. End with a concluding remark.
   _____

F. テキストチャット 「日本の製品〔せいひん〕」：ペアワーク→クラスワーク

You will have a conversation with Mr. Watanabe, a Japanese college student who is interviewing American high school students about Japanese products.

First, read this text chat conversation with your partner. Next, read the questions and your partner will respond without looking at the book. Give original answers to the questions. For each question, answer in 20 seconds. Take turns asking and answering questions.

20課

1. 渡辺：こんにちは。今日は日本の製品について意見を聞かせて下さい。
   私　：こんにちは。日本の製品についての意見ですか。分かりました。出来るだけ答えてみますから、何でも聞いて下さい。
2. 渡辺：今持っている物の中に、どんな日本製の物がありますか。
   私　：私が今持っている日本製の物では、ボールペンや鉛筆や消しゴムなどがあります。日本製の物はかわいいし、格好いいので、大好きです。
3. 渡辺：日本からの輸入品の中で、アメリカで何が一番人気がありますか。
   私　：そうですねえ。いろいろな物がありますが、若者に一番人気があるのは、日本のアニメでしょう。多くの友達が日本のアニメのＤＶＤを持っています。大人は日本製の車や電気製品が好きなようですが。
4. 渡辺：日本の製品とほかの国の製品を比べて、何が違うと思いますか。
   私　：そうですねえ。日本の物はもっと質がいいと思います。よく作られています。いろいろな工夫がされているので、使うのが楽しいです。
5. 渡辺：今一番ほしい日本製の物は何ですか。なぜですか。
   私　：私は車がほしいんですが、車なら日本製がほしいです。それも、電気で動く車がいいですねえ。エコ車は環境にやさしいと思います。
6. 渡辺：何か日本の製品についての希望を教えて下さい。どうも貴重な答を有難うございました。
   私　：私の希望は、日本の製品はちょっと値段が高いので、もっと安ければ嬉しいです。このチャットは楽しかったです。有難うございました。

G. Compare & Contrast「日本の文化とアメリカの文化」：ペアワーク→クラスワーク

a. First, read this compare and contrast passage with your partner.

　これから、日本の文化とアメリカの文化を比べてみます。たくさん違うことがありますが、三つの違いを述べます。
　まず、一つ目の大きな違いは、日本には一つの文化がありますが、アメリカにはいろいろな文化があります。日本に住んでいる人はほとんど日本人ですが、アメリカはいろいろな国からの移民が住んでいる多人種の国なので、いろいろな文化が共存しています。
　次に、二つ目の違いは、日本は神道と仏教の文化の国ですが、アメリカはキリスト教の文化が強い国だと思います。ですから、国の祝日はとても違います。日本ではお正月が一番大事な祝日ですが、アメリカではクリスマスが一番大事な祝日です。
　最後に、三つ目の違いは、日本は歴史が長いので、伝統的な文化が多くありますが、

20課

アメリカの歴史は短いので、伝統的な文化はあまりありません。日本には、茶道や書道や生け花や俳句や柔道や剣道などの伝統を大事にしている文化があります。
　結論として、私は日本の文化の方がアメリカの文化より好きです。なぜなら、私は柔道を始めて、体だけでなく心も大事だと習ったので、そんな文化を大事にするべきだと思います。

b. Next, work with your partner and together compare and contrast this aspect of Japanese and American culture. Identify a total of three similarities and/or differences. For each, elaborate on your statement. Finally, state your preference for either and give a reason why you think so. Share your presentation with your class.

Introduction:
_____

Three similarities/differences:
1. _____
2. _____
3. _____

Your preference and reason:
_____
_____

H. 会話「選挙〔せんきょ〕」：ペアワーク→クラスワーク

First, read this conversation with your partner. Next, read the questions and your partner will respond without looking at the book. Repeat the underlined parts and give your own answers to the questions. For each question, answer in 20 seconds. Take turns asking and answering questions. You will have an interview with Ms. Ito, a Japanese newspaper reporter from the *Nihon Shinbun*, about elections.

1. 質問　：初めまして。日本新聞の伊藤です。少し質問してもいいですか。
　　答(例)：初めまして。(last name)と申します。どうぞよろしく。どんな質問でしょうか。
　　　　　　出来るだけ答えますので、何でも聞いて下さい。

2. 質問　：アメリカでは高校生でも大統領の選挙に投票出来るそうですが、本当ですか。
　　答(例)：大統領の選挙ですか。アメリカでは１８歳になれば選挙出来るので、１８歳の
　　　　　　高校生も選挙出来るはずです。私は来年１８歳になるので、来年選挙出来ます。

3. 質問　：そうですか。今の大統領について、どんな意見を持っていますか。
　　答(例)：今の大統領ですか。今の大統領の考えにはだいたい賛成していますが、戦争は
　　　　　　出来るだけ早く止めてほしいと願っています。

4. 質問　：そうですか。どうも有難うございました。日本の政治について何か質問など
　　　　　　ありませんか。

20課

答(例)：日本の政治ですか。日本の政治のことは全然知りませんが、今の総理大臣は誰ですか。そして、いい総理大臣ですか。どうも有難うございました。

I. 文化発表「日本への海外からの影響〔えいきょう〕」：ペアワーク→クラスワーク

a. Fill in the blanks with the appropriate responses from the list below.

　　これから、日本への海外からの影響について発表します。日本は歴史の中でいつも外国からいろいろなものを取り入れて来ました。
　　まず第一に、日本が一番影響を受けた国は、中国でしょう。日本人は中国から(1.)を習い、ひらがなとカタカナを作りました。孔子の教えから礼儀も習いました。奈良と京都も中国の都市を真似して作りました。建築や着物も中国から習いました。
　　第二に、韓国からの影響も大きいです。いろいろな物が韓国を通って日本に行きました。(2.)はインドで産まれましたが、中国、韓国を通って、日本に渡りました。お米の作り方も音楽も工芸品も韓国から日本に渡りました。
　　第三に、ポルトガルからも影響を受けました。１６世紀の中ごろに(3.)が日本に行き、キリスト教や鉄砲や印刷などを伝えました。パンやタバコという言葉もポルトガル人が日本に持って行きました。
　　第四に、オランダです。オランダは(4.)時代に日本が鎖国をしていた時にも、日本との貿易を許可されていました。医学、地理、科学、軍事、美術などを日本に伝えました。ビールやコーヒーやガラスもオランダ人が伝えました。
　　第五に、アメリカの影響は近年とても大きいです。1987年にペリーが黒船で日本へ行き、日本の鎖国を止めさせました。日本はその時から、(5.)からいろいろなことを学び始めました。日本が第二次世界大戦で敗けた後、教育や政治や経済などはアメリカから大きな影響を受けました。
　　結論として、日本人は歴史的にいろいろな(6.)から新しいことを習い、より良いものを作り続けて来ました。日本人の器用さと(7.)が、現在の日本を作って来たのだと思います。

1.(　) 2.(　) 3.(　) 4.(　) 5.(　) 6.(　) 7.(　)

a. 仏教　b. 江戸　c. 国　d. 宣教師　e. まじめさ　f. 西洋　g. 漢字

b. Discuss your view and perspective on the influence Japan has received from other countries.

_____
_____

20課

<20課 - 聞く>
Listening: World Peace

12秒×5

【You may take notes while listening. Do not look at the questions below before listening. You will have 12 seconds to answer each question. You may NOT move back and forth among questions.】

(Narrator) Now you will listen to a speech given by Sadako's older brother who attended the 9/11 memorial service in New York in 2007. It will be read once.

(Narrator) Now answer the questions for this selection.

1. Why wasn't Sadako's father wearing his wristwatch when visited Sadako?
    (A) He left it at home.
    (B) He sold it.
    (C) He lost it.
    (D) He gave it to Sadako.

2. How did Sadako deal with her disease?
    (A) She cried in front of her father.
    (B) She expressed her fears to her father.
    (C) She complained about her pain to the nurse.
    (D) She showed her tears only once when her mother was about to leave.

3. How did Sadako deal with her imminent death?
    (A) She knew she was dying.
    (B) She was not aware of her imminent death.
    (C) She could not tell anyone about her death because of her fear of death.
    (D) She told people around her about her imminent death.

4. What was found under Sadako's bed after she passed away?
    (A) a letter to her parents
    (B) her father's watch
    (C) *origami* cranes
    (D) a memo about her white blood cell count

5. What message did Sadako's older brother want to give to his audience?
    (A) to make paper cranes
    (B) to be considerate of others
    (C) to wish for a bright future
    (D) all of the above

<20課 - 読む>

Reading: Environment

【You may move back and forth among all the questions.】

　野口健さんは登山家です。１９９７年に世界７大陸最高峰の登頂という冒険に成功しました。野口さんが登山家になろうと思ったきっかけはある本でした。その本は冒険家の植村直樹さんが書いた「青春を山にかけて」という本でした。落ちこぼれだった植村さんが山登りをして、世界的な冒険を成功させ、自信を取り戻すという話です。野口さんも落ちこぼれだったので、この本を読んで、山に登りたくなりました。

　ある日、野口さんは外国人の登山家たちに一緒にゴミ拾いをしないかと誘われました。その時、エベレストに大量のゴミが捨てられていることを知りました。そして、その多くが日本の登山隊のゴミだったと知りました。「日本は経済は一流だけど、マナーは三流だね。」と外国人の登山家に言われました。富士山にもゴミがたくさんあることを知りました。野口さんはとてもびっくりし、何かをしないといけないと思い、ゴミ拾いを始めました。そこから、地球を守るという次の冒険が始まりました。

　野口さんがエベレストや富士山などでゴミ拾いを始めた時には、手伝ってくれる人はあまりいなくて、とても大変でした。野口さんはたくさんの演説をし、だんだんと手伝ってくれる人が集まり、山は少しずつきれいになりました。野口さんは「あきらめないこと、それが冒険だ。」と言っています。かけがえのないこの自然を次の世代に残すため、彼の活動はこれからも続いていきます。

参考：学習研究社　野口健著「あきらめないこと、それが冒険だ」

<20課 - 読む (質問)>

Reading: Environment

(Narrator) Now answer the questions for this section.

1. What kind of child was Mr. Noguchi?
   (A) He was a good student.
   (B) He was a school dropout.
   (C) He loved mountain climbing.
   (D) He was very self-confident.

2. What made Mr. Noguchi want to become a mountain climber?
   (A) He saw pictures of mountains.
   (B) His father took him to the mountains when he was young.
   (C) He joined a mountain climbing club in college.
   (D) He was inspired by a book written by a mountain climber.

3. Which of the following was NOT mentioned as a motivating factor for Mr. Noguchi to pick up trash on Mt. Everest and Mt. Fuji?
   (A) He saw the news of foreign mountain climbers picking up trash on Mt. Everest.
   (B) He learned about all of the trash that was left behind on Mt. Everest by Japanese climbers.
   (C) Other foreign mountain climbers told him "The Japanese economy is first class, but Japanese manners are third class."
   (D) He learned that there was lots of trash on Mt. Fuji.

4. How did Mr. Noguchi recruit people to pick up trash on Mt. Everest and Mt. Fuji?
   (A) He put an advertisement in the newspaper and asked for cooperation from the public.
   (B) He started a trash pick-up club at the college where he teaches.
   (C) He gave speeches at many places.
   (D) He made a web page and asked people for their cooperation.

5. What is Mr. Noguchi's definition of "adventure"?
   (A) Don't give up picking up trash.
   (B) Recruit more people to pick up trash.
   (C) Climb Mt. Fuji and pick up trash.
   (D) Do trash pick-up campaigns through the media.

<20課 - 書く (テキストチャット)>

Text Chat: Japanese Products

90秒×6

You will participate in a simulated exchange of text-chat messages. Each time it is your turn to write, you will have 90 seconds. You should respond as fully and as appropriately as possible.

You will have a conversation with Watanabe, a Japanese college student who is interviewing American high school students about Japanese products.

1. Respond. (90 seconds)
   こんにちは。今日は日本の製品について意見を聞かせて下さい。
2. Give a specific example. (90 seconds)
   今持っている物の中に、どんな日本製の物がありますか。
3. Give a specific example. (90 seconds)
   日本からの輸入品の中で、アメリカで何が一番人気がありますか。
4. Respond and describe. (90 seconds)
   日本の製品とほかの国の製品を比べて、何が違うと思いますか。
5. Give a specific example and give a reason. (90 seconds)
   今一番ほしい日本製の物は何ですか。なぜですか。
6. Suggest. (90 seconds)
   何か日本の製品についての希望を教えて下さい。どうも貴重な答を有難うございました。

<20課 - 書く (比較と対比)>

Compare & Contrast Article: Japanese Culture and American Culture

20分

Directions: You are writing an article for the student newspaper of your sister school in Japan. Write an article in which you compare and contrast similarities and differences between Japanese culture and American culture. Based on your personal experience, describe at least THREE aspects of each and highlight the similarities and/or differences between Japanese culture and American culture. Also state your preference for either and give reasons for it.

Your article should be 300 to 400 characters or longer. Use the *desu/masu* or *da* (plain) style, but use one style consistently. Also, use *kanji* wherever *kanji* from the AP® Japanese *kanji* list is appropriate. You have 20 minutes to write.

【NOTES/OUTLINE: 自分の作文のアウトラインを書こう！】

Introduction: _____

Three similarities/differences:

1. _____
2. _____
3. _____

Your preference and give reason(s):
_____
_____

20課

<20課 - 話す (会話)>

Conversation: Elections

20秒×4

You will participate in a simulated conversation. Each time it is your turn to speak, you will have 20 seconds to record. You should respond as fully and as appropriately as possible.

You will have an interview with Ms. Ito, a Japanese newspaper reporter from the *Nihon Shinbun*, about elections.

(Female)
(20 seconds)
(Female)
(20 seconds)
(Female)
(20 seconds)
(Female)
(20 seconds)

<20課 - 話す (日本文化)>

Cultural Perspective Presentation: Foreign Influences in Japan

4分+2分

Directions: Imagine you are making an oral presentation to your Japanese class. First, you will read and hear the topic for your presentation. You will have 4 minutes to prepare your presentation. Then you will have 2 minutes to record your presentation. Your presentation should be as complete as possible.

Present your own view or perspective of foreign influences in Japan. Discuss at least FIVE aspects or examples of foreign influences in Japan.

Begin with an appropriate introduction, give details, explain your own view or perspective, and end with a concluding remark.

【Let's take notes!】

1. Begin with an appropriate introduction.

___

2. Discuss five aspects/examples of the topic.

    1.) ___
    2.) ___
    3.) ___
    4.) ___
    5.) ___

3. Explain your view or perspective.

___

4. End with a concluding remark.

___

20課

Verb Conjugation Charts

	NAI form	MASU form	Dic. form	BA form	OO form	TE form	TA form
	informal, neg., nonpast	formal, nonpast	informal, nonpast	conditional	informal, volitional		informal, past
I. Group 1 Verbs							
み	のまない / nomanai	のみます / nomimasu	のむ / nomu	のめば / nomeba	のもう / nomoo	のんで / nonde	のんだ / nonda
に	しなない / shinanai	しにます / shinimasu	しぬ / shinu	しねば / shineba	しのう / shinoo	しんで / shinde	しんだ / shinda
び	あそばない / asobanai	あそびます / asobimasu	あそぶ / asobu	あそべば / asobeba	あそぼう / asoboo	あそんで / asonde	あそんだ / asonda
い	かわない / kawanai	かいます / kaimasu	かう / kau	かえば / kaeba	かおう / kaoo	かって / katte	かった / katta
ち	またない / matanai	まちます / machimasu	まつ / matsu	まてば / mateba	まとう / matoo	まって / matte	まった / matta
り	かえらない / kaeranai	かえります / kaerimasu	かえる / kaeru	かえれば / kaereba	かえろう / kaeroo	かえって / kaette	かえった / kaetta
	*ない / * nai	あります / arimasu	ある / aru	あれば / areba		あって / atte	あった / atta
き	かかない / kakanai	かきます / kakimasu	かく / kaku	かけば / kakeba	かこう / kakoo	かいて / kaite	かいた / kaita
	いかない / ikanai	いきます / ikimasu	いく / iku	いけば / ikeba	いこう / ikoo	*いって / * itte	*いった / * itta
ぎ	およがない / oyoganai	およぎます / oyogimasu	およぐ / oyogu	およげば / oyogeba	およごう / oyogoo	およいで / oyoide	およいだ / oyoida
し	はなさない / hanasanai	はなします / hanashimasu	はなす / hanasu	はなせば / hanaseba	はなそう / hanasoo	はなして / hanashite	はなした / hanashita
II. Group 2 Verbs							
-e	たべない / tabenai	たべます / tabemasu	たべる / taberu	たべれば / tabereba	たべよう / tabeyoo	たべて / tabete	たべた / tabeta
◻	みない / minai	みます / mimasu	みる / miru	みれば / mireba	みよう / miyoo	みて / mite	みた / mita

Special verbs: おきます get up; happen, かります borrow, おります get off; go down, できます can do, -すぎます too ~, (シャワーを)あびます take a shower, いきます to live, おちます to fall, かんじます to feel

III. Group 3 Irregular verbs							
する (do)	しない / shinai	します / shimasu	する / suru	すれば / sureba	しよう / shiyoo	して / shite	した / shita
くる (come)	こない / konai	きます / kimasu	くる / kuru	くれば / kureba	こよう / koyoo	きて / kite	きた / kita

＊Exceptional form.

	NAKATTA form informal, neg., past	(Honorific-Passive)	Causative Permissive	Polite Command	Neg. Command	Potential (Group 2 verb)	Command
I. Group 1 Verbs							
み	のまなかった nomanakatta	のまれる nomareru	のませる nomaseru	のみなさい nominasai	のむな nomuna	のめる nomeru	のめ nome
に	しななかった shinanakatta	しなれる shinareru	しなせる shinaseru	しになさい shininasai	しぬな shinuna	しねる shineru	しね shine
び	あそばなかった asobanakatta	あそばれる asobareru	あそばせる asobaseru	あそびなさい asobinasai	あそぶな asobuna	あそべる asoberu	あそべ asobe
い	かわなかった kawanakatta	かわれる kawareru	かわせる kawaseru	かいなさい kainasai	かうな kauna	かえる kaeru	かえ kae
ち	またなかった matanakatta	またれる matareru	またせる mataseru	まちなさい machinasai	まつな matsuna	まてる materu	まて mate
り	かえらなかった kaeranakatta *なかった * nakatta	かえられる kaerareru	かえらせる kaeraseru	かえりなさい kaerinasai	かえるな kaeruna	かえれる kaereru	かえれ kaere
き	かかなかった kakanakatta	かかれる kakareru	かかせる kakaseru	かきなさい kakinasai	かくな kakuna	かける kakeru	かけ kake
	いかなかった ikanakatta	いかれる ikareru	いかせる ikaseru	いきなさい ikinasai	いくな ikuna	いける ikeru	いけ ike
ぎ	およがなかった oyoganakatta	およがれる oyogareru	およがせる oyogaseru	およぎなさい oyoginasai	およぐな oyoguna	およげる oyogeru	およげ oyoge
し	はなさなかった hanasanakatta	はなされる hanasareru	はなさせる hanasaseru	はなしなさい hanashinasai	はなすな hanasuna	はなせる hanaseru	はなせ hanase
II. Group 2 Verbs							
-e	たべなかった tabenakatta	たべられる taberareru	たべさせる tabesaseru	たべなさい tabenasai	たべるな taberuna	たべられる taberareru	たべろ tabero
☐	みなかった minakatta	みられる mirareru	みさせる misaseru	みなさい minasai	みるな miruna	みられる mirareru	みろ miro

Special verbs: おきます get up; happen, かります borrow, おります get off; go down, できます can do, -すぎます too ~, (シャワーを)あびます take a shower, いきます to live, おちます to fall, かんじます to feel

III. Group 3 Irregular verbs							
する (do)	しなかった shinakatta	される sareru	させる saseru	しなさい shinasai	するな suruna	できる dekiru	しろ shiro
くる (come)	こなかった konakatta	こられる korareru	こさせる korareru	きなさい kinasai	くるな kuruna	こられる korareru	こい koi

*Exceptional form.

Verb Conjugation

REFERENCES

AP® Japanese Language and Culture Course Description, College Board®, May 2007

Makino, Seiichi and Tsutsui, Michio. *A Dictionary of Basic Japanese Grammar.* Tokyo: The Japan Times 1998

Makino, Seiichi and Tsutsui, Michio. *A Dictionary of Intermediate Japanese Grammar.* Tokyo: The Japan Times 1998

The Modern Reader's Japanese-English Character Dictionary, Tokyo: Tuttle Publishing 1962

「小学生のための漢字をおぼえる辞典」川嶋優　旺文社 1975 Tokyo

マイロク先生の地球一よく分かる！温暖化問題　www.team-6.net/-6sensei/

「となりのトトロ」徳間書店 Tokyo 1988

「あきらめないこと、それが冒険だ―エベレストに登るのも冒険、ゴミ拾いも冒険！」野口健著　学習研究社、２００７年発行

野口健著「あきらめないこと、それが冒険だ」学習研究社 Tokyo, 2006

Carlyn Tani, "*A kid called Barry: Barack Obama '79,*" Punahou Bulletin 2007

Web pages:
資源ゴミ　http://www11.synapse.ne.jp/hishikaricho/kankyou/bunbetu.htm